D0947314

CONTROVERSIES IN PHILOSOPHY

General Editor: A. G. N. Flew

Each volume in this series deals with a topic that has been, and still is, the subject of lively debate among philosophers. The sort of issues that they embrace are only partially covered, if covered at all, by the usual collections of reprinted work.

The series consists largely but not entirely of material already published elsewhere in scattered sources. It is as a series distinguished by two guiding ideas. First, the individual editors of the various constituent volumes select and collect contributions to some important controversy which in recent years has been, and which still remains, alive. The emphasis is thus upon controversy, and upon the presentation of philosophers in controversial action. Second, the individual editors are encouraged to edit extensively and strongly. The idea is that they should act as firm, fair and constructive chairmen. Such a chairman gives shape to a discussion and ensures that the several contributors are not merely heard, but heard at the moment when their contributions can be most relevant and most effective. With this in mind the contributions as they appear in these volumes are arranged neither in the chronological order of their first publication nor in any other possibly arbitrary sequence, but in such a way as to provide and to reveal some structure and development in the whole argument. Again, and for similar reasons, the editorial introductions are both substantial and forthcoming.

Although most of the contributions in each volume have been published before as articles in journals, the editors are asked not to confine themselves to this source. There will be a fair element of previously unpublished material and, even more frequently, extracts will be taken from books.

CONTROVERSIES IN PHILOSOPHY

General Editor A. G. N. Flew

Philosophy and Linguistics

EDITED BY

Colin Lyas

CONTRIBUTORS
W. P. Alston, J. L. Austin, S. Cavell, A. G. N. Flew, J. Fodor,
R. M. Hare, Richard Henson, J. J. Katz, B. Mates, C. G. New,
Gilbert Ryle, J. R. Searle, Z. Vendler

MACMILLAN
ST MARTIN'S PRESS

First published 1971 by
MACMILLAN AND CO LTD
London and Basingstoke
Associated companies in New York Toronto
Dublin Melbourne Johannesburg and Madras

Library of Congress catalog card no. 76–147781

SBN 333 10513 3 (hard cover)
SBN 333 10534 6 (paper cover)

Printed in Great Britain by
WESTERN PRINTING SERVICES LTD
Bristol

Foreword by the General Editor

In at any rate the English-speaking countries the idea that philosophy is in some way essentially concerned with language has since the end of the Second World War become commonplace. The controversy which Colin Lyas presents in this volume deals with the consequent questions of the relations between philosophy so conceived and linguistic science. Since the conception seems to have achieved its common currency without thereby ceasing to appear as some sort of public scandal, it is fortunate that the presentation of the consequent controversy has to begin with a Part I on 'The Philosophical Appeal to Language'. An initial study of that Part, followed by a reading or rereading in Part II of J. L. Austin's methodological manifesto, should do their mite to dispel the stubbornly persistent prejudice that linguistic philosophy is something radically distinct from traditional: the former dealing merely with words, and being ultimately frivolous; whereas the latter was, of course, engaged with the deepest and entirely non-verbal realities.

The truth is, rather, that if linguistic is to be distinguished from traditional philosophy, it must be in terms of differences in the degree of awareness of the inseparability of conceptual questions from questions about the use of words; and also, perhaps, of differences in the strength of the inclination to flaunt any such awareness. Certainly it would be perverse to pretend that the inquiries of Austin's 'A Plea for Excuses' are of a different kind from those reported by Aristotle in chapter 1 of bk iii of his *Nicomachean Ethics*; or that the subject of Sir Alfred Ayer's *The Problem of Knowledge* (London, 1956) is not the same as that of Plato's *Theaetetus*. It is, therefore, perhaps significant that the author of the most widely circulated polemic against 'Linguistic Philosophy' – not being himself, presumably, ignorant of such philosophical classics – is careful always to avoid saying anything substantial and precise about the tradition which he is supposed to be defending. (See E. A. Gellner, *Words and Things* (London, 1959; Harmondsworth, 1968).)

But the challenge with which the present volume is mainly concerned comes from a quite different direction. If it is once granted that philosophy is a conceptual inquiry, and hence concerned in some way with the uses of words, then the question arises of what are its proper relations with linguistic science. If they are competitors, then does not this put the philosopher in the uneasy position of the witch-doctor confronted by the scientifically qualified medico, the untrained manager up against the graduate of the Harvard Business School? Even if he and the philosopher are not direct rivals, surely the findings and the methods of the modern linguistic scientist must be indispensibly relevant to the philosopher? In that case all philosophers, and not only those who resonate in sympathy with his politics, need to wait on the words of Noam Chomsky.

The present volume is the fifth and, at least temporarily, the last of a series on 'Controversies in Philosophy'. This is as a series distinguished by two guiding ideas. First, the individual editors of the various constituent volumes select and collect contributions to some important controversy which in recent years has been, and which still remains, alive. They are not restricted to what has already appeared in article form. Second, the editors are encouraged to edit extensively and strongly. The idea is that they should act as firm, fair and constructive chairmen. Such a chairman gives shape to a discussion and ensures that the several contributors are not merely heard, but heard at the moment when their contributions can be most relevant and most effective. For similar reasons the editorial introductions are both substantial and forthcoming. This all involves an uninhibited and self-aware acceptance of the role of teacher, and a corresponding rejection of the suspiciously comfortable doctrine that helpful but hard work by the teacher constitutes always an undesirable spoon-feeding of the taught.

Whether there will be other volumes in the present series in addition to the original five depends entirely on the response which these meet. Certainly as General Editor I shall be glad to hear of other possible members, whether the suggestions come from colleagues who would like to undertake the editorial job themselves, or whether they are made by those who – in whatever capacity – feel a need which they would like someone else to fill.

ANTONY FLEW

University of Keele,
Staffordshire,
England

Contents

Acknowledgements

Chapter I was first published in *The Concept of Mind* (London: Hutchinson, 1949; New York: Barnes & Noble, 1949) ch. 3, s. 3. Thanks are due to Messrs Hutchinson and Barnes & Noble for permission to reprint this material. Chapters II, IX, X and XVII appeared originally in the *Philosophical Review* (Chapter II in vol. LXII (1953), Chapter IX in vol. LXXI (1962), Chapter X in vol. LXXII (1963) and Chapter XVII in vol. LXXIII (1964)) and are reprinted with the permission of the editors and of Messrs Ryle, Cavell, Fodor and Katz. Chapters III and V appeared originally in the *Proceedings of the Aristotelian Society* (Chapter III in supp. vol. XXXV (1961) and Chapter V in the *Proceedings*, vol. LVII (1956–7)) and are reprinted by courtesy of the editor of the Aristotelian Society. They are, respectively, copyright © 1961 and copyright © 1956–7 of the Aristotelian Society. Chapter IV appeared first in the volume *Essays in Conceptual Analysis* (Macmillan, 1956) and is reprinted with permission from Professor Flew and the publishers. Chapters VI and XII appeared first in *Mind* (Chapter XII in vol. LXIX (1960) and Chapter VI in vol. LXXV (1966)) and are reprinted with the permission of the editor of *Mind* and Messrs Hare and New. Chapters VII, VIII and XIII appeared first in *Inquiry* (Chapters VII and VIII in vol. 1 (1958) and Chapter XIII in vol. V (1962)) and are reprinted by permission of the editors. Chapters XV and XVI appeared originally in the *Journal of Philosophy* (Chapter XV in vol. LIX (1962) and Chapter XVI in vol. LXI (1964)) and are reprinted by permission of the editors of the *Journal* and of Messrs Alston and Katz. Chapter XIII appeared first in Professor Searle's *Speech Acts* (Cambridge, 1969) pp. 12–15 and is reprinted by permission of Professor Searle and the Cambridge University Press. Chapter XIV was the first chapter of Vendler's *Linguistics in Philosophy* (Ithaca, N.Y., 1967) pp. 1–32 and is reprinted by courtesy of the Cornell University Press. Professor Cavell has asked that attention be drawn to the fact that the writings by him in the present volume are now also to be found in his collection *Must We Mean What We Say?* (New York:

Scribner's, 1969). Chapter XI first appeared in the *American Philosophical Quarterly*, vol. 2, no. 1 (1965) and is reprinted by permission of the editor and Professor Henson.

Editor's Introduction

There are at least two reasons why language has always been an intriguing object of study. First, there is the supposition that language is a distinctively human possession, one that marks us off in some way from other inhabitants of the animal kingdom. Given this supposition, it is not unnatural for there to be a belief that to achieve an understanding of language is to make a significant step towards an understanding of our own nature. Second, language has been studied for the more practical reason that many difficulties arise from its misuse. The hope here is that an understanding of language will lead to an understanding and avoidance of these difficulties.

The interest in language is not an interest of recent origin but is one shown by a distinguished and unbroken line of investigators running from the pre-Socratics to the most recent followers of Noam Chomsky. In recent years, however, we have witnessed remarkable advances in the study of language. This is not only a matter of the development of empirical methods for penetrating and recording different languages. Nor is it merely a development of methods by which to investigate the acquisition of language and the way in which language operates as a psychological and social influence. It is also, very importantly, the development of highly complex theories that explain the nature of language by means of an explanation of the structure any language must have. There is some evidence that the outcome of these developments may not only be an understanding of the ways in which difficulties arise from the various misuses of language, but may also be a partial realisation of the hope of understanding man by means of an understanding of his language.[1]

The striking developments in linguistics have had implications for philosophers, for they too have claimed the study of language as a legitimate task. It has seemed, however, to some linguistic scientists that these philosophical investigations, subtle though they may be, have not been carried out with the new and very sophisticated methods of analysis recently developed for the study of language. Given the development of linguistics, the temptation is to claim, justly or not, that the linguistic scientist is now equipped to do with proper professionalism what the philosopher has in the past done in a more amateurish and piecemeal way.

Linguistics as a subject appears, then, to compete with philosophy as a subject. This book is a record of some of the disputes that have taken place as the result of this apparent competition. In the remainder of this introduction I shall try to explore some of these matters in a way that may aid an understanding of the disputes. I shall first explain three of the ways in which the philosopher is involved with language and hence with the problem of working out a *modus vivendi* with linguistics.

I

In order to understand the first philosophical involvement with language I shall mention, it is necessary to realise that the philosopher is not in competition with what might be called the 'first-order' specialist disciplines (subjects such as chemistry, physics, psychology, literary criticism and mathematics) in explaining, interpreting and predicting things about our environment. Were philosophical inquiry on a level with these, it would, in all likelihood, long since have been absorbed into one or other of them. If there is not to be such an assimilation, there must be tasks for the philosopher that would not lead him into competition with practitioners of the special disciplines. We can find such a task if we think of philosophy not as merely another 'first-order' discipline inquiring into some aspect of our environment, but as the subject in which these first-order disciplines are *themselves* made objects of study. Hence the description of philosophy as a 'higher-' or 'second-order' discipline, and hence such branches of the subject as the philosophy of science, the philosophy of mathematics and philosophical psychology.

One important reason why the philosopher studies the special disciplines is to get clear about the meaning of the terms used in them. Thus, for example, the psychologist *uses* the term 'interpretation' when talking of dreams, the physicist *uses* the term 'cause' when explaining events and the critic *uses* the term 'style' in talking of the products of an artist. The philosopher asks what these terms *mean* as used by the practitioners of the special inquiries. This is not to ask, as psychologists, physicists or critics ask, questions about dreams, events or novels. It is to ask about the investigations that are pursued into these things and in particular about the meaning of the terms used in such inquiries. Often the task of clarification here is quite essential. Thus the question 'Is the fact that actions are caused compatible with the freedom of the will?' cannot be answered by *anyone*, let alone the psychologist, unless we are first clear what is meant by 'cause' and 'free'.

Obviously philosophy conceived as the higher-order study of the special disciplines is reasonably safe from challenge by developments in those special disciplines. No amount of progress in physics, for instance, can eliminate the need for a watching brief on the activities of physicists. The interesting point, to which I now turn, is that the development of one special discipline, linguistics, may present problems for philosophy conceived as a second-order subject. I shall now show that given the view that philosophy is, at least in part, a study of the special disciplines, there is possible reason for both optimism and pessimism as we consider the relations between philosophy and linguistics.

First, we have reason for optimism. If the philosophical investigation of the conceptual underpinnings of a special discipline is a useful task, and if linguistic science is a special discipline, then there will be an opportunity for a second-order philosophical investigation of it. Far from undermining the philosophical enterprise, the development of linguistics will provide an opening for more philosophy in the form of the philosophy of linguistics.[2] What is called theoretical linguistics is often such a study.

There is, however, also some reason for disquiet. The second-order task I have outlined for the philosopher is a conceptual inquiry, an inquiry into the meaning of terms. However, it is just over inquiries into meaning that the development of linguistics seems to present a problem to the philosopher. For the linguistic scientist will presumably claim that he has developed methods for the determination of meaning which supersede those hitherto used by the philosopher. This being so, it will not be enough to argue that there is a valuable second-order task, the investigation of the terms of art of the special disciplines. We shall also have to show why the philosopher rather than the linguistic scientist is best qualified to discuss such questions about meaning.

II

The first involvement of philosophy with language arises from the fact that philosophy is, at least in part, an investigation into the meaning of terms used in the special disciplines. However, in addition to any activities we may pursue as exponents of the special disciplines, we have as well a very wide range of ordinary non-specialist concerns. These may include feeding the cat, banking the fire, offering consolation and reproving thoughtlessness. True, these too may be studied by sociologists, psychologists, specialists in ergonomics and the like, but even these experts from time to time leave aside their specialist activities and take part in the ordinary human concerns.

There is, then, in our lives a central core of non-specialist activities, and from human reflections upon these activities there have arisen what have traditionally been some of the profoundest problems in philosophy. Of late, however, the philosopher's way of dealing with these problems has given rise to comment by those conversant with the methods of the linguistic scientist. I shall now explain how this has happened and I begin by showing how philosophical problems may arise from quite ordinary happenings of the sort I have just mentioned.

Our ordinary non-specialist doings are centred about two, not necessarily discrete, groups of entities, namely, persons and things. Our day-to-day confrontations with these issue in such activities as promising, giving, threatening, exhorting, wishing, moving, touching, hoping and arguing. They also issue in the many judgements, statements and assertions we make about the persons and things we encounter. Out of our reflections on all these, philosophical problems can arise. I mention two examples.

First, we normally realise with no sense of difficulty that someone is worried, hopeful or in pain. We succeed in knowing of the doings and feelings of others. When we reflect upon this knowledge, however, we can come to doubt our right to claim to know what we ordinarily think we know. We are led to ask, for example, 'How can I *really* know what a person is feeling or thinking when all I can see is the movement of a body?' 'What', we may ask, 'does it *mean* to attribute states of mind to others?'[3]

Again, with no sense of strain, we identify coats, chairs and other such objects and we do such ordinary things as to tell people to bring them to us. Again, however, when we reflect upon our knowledge of objects we can come to doubt that we are entitled to it. We think of the delusions and illusions which have betrayed the confidence of others and may be led to ask 'What does it *mean* to say that we encounter publicly observable things?'

Before I say why the philosopher's handling of such problems is affected by the development of linguistics, a particular feature of these doubts should be noted. In our philosophical speculations we can come to doubt what, when the philosophical mood is not upon us, we do and say with no difficulty. In these doubts, therefore, we come to doubt ourselves and our status in a world of persons and things. This doubt is a self-doubt, and the answer to it is at least in part a matter of self-discovery (Chapter IX). I shall return to this point later (section IX below).

In order to show why philosophical concerns of the sort I have just described are affected by developments in linguistics, we need first to explain the distinction between the material and the formal modes of speech. This distinction is best illustrated by an example. Thus the statement 'We make a gift voluntarily' is in the material mode, whereas the statement 'We may say "We make a gift voluntarily"' is in the formal mode. In the move from the material mode to the formal mode we make a shift from talking about things happening in the world about us to talking about the way language is used to talk about things happening in this world. A characteristic of much philosophical discussion is a predilection for talking in the formal rather than the material mode. The belief is that if we are puzzled, say about the status of our knowledge of the mental states of others, we can pursue this question equally well by asking under what conditions it is proper to *say* that someone is in a particular mental state.

Two problems now arise. First, we might ask *why* we can move from the material to the formal mode with such facility. Secondly, we can ask why one *should* make this move, granted that it is a possible one.

A reason why we *can* make the move is given by Cavell (Chapter VIII):

If this [*sc.* the move from the material to the formal mode] seems surprising, perhaps it is because we forget that we learn language and the world *together*, that they become elaborated and distorted together, and in the same places.

Cavell also suggests some reasons why there may be an advantage, on occasion, in moving from the material to the formal mode (Chapter VIII). A full account of the thinking that lies behind an inclination towards formal-mode discussions would be a discussion of nearly all the thinking that lies behind much recent and not so recent philosophy. For my present purposes it is sufficient to point out that there is a widespread tendency to produce statements in the formal mode, to move, for example, from asking what voluntary action is to asking what the conditions are in which we may *call* an action voluntary. For once the attention of the philosopher *is* thus focused upon language, it might begin to seem that a philosophical inquiry is an inquiry that could also be made by the linguistic scientist, and it is open to the linguistic scientist to claim that he has developed and refined the very methods by which such inquiries are best to be pursued.

III

I want, finally, to indicate one last area in which there is a philosophical interest in language. I mention this area because it is not clear what contribution can here be made by the linguistic scientist.

I have suggested above that philosophers might direct themselves to the analysis of terms used in the special disciplines and also to puzzles which arise out of reflection upon our dealings with the persons and things we encounter in our ordinary lives. There is, however, an interesting area, common to neither of these interests, in which problems may arise. I have in mind here problems that arise when we consider the ways in which advances in some special disciplines, say psychology or physics, affect what we say in our ordinary non-specialist language. Sometimes the problems that arise here are rather peripheral, as for example the dispute as to whether we can say that anything is really *solid* given the truth of some scientific accounts of matter.[4] Sometimes the disputes here are much more important. Thus, as the psychologist progresses in the explanation and prediction of human behaviour, people may come to wonder more and more whether they are entitled to go on saying that human actions are free.

In such a case one task must be performed first. That is the determination, as far as possible, of the conditions that do govern our use of terms such as 'free' and 'voluntary' in so far as we are as yet unaffected by developments in psychology. When we have done this, however, we still have to discuss what to say in the light of advances in psychology. In the paper reprinted in this volume, Flew adopts one particular argument, the paradigm case argument.[5] The line taken is that prior to the developments in psychology, we have some agreement on the conditions under which we will call an action free, and we teach the use of 'free' by teaching people to apply it only when these conditions are fulfilled. Thus a man is not free if he acts under duress, say when a gun is held to his head. Given that there are such agreed conditions, and given that we teach the meaning of 'free' by reference to them, Flew seems to conclude that there are such things as free acts.

We might query, however, whether this sort of line takes account of the problem in which we are interested, namely the problem of what to do when a new discipline tempts us to *alter* our view of the conditions governing the use of a word.[6] Flew's proposal seems to amount to the claim that we can be secure in our belief that there are free actions because we *now* have an agreement about the conditions governing the use of this term. What for Flew appears to fix the meaning of 'free', therefore, is some sort of agreement that if certain conditions are met, an act is free. This seems right. The question is what happens if the agreement alters. This might happen when people who understand Flew's use of 'free' and have hitherto assented to it, come to feel that psychologists and sociologists have shown that people are conditioned in certain ways, and then agree among themselves that these conditionings are not *different in kind* from those other conditions under which even Flew would claim that actions are not free.[7]

Faced with such a proposed change in agreement, one might do various things. One might try to argue that the various sorts of conditionings referred to above *do* differ in kind from the conditions we have hitherto thought incompatible with the freedom of an act. There is no guarantee that this line will work. If this line fails, one might look round for another sense of 'free' in which human actions can be said to be free. Failing that, one might just say that as a matter of fact agreements may alter, and when they change they represent new ways of viewing ourselves, or, in the Wittgensteinian idiom, new 'forms of life'.[8]

Whatever we *do* say about such problems, it does not seem to me that the linguistic scientist has any special advantage over the philosopher in discussing them. As I have said, advances in special disciplines may lead to alteration in our agreements as to conditions under which a word may be used. If this happens, no amount of information the linguistic scientist has accumulated about the agreements there in fact are about the conditions governing the use of words can be of help, for the *status* of those agreements is being called into question. One might further add that not only does the linguistic scientist not seem to be at any special advantage here, but that those who have most penetratingly investigated the nature of the agreements that establish the conditions of proper use have been philosophers – in particular, as Cavell points out (Chapter IX), Wittgenstein.

IV

I have tried so far to indicate in a preliminary way the manner in which the philosopher becomes involved with language. I want now, as a prelude to the more detailed discussion of these involvements, to define more precisely the area of language study in which the linguistic scientist challenges the philosopher.

The work of the philosopher has as its *aim* the understanding, and possibly the solution of certain sorts of puzzles, notably, as I have tried to show, puzzles arising from obscurities in the meaning of terms used in the special disciplines and puzzles arising from our reflections on what we ordinarily say and do. As well as this aim there is a *method*, and this often involves an examination of the use of language, the belief being that difficulties that concern the philosopher have their root there and may be understood, and possibly settled, when facts about the use of language are clear.

Given that there is an aim and a method, it would seem that a challenge from the linguistic scientist can be directed either to the aims of the philosopher or to his methods. I shall first show that the aims of the philosopher have not *in fact* been undermined or appropriated by the linguistic scientists, nor, moreover, *could* they be invalidated by developments in linguistics.

First, in order to show that the aims of the philosopher are not in fact appropriated or undermined, we need only to observe that the aims of the linguistic scientist are very different from the aims of the philosopher. The linguistic scientist wishes to do such things as reconstruct the system of rules 'internalised' by the speaker, and which allow the speaker to produce and understand infinitely many meaningful utterances (Chapter XV). Again, he wishes to devise methods that will allow him to achieve such varied aims as the effective penetration of foreign languages, the construction of machines for automatic translation, the efficient teaching of language and the understanding of language as an influence on behaviour. These aims are markedly different from the sorts of aims I have been attributing to the philosopher. Put very roughly, one might say that the linguistic scientist is usually content to accept in a non-sceptical way that language is a justified ongoing enterprise, albeit with the occasional malfunction. He wishes to articulate the mechanisms of this enterprise for various practical and theoretical purposes. The philosophical problems are not uncommonly more deeply sceptical doubts about the justifiability of our saying and doing what we ordinarily say and do. These doubts are often, indeed, doubts as to the very possibility of language.[9]

It is no mere matter of fact that the aims of the philosopher and the aims of the linguistic scientist are different. The philosophical aims I have been discussing *could* not be eliminated by *any* development in linguistic science. Even if the science of linguistics appropriated these aims, that would at most mean that linguistic science had to some extent become philosophy and that its aims included some philosophical aims. (To some extent, by branching out into theoretical linguistics, linguistic science *has* become, in part, philosophy.)

If what I have said is correct, a linguistic challenge to the philosopher is no challenge to his aims. It can at most be a challenge to his methods. Here, indeed, there *is* an interesting confrontation. For the advances in linguistics have been advances in the *methods* by which language is investigated, advances in the ways of determining the structure of language (its syntax) and its meanings (its semantics). Suppose now the linguistic scientist did succeed in providing a means whereby to determine the structure of language, a syntactical or grammatical theory, and suppose he also provided a semantic theory in terms of which one might determine the meaning or proper use of the various utterances of a language. Then, in such a case, the linguistic scientist would not only have achieved many of his own aims but would also offer to the philosopher powerful methods by which to achieve *his* language-oriented aims. An ignorance of such methods, if they were available, would indeed be an admission of amateurism.

The linguistic challenge to the philosopher is therefore a demand that he look to his *methods* and consider in what way advances in linguistics can assist his task. The philosophers in this book accept this challenge. One even goes so far as to say:

. . . structural linguistics might be of real importance to philosophy. And, of course, if and when semantics is developed and integrated into structural linguistics along with grammar, the differences between the two sorts of inquiry in methods and status of conclusions, though not in ultimate aim, may well be reduced to vanishing point (Alston, p. 295 below).

What I shall do now is explain in a little more detail the debates that there have been over the linguistic challenge as a methodological challenge. I shall discuss three matters. First I shall explain the line said to be taken by Ryle (Chapters II and III) that the linguistic scientist and the philosopher are not in competition since the philosopher is interested in the *use* of language (speech) whereas the linguistic scientist is interested in its *usage* (*what* is used, or language). This is not entirely a separate matter from the second issue I wish to discuss, namely the extent to which philosophical statements about language are *empirical* statements and hence in need of verification in various ways. Finally I shall discuss briefly the ways in which new developments in syntactic and semantic theory might affect the philosophical method.

V

One way in which philosophers have attempted to meet the intrusions of linguistic scientists is to argue that the philosopher is interested in the proper use of language and that the linguistic scientist is interested in its usage. The same point is often made in terms of a distinction between a philosophical interest in speech (the use of language) and a linguistic interest in language (what is used). (Chapter III). The former, it is said, is a normative matter (Chapters II and IX), the latter is a matter of fact. Granted this distinction, it might then be claimed that the interests are *in fact* different. Some might even go so far as to say that the interests *must* be different. For since from a matter of fact no statement of value is said to follow,[10] nothing the linguist discovers about the facts of usage could affect philosophical statements about the rights of use.

I shall first show that it is right to claim, on the basis of a use/usage, speech/language distinction, that philosophy and *philology* (or lexicography) are indeed different (Chapter II). I shall then point out that even if philosophy and philology are different subjects, it does not follow that philosophy and linguistic science (where this is thought of as a more general subject than philology) differ in their methods of approaching the use of language.

Let us first ask what Ryle, for example, was up to in making the distinction between use and usage, speech and language. It is important here to realise that language speakers do not, typically, *just* produce strings of sounds but produce sequences of sounds or marks in order to *do* something.[11] Speakers use words in order to do such things as stating, warning, promising, threatening and so on. Thus, in English, one might produce the string of phonemes corresponding to the written utterance 'Your brakes are worn' in order to tell or warn someone that his brakes are worn. These jobs are not, of course, just a matter for English speakers. Frenchmen, for example, can do them too, only as a matter of fact they use different sounds in doing them. Even in English it merely happens to be the case that we use the sounds and marks we do. Things could have been different, and in different English dialects often are.

There is then on the one hand the job done by the *use* of language and on the other the pieces of language that are used in doing these jobs. What Ryle apparently wishes to claim is that the philosopher is interested in the language-neutral conditions that govern the jobs or uses to which a particular piece of language can be put, the conditions, for example, which govern jobs such as stating something, whether they can be done by English speakers or speakers in any other language. The philosopher is not, however, primarily interested in the language-specific units that are pressed into service in the performance of the tasks. Recording these is a job for the philologist or lexicographer. (But see Flew on the use/usage distinction for an important qualification, pp. 65–6 below.)

It is of course true that part of linguistics is concerned with the units of a language, as when dialects, idioms and the like are recorded. Linguistic science thus *includes* lexicography and philology. But although Ryle has shown that *these* interests do not affect the philosopher, his arguments leave it an open question whether the philosopher should take account of the methods developed in those parts of linguistics other than philology and lexicography.

Clearly there will be at least a prima facie case for saying that these other linguistic methods impinge on philosophy if those who use them are interested in conditions for the proper use of language and have devised these methods in order to determine such questions. And there can be little doubt that the linguistic scientist *is* interested in conditions for proper use, for one of his aims is the penetration of foreign languages. To succeed in this *is* to discover the proper use of the words of the language under investigation. Only so can one learn to speak that language.

Linguistic science, then, taken more generally concerns itself not only with language but with speech, with use as well as usage. For various practical reasons, e.g. translation, the linguistic scientist must ask questions about the conditions under which a word may properly be used, and he has had to develop methods by which such questions might be determined. Our question is whether these methods might be of interest to the philosopher. In order to decide this matter we need to know more about these methods and more about the reasons why the linguistic scientist has criticised the philosopher for ignoring them. Discussion of these matters leads naturally on to the second main issue I wish to discuss, namely the question whether the philosopher's discoveries and statements about language are empirical discoveries and statements.

VI

The questions at issue here are 'Does the philosopher make empirical statements about the use of language, and if so *how* are they discovered and *how* are they verified?'

Confusion can be caused here by a failure to notice ambiguities in the question 'Is the philosopher's statement about the use of language an empirical statement?' This may mean 'Is the philosopher's statement about the use of language, if true, *necessarily* true?', or it may mean 'Is the discovery that such a statement is true an empirical discovery?' If these questions are kept distinct, much of the debate between Fodor, Katz and Cavell becomes clearer.

The first question here is about the *status*, empirical or otherwise, of the philosopher's claim that a word may, in a particular language, be used to do a certain job only in certain conditions. Such a statement may be expressed in various ways.

First the philosopher may use the material mode and say, e.g., 'If a person is truly said to know that something is the case, he must (i) feel sure about it, (ii) it must *be* the case (and so on through the conditions under which someone may be said to know something)' (see Flew, pp. 61–2 below).

Secondly the philosopher may use a formal-mode statement and claim 'One may only *say* "I know that something is the case" if one feels sure, etc.' A note is here needed on the word 'say', for someone might ask 'Can't I say what I want in whatever conditions I want?' If one means by 'say' here 'utter certain sounds', of course one can. We are, however, interested in saying in some fuller sense such as 'utter, mean and communicate', and then of course, if the philosopher is right in his claim about our language, one can only *say* 'I know that such and such' if one sticks to the agreed conditions for the use of 'I know that such and such'.

There is a third way in which the philosopher may express his findings about language (Chapter IX). If one assumes that language rests on an agreement that certain words are only used in certain conditions, and assumes also a general wish on the part of language users to sustain these conditions in the interests of communication, then the use of words will generally imply that the speaker believes that the conditions governing the use of the words he produces have been met. So the philosopher may express himself by saying: 'When we say "I know that something is the case" we *imply* that we feel sure, etc.' or 'When S says of another "he knows that p", S's utterance implies that S believes that p is true' (although S does not, strictly speaking, say or utter 'I believe that p is true').

The philosopher then may make, in addition to material-mode statements, statements about language use such as 'One may say "x" only if conditions C are fulfilled' or 'If S says "x" he implies that conditions C are the case'. The question then is, are such statements, if true, necessarily true. To this Cavell and Vendler, for example, are inclined to give the answer 'Yes'. With one qualification I am inclined to agree with them. The qualification is needed because I said above in section III that the agreed conditions for the use of a word may alter, even though, after the alteration, it does not seem unnatural to say that we mean the same by the use of that word. (There is some discussion of this in Chapter IX.) Because there is this disposition to believe that the philosopher's statements about language are, if true, necessarily true, and yet also some tendency to believe that if agreements change, these statements may alter, it has not seemed unnatural to some to ask whether these statements are *synthetic a priori* (see Chapters VIII, XII and XIV).

VII

There are in this book impressive arguments that the philosophical statements about language are, if true, necessarily true, or at the very least are not straightforwardly empirical statements. But this of itself does not rule out challenges from linguistic scientists of an empirical turn of mind. For although a statement may be necessarily true, the fact that it *is* necessarily true may have to be determined by empirical investigation. Thus suppose we consider the statement 'Whales are mammals'. Someone might wonder if this was true by definition. If he knows that the definition of 'mammal' includes the notion of being warm-blooded, he might then discover by empirical investigation that whales are warm-blooded and hence be led to the conclusion that it is true by definition that a whale is a mammal. That something is necessarily true may be established, at least in part, as the result of inquiry. Moreover, one may think that something is necessarily true and be wrong, and may discover one's error as the result of empirical inquiry. (Consider the case of a man who, not unnaturally, thinks that 'A whale is not a mammal' is true by definition.) The upshot is that a statement may be necessarily true, but the statement that it *is* necessarily true may need proof. It follows, then, that although the philosopher's statement about the use of language may be necessarily true, his *claim* that this statement is necessarily true may or may not be justified, and the determination of its justifiability *may* need some empirical investigation.

The philosopher is, therefore, bound to admit that in some sense of 'find out' he finds out things about the use of language and may go wrong in claims he makes as the result of his finding out. He may mischaracterise his language. As Fodor and Katz point out, the best reporter of the use of language might not be a speaker reflecting on his use of language (Chapter X).

It does not seem to me that many recent philosophers could deny that people can make mistaken claims about language. Philosophers of late have been the first to maintain that philosophical problems can arise just because people go wrong in their reflections upon the conditions which govern the use of a word, e.g. because they misdescribe how such philosophically important words as 'know' are used. If the philosopher wishes to maintain this, he must address himself to questions about the verification of philosophical statements about language. He must show under what conditions he can *know* he is right in his characterisation of language and under what conditions he can know that someone else is wrong. However, when we investigate this matter we again encounter the challenge from the linguistic scientist. His claim will be that the verification of linguistic characterisations, be these necessary or not, is a matter of an empirical study of language use, and he will presumably further claim that empirical linguistics has devised the best methods for such a study.

In discussing this challenge I wish to make two sets of remarks. First I shall mention possible answers the philosopher might make when his statements about language are challenged. I shall then make a set of remarks on the linguistic methods which the empirical linguist is said to offer the philosopher.

VIII

The claim then is that the philosopher, since he might be wrong in what he claims about language, must discuss methods of verification of these statements. I shall show that philosophers have not been unaware of these problems and, given that some counter-example is produced to his claim that we may or may not say something by the use of certain words, I shall mention various responses that the philosopher might make.

First, it is worth noting that those acquainted with the doings and findings of the empirical linguist often tell us that philosophers have made some important and essential discoveries about language (Chapter XIV).[12] This might give us some hope that the philosopher is not *that* incompetent in his investigations of the use of language.

Secondly, we must resist the suggestion that might be made by empirically-minded linguistic scientists that the typical philosopher produces his results after a crude and facile piece of armchair introspection. The reported methods of Austin, for example, give the lie direct to this and tell of a careful, laborious, group inquiry into the meaning of terms. These results are derived by something like an empirical investigation.[13] (I shall come later to the charge that the group involved is insufficiently representative (section IX below). Here I remark only that in so far as such a group manages to communicate at will with others, there is reason to suppose them competent, in principle, to make true statements about the use of language.)

Thirdly, the philosopher has not been helpless when confronted with apparent objections to his statements about language (Chapter IV). I mention three possible responses that might be made. First, as Cavell points out (Chapter VIII), the philosopher may just admit that he is wrong and amend his account. If someone here is inclined to ask 'How does the philosopher know that he is right in this admission?', an answer is that he might not be. To that, however, we may add that a counter-example can convince a speaker that he is wrong in his statement about language because he is by hypothesis a competent speaker of his language and hence can be reminded of the facts about it he may have overlooked. (For an important discussion of linguistic discovery as a matter of recollection, see Hare's paper reprinted below.) True, the philosopher might make an over-hasty admission, but granted he is a competent speaker and granted that he thinks carefully, it would be rare if this sort of admission were the rule.

The philosopher is prepared to consider counter-examples and possibly to amend his claims. This is not his only possible line. As Flew points out, he can always ask whether the apparent counter-example does not merely establish the point that the philosopher is trying to make. This may happen when the suggested locution is in fact a use of language that can only be ironical or sarcastic, as when we say 'So you knew wrong'. Not every counter-example need be allowed.

A third possible response by the philosopher to a counter-example is just to show that the counter-example itself rests on a mistake (pp. 67–8 below). Thus suppose the philosopher says 'We may not say that statements *infer* that something is the case', and suppose someone says 'But people (possibly a majority) do *say* that statements infer things'. A useful reply here is to point out that the mere fact that people *do* say certain things does not establish what we are interested in, namely, that they are *right* so to speak. For this reason surveys of what people in fact say, no matter how well documented, are as yet nothing to the point. The majority may misuse language, but a majority misuse no more undermines the philosopher's statement about proper use than a majority ignorance about wine establishes the superiority of a home-brewed wine over the products of the Château Mouton Rothschild.

Thus in the case of inference, the philosopher may point out that since inference is a performance, something which *people* do, it is right to say 'Jones inferred that . . .', but wrong to say 'Statements infer that . . .'. He might add that 'implication' is the word we have to characterise relations of statements, so that it is right to say 'Statement S implies that . . .'. To be sure, inference and implication are related, for an inference of B from A is fully justified if A implies B. The two are, however, not identical and paradoxes can arise from their confusion.[14]

Given the distinction between inference and implication, what shall we say about a person who speaks of a statement as inferring something? Two cases may be distinguished. First, granted that there is a distinction between inference and implication, one thing will be wrong, that is the use of 'infer' to cover both cases just because one does not know that there is a difference. This is the usual case with new students in logic, for example, and experience shows that once they are *shown* the difference they *want* to use the proper words to mark it. Secondly, there is the case of the person who recognises the difference between inference and implication yet uses 'infer' to cover both cases. In a sense there is nothing wrong with this. *He* knows what he means, and he usually succeeds in making it clear to others what he means. In another way such use is not happy. If it is important to keep inference and implication separate, to avoid paradoxes perhaps, then a tendency to use 'infer' indiscriminately to cover both cases will lead to a temptation to ignore the difference between them.[15]

IX

I have tried to show so far that philosophers have *some* answers when objections are made to their statements about the proper use of language. I come now to the more direct reply to the linguistic scientist, a reply that rests on an examination of claims made on behalf of the methods by which the empirical linguist determines questions of use, and which the philosopher is being advised to borrow.

A first difficulty here is that philosophers, e.g. Fodor and Katz, who claim that philosophers ought to be acquainted with the field methods of the linguist, do not tell us precisely what these methods are or precisely how their use would facilitate the philosopher's task. Moreover, in their own writing, the conclusions that they present do not appear to have been obtained as the result of the intensive use of empirical field methods. Thus when in a recent paper Katz makes his remarks on the word 'good', he seems to rely as much on investigation of his understanding of the term as on any philosophical discussion of language (see reference in note 33 below).

Next we need to point out that many of the methods the empirical linguist has at his disposal have been developed and refined because of a need to penetrate *foreign* languages. Techniques for doing this *have* been greatly improved. The question we need to ask, however, is to what extent methods designed to determine the proper use of a foreign language (as yet not mastered) are of use when we are concerned with our own, long mastered, native language.

In order to determine the answer to this question, let us begin with the translator confronted with an unknown language.[16] Mastering this language will be a matter of coming to master the proper use of its words, and the investigator proceeds in various ways. An initial stage may well be a phonemic analysis of the language in order to determine what the various units (phonemes, roughly speaking words) are.[17] This may show the investigator not only what the units of the language are but also tell him something about the way in which they are permuted in the various utterances. Without going into the need for such an analysis, and without wishing to deny the subtlety with which it is performed, the method of phonemic analysis does not seem of any obvious relevance to the work of the philosopher. For he *already* knows how to recognise the discrete elements (words) of his own language.[18]

Another important step is the pairing of utterances with the features or situations in the vicinity of the native informant that may have occasioned them. For as Quine remarks:

> All the objective data that he [the translator] has to go on are the forces that he sees impinging on the native's surfaces and the observable behaviour, vocal or otherwise, of the native. . . . The utterances first and most surely translated in such a case are ones keyed to present events that are conspicuous to the linguist and his informant. A rabbit scurries by, the native says 'Gavagai' and the linguist notes down the sentence 'Rabbit' (or 'Lo, a rabbit') as tentative translation.[19]

Various practical difficulties may arise here.[20]   Thus suppose the linguist has noticed that the presence of rabbits tends to elicit the word 'gavagai' and makes a tentative pairing of 'rabbit' and 'gavagai' in his dictionary. Then, however, he may be puzzled by utterances of 'gavagai' when there are *no* rabbits present, when the word is used in telling a story, or when the native speaker has seen a rabbit which is not in the field of vision of the translator.

These are practical problems and require ingenuity and patience on the part of the investigator if they are to be dealt with. But again such practical difficulties do not seem to be problems solved by methods that might interest the philosopher who is addressing himself to his own language. When these sorts of questions arise for speakers in a common language, they can just ask such questions as 'Why did you say you saw a rabbit? I don't see one.' The practical problems I have mentioned that the linguist has to overcome, arise because an unmastered *foreign* language is being studied. They are not obviously problems that need concern a philosopher interested in his own language.

So far I have confined a discussion of translation to the more basic terms of a language, where it is possible to some extent to match observable events to speech dispositions. There comes a stage, however, at which the linguist may wish to move away from the basic language of rabbits and the like and wishes to find out translations for such words as 'intend', 'pretend', 'good', 'duty', 'right', 'hope', 'meaning', 'cause', 'know', 'same', 'promise', 'time', 'property', 'perception', 'graceful', 'free', 'infer', 'imply', and the like.

One interesting problem here is that the native speakers may not have a word in their language corresponding to each of these terms, in which case the investigator must discover whether they *do* recognise such notions even though they do not have words for them. He may, of course, discover that the native speaker of the language he is investigating does *not* recognise many of these notions, and that raises the interesting question whether he *can* be brought to understand them. Such questions touch on the problem of linguistic relativity and the Sapir–Whorf hypothesis, which, regrettably, I cannot here discuss.[21]

I shall assume that the language does have words that may be used for these notions and the problem of the linguist is to correlate the words in his language to equivalent words in the language being studied. My question is about the methods the linguist might here use. *These* methods for determining proper use are more likely to be of interest to the philosopher, for the terms whose translation we are now considering are the sort of terms that the philosopher is interested in.

First, the linguist might just make a shrewd guess that a certain word in the foreign language does mean the same as some word, such as 'pretend', in his own language. He then uses this native word where he would use 'pretend', and if this works then he has some reason to believe that his translation is correct. This method is of no help to the philosopher, for it assumes that the use of 'pretend', to use the present example, is already known to the linguist. Obviously this approach is of no use when the proper use of a word in one's own language is in doubt.

Next, suppose that the linguist does not guess but decides to find out in some other way whether a certain word in the foreign language corresponds to, say, 'know' in English. One thing he must do to begin with is to determine the conditions governing the proper use of 'know' in English and then find ways of discovering whether the foreign word in question is used in those conditions. Thus suppose one decides that one must not say 'He knows that *p*' if one believes that *p* is not the case. One might then wait until a native informant is proved *wrong* about something, call it *q*, and then say 'So you knew that *q*'. If this does not prove acceptable to native informants, one has at least some ground for believing that the word in the language in question means 'know'. Again there may be difficulties. The informants may in fact be misusers of the language (compare the case of 'infer' discussed above). Again the speaker may show surprise at the utterance because of its obviousness rather than because of its deviance, and so on. Leaving these aside for the moment, consider the procedure as so far outlined. What I have been suggesting is that if the linguist is to do anything other than guess shrewdly, he must first determine the meaning of a term in his own language. He must do this before he can ever start asking questions about the proper use of a term in another language – indeed, before he can ever know what questions to ask. But then, what is the point of saying that methods developed in the field, in translating foreign languages, are models for the philosopher as he struggles with the problem of clarifying the proper use of questions in his own language?

The claim of the linguistic scientist must therefore be amended. The claim must now be that empirical investigations into our own language by the linguistic scientist have shown the philosopher certain advantageous methods of procedure. Certainly some such investigations have been made, e.g. by those attempting to do field work on the grammatical theories of Noam Chomsky.[22]

When the claim is put thus, I see two issues only. First, there is the problem of the relation of these linguistic methods to philosophical methods. Second, there are certain theoretical problems about these methods raised by the linguistic scientist.

On the first issue I would claim that the methods the linguist might use in his investigation of our use of our language do not seem to differ greatly from methods for determining use that have been used by philosophers, in more or less sophisticated ways, from the time of Plato's development of a dialectical method (Chapter XII). The method is very simply to ask the speaker if he would agree that such and such is a clear case of the use of the word in question, to think up possible counter-examples, to devise border-line cases and puzzle cases that might, when put to the speaker, throw light on the matter. One will also try to collect and analyse examples of the actual use of the word. One thereby displays the use of the word in as many varied contexts as possible, hoping to reveal the way in which it functions. In so doing one assumes that the speaker can use properly such words as 'know', 'intend', 'pretend' and so on. Both the linguist and the philosopher are here assuming a competence and attempting, for different reasons, to make it plain (Chapter IX).[23] Their methods are not in principle different. The upshot seems to be, then, that there is not one method used by the linguistic scientist and another used by the philosopher for determining the conditions in which a word may be properly used. There is one method used by them both. That is why it is not surprising that linguists have to admit that philosophers, too, have come up with characterisations of language which are of the first importance.

Granted these are the sorts of things that go on in the investigations of linguists and philosophers, we may make another remark on philosophical method (Chapters VIII and IX). If we assume that the language we speak is a common property, then given sufficient care, imagination and inventiveness there is no reason why the philosopher should not work on his own idiolect. What he would find out by the investigation of the language of others could, in principle, be found out by reflection on what he says himself. The same methods applied to his own speech dispositions *could* yield the same results as an examination of the speech dispositions of others. Moreover it is not unnatural to start with oneself here. For the doubts that prompt the genuine philosopher are *his* doubts and are settled, or at least understood, by self-discovery (Chapter IX). This, however, represents an ideal. For there may be a positive gain in taking advantage of the co-operative inventiveness and imagination that a group investigation can bring.

One final remark may be made on these methods of linguistic inquiry. There is a temptation to say that the philosopher is relying ultimately on his intuitions about language. It is important to realise that the linguist's method is ultimately no less intuitive and rests ultimately upon what someone or other does or does not accept as a characterisation of what we may say by the use of words.

This brings me to the second main problem that I wish to discuss, namely, the theoretical problems that arise when we reflect upon the methods of the linguist and the philosopher. Sometimes when the linguistic scientist criticises the philosopher it is not *really* because he thinks the methods of the philosopher are amateurish, but because he thinks philosophers do not realise *theoretical* problems that arise from the *use* of the methods. I mention one problem in particular, the so called 'problem of acceptability'.

Both the linguist's and the philosopher's methods as I have reported them rely on the presentation of cases to oneself and others in order to test their acceptability. There is nothing wrong with this, for language ultimately rests upon agreements to accept some things as correct and others as incorrect. When one reflects upon the notion of acceptability, however, doubts can arise about it. Not only may one ask for a distinction between the different sorts of acceptability (Chapter XVI), but one may also ask how we know that someone was right to accept or not to accept some locution that is offered to him.[24] Two things may be said on theoretical problems of this sort.

First, the sort of problems we are now discussing arise because of doubts *about* a concept used in linguistic and philosophical inquiry, namely the concept of acceptability. These doubts are therefore second-order doubts and, as I argued above, such doubts are philosophical doubts.[25] The linguistic scientist in accusing the philosopher of ignoring them is not accusing the philosopher of ignoring the methods of empirical linguistics but of ignoring some *philosophy* that he ought to be doing.

Secondly, it is quite true that all sorts of possible disagreements can occur. What one speaker may find acceptable another may reject. I do not, therefore, wish to deny that there are here problems about the methods of linguistics and philosophy and that the determination of meaning by these methods is an intricate and difficult task. Even granted, however, that there may be all sorts of disagreements as to whether some locution or other is acceptable, it is still worth remarking that many significant philosophical conclusions are not open to *this* sort of disagreement. Thus, in one recent dispute, J. L. Austin produced cases to show that the way in which Bedford would have us use the word 'pretend' is unacceptable. These cases as far as I know remove any temptation on anyone's part to call Bedford's remarks on the meaning of 'pretend' acceptable. The destructive remarks are compelling. The false analysis is removed by the production of clear cases of pretending which do not fit it,[26] by a method that has *always* been used in philosophy (Chapter XII).

It may seem here as if I am suggesting that the problem of acceptability is solved for the philosopher by his production of examples that no one is inclined to reject as clear cases of the use of a word. There is something in this (although a closer investigation than I can here give is needed of the various sorts of agreements and disagreements that are possible). After all, we are dealing with people, including ourselves, who have a mastery of the language and, moreover, the concepts that we are investigating are often very familiar ones – pretending, hoping, promising, intending and the like. Because of this we are in a position to recognise, often immediately, whether a philosopher is right in claiming that something is a clear case of what we call, say, pretending. This is why Wittgenstein is led to say:

> The aspects of things that are most important for us are hidden because of their simplicity and familiarity. (One is unable to notice something because it is always before one's eyes.) The real foundations of his inquiry do not strike a man at all. Unless *that* fact has at some time struck him. And this means: we fail to be struck by what, once seen, is most striking and most powerful.[27]

If someone now asks, 'Can't it *seem* obvious to us all that something is a clear case of what we call pretending when in fact it isn't?', the answer is that this may be *possible*, just as it may be *possible* that what we all agree is a chair might be some sort of illusion. This doubt, however, is a more deeply sceptical doubt and if the linguistic scientist wishes to raise it, he wishes to do philosophy. Then he might be directed to discussions by philosophers of various sorts of sceptical doubts, discussions which will almost certainly include an examination of the various means of 'possible'.[28]

X

In the *Tractatus Logico-Philosophicus* Wittgenstein writes: 'All philosophy is "Critique of Language". . . . Russell's merit is to have shown that the apparent logical form of the proposition may not be its real form.'[29]

The insight of Russell as reported here has, in various ways, been exploited by recent philosophers. Thus Ryle has argued that we may be led into philosophical bewilderment if we are led by superficial grammatical similarities to assimilate utterances that are different in type.[30] Similarly Moore has argued, for instance, that we can be misled by the superficial grammatical similarity of 'Tame tigers exist' and 'Tame tigers growl' into various sorts of confusion.[31] (Vendler in Chapter XIV claims that Moore was himself misled by the superficial grammatical similarity between 'This book is good' and 'This book is yellow'.) Given the possibility that errors may arise from the failure to notice that grammatical similarities may overlay more basic dissimilarities, it has seemed a useful philosophical task to display the dissimilarity of utterances that are grammatically similar.

This philosophical task has been affected by developments in the theory of grammar associated with Noam Chomsky. It is a fundamental thesis of Chomsky's that we must recognise a distinction between the superficial grammatical structure and the more basic structure of an utterance. There is on the one hand the 'surface grammar' of an utterance and on the other its 'deep grammar', and a vast amount of work has been done in an effort to make the distinction clear and to provide a grammatical theory that will allow the transformation of utterances in order to reveal their real structure. This is the so-called 'transformational grammar'.

Some philosophers have not been slow to realise that an application of these grammatical theories might assist the task of investigating the distinction between the grammatical form of a sentence and its real form in order to avoid difficulties that arise when superficial grammatical similarities bemuse us. One contributor to this volume, Vendler, has, in the work from which his contribution is taken, made a special effort to apply developments in grammatical theory to philosophical problems.

I make two comments on the impact of grammatical theories on the work of the philosopher. First, regardless of the possible help that might be provided to the philosopher by advances in grammatical theory, there might also be room for a helpful contribution by the philosopher to the discussion of such theories. Second-order investigations of the theory of grammar are still needed.[32]

Secondly, although some philosophical difficulties might be alleviated by an attention to syntactical considerations, some will not. The problems which will not be affected will be those that depend on the philosopher's investigation of the *meaning* of some philosophically difficult term. True, as some point out, the grammatical function of a word is often an important factor in determining its meaning. Thus as Strawson points out:

> To appreciate the difference in sense between 'John loves Mary' and 'Mary loves John' . . . *is* to grasp those structural facts which are expressed in the terminology of grammar by saying that 'John' is the subject and 'Mary' the object of the verb in the first sentence and vice versa in the second (op. cit.).

Knowing how terms function, whether they are verbs, adverbs, nouns, subjects or predicates, is, then, part of what is needed for an understanding of utterances. As well as knowing the syntactic status of a word, however, one needs also to know its meaning. As well as syntax there is semantics.

Granted this, the philosopher might say that even though advances have been made in syntactical theory, still, since the philosophical task is concerned importantly with meaning, or semantics, there is a large area left to him into which linguistic theory has not penetrated (Chapter XIV). Two things are wrong with this reply. First, such a line is always a risky one to take. Even though the linguist might not yet have produced a semantic theory he might soon do so, and one should therefore try to work out in advance the sort of thing that might be said when that happens.

Secondly, some linguistic theorists, notably Katz, *have* attempted to provide semantic theories, and Katz has argued that his semantic theory does have repercussions for the philosopher. A discussion of these semantic theories would unfortunately take us beyond the space allowed in the present work. Suffice it here to say that they open up new possibilities of mutually helpful discussion between philosophers and linguistic scientists and that a study of the issues raised by these theories will show that debates between philosophers and linguistic scientists are far from over.[33]

PART ONE

The Philosophical Appeal to Language

We begin with an example, taken from Ryle's *The Concept of Mind*, of a philosopher attempting to throw light on a philosophical problem by means of appeals to the use of language. There follows some discussion by Ryle of the exact nature of this appeal, in which Ryle, by means of a distinction between use and usage, speech and language, attempts to show that the linguistic philosopher is no mere philologist or lexicographer. The first part concludes with a detailed examination by Flew of some of the misconceptions that might be held about the appeal to the use of language. An important part of this paper is an account of what the philosopher might say when counter-examples to his analyses are produced. There also appears in this paper an early formulation of the paradigm case argument, itself a source of some philosophical controversy (see my Introduction, note 5).

I An appeal to language

Gilbert Ryle

It should be noticed that while ordinary folk, magistrates, parents and teachers, generally apply the words 'voluntary' and 'involuntary' to actions in one way, philosophers often apply them in quite another way.

In their most ordinary employment 'voluntary' and 'involuntary' are used, with a few minor elasticities, as adjectives applying to actions which ought not to be done. We discuss whether someone's action was voluntary or not only when the action seems to have been his fault. He is accused of making a noise, and the guilt is his, if the action was voluntary, like laughing; he has successfully excused himself, if he satisfies us that it was involuntary, like a sneeze. In the same way in ordinary life we raise questions of responsibility only when someone is charged, justly or unjustly, with an offence. It makes sense, in this use, to ask whether a boy was responsible for breaking a window, but not whether he was responsible for finishing his homework in good time. We do not ask whether it was his fault that he got his long-division sum right, for to get a sum right is not a fault. If he gets it wrong, he may satisfy us that his failure was not his fault, perhaps because he had not yet been shown how to do such calculations.

In this ordinary use, then, it is absurd to discuss whether satisfactory, correct or admirable performances are voluntary or involuntary. Neither inculpation nor exculpation is in point. We neither confess to authorship nor adduce extenuating circumstances; neither plead 'guilty' nor plead 'not guilty'; for we are not accused.

But philosophers, in discussing what constitutes acts voluntary or involuntary, tend to describe as voluntary not only reprehensible but also meritorious actions, not only things that are someone's fault but also things that are to his credit. The motives underlying their unwitting extension of the ordinary sense of 'voluntary', 'involuntary' and 'responsible' will be considered later.[1] For the moment it is worth while to consider certain consequences which follow from it. In the ordinary use, to say that a sneeze was involuntary is to say that the agent could not help doing it, and to say that a laugh was voluntary is to say that the agent could have helped doing it. (This is not to say that the laugh was intentional. We do not laugh on purpose.) The boy could have got the sum right which he actually got wrong; he knew how to behave, but he misbehaved; he was competent to tie a reef-knot, though what he unintentionally produced was a granny-knot. His failure or lapse was his fault. But when the word 'voluntary' is given its philosophically stretched use, so that correct as well as incorrect, admirable as well as contemptible acts are described as voluntary, it seems to follow by analogy with the ordinary use, that a boy who gets his sum right can also be described as having been 'able to help it'. It would then be proper to ask: Could you have helped solving the riddle? Could you have helped drawing the proper conclusion? Could you have helped tying a proper reef-knot? Could you have helped seeing the point of that joke? Could you have helped being kind to that child? In fact, however, no one could answer these questions, though it is not at first obvious why, if it is correct to say that someone could have avoided getting a sum wrong, it is incorrect to say that he could have avoided getting it right.

The solution is simple. When we say that someone could have avoided committing a lapse or error, or that it was his fault that he committed it, we mean that he knew how to do the right thing, or was competent to do so, but did not exercise his knowledge or competence. He was not trying, or not trying hard enough. But when a person has done the right thing, we cannot then say that he knew how to do the wrong thing, or that he was competent to make mistakes. For making mistakes is not an exercise of competence, nor is the commission of slips an exercise of knowledge *how*; it is a failure to exercise knowledge *how*. It is true in one sense of 'could' that a person who had done a sum correctly could have got it wrong; in the sense, namely, that he is not exempt from the liability to be careless. But in another sense of 'could', to ask, 'Could you have got it wrong?' means 'Were you sufficiently intelligent and well-trained and were you concentrating hard enough to make a miscalculation?', and this is as silly a question as to ask whether someone's teeth are strong enough to be broken by cracking nuts.

The tangle of largely spurious problems, known as the problem of the Freedom of the Will, partly derives from this unconsciously stretched use of 'voluntary' and these consequential misapplications of different senses of 'could' and 'could have helped'.

The first task is to elucidate what is meant in their ordinary undistorted use by 'voluntary', 'involuntary', 'responsible', 'could not have helped' and 'his fault', as these expressions are used in deciding concrete questions of guilt and innocence.

If a boy has tied a granny-knot instead of a reef-knot, we satisfy ourselves that it was his fault by first establishing that he knew how to tie a reef-knot, and then by establishing that his hand was not forced by external coercion and that there were no other agencies at work preventing him from tying the correct knot. We establish that he could tie reef-knots by finding out that he had been taught, had had practice, usually got them right, or by finding that he could detect and correct knots tied by others, or by finding that he was ashamed of what he had done and, without help from others, put it right himself. That he was not acting under duress or in panic or high fever or with numb fingers, is discovered in the way in which we ordinarily discover that highly exceptional incidents have not taken place; for such incidents would have been too remarkable to have gone unremarked, at least by the boy himself.

The first question which we had to decide had nothing to do with the occurrence or non-occurrence of any occult episode in the boy's stream of consciousness; it was the question whether or not he had the required higher-level competence, that of knowing how to tie reef-knots. We were not, at this stage, inquiring whether he committed, or omitted, an extra public or private operation, but only whether he possessed or lacked a certain intelligent capacity. What satisfied us was not the (unattainable) knowledge of the truth or falsity of a particular covert cause-overt effect proposition, but the (attainable) knowledge of the truth or falsity of a complex and par-tially general hypothetical proposition – not, in short, that he did tie a shadowy reef- or granny-knot behind the scenes, but that he could have tied a real one with this rope and would have done so on this occasion, if he had paid more heed to what he was doing. The lapse was his fault because, knowing how to tie the knot, he still did not tie it correctly.

Consider next the case of a act which everyone would decide was not the agent's fault. A boy arrives late for school and on inquiry it turns out that he left home at the usual time, did not dally on his way to the omnibus halt and caught the usual omnibus. But the vehicle broke down and could not complete the journey. The boy ran as fast as he could the rest of the way, but was still late. Clearly all the steps taken by the boy were either the same as those which normally bring him to school in time, or were the only steps open to him for remedying the effects of the breakdown. There was nothing else that he could have done and his teacher properly recommends him to follow the same routine on future occasions. His late arrival was not the result of a failure to do what he was capable of doing. He was prevented by a circumstance which was not in his power to modify. Here again the teacher is judging an action with reference to the capacities and opportunities of the agent; his excuse is accepted that he could not have done better than he did. The whole question of the involuntariness of his late arrival is decided without the boy being asked to report any deliverances of consciousness or introspection about the execution or non-execution of any volitions.

It makes no difference if the actions with which the agent is charged either are or embody operations of silent soliloquy or other operations with verbal or non-verbal images. A slip in mental arithmetic is the pupil's fault on the same grounds as a slip made in written arithmetic; and an error committed in matching colours in the mind's eye may merit the reproach of carelessness in the same way as an error committed in matching colours on the draper's counter. If the agent could have done better than he did, then he could have helped doing it as badly as he did.

Besides considering the ordinary senses of 'voluntary', 'involuntary', 'responsible', 'my fault' and 'could' or 'could not help', we should notice as well the ordinary uses of such expressions as 'effort of will', 'strength of will' and 'irresolute'. A person is described as behaving resolutely when in the execution of difficult, protracted or disagreeable tasks he tends not to relax his efforts, not to let his attention be diverted, not to grumble and not think much or often about his fatigue or fears. He does not shirk or drop things to which he has set his hand. A weak-willed person is one who is easily distracted or disheartened, apt to convince himself that another time will be more suitable or that the reasons for undertaking the task were not after all very strong. Note that it is no part of the definition of resoluteness or of irresoluteness that a resolution should actually have been formed. A resolute man may firmly resist temptations to abandon or postpone his task, though he never went through a prefatory ritual-process of making up his mind to complete it. But naturally such a man will also be disposed to perform any vows which he has made to others or to himself. Correspondingly the irresolute man will be likely to fail to carry out his often numerous good resolutions, but his lack of tenacity of purpose will be exhibited also in surrenders and slacknesses in courses of action which were unprefaced by any private or public undertakings to accomplish them.

Strength of will is a propensity the exercises of which consist in sticking to tasks; that is, in not being deterred or diverted. Weakness of will is having too little of this propensity. The performances in which strength of will is exerted may be performances of almost any sort, intellectual or manual, imaginative or administrative. It is not a singe-track disposition or, for that and other reasons, a disposition to execute occult operations of one special kind.

By 'an effort of will' is meant a particular exercise of tenacity of purpose, occurring when the obstacles are notably great, or the counter-temptations notably strong. Such efforts may, but need not, be accompanied by special processes, often of a ritual character, of nerving or adjuring oneself to do what is required; but these processes are not so much ways in which resoluteness is shown as ways in which fear of irresoluteness manifests itself.

Before we leave the concept or concepts of voluntariness, two further points need to be made. (1) Very often we oppose things done voluntarily to things suffered under compulsion. Some soldiers are volunteers, others are conscripts; some yachtsmen go out to sea voluntarily, others are carried out to sea by the wind and tide. Here questions of inculpation and exculpation need not arise. In asking whether the soldier volunteered or was conscripted, we are asking whether he joined up because he wanted to do so, or whether he joined up because he had to do so, where 'had to' entails 'no matter what he wanted'. In asking whether the yachtsman went out to sea of his own accord or whether he was carried out, we are asking whether he went out on purpose, or whether he would still have gone out as he did, even if he had meant not to do so. Would bad news from home, or a warning from the coastguard, have stopped him?

What is involuntary, in this use, is not describable as an act. Being carried out to sea, or being called up, is something that happens to a person, not something which he does. In this respect, this antithesis between voluntary and involuntary differs from the antithesis we have in mind when we ask whether someone's tying of a granny-knot, or his knitting of his brows, is voluntary or involuntary. A person who frowns involuntarily is not forced to frown, as a yachtsman may be forced out to sea; nor is the careless boy forced to tie a granny-knot, as the conscript is forced to join the army. Even frowning is something that a person does. It is not done to him. So sometimes the question 'Voluntary or involuntary?' means 'Did the person do it, or was it done to him?'; sometimes it presupposes that he did it, but means 'Did he do it with or without heeding what he was doing?' or 'Did he do it on purpose or inadvertently, mechanically, or instinctively, etc.?'

(2) When a person does something voluntarily, in the sense that he does it on purpose or is trying to do it, his action certainly reflects some quality or qualities of mind, since (it is more than a verbal point to say) he is in some degree and in one fashion or another minding what he is doing. It follows also that, if linguistically equipped, he can then tell, without research or conjecture, what he has been trying to accomplish. But these implications of voluntariness do not carry with them the double-life corollaries often assumed.[2] To frown intentionally is not to do one thing on one's forehead and another thing in a second metaphorical place; nor is it to do one thing with one's brow-muscles and another thing with some non-bodily organ. In particular, it is not to bring about a frown on one's forehead by first bringing about a frown-causing exertion of some occult non-muscle. 'He frowned intentionally' does not report the occurrence of two episodes. It reports the occurrence of one episode, but one of a very different character from that reported by 'he frowned involuntarily', though the frowns might be photographically as similar as you please.

II Use and usage

Gilbert Ryle

Use

The phrase 'the ordinary (i.e. stock) use of the expression "..." '
is often so spoken that the stress is made to fall on the word 'expression' or else on the word 'ordinary' and the word 'use' is slurred
over. The reverse ought to be the case. The operative word is *'use'*.

Hume's question was not about the word 'cause'; it was about the
use of 'cause'. It was just as much about the *use* of 'Ursache'. For
the use of 'cause' is the same as the use of 'Ursache', though 'cause'
is not the same word as 'Ursache'. Hume's question was not a
question about a bit of the English language in any way in which it
was not a question about a bit of the German language. The job
done with the English word 'cause' is not an English job, or a
continental job. What I do with my Nottingham-made boots –
namely walk in them – is not Nottingham-made; but nor is it
Leicester-made or Derby-made. The transactions I perform with a
sixpenny-bit have neither milled nor unmilled edges; they have no
edges at all. We might discuss what I can and cannot do with a
sixpenny-bit, namely what I can and cannot buy with it, what
change I should and should not give or take for it, and so on; but
such a discussion would not be a discussion about the date, ingredients, shape, colour or provenance of the coin. It is a discussion
about the purchasing power of this coin, or of any other coin of the
same value, and not about *this coin*. It is not a numismatic discussion, but a commercial or financial discussion. Putting the stress
on the word 'use' helps to bring out the important fact that the
inquiry is an inquiry not into the other features or properties of the
word or coin or pair of boots, but only into what is done with it, or
with anything else with which we do the same thing. That is why
it is so misleading to classify philosophical questions as linguistic
questions – or as non-linguistic questions.

It is, I think, only in fairly recent years that philosophers have
picked up the trick of talking about the use of expressions, and even
made a virtue of so talking. Our forefathers, at one time, talked

instead of the *concepts* or *ideas* corresponding to expressions. This was in many ways a very convenient idiom, and one which in most situations we do well to retain. It had the drawback, though, that it encouraged people to start Platonic or Lockean hares about the status and provenance of these concepts or ideas. The impression was given that a philosopher who wanted to discuss, say, the concept of *cause* or *infinitesimal* or *remorse* was under some obligation to start by deciding whether concepts have a supramundane or only a psychological existence; whether they are transcendent intuitables or only private introspectibles.

Later on, when philosophers were in revolt against psychologism in logic, there was a vogue for another idiom, the idiom of talking about the *meanings* of expressions, and the phrase 'the concept of cause' was replaced by the phrase 'the meaning of the word "cause" or of any other with the same meaning'. This new idiom was also subject to anti-Platonic and anti-Lockean cavils; but its biggest drawback was a different one. Philosophers and logicians were at that time the victims of a special and erroneous theory about meaning. They construed the verb 'to mean' as standing for a relation between an expression and some other entity. The meaning of an expression was taken to be an entity which had that expression for its name. So studying the meaning of the phrase 'the solar system' was supposed or half-supposed to be the same thing as studying the solar system. It was partly in reaction against this erroneous view that philosophers came to prefer the idiom 'the use of the expressions ". . . caused . . ." and ". . . the solar system"'. We are accustomed to talking of the use of safety-pins, banisters, table knives, badges and gestures; and this familiar idiom neither connotes nor seems to connote any queer relations to any queer entities. It draws our attention to the teachable procedures and techniques of handling or employing things, without suggesting unwanted correlates. Learning how to manage a canoe-paddle, a traveller's cheque or a postage stamp is not being introduced to an extra entity. Nor is learning how to manage the words 'if', 'ought' and 'limit'.

There is another merit in this idiom. Where we can speak of managing, handling and employing we can speak of mismanaging, mishandling and misemploying. There are rules to keep or break, codes to observe or flout. Learning to use expressions, like learning to use coins, stamps, cheques and hockey-sticks, involves learning to do certain things with them and not others; when to do certain things with them, and when not to do them. Among the things that we learn in the process of learning to use linguistic expressions are what we may vaguely call 'rules of logic'; for example, that though Mother and Father can both be tall, they cannot both be taller than one another; or that though uncles can be rich or poor, fat or thin, they cannot be male or female, but only male. Where it would sound implausible to say that concepts or ideas or meanings might be meaningless or absurd, there is no such implausibility in asserting that someone might use a certain expression absurdly. An attempted or suggested way of operating with an expression may be logically illegitimate or impossible, but a universal or a state of consciousness or a meaning cannot be logically legitimate or illegitimate.

'USE' AND 'UTILITY'

On the other hand there are inconveniences in talking much of the *uses* of expressions. People are liable to construe 'use' in one of the ways which English certainly does permit, namely as a synonym of 'utility' or 'usefulness'. They then suppose that to discuss the use of an expression is to discuss what it is useful for or how useful it is. Sometimes such considerations are philosophically profitable. But it is easy to see that discussing the use (versus uselessness) of something is quite different from discussing the use (versus misuse) of it, i.e. the way, method or manner of using it. The female driver may learn what is the utility of a spark plug, but learning this is not learning how to operate with a spark plug. She does not have or lack skills of competences with spark plugs, as she does with steering wheels, coins, words and knives. Her spark plugs manage themselves; or, rather, they are not managed at all. They just function automatically, until they cease to function. They are useful, even indispensable to her. But she does not manage or mismanage them.

Conversely, a person who has learned how to whistle tunes may not find the whistling of tunes at all useful or even pleasant to others or to himself. He manages, or sometimes mismanages, his lips, tongue and breath; and, more indirectly, manages or mismanages the notes he produces. He has got the trick of it; he can show us and perhaps even tell us how the trick is performed. But it is a useless trick. The question 'How do you use your breath or your lips in whistling?' has a positive and complicated answer. The

question 'What is the use, or utility, of whistling?' has a negative
and simple one. The former is a request for the details of a technique; the latter is not. Questions about the use of an expression
are often, though not always, questions about the way to operate
with it; not questions about what the employer of it needs it for.
They are How-questions, not What-for-questions. This latter sort of
question can be asked, but it is seldom necessary to ask it, since the
answer is usually obvious. In a foreign country, I do not ask what a
centime or a peseta is for; what I do ask is how many of them I have
to give for a certain article, or how many of them I am to expect to
get in exchange for a half-crown. I want to know what its purchasing power is; not that it is for making purchases with.

'USE' AND 'USAGE'

Much more insidious than this confusion between the way of
operating with something and its usefulness is the confusion between
a 'use', i.e. a way of operating with something, and a 'usage'. Lots
of philosophers, whose dominant good resolution is to discern logico-
linguistic differences, talk without qualms as if 'use' and 'usage'
were synonyms. This is just a howler, for which there is little excuse
except that in the archaic phrase 'use and wont', 'use' could, perhaps, be replaced by 'usage'; that 'used to' does mean 'accustomed
to'; and that to be hardly used is to suffer hard usage.

A usage is a custom, practice, fashion or vogue. It can be local or
widespread, obsolete or current, rural, or urban, vulgar or academic.
There cannot be a misusage any more than there can be a miscustom
or a misvogue. The methods of discovering linguistic usages are the
methods of philologists.

By contrast, a way of operating with a razor-blade, a word, a
traveller's cheque, or a canoe-paddle is a technique, knack, or
method. Learning it is learning how to do the thing; it is not finding
out sociological generalities, not even sociological generalities about
other people who do similar or different things with razor-blades,
words, travellers' cheques, or canoe-paddles. Robinson Crusoe
might find out for himself how to make and how to throw boomerangs; but this discovery would tell him nothing about those
Australian aborigines who do in fact make and use them in the
same way. The description of a conjuring-trick is not the description
of all the conjurors who perform or have performed that trick. On

the contrary, in order to describe the possessors of the trick, we should have already to be able to give some sort of description of the trick itself. Mrs Beeton tells us how to make omelets; but she gives us no information about Parisian chefs. Baedeker might tell us about Parisian chefs, and tell us which of them make omelets; but if he wanted to tell us how they make omelets, he would have to describe their techniques in the way that Mrs Beeton describes the technique of making omelets. Descriptions of usages presuppose descriptions of uses, i.e. ways or techniques of doing the thing, the more or less widely prevailing practice of doing which constitutes the usage.

There is an important difference between the employment of boomerangs, bows and arrows, and canoe-paddles on the one hand and the employment of tennis rackets, tug-of-war ropes, coins, stamps and words on the other hand. The latter are instruments of interpersonal, i.e. concerted or competitive actions. Robinson Crusoe might play some games of patience; but he could not play tennis or cricket. So a person who learns to use a tennis racket, a stroke-side oar, a coin or a word is inevitably in a position to notice other people using these things. He cannot master the tricks of such interpersonal transactions without at the same time finding out facts about some other people's employment and misemployment of them; and normally he will learn a good many of the tricks from noticing other people employing them. Even so, learning the knacks is not and does not require making a sociological study. A child may learn in the home and the village shop how to use pennies, shillings and pound notes; and his mastery of these slightly complex knacks is not improved by hearing how many people in other places and years have managed and now manage or mismanage their pennies, shillings and pound notes. Perfectly mastering a use is not getting to know everything, or even much, about a usage, even when mastering that use does casually involve finding out a bit about a few other people's practices. We were taught in the nursery how to handle a lot of words; but we were not being taught any historical or sociological generalities about employers of these words. That came later, if it came at all.

Before passing on we should notice one big difference between using canoe-paddles or tennis rackets on the one hand and using postage stamps, safety pins, coins and words on the other. Tennis rackets are wielded with greater or less skill; even the tennis champion studies to improve. But, with some unimportant reservations, it is true to say that coins, cheques, stamps, separate words, buttons and shoelaces offer no scope for talent. Either a person knows or he does not know how to use and how not to misuse them. Of course literary composition and argumentation can be more or less skilful; but the essayist or lawyer does not know the meaning of 'rabbit' or 'and' better than Everyman. There is no room here for 'better'. Similarly, the champion chess player manœuvres more skilfully than the amateur; but he does not know the permitted moves of the pieces better. They both know them perfectly, or rather they just know them.

Certainly, the cultured chess player may describe the permitted moves better than does the uncultured chess player. But he does not make these moves any better. I give change for a half-crown no better than you do. We both give the correct change. Yet I may describe such transactions more effectively than you can describe them. Knowing how to operate is not knowing how to tell how to operate. This point becomes important when we are discussing, say, the stock way (supposing there is one) of employing the word 'cause'. The doctor knows how to make this use of it as well as anyone, but he may not be able to answer any of the philosopher's inquiries about this way of using it.

In order to avoid these two big confusions, the confusion of 'use' with 'usefulness' and the confusion of 'use' with 'usage', I try nowadays to use, *inter alia*, 'employ' and 'employment' instead of the verb and noun 'use'. So I say this. Philosophers often have to try to describe the stock (or, more rarely, some non-stock) manner or way of employing an expression. Sometimes such an expression belongs to the vernacular, sometimes to some technical vocabulary; sometimes it is betwixt and between. Describing the mode of employment of an expression does not require and is not usually helped by information about the prevalence or unprevalence of this way of employing it. For the philosopher, like other folk, has long since learned how to employ or handle it, and what he is trying to describe is what he himself has learned.

Techniques are not vogues – but they may have vogues. Some of them must have vogues or be current in some other way. For it is no accident that ways of employing words, as of employing coins, stamps and chessmen, *tend* to be identical through a whole community and over a long stretch of time. We want to understand and be understood; and we learn our native tongue from our elders. Even without the pressure of legislation and dictionaries, our vocabularies tend towards uniformity. Fads and idiosyncrasies in these matters impair communication. Fads and idiosyncrasies in matters of postage stamps, coins and the moves of chessmen are ruled out by explicit legislation, and partly analogous conformities are imposed upon many technical vocabularies by such things as drill-manuals and textbooks. Notoriously these tendencies towards uniformity have their exceptions. However, as there naturally do exist many pretty widespread and pretty long-enduring vocabulary usages, it is sometimes condonable for a philosopher to remind his readers of a mode of employing an expression by alluding to 'what everyone says' or 'what no one says'. The reader considers the mode of employment that he has long since learned and feels strengthened, when told that big battalions are on his side. In fact, of course, this appeal to prevalence is philosophically pointless, besides being philologically risky. What is wanted is, perhaps, the extraction of the logical rules implicitly governing a concept, i.e. a way of operating with an expression (or any other expression that does the same work). It is probable that the use of this expression, to perform this job, is widely current; but whether it is so or not is of no philosophical interest. Job-analysis is not Mass Observation. Nor is it helped by Mass Observation. But Mass Observation sometimes needs the aid of job-analysis.

Before terminating this discussion of the use of the expression 'the use of the expression ". . ."'. I want to draw attention to an interesting point. We can ask whether a person knows how to use and how not to misuse a certain word. But we cannot ask whether he knows how to use a certain *sentence*. When a block of words has congealed into a phrase we can ask whether he knows how to use the phrase. But when a sequence of words has not yet congealed into a phrase, while we can ask whether he knows how to use its ingredient words, we cannot easily ask whether he knows how to use that sequence. Why can we not even ask whether he knows how to use a certain sentence? For we talk about the meanings of sentences, seemingly just as we talk of the meanings of the words in it; so, if knowing the meaning of a word is knowing how to use it, we might have expected that knowing the meaning of a sentence was knowing how to use the sentence. Yet this glaringly does not go.

A cook uses salt, sugar, flour, beans and bacon in making a pie. She uses, and perhaps misuses, the ingredients. But she does not, in this way, use the pie. Her pie is not an ingredient. In a somewhat different way, the cook uses, and perhaps misuses, a rolling-pin, a fork, a frying-pan and an oven. These are utensils with which she makes her pie. But the pie is not another utensil. The pie is (well or badly) composed out of the ingredients, by means of the utensils. It is what she used them for; but it cannot be listed in either class of them. Somewhat, but only somewhat, similarly a sentence is (well or badly) constructed out of words. It is what the speaker or writer uses them for. He composes it out of them. His sentence is not itself something which, in this way, he either uses or misuses, either uses or does not use. His composition is not a component of his composition. We can tell a person to say something (e.g. ask a question, give a command or narrate an anecdote), using a specified word or phrase, and he will know what he is being told to do. But if we just tell him to pronounce or write down, by itself, that specified word or phrase, he will see the difference between this order and the other one. For he is not now being told to use, i.e. *incorporate*, the word or phrase, but only to pronounce it or write it down. Sentences are things that we say. Words and phrases are what we say things *with*.

There can be dictionaries of words and dictionaries of phrases. But there cannot be dictionaries of sentences. This is not because such dictionaries would have to be infinitely and therefore impracticably long. On the contrary, it is because they could not even begin. Words and phrases are there, in the bin, for people to avail themselves of when they want to say things. But the sayings of these things are not some more things which are there in the bin for people to avail themselves of, when they want to say these things. This fact that words and phrases can, while sentences cannot, be misused, since sentences cannot be, in this way, used at all, is quite consistent with the important fact that sentences can be well or ill constructed. We can say things awkwardly or ungrammatically and we can say things which are grammatically proper, but do not make sense.

It follows that there are some radical differences between what is meant by 'the meaning of a word or phrase' and what is meant by 'the meaning of a sentence'. Understanding a word or phrase is knowing how to use it, i.e. make it perform its role in a wide range of sentences. But understanding a sentence is not knowing how to make it perform its role. The play has not got a role.

We are tempted to suppose that the question 'How are word-meanings related to sentence-meanings?' is a tricky but genuine question, perhaps, rather like 'How is the purchasing power of my shilling related to the purchasing power of the contents of my pay-envelope?' But this model puts things awry from the start.

If I know the meaning of a word or phrase I know something

like a body of unwritten rules, or something like an unwritten code or general recipe. I have learned to use the word correctly in an unlimited variety of different settings. What I know is, in this respect, somewhat like what I know when I know how to use a knight or a pawn at chess. I have learned to put it to its work anywhen and anywhere, if there is work for it to do. But the idea of putting a sentence to its work anywhen and anywhere is fantastic. It has not got a role which it can perform again and again in different plays. It has not got a role at all, any more than a play has a role. Knowing what it means is not knowing anything like a code or a body of rules, though it requires knowing the codes or rules governing the use of words or phrases that make it up. There are general rules and recipes for constructing sentences of certain kinds; but not general rules or recipes for constructing the particular sentence 'Today is Monday'. Knowing the meaning of 'Today is Monday' is not knowing general rules, codes or recipes governing the use of this sentence, since there is no such thing as the utilisation or, therefore reutilisation of this sentence. I expect that this ties up with the fact that sentences and clauses make sense or make no sense, where words neither do nor do not make sense, but only have meanings; and that pretence-sentences can be absurd or nonsensical, where pretence-words are neither absurd nor nonsensical, but only meaningless. I can say stupid things, but words can be neither stupid nor not stupid.

III Use, usage and meaning

Gilbert Ryle

In 1932 Mr (now Sir) Alan H. Gardiner published *The Theory of Speech and Language* (Clarendon Press). A central theme of his book was what, with some acknowledged verbal artificiality, he labelled the distinction between 'Language' and 'Speech'. I shall draw, develop and apply this distinction in my own way.

A language, such as the French language, is a stock, fund or deposit of words, constructions, intonations, cliché phrases and so on. 'Speech', on the other hand, or 'discourse' can be conscripted to denote the activity or rather the clan of activities of saying things, saying them in French, it may be, or English or some other language. A stock of language-pieces is not a lot of activities, but the fairly lasting wherewithal to conduct them; somewhat as a stock of coins is not a momentary transaction or set of momentary transactions of buying, lending, investing, etc., but is the lasting wherewithal to conduct such transactions. Roughly, as Capital stands to Trade, so Language stands to Speech.

A language is something to be known, and we get to know it by learning it. We learn it partly by being taught it, and partly by picking it up. For any given part of a language, a learner may not yet have learned that part; or he may have learned it and not forgotten it, or he may have learned it and forgotten it, or he may have half-learned it; or he may have half-forgotten it. A language is a corpus of teachable things. It is not, of course, a static corpus until it is a dead language. Nor would two teachers of it always agree whether something should be taught as a part of that language. Is French literary-style to be taught by teachers of the French Language or by teachers of French Literature? Just when does an acceptable turn of phrase become an idiom? How old can a neologism be? What about slang?

Saying something in a language involves but does not reduce to knowing the requisite pieces of that language. The speaker is here and now employing what he had previously acquired and still possesses. He is now in the act of operating with things of which he has, perhaps for years, been the possessor. The words, constructions, intonations, etc., that he employs in saying what he says in these words, constructions, etc., is not another part of that language. It is a momentary operation *with* parts of that language, just as the buying or lending that I do with part of my capital is not itself a part of that capital, but a momentary operation with a part of it. That, indeed, is what my capital is for, namely, to enable me to make purchases, benefactions, loans, etc., with parts of it whenever I wish to do so. It is a set of moderately permanent possibilities of making particular momentary transactions.

If I say something in French, then, even though what I say has never been said before, I do not thereby enlarge the French language, i.e. increase the amount to be learned by a student of the French language. The fact that he does not know what I said does not entail that there is a bit of the French language that he has still to learn. Dicta made in French are not parts of the French language. They are things done with parts of the French language. You might utilise the same parts in saying something identical with or quite different from what I said. Your act of saying it is not mine, and neither is a part of the fund on which we both draw. But dicta can notoriously fossilise into clichés. '*Je ne sais quoi*' can now be used as a noun; and '*Rest and be Thankful*' can be a proper name.

We are tempted to treat the relation between sentences and words as akin to the relation between faggots and sticks. But this is entirely wrong. Words, constructions, etc., are the atoms of a Language; sentences are the units of Speech. Words, constructions, etc., are what we have to learn in mastering a language; sentences are what we produce when we say things. Words have histories; sentences do not, though their authors do. I must have learned the words that I utter when I say something with them. I need not, and, with reservations, cannot have learned the sentence that I come out with when I say something. It is something that I compose, not something that I have acquired. I am its author, not its employer. Sentences are not things of which I have a stock or fund. Nor are my buyings and lendings things of which I have a hoard or purseful.

In daily life we do not often mention as such the sentences that people produce. We speak instead of their allegations, complaints, promises, verdicts, requests, witticisms, confessions and commands. It is, in the main, people like grammarians, compositors, translators, amanuenses and editors who need to refer to the things that people say as 'sentences', since they are *ex officio* concerned with such matters as page-space, punctuation, syntax, plagiarisation, and so on. None the less, what they are interested in are instances of someone, actual or imagined, alleging, complaining, warning, joking, etc., though their special concern is with the punctuation of them and not with their humorousness; with their length and not with their truth; with their moods and tenses and not with their relevance or rudeness.

When Caesar said '*Veni*; *vidi*; *vici*', he said three things, though he used only three Latin words. Then is '*Vici*' a word or a sentence? The queerness of this disjunctive question is revealing. What Caesar produced, orally or in writing, on a certain day, was a laconic sentence, if a sentence is an instance of someone saying something. In this instance Caesar said something which was true. But he said it using only one Latin word, a word which had long been there for anyone to use anywhen in saying all sorts of considerably different things. The word was not true, or, of course, false either. Caesar boasted '*Vici*', but the dictionary's explanation of the verb '*Vici*' need say nothing about Caesar boasting. What it describes was, perhaps, also used by, *inter alios*, some concussed gladiator asking anxiously '*Vici?*' The boast '*vici*' was a different sentence from the question '*vici?*', though the authors of both used the same Latin word, of which neither was the inventor. The word '*vici*' was there, in their common fund, to be employed, misemployed or left unemployed by anyone anywhen. The boast '*vici*' and the query '*vici?*' were two momentary speech-acts in which this one word was utilised for saying different things. Our question 'Is "*vici*" a word or a sentence?' was queer because its subject was ambiguous. Was it about a speech-episode, like a boast or a query, or was it about an inflected Latin verb? It was queer also because '. . . a word or a sentence?' was a disjunction between predicates of quite different categories, on a par with '. . . a bat or a stroke?'

Is the interrogative sentence '*vici?*' a part of the Latin language? Well, would a student still have some Latin to learn who had never met it? Surely not. What he had learned is enough to enable him to construe it if he should ever meet it. What he construes are employments of Latin words, constructions, etc.; what he must know in order to construe or understand these employments are the Latin words, inflections, constructions, etc. He must know the word in order to understand the one-word boast or question; but that knowing is not this understanding; what he had long since known is not what he has just understood or misunderstood. As we employ coins to make loans, but do not employ lendings, so we employ words, etc., in order to say things, but we do not employ the sayings of things – or misemploy them or leave them unemployed either.

Dictions and dicta belong to different categories. So do roads and journeys; so do gallows and executions.

Sometimes a person tries to say something and fails through ignorance of the language. Perhaps he stops short because he does not know or cannot think of the required words or constructions. Perhaps he does not stop, but produces the wrong word or construction, thinking it to be the right one, and so commits a solecism. Perhaps his failure is of lesser magnitude; he says something unidiomatically or ungrammatically; or he gets the wrong intonation or he mispronounces. Such failures show that he has not completely mastered, say, the French language. In the extended sense of 'rule' in which a rule is anything against which faults are adjudged to be at fault, solecisms, mispronunciations, malapropisms, and unidiomatic and ungrammatical constructions are breaches of the rules of, e.g., the French language. For our purposes we do not need to consider the sources or the status of rules of this kind, or the authorities whose censures our French instructor dreads. Solecisms are in general philosophically uninteresting. Nor, for obvious reasons, do we often commit solecisms, save when young, ill-schooled, abroad or out of our intellectual depth.

The reproof 'You cannot say that and speak good French' is generically different from the reproof 'You cannot say that without absurdity'. The latter is not a comment on the quality of the speaker's French, since it could be true though the speaker had spoken in flawless French, or had not been speaking in French at all, but in English or Greek instead. The comment, if true, would be true of what was said whatever language it was said in, and whether it was said in barbarous or impeccable French or English. A mispronunciation or a wrong gender may be a bit of faulty French, but a self-contradiction is not a fault-in-French. Cicero's *non sequiturs* were not lapses from good Latin into bad Latin. His carelessness or incompetence was not linguistic carelessness or incompetence, if we tether the adjective 'linguistic' to the noun 'Language' as this is here being contrasted with 'Speech'.

There is an enormous variety of disparate kinds of faults that we can find or claim to find with things that people say. I can complain, justly or else unjustly, that what you said was tactless, irrelevant, repetitious, false, inaccurate, insubordinate, trite, fallacious, ill-timed, blasphemous, malicious, vapid, uninformative, over-informative, prejudiced, pedantic, obscure, prudish, provocative, self-contradictory, tautologous, circular or nonsensical, and so on indefinitely. Some of these epithets can be appropriate also to behaviour which is not speech-behaviour; some of them cannot. Not one of them could be asserted or denied of any item in an English or French dictionary or Grammar. I can stigmatise what you said with any one of these epithets without even hinting that what you said was faulty in its French or whatever other language you said it in. I grumble at your dictum but not at your mastery of the language that it was made in. There are countless heterogeneous disciplines and corrections which are meant to train people not to commit these Speech-faults. Not one of them belongs to the relatively homogeneous discipline of teaching, say, the French language. Speech-faults are not to be equated with Language-faults. Nothing need be wrong with the paints, brushes and canvas with which a portrait is bungled. Painting badly is not a pot of bad paint.

Logicians and philosophers are, *ex officio*, much concerned with kinds of things that people say or might be tempted to say. Only where there can be fallacies can there be valid inferences, namely in arguments; and only where there can be absurdities can there be non-absurdities, namely in dicta. We are presented with *aporiai* not by the telescope or the trawling-net, but by passages in books or by ripostes in debates. A fallacy or an impossible consequence may indeed have to be presented to us in French or English, etc. But it does not follow from this that what is wrong with it is anything faulty in the French or English in which it is presented. It was no part of the business of our French or English instructors to teach us that if most men wear coats and most men wear waistcoats it does not follow that most men wear both. This is a different sort of lesson and one which we cannot begin until we have already learned to use without solecism 'most', 'and', 'if', etc. There are no French implications or non-implications, so though 'p' may be said in French and 'q' may be said in French, it is nonsense to say 'q does not follow from p in the best French'. Similarly, what is impossible in 'The Cheshire Cat vanished, leaving only her grin behind her' is not any piece of intolerably barbarous English. Carroll's wording of the impossible story could not be improved, and the impossibility of his narrated incident survives translation into any language into which it can be translated. Something was amusingly wrong with what he said, but not with what he said it in.

I have a special reason for harking on this point that what someone says may be fallacious or absurd without being in any measure solecistic; i.e. that some Speech-faults, including some of those which matter to logicians and philosophers, are not and do not carry with them any Language-faults. Some philosophers, oblivious of the distinction between Language and Speech, or between having words, etc., to say things with and saying things with them, give to sentences the kind of treatment that they give to words, and, in particular, assimilate their accounts of what a sentence means to their accounts of what a word means. Equating the notion of the meaning of a word with the notion of the use of that word, they go on without apparent qualms to talking as if the meaning of a sentence could equally well be spoken of as the use of that sentence. We hear, for example, that nonsensical English sentences are sentences that have no use in English; as if sentences could *be* solecisms. Should we expect to hear that a certain argument is henceforth to contain an Undistributed Middle in B.B.C. English?

My last sentence but three, say, is not something with which I once learned how to say things. It *is* my saying something. Nor is an execution something erected to hang people on. It *is* the hanging of somebody. Part of what we learn, in learning the words of a language, is indeed how to employ them. But the act of exercising this acquired competence, i.e. the saying something with them, is not in its turn an acquired wherewithal to say things. It neither has nor lacks a use, or, therefore, a use in English.

The famous saying, 'Don't ask for the meaning; ask for the use', might have been and I hope was a piece of advice to philosophers, and not to lexicographers or translators. It advised philosophers, I hope, when wrestling with some *aporia*, to switch their attention from the trouble-giving words in their dormancy as language-pieces or dictionary-items to their utilisations in the actual sayings of things; from their general promises when on the shelf to their particular performances when at work; from their permanent purchasing power while in the bank to the concrete marketing done yesterday morning with them; in short, from these words *qua* units of a Language to live sentences in which they are being actively employed.

More than this; the famous saying, in association with the idea of Rules of Use, could and I think should have been intended to advise philosophers, when surveying the kinds of live dicta that are or might be made with these trouble-giving words, to consider especially some of the kinds of non-solecistic Speech-faults against which the producer of such live dicta ought to take precautions, e.g. what sorts of dicta could not be significantly made with them, and why; what patterns of argument pivoting on these live dicta would be fallacious, and why; what kinds of verification-procedures would be impertinent, and why; to what kinds of questions such live dicta would be irrelevant, and why; and so on. To be clear about the 'how' of the employment of something we need to be clear also about its 'how not to', and about the reasons for both.

Early in this century Husserl and later Wittgenstein used the illuminating metaphors of 'logical syntax' and 'logical grammar'. Somewhat as, say, indicative verbs used instead of subjunctive verbs render some would-be Latin sentences bad Latin, so certain category-skids and logical howlers render dicta, said in no matter which tongue, nonsensical or absurd. A so-called Rule of Logical Syntax is what a nonsensical dictum is in breach of. But the analogy must not be pressed very far. The rules of Latin syntax are part of what we must learn if we are to be able to produce or construe Latin dicta. They are parts of the equipment to be employed by someone if he is to say either sensible or silly things in decent Latin. The Rules of Logical Syntax, on the other hand, belong not to a Language or to Languages, but to Speech. A person who says something senseless or illogical betrays not ignorance but silliness, muddle-headedness or, in some of the interesting cases, over-cleverness. We find fault not with his schooling in years gone by but with his thinking here and now. He has not forgotten or misremembered any of his lessons; he has operated unwarily or over-ingeniously in his execution of his momentary task. In retrospect he will reproach not his teachers, but himself; and he will reproach himself not for never having known something but for not having been thinking what he was saying yesterday.

The vogue of using 'Language' and 'linguistic' ambivalently both for dictions and for dicta, i.e. both for the words, etc., that we say things in and for what we say in them, helps to blind us to the wholesale inappropriateness of the epithets which fit pieces of language to the sayings of things with those pieces; and to the wholesale and heterogeneous inappropriateness of the variegated epithets which fit things said to the language-pieces and language-patterns that they are said in.

It remains true that philosophers and logicians do have to talk about talk, or, to put it in a more Victorian way, to discourse about discourse. But it is not true that they are *ex officio* concerned with what language teachers are *ex officio* concerned with.

IV Philosophy and language[1]

A. G. N. Flew

I propose to attack a miscellany of popular misconceptions, trying incidentally to illuminate various possibly puzzling practices. A very typical passage from Aristotle's *Nicomachean Ethics* will serve as a text:

> We must also grasp the nature of deliberative excellence – εὐβουλία – and find whether it is a sort of knowledge, or of opinion, or of skill at guessing – εὐστοχία – or something different from these in kind. Now it is not knowledge: for men do not investigate – ζητοῦσι – matters about which they know, whereas deliberative excellence is a sort of deliberation, and deliberating implies investigating and calculating. But deliberation is not the same as investigation: it is the investigation of a particular subject [i.e. conduct – A.F.]. Nor yet is it skill at guessing: for this operates without conscious calculation, and rapidly, whereas deliberating takes a long time. . . . Correctness cannot be predicated of knowledge, any more than can error, and correctness of opinion is truth (bk vi, ch. 9: 1142 a32 ff.).

Objections: (i) 'But imagine that a man knew that there was a body buried in his back garden, and nevertheless joined with the police in their investigations: would that not be investigating a matter about which he already knew?'

(ii) 'But surely it is sometimes all right to speak of erroneous knowledge, as when sarcastically I say: "He knew the winner of the two-thirty, but he knew wrong"?'

Replies: (i) 'No, it would in his case, but not that of the police, only be *pretending* to investigate, a matter of "investigating" (in inverted commas, making the protest that this is a bogus case of investigation). To anyone who knows that the man knows that the body is there, and yet sincerely persists in saying that that man is investigating, and not pretending to investigate or "investigating" (in snigger quotes), what else can we say but "You just do not know the meaning of the word 'investigate' "?'

(ii) 'You are quite right, of course: but your exception is one which, properly understood, only helps to reinforce Aristotle's thesis. For the whole sarcastic point of the use of the expression "knew wrong" and of saying "he 'knew'" (in that sniggering inverted-comma tone of voice) depends absolutely on the (logical) fact that "He knows p" entails "p"; that it is incorrect to say "He knows p" unsarcastically if you or he to your knowledge have reason to doubt p.[2] And again, if anyone has reason to doubt p (or, still better, knows not p), and yet sincerely and unsarcastically insists "He (there) knows p", what else can we say but "Either you do not know the meaning of the word 'know' and are ignorantly misusing it; or else you have your own peculiar use for the word which I wish you would explain and try to justify"?'

Notes: (i) It is appropriate to build our basic example here upon a passage of the *Nicomachean Ethics*, since most of the *avant-garde* of Oxford philosophy since the war (Austin, Hart, Hare and Urmson, for instance) are soaked in this book, and there is a very strong analogy between their work and it.

(ii) When someone like Ryle says 'We don't say' or 'We can't say' or uses any of the semi-equivalent expressions of the material mode of speech, and we can think of occasions on which we might and do intelligibly and not incorrectly say precisely what he says we cannot say, it is a good rule to consider whether these exceptions do not in fact actually reinforce the point he is really concerned to make, or whether, if not, they are really relevant to it, involving the same use of the word. No one is infallible, and certainly not Ryle in this matter, but we should allow for the fact that a self-contradictory or otherwise logically improper expression *may* get a piquancy precisely as such, and can thus acquire a use, a point, which depends entirely on the fact that it is a misuse, and is thus parasitical on the logico-linguistic rule to which it is an exception. 'He knew but he knew wrong', 'bachelor husband', and 'the evidence of my own eyes' all get their piquancy in this way.

(A) 'But Aristotle was not concerned with *mere words*: whereas your replies to objections involve nothing else.' A closer look at the example will show that and how this antithesis is here crucially misleading. The replies are not about words in the way in which protests at the replacement of 'men (and women)' or 'people' by '(male and female) personnel' are about words.[3] Nor do they concern English words to the exclusion of equivalents in Greek or Chocktaw. Nor do they even concern words as opposed to non-verbal signs doing the same jobs. (Consider the camp-fire version of 'Under-

neath the Spreading Chestnut Tree', of which our late King was
so fond, in which gestures replace some of the words.) Rather they
are about the *uses* of certain words, the *jobs* they do, the *point* of
employing them: their *meaning*, and the *implications* which they
carry.

Thus it would be no more necessary to mention the particular
English words 'investigate' and 'know' in translating the replies
into another language than it is to mention ζήτησις and ἐπιστήμη
in rendering Aristotle's argument from the Greek. Though English-
speaking philosophers sometimes speak of correct or standard
English, this must not be mistaken to imply that they are concerned
with English as opposed to other languages (usually: but see (B)
below).[4] The replies, like Aristotle's theses and the objections to
them, are all equally concerned with logic as much as with language.
The whole inquiry is logical rather than philological, an examination of the 'informal logic'[5] of two workaday concepts. Hence the
fashion for expressions such as 'the *logic* of (our) language', '*logic*
and language', 'the *logic* of "probable"', 'the *logical* behaviour of
"God"-sentences', and even '*logical* geography', is not necessarily
just a pointless irritating fad; though nothing we have to say will
do anything to justify 'The Logic of British and American Industry'
or 'The Logic of Liberty' when used of inquiries neither in the linguistic idiom nor even conceptual.

(B) This suggests why philosophers given to talking about correct
English 'seem to take little account of the existence of other languages whose structure and idiom are very different from English
. . . but which seem equally if not more capable of engendering
metaphysical confusion'.[6] Being, like their colleagues, concerned
with conceptual matters, their protests against the misuse of English
are not primarily motivated by a concern for correct *English* as
opposed to faultless Eskimo. But the matters should not be allowed
to rest there. The existence of other natural languages whose
structure, idiom, and vocabulary are not completely congruent
with those of our own, is philosophically relevant in at least three
ways.

(i) They provide concepts not available in the stock of our language group. Notoriously there are in all languages words un-
translatable into English: no English words, that is, have precisely
the same use. And many of the concepts concerned are of philosophic
interest: either directly in themselves, or indirectly because it is
necessary to master them in order to understand some philosopher
who used or discussed the concept in question. Perhaps the best

examples are ethical, such as ὕβρις, ἀρετή, or *tabu*.

(ii) Different languages offer different temptations. J. S. Mill must have been beguiled into his disastrous argument from what is in fact desired to what is in morals desirable by the 'grammatical' analogy between English words like 'audible' and 'visible' and the English word 'desirable'.[7] (There might be a language in which there was no such morphological analogy between a class of words meaning 'able as a matter of fact to be somethinged' and one meaning 'ought as a matter of value to be somethinged'.) The misconstruction of 'infinity' as being the word for a gigantic number is made attractive by the morphological analogy between the expression 'to infinity' and such as 'to one hundred'. If we always said 'for ever' or 'indefinitely' instead of 'to infinity', and if 'alephnought' did not happen to sound like the word for a colossal number, then this temptation would disappear.[8] It has been said that it is hard to make Hegel's dialectic plausible or even intelligible in English for the lack of any word with ambiguities parallel to those of the German *aufheben*.[9] Kant, in a significantly phrased passage, noted:

> The German language has the good fortune to possess expressions which do not allow this difference [between the opposites of *das Übel* and *das Böse* – A.F.] to be overlooked. It possesses two very distinct concepts, and especially different expressions, for that which the Latins express by a single word *bonum*.[10]

Lastly, the Greek way of forming abstract noun substitutes from the neuter of the definite article and the adjective does something, though not of course very much to explain the attractions for Plato of the Theory of Forms.[11]

(iii) The existence of natural languages with radically different logical characteristics gives the opportunity for logical explorations of ways of thinking far more diverse than those embraced in most of these singly – for, as it were, logico-linguistic travel, which can broaden the mind and stimulate the imagination and so provide benefits of the sort which alert people are able to get from physical travel.

Consider, for example, the analogy between the recognition of the legitimate existence of non-Euclidean geometries, which helps to undermine rationalist hopes of a quasi-geometrical deductive system of knowledge about the world based on self-evident necessary premisses; and the realisation that there actually are natural languages to which the subject-predicate distinction can scarcely be applied, which are not saturated with the concept of cause, and which provide words to pick out different differences and likenesses from those which English, and indeed most European languages, are equipped to mark. To realise this is to discredit ideas that the subject–predicate distinction must be inextricably rooted in the non-linguistic world,[12] that the notion of cause is an indispensable category of thought,[13] and that language must reflect the ultimate nature of reality.[14] Of course, it is theoretically possible simply to imagine other conceptual systems and categories of concept.[15] But this is excessively difficult, as witness the calibre of some of the philosophers who have assumed or even asserted contingent, though perhaps admirable, characteristics of their particular languages to be necessities of thought. In any case there is actual material waiting to be studied;[16] and there is much to be said for the use of real, as opposed to imaginary, examples in philosophy. It can add vitality to discussion and help to break down the idea that philosophical training and philosophical inquiry can have no relevance or value in the world outside our cloistered classrooms.

(C) The *use* of a word is not the same as, though it is subtly connected with, the *usage* of that word. The former (see above) is language-neutral: if we inquire about the *use* of 'table', then we are simultaneously and equally concerned with the *use* of 'tavola' and other equivalents in other languages – with, if you like, the concept of table. The latter is language-specific: if we inquire about the *usage* of 'table' then we are concerned with how that particular *English* word is (or ought to be) employed by those who employ that word, and not 'tavola'.

But the two are crucially related. No word could be said to have a use except in so far as some language group or sub-group gives it a use and recognises as correct the usage appropriate to that use. For the sounds we use as words are all, intrinsically and prior to the emergence of any linguistic conventions about them, almost equally suitable to do any linguistic job whatever. Whereas a knife, say, could not be used, or even misused, as a tent, 'glory' might have been given the use we have in fact given to 'a nice knock-down argument'.

The *uses* of words depend subtly on the correct *usages* of words. Humpty Dumpty can only be accused of *misusing* 'glory' because the accepted, standard, correct *usage* of Lewis Carroll's language group was radically different from the private usage of Humpty Dumpty. It was perverse, ill-mannered, misleading, and endangered the possibility of linguistic communication, thus wantonly and without explanation to flout the linguistic conventions. (No doubt, like contemporary 'prophets of a new linguistic dispensation',[17] he regarded such linguistic conventions as 'preposterous restrictions upon free speech'.[18]) Furthermore, as academic philologists[19] and people concerned with maintaining and increasing the efficiency of the English language[20] (and others) have often urged, what is *correct* usage of any language group depends ultimately upon *actual* usage. It is because *use* depends on *correct usage* while this in turn depends ultimately upon *actual usage* that changes in actual usage can enrich or impoverish the conceptual equipment provided by a language. If a new usage is established by which a new use is given to a word, a use not previously provided for, then to that extent the language concerned is enriched.[21] Whereas if an old usage whereby two words had two different uses is replaced by a new one in which one of them loses its job to become a mere synonym of the other, then similarly there is a proportionate impoverishment. Since the actual usage of any language group or sub-group is never in fact completely static, both processes are usually going on, and together constitute a considerable part of the history of any language. ('The history of language . . . is little other than the history of corruptions': Lounsbury was writing as a grammarian, but the same is true from a logical point of view, though 'corruption' must be taken as value-neutral here.)

To come at the matter from a new angle: consider how the historical theologian studies the concept of *nephesh* in Israel. He has and can have no other method but the examination of the occurrences of the word '*nephesh*' in his texts: the attempt to discover from a survey of usage what was its use, what job this word did in the vocabulary of the people who employed it. Or, again, consider how Professor H. J. Paton objects decisively to the translation of *abgeleitet* as 'deducted' because 'an examination of Kant's usage will show that it seldom or never means this' (*The Categorical Imperative*, p. 134 n.). Or consider how the cryptographer tries to discover the meaning of an unknown element in a code. He has and can have no other method but a similar examination of its occurrences, hoping by a study of usage to hit upon its use, its meaning. Appeals to *use* and *usage* in creative philosophy can be regarded as a belatedly explicit application of the tried and necessary methods of the historians of ideas.

Before passing to section (D), there are various minor points to be made. First, 'linguistic conventions' here means those by which we use 'pod' rather than 'pid' or 'nup' to mean pod; and so forth. Second, 'language-group or sub-group' is not here a precise expression. It is intended to cover the users of recognised languages, of their dialects, of jargons and private languages of all kinds, down to and including individuals who develop terminologies private to themselves and their readers and interpreters, if any. Our point is one about the presuppositions of linguistic communication. Third, not all features of the usage of a word will be relevant to questions about its use. That the personal pronouns 'I', 'he', and 'she' are subject to radical morphological transformation in other cases is of concern to Fowler, but not to the philosopher. For their use would be unaffected if usage were to send these transformations the way of other unnecessary case-indications. But this is a matter for caution, for it is hard to be sure without examination what will turn out to be relevant. Fowler would be concerned with the spread of the usage which makes 'contact' a transitive verb, but perhaps this change also subtly affects the notion of contact.[22] Fourth, it is possible for people to communicate, in a way which depends partly on words (or other conventional signs), in spite of misusing many of the words (or other conventional signs) they employ; for the intelligent appreciation of context (in the widest sense) can do much to compensate for such deficiencies. But to the precise extent that such compensation is necessary, communication is thereby not depending upon words (or other conventional signs). Fifth, this stress on *use* derives mainly from Wittgenstein: the idea is present unexploited in the *Tractatus Logico-Philosophicus*: 'In philosophy the question "For what purpose do we really use that word . . .?" constantly leads to valuable results' (6.211, cf. also 3.328, 3.326 and 5.47321); and it became the slogan 'Don't ask for the *meaning*, ask for the *use*' in the early thirties after his return to Cambridge.[23] The explicit concern with correct *usage* as the determinant of *use* seems to derive mainly from J. L. Austin.[24]

(D) Notoriously there is often a gap between actual and correct usage. It is possible for some usage which is (even much) more honoured in the breach than the observance to be one which defaulters are prepared to acknowledge as correct, mainly because certain people and reference books are recognised as generally authoritative. There is still, in Britain at any rate, no question as to what is the correct usage of such non-technical logical terms as 'refute', 'imply', and 'infer'. But it seems most unlikely that the actual usage of the majority (even of first-year university students) conforms with it. This gap is of the greatest importance to anyone

who wishes to understand 'what is at the bottom of all this terminological hyperaesthesia, and all the whistle-blowing and knuckle-
rapping and scolding that goes along with it'.[25]

(i) It enables a piece of 'logical geographising', telling us only
what most of us in a way know, making no distinction not already
provided for in familiar words, to be an exercise in precisification of
thought and in improvement of usage for all those who work
through it; and not merely for those, like the students mentioned
above, whose word training has been conspicuously deficient. Consider the effects of describing the differences and analogies between
threats, *promises* and *predictions*, to draw example from a recent
Oxford examination paper. Often, however, such examinations of
present correct usage will show that we need not only to bring our
actual usage more into line with correct usage, but also to go
further by suggesting improvements. 'Essential though it is as a
preliminary to track down the detail of our ordinary uses of words,
it seems that we shall in the end always be compelled to straighten
them out to some extent' (Austin).[26]

(ii) It gives ground for hope that philosophers, including always
and especially ourselves, who misuse or tolerate the misuse of
certain words and expressions,[27] or who give or accept incorrect
accounts of their *rationes applicandi*, may be led by suitable
attention to their correct usage and actual use to realise and
remedy their mistakes. This phrase *ratio applicandi* is modelled deliberately upon the *ratio decidendi* of the lawyers: the principle
under which all previous decisions can be subsumed and upon
which, as the fiction has it, they were in fact made. For just as it is
perfectly possible to make decisions consistent with such a principle
without having actually formulated it, so it is possible, and even
usual, to be able to apply a word correctly in unselfconscious
moments, without being able to discern its *ratio applicandi*, or even
to do so when positively in error about it; though of course anyone
making such a mistake will have some inclination to misuse the
word.

(iii) But it also makes it possible to misrepresent present *correct*
usage as nicer, more uniform, and more stable than it in fact is: 'the
assumption being that the necessary rules and regulations are
already embodied in ordinary parlance, requiring only inspection, or
the production of a few trivial examples, to make clear what is
allowable and what is not'.[28] To do this is especially tempting
perhaps for philosophers in strong reaction against the contempt
shown by many of their mathematically-minded colleagues for the

rich and subtle instruments provided to those willing and able to use them with care and skill by all but the most beggarly of the natural languages (see (v) below). The extent to which the 'logical geographers' have in fact succumbed has perhaps been exaggerated; but it is well to be on guard.

(iv) It is this alone which makes it possible to speak at all of *misuses*. When philosophers are attacked for misusing an ordinary, or even an extraordinary, word, this is rarely an 'attempt to convict perfectly respectable philosophers of illiteracy, or of the perpetration of ungrammatical gibberish. Instead 'what is complained of is not lack of *grammar*, even [*sic*] in the text-book sense, but incoherence or absence of meaning' (my italics); even though some (like Wittgenstein who perhaps discovered it) given to pressing 'the familiar and overworked analogy between logical and grammatical rules',[29] occasionally omit the prefix 'logical' where the context makes clear that it is *logical* grammar that is at issue. The point is, usually, that the philosopher under attack has somehow been misled into misusing a word in a way which generates paradox, confusion and perplexity. Hume was scandalised that a controversy 'canvassed and disputed with great eagerness since the first origin of science and philosophy' had 'turned merely upon words'.[30] But the skeleton solution he suggested depended, fairly explicitly, upon recalling to mind, with the help of simple concrete examples, just what the ordinary use of the word 'free' actually is; and that it is not its ordinary job (not what it ordinarily means), not yet any part of its ordinary job (nor yet part of what it implies), to attribute to actions unpredictability in principle.[31] If this is so, then it is not contradictory to say that some action was both predictable and performed of the agent's own free will – always assuming, of course, that the key words are being used in their ordinary senses. And in any case complaints about 'pseudo-problems',[32] 'a petty word-jugglery',[33] or the tendency 'for philosophers to encroach upon the province of grammarians, and to engage in disputes of words, while they imagine they are handling controversies of the deepest importance and concern'[34] all miss the point. For Hume is broaching a conceptual solution to a philosophical problem, which cannot thereby lose whatever importance it may have had before.

Such a brief outline example may suggest facile crudity: 'a very simple way of disposing of immense quantities of metaphysical and other argument, without the smallest trouble or exertion'.[35] This is inevitable perhaps in the terse cartoon simplicity needed in incidental illustrations. But the suggestion could scarcely survive: *either* an examination of such contributions to the free will problems as R. M. Hare's 'The Freedom of the Will',[36] W. D. Falk's 'Goading and Guiding',[37] and H. L. A. Hart's 'Ascription of Responsibility and Rights';[38] *or* an awakening to the fact that no one has asked to be excused from dealing with whatever arguments may be deployed in support of such philosophers' misuses. Perhaps Kant was discouraged from recognising the merit in Hume here by Hume's own misleading talk about mere words as well as by the aggressive way in which Hume misrepresented a good start as the end of the affair. Certainly we find Kant two pages later very grudgingly conceding part of Hume's point, but insisting that at any rate *transcendental* freedom cannot thus be reconciled with scientific determinism.[39]

(v) After so much has been said about misuses and misconstructions, it must be mentioned that interest originally directed at the uses of words only inasmuch as this brought out what were misuses and misconstructions, is sometimes, by a familiar psychological process, partly diverted to the study of use for its own sake. Before suggesting that, however psychologically understandable, such interests do not become a philosopher in his working hours, we should cast our minds back to Aristotle and reflect whether all his studies of the concepts of moral psychology were in fact wholly directed to some ulterior end even within philosophy; or, more generally, ask ourselves whether an interest in concepts is not one of the things which makes a philosopher.

But whatever are the rights and wrongs about ulterior and ultimate ends, and whatever the jurisdictional proprieties, disputes about these here turn out to be largely unnecessary. For in elucidating the ordinary uses (as opposed to philosophers' suspected misuses) of some of the rather limited range of words around which our controversies tend to cluster,[40] it has been noticed that the conceptual equipment provided by ordinary (here opposed particularly to technical) language is amazingly rich and subtle; and that even the classical puzzles cannot be fully resolved without elucidating not merely the formerly fashionable elite of notions but also all their neglected logical hangers-on. In formulating and attacking free will puzzles, philosophers, with the outstanding exception of Aristotle, have been inclined to concentrate on a few ideas: *free will, compulsion, choice, necessity, responsible,* and one or two others. Whereas we have available in our ordinary vocabulary of extenuation and responsibility a great range of notions, which it would be wise to master and exhaust before thinking of adaptation or invention:[41] *automatically, by mistake, unintentionally, by force of habit, involuntarily, unwillingly, on principle, under provocation,* to mention a few. Philosophers have tended to ignore all this richness and variety, assuming that it could all be satisfactorily assimilated to a few most favoured notions. But to do this is clumsy and slovenly. Furthermore, proposals to jettison ordinary language in favour of new-minted terms overlook the crucial primacy of the vernacular: ordinary, as opposed to technical, language is fundamental in the sense that the meaning of terms of art can only be explained with its aid; and it is a perennial complaint against such lovers of jargon as Kant and the Scholastics that this essential work is so often botched, skimped, or altogether neglected. The upshot of all this is that it is improbable that the elucidation of the logic of any term at all likely to engage any philosopher's attention will fail some day to find application to some generally recognised philosophical problem, however 'pure' his own interests may have been: the implied comparison with the pure scientific research which so frequently finds unexpected and unintended application is suggestive and, up to a point, apposite. It is to such often seemingly indiscriminate interest in the uses of words that we owe such fruitful logical explorations of neglected territory as R. M. Hare's 'Imperative Sentences',[42] and J. L. Austin on performatory language in 'Other Minds'. Contrast the old 'fetich of the indicative sentence' (Ryle) formulated by Hobbes: 'In philosophy there is but one kind of speech useful . . . most men call it *proposition,* and [it] is the speech of those that affirm or deny, and expresseth truth and falsity' (*Works,* vol. 1 p. 30).

If one quoted to those who have learnt most from Austin:

> Other apart sat on a hill retired
> In thoughts more elevate, and reasoned high
> Of providence, foreknowledge, will and fate;
> Fixt fate, free will, foreknowledge absolute
> And found no end, in wandering mazes lost
> > (Milton, *Paradise Lost,* bk ii)

the reply would be that the Devils in Pandemonium found no end *precisely because* they insisted on 'reasoning high'; that they should have begun with a meticulous and laborious study of the use of 'free will' and all the terms with which it is logically associated. Such an examination, which is certainly no quick and easy matter, is, as Austin has said, if not the be-all and end-all, at least the begin-all of philosophy.

(E) A derisive brouhaha has been raised about the notion of 'Standard English' – 'Why it should have been thought to deserve consideration as a philosophical principle it is by no means easy to imagine'.[43] Those who have emphasised the frequent philosophical importance of 'unexplained and unnoticed distortions of standard English' and 'deviations from standard English to which no sense has been attached'[44] have not, of course, been claiming that there is or ought to be an absolute, unchanging, universal, inflexible standard of correctness applicable to all users of the English language, past, present, and to come. The strange idea that they have seems to derive partly from failing to appreciate the force of the emphasis on *uses*, etc. (see (A) and (C) above); partly from a significant though perhaps seemingly trivial misrepresentation, whereby a concern for 'Standard English' is attributed to those who have in fact written of 'standard English';[45] and partly from the sheer errors that standards must necessarily be universal, inflexible, unchanging, and absolute. These last may be dispelled by the reflection that makers of cars may offer fresh standard models yearly, different ones for different markets, and with a standard choice of fittings and colours for each. About standards such as these there is presumably nothing normative, whereas with standard linguistic usage there certainly is. For, for the reasons already given (see (C) *ad init.*), everyone ought in general to conform with the usage accepted as correct by the language group or sub-group of which his linguistic and non-linguistic behaviour makes it reasonable to presume he is, tacitly or explicitly, claiming membership. This is *not* to say that usage ought to be absolutely rigid, uniform, and static among all users of any language; this would be to impose an embargo on improvisation and innovation, growth and decay.

It is common enormously to exaggerate the amount of variation in usage which there in fact is. People often write as if usage were so fluid, irregular, and varied that it must be impossible to say anything about the meaning of any word, except perhaps as employed by one particular person on one particular occasion. As we have argued above (in (C)) and elsewhere,[46] if this were in fact the case, verbal communication would be impossible. These exaggerations, like the linguists' analogue that different languages are all so very different that there is no equivalent of any word at all in any other language, arise from the understandable and inevitable preoccupation of philologists with differences and changes, and of translators with their more intractable difficulties. Such exaggerations are perhaps encouraged by vested interests, in obfuscation generally, and in the pretence that knowledge of foreign languages is even more important than it actually is.

(F) Ryle has so recently distinguished again between, and redeployed some of the arguments in favour of, the various policies which have sometimes been confused together as 'the appeal to ordinary language' that there is no need here to develop at length the relations and differences between these.[47] First, appealing to the ordinary use(s) of terms to elucidate philosophers' possible misuses. Second, appealing for plain English as opposed to jargon and high abstraction in philosophical prose. Not that anyone is suggesting an embargo on technical terms and abstraction: only a bias against, except where they prove essential. Third, concentrating upon everyday as opposed to technical concepts and their problems. Yet the fact that a large proportion of classical problems centre round such notions as *cause, mistake, evidence, knowledge, ought, can,* and *imagine* is no reason at all for neglecting those which arise from *psi-phenomena, collective unconscious, transubstantiation, economic welfare,* and *infinitesimal.* But whereas (most of) the former group can be tackled with no knowledge other than that minimum common to all educated men, even to understand the latter one must acquire some smattering of the disciplines to which the notions belong. Fourth, a protest 'that the logic of everyday statements and even . . . of scientists, lawyers, historians, and bridge-players cannot in principle be adequately represented by the formulae of formal logic'.[48] Oxford philosophers who incline to all four policies together may be thought of as trying to preserve a balance: between this 'formaliser's dream' that non-formalised language really is, or ought to be replaced by, a calculus;[49] and the Humpty Dumpty nightmare that there is, at least in those parts of it which most concern philosophers, no logic or order at all.

One pattern of argument, a particular application of the first policy, demands special attention. Talk, mainly deriving from Moore, of the Plain Man and his Common Sense, has now been largely replaced by emphasis upon the ordinary uses of words. But many philosophers have been as reluctant to abandon their reasoned paradoxes because they offend the Plain Man in his capacity as arbiter of ordinary language as they were to abdicate in face of Moore's protests on behalf of his common sense. And not without reason. The clue to the whole business now seems to lie in mastering what has recently been usefully named the Argument of the Paradigm Case.[50] Crudely: if there is any word the meaning of which can be taught by reference to paradigm cases, then no argument whatever could ever prove that there are no cases whatever of whatever it is. Thus, since the meaning of 'of his own free will' can be taught by reference to such paradigm cases as that in which a man, under no social pressure, marries the girl he wants to marry (how else *could* it be taught?), it cannot be right, on any grounds whatsoever, to say that no one *ever* acts of his own free will. For cases such as the paradigm, which must occur if the word is ever to be thus explained (and which certainly do in fact occur), are not in that case specimens which might have been wrongly identified: to the extent that the meaning of the expression is given in terms of them they are, by definition, what 'acting of one's own free will' is. As Runyon might have said: If these are not free actions they will at least do till some come along. A moment's reflection will show that analogous arguments can be deployed against many philosophical paradoxes.

What such arguments by themselves will certainly not do is to establish any matter of value, moral or otherwise: and almost everyone who has used them, certainly the present writer, must plead guilty to having from time to time failed to see this. For one cannot *derive* any sort of value proposition from *either* a factual proposition about what people value, *or* from definitions, however disguised, of value terms. This applies to any sort of value: indeed we might distinguish a Special (in ethics) from a General (anywhere) Naturalistic Fallacy. There is a world of difference between saying that it is reasonable in certain circumstances to act inductively (which is a value matter, one of commending a certain sort of behaviour), and saying that most people regard it as reasonable so to act (which is a factual matter, one of neutrally giving information about the prevalence of that kind of ideal). Thus that too short way with the problem of induction, which tries to *deduce* that induction is reasonable from the premise that people regard it as so, or even that they make inductive behaviour part of their paradigm of reasonableness, will not do. It is necessary for each of us tacitly or explicitly actually to make our personal value commitments here. Most of us are in fact willing to make that one which is involved in making inductive behaviour part of our paradigm of reasonableness. But as philosophers we must insist on making it explicitly and after examining the issues. With appropriate alterations, the same applies to attempts to derive ethical conclusions simply from what we (as a matter of fact) call reasonable behaviour or good reasons to act, without the introduction of an explicit commitment to accepted moral standards. These must involve versions of the (Special) Naturalistic Fallacy.[51]

To see the power, and the limitations, of the Argument of the Paradigm Case is to realise how much of common sense can, and how much cannot, be defended against philosophical paradoxes by simple appeal to the ordinary use of words, and why.

PART TWO

Austin's Appeal to Language

This section begins with Austin's classic statement of the methods of his philosophy. It is followed by New's criticisms of Austin from the point of view of the linguistic scientist.

V A plea for excuses

J. L. Austin

The subject of this paper, *Excuses,* is one not to be treated, but only to be introduced, within such limits. It is, or might be, the name of a whole branch, even a ramiculated branch, of philosophy, or at least of one fashion of philosophy. I shall try, therefore, first to state *what* the subject is, *why* it is worth studying, and *how* it may be studied, all this at a regrettably lofty level; and then I shall illustrate, in more congenial but desultory detail, some of the methods to be used, together with their limitations, and some of the unexpected results to be expected and lessons to be learned. Much, of course, of the amusement, and of the instruction, comes in drawing the coverts of the microglot, in hounding down the minutiae, and to this I can do no more here than incite you. But I owe it to the subject to say, that it has long afforded me what philosophy is so often thought, and made, barren of – the fun of discovery, the pleasures of co-operation, and the satisfaction of reaching agreement.

What, then, is the subject? I am here using the word 'excuses' *for a title,* but it would be unwise to freeze too fast to this one noun and its partner verb: indeed for some time I used to use 'extenuation' instead. Still, on the whole 'excuses' is probably the most central and embracing term in the field, although this includes others of importance – 'plea', 'defence', 'justification', and so on. When, then, do we 'excuse' conduct, our own or somebody else's? When are 'excuses' proffered?

In general, the situation is one where someone is *accused* of having done something, or (if that will keep it any cleaner) where someone is *said* to have done something which is bad, wrong, inept, unwelcome, or in some other of the numerous possible ways untoward. Thereupon he, or someone on his behalf, will try to defend his conduct or to get him out of it.

One way of going about this is to admit flatly that he, X, did do that very thing, A, but to argue that it was a good thing, or the right or sensible thing, or a permissible thing to do, either in general or at least in the special circumstances of the occasion. To take this line is to *justify* the action, to give reasons for doing it: not to say, to brazen it out, to glory in it, or the like.

A different way of going about it is to admit that it wasn't a good thing to have done, but to argue that it is not quite fair or correct to say *baldly* 'X did A'. We may say it isn't fair just to say X did it; perhaps he was under somebody's influence, or was nudged. Or, it isn't fair to say baldly he *did* A; it may have been partly accidental, or an unintentional slip. Or, it isn't fair to say he did *simply* A – he was really doing something quite different and A was only incidental, or he was looking at the whole thing quite differently. Naturally these arguments can be combined or overlap or run into each other.

In the one defence, briefly, we accept responsibility but deny that it was bad; in the other, we admit that it was bad but don't accept full, or even any, responsibility.

By and large, justifications can be kept distinct from excuses, and I shall not be so anxious to talk about them because they have enjoyed more than their fair share of philosophical attention. But the two certainly can be confused, and can *seem* to go very near to each other, even if they do not perhaps actually do so. You dropped the tea tray: Certainly, but an emotional storm was about to break out: or, Yes, but there was a wasp. In each case the defence, very soundly, insists on a fuller description of the event in its context; but the first is a justification, the second an excuse. Again, if the objection is to the use of such a dyslogistic verb as 'murdered', this may be on the ground that the killing was done in battle (justification) or on the ground that it was only accidental, if reckless (excuse). It is arguable that we do not use the terms 'justification' and 'excuse' as carefully as we might; a miscellany of even less clear terms, such as 'extenuation', 'palliation', 'mitigation', hovers uneasily between partial justification and partial excuse; and when we plead, say, provocation, there is genuine uncertainty or ambiguity as to what we mean – is *he* partly responsible, because he roused a violent impulse or passion in me, so that it wasn't truly or merely me acting 'of my own accord' (excuse)? Or is it rather that, he having done me such injury, I was entitled to retaliate (justification)? Such doubts merely make it the more urgent to clear up the usage of these various terms. But that the defences I have for convenience labelled 'justification' and 'excuse' are in principle distinct can scarcely be doubted.

This then is the sort of situation we have to consider under 'excuses'. I will only further point out how very wide a field it covers.

We have, of course, to bring in the opposite numbers of excuses – the expressions that *aggravate*, such as 'deliberately', 'on purpose', and so on, if only for the reason that an excuse often takes the form of a rebuttal of one of these. But we have also to bring in a large number of expressions which at first blush look not so much like excuses as like accusations – 'clumsiness', 'tactlessness', 'thoughtlessness', and the like. Because it has always to be remembered that few excuses get us out of it *completely*: the average excuse, in a poor situation, gets us only out of the fire into the frying-pan – but still, of course, any frying-pan in a fire. If I have broken your dish or your romance, maybe the best defence I can find will be clumsiness.

Why, if this is what 'excuses' are, should we trouble to investigate them? It might be thought reason enough that their production has always bulked so large among human activities. But to moral philosophy in particular a study of them will contribute in special ways, both positively towards the development of a cautious, latter-day version of conduct, and negatively towards the correction of older and hastier theories.

In ethics we study, I suppose, the good and the bad, the right and the wrong, and this must be for the most part in some connection with conduct or the doing of actions. Yet before we consider what actions are good or bad, right or wrong, it is proper to consider first what is meant by, and what not, and what is included under, and what not, the expression 'doing an action' or 'doing something'. These are expressions still too little examined on their own account and merits, just as the general notion of 'saying something' is still too lightly passed over in logic. There is indeed a vague and comforting idea in the background that, after all, in the last analysis, doing an action must come down to the making of physical movements with parts of the body; but this is about as true as that saying something must, in the last analysis, come down to making movements of the tongue.

The beginning of sense, not to say wisdom, is to realise that 'doing an action', as used in philosophy,[1] is a highly abstract expression – it is a stand-in used in the place of any (or almost any?) verb with a personal subject, in the same sort of way that 'thing' is a stand-in for any (or when we remember, almost any) noun substantive, and 'quality' a stand-in for the adjective. Nobody, to be sure, relies on such dummies quite implicitly quite indefinitely. Yet notoriously it is possible to arrive at, or to derive the idea for, an oversimplified metaphysics from the obsession with 'things' and their 'qualities'. In a similar way, less commonly recognised even in these semi-sophisticated times, we fall for the myth of the verb. We treat the expression 'doing an action' no longer as a stand-in for a verb with a personal subject, as which it has no doubt some uses, and might have more if the range of verbs were not left unspecified, but as a self-explanatory, ground-level description, one which brings adequately into the open the essential features of everything that comes, by simplest inspection, under it. We scarcely notice even the most patent exceptions or difficulties (is to think something, or to say something, or to try to do something, to do an action?), any more than we fret, in the *ivresse des grandes profondeurs*, as to whether flames are things or events. So we come easily to think of our behaviour over any time, and of life as a whole, as consisting in doing now action A, next action B, then action C, and so on, just as elsewhere we come to think of the world as consisting of this, that, and the other substance or material thing, each with its properties. All 'actions' are, as actions (meaning what?), equal, composing a quarrel with striking a match, winning a war with sneezing: worse still, we assimilate them one and all to the supposedly most obvious and easy cases, such as posting letters or moving fingers, just as we assimilate all 'things' to horses or beds.

If we are to continue to use this expression in sober philosophy, we need to ask such questions as: Is to sneeze to do an action? Or is to breathe, or to see, or to checkmate, or each one of countless others? In short, for what range of verbs, as used on what occasions, is 'doing an action' a stand-in? What have they in common, and what do those excluded severally lack? Again we need to ask how we decide what is the correct name for 'the' action that somebody did – and what, indeed, are the rules for the use of 'the' action, 'an' action, 'one' action, a 'part' or 'phase' of an action and the like. Further, we need to realise that even the 'simplest' named actions are not so simple – certainly are not the mere makings of physical movements – and to ask what more, then, comes in (intentions? conventions?) and what does not (motives?), and what is the detail of the complicated internal machinery we use in 'acting' – the receipt of intelligence, the appreciation of the situation, the invocation of principles, the planning, the control of execution and the rest.

In two main ways the study of excuses can throw light on these fundamental matters. First, to examine excuses is to examine cases where there has been some abnormality or failure: and as so often, the abnormal will throw light on the normal, will help us to penetrate the blinding veil of ease and obviousness that hides the mechanisms of the natural successful act. It rapidly becomes plain that the breakdowns signalised by the various excuses are of radically different kinds, affecting different parts or stages of the machinery, which the excuses consequently pick out and sort out for us. Further, it emerges that not *every* slip-up occurs in connection with *every*thing that could be called an 'action', that not every excuse is apt with every verb – far indeed from it – and this provides us with one means of introducing some classification into the vast miscellany of 'actions'. If we classify them according to the particular selection of breakdowns to which each is liable, this should assign them their places in some family group or groups of actions, or in some model of the machinery of acting.

In this sort of way, the philosophical study of conduct can get off to a positive fresh start. But by the way, and more negatively, a number of traditional cruces or mistakes in this field can be resolved or removed. First among these comes the problem of Freedom. While it has been the tradition to present this as the 'positive' term requiring elucidation, there is little doubt that to say we acted 'freely' (in the philosopher's use, which is only faintly related to the everyday use) is to say only that we acted *not* unfreely, in one or another of the many heterogeneous ways of so acting (under duress, or whatnot). Like 'real', 'free' is only used to rule out the suggestion of some or all of its recognised antitheses. As 'truth' is not a name for a characteristic of assertions, so 'freedom' is not a name for a characteristic of actions, but the name of a dimension in which actions are assessed. In examining all the ways in which each action may not be 'free', i.e. the cases in which it will not do to say simply 'X did A', we may hope to dispose of the problem of Freedom. Aristotle has often been chidden for talking about excuses or pleas and overlooking 'the real problem': in my own case, it was when I began to see the injustice of this charge that I first became interested in excuses.

There is much to be said for the view that, philosophical tradition apart, Responsibility would be a better candidate for the role here assigned to Freedom. If ordinary language is to be our guide, it is to evade responsibility, or full responsibility, that we most often make excuses, and I have used the word myself in this way above. But in fact 'responsibility' too seems not really apt in all cases: I do not exactly evade responsibility when I plead clumsiness or tactlessness, nor, often, when I plead that I only did it unwillingly or reluctantly, and still less if I plead that I had in the circumstances no choice: here I was constrained and have an excuse (or justification), yet may accept responsibility. It may be, then, that at least two key terms, Freedom and Responsibility, are needed: the relation between them is not clear, and it may be hoped that the investigation of excuses will contribute towards its clarification.[2]

So much, then, for ways in which the study of excuses may throw light on ethics. But there are also reasons why it is an attractive subject methodologically, at least if we are to proceed from 'ordinary language', that is, by examining *what we should say when*, and so why and what we should mean by it. Perhaps this method, at least as *one* philosophical method, scarcely requires justification at present – too evidently, there is gold in them thar hills: more opportune would be a warning about the care and thoroughness needed if it is not to fall into disrepute. I will, however, justify it very briefly.

First, words are our tools, and, as a minimum, we should use clean tools: we should know what we mean and what we do not, and we must forearm ourselves against the traps that language sets us. Secondly, words are not (except in their own little corner) facts or things: we need therefore to prise them off the world, to hold them apart from and against it, so that we can realise their inadequacies and arbitrariness, and can relook at the world without blinkers. Thirdly, and more hopefully, our common stock of words embodies all the distinctions men have found worth drawing, and the connections they have found worth marking, in the lifetimes of many generations: these surely are likely to be more numerous, more sound, since they have stood up to the long test of the survival of the fittest, and more subtle, at least in all ordinary and reasonably practical matters, than any that you or I are likely to think up in our armchairs of an afternoon – the most favoured alternative method.

In view of the prevalence of the slogan 'ordinary language', and of such names as 'linguistic' or 'analytic' philosophy or 'the analysis of language', one thing needs specially emphasising to counter misunderstandings. When we examine what we should say when, what words we should use in what situations, we are looking again not *merely* at words (or 'meanings', whatever they may be) but also at the realities we use the words to talk about: we are using a sharpened awareness of words to sharpen our perception of, though not as the final arbiter of, the phenomena. For this reason I think it might be better to use, for this way of doing philosophy, some less misleading name than those given above – for instance, 'linguistic phenomenology', only that is rather a mouthful.

Using, then, such a method, it is plainly preferable to investigate a field where ordinary language is rich and subtle, as it is in the pressingly practical matter of Excuses, but certainly is not in the matter, say, of Time. At the same time we should prefer a field which is not too much trodden into bogs or tracks by traditional philosophy, for in that case even 'ordinary' language will often have become infected with the jargon of extinct theories, and our own prejudices too, as the upholders or imbibers of theoretical views, will be too readily, and often insensibly, engaged. Here too Excuses form an admirable topic; we can discuss at least clumsiness, or absence of mind, or inconsiderateness, even spontaneousness, without remembering what Kant thought, and so progress by degrees even to discussing deliberation for once without remembering Aristotle or self-control without Plato. Granted that our subject is, as already claimed for it, neighbouring, analogous, or germane in some way to some notorious centre of philosophical trouble, then, with these two further requirements satisfied, we should be certain of what we are after: a good site for *field work* in philosophy. Here at last we should be able to unfreeze, to loosen up and get going on agreeing about discoveries, however small, and on agreeing about how to reach agreement.[3] How much it is to be wished that similar field work will soon be undertaken in, say, aesthetics; if only we could forget for a while about the beautiful and get down instead to the dainty and the dumpy.

There are, I know, or are supposed to be, snags in 'linguistic' philosophy, which those not very familiar with it find, sometimes not without glee or relief, daunting. But with snags, as with nettles, the thing to do is to grasp them – and to climb above them. I will mention two in particular, over which the study of excuses may help to encourage us. The first is the snag of Loose (or Divergent or Alternative) Usage; and the second the crux of the Last Word. Do we all say the same, and only the same, things in the same situations? Don't usages differ? And why should what we all ordinarily say be the only or the best or final way of putting it? Why should it even be true?

Well, people's usages do vary, and we do talk loosely, and we do say different things apparently indifferently. But first, not nearly as much as one would think. When we come down to cases, it transpires in the very great majority that what we had thought was our wanting to say different things of and in *the same* situation was really not so – we had simply imagined the situation *slightly* differently: which is all too easy to do, because of course no situation (and we are dealing with *imagined* situations) is ever 'completely' described. The more we imagine the situation in detail, with a background of story – and it is worth employing the most idiosyncratic or, sometimes, boring means to stimulate and to discipline our wretched imaginations – the less we find we disagree about what we should say. Nevertheless, *sometimes* we do ultimately disagree: sometimes we must allow a usage to be, though appalling, yet actual; sometimes we should genuinely use either or both of two different descriptions. But why should this daunt us? All that is happening is entirely explicable. If our usages disagree, then you use 'X' where I use 'Y', or more probably (and more intriguingly) your conceptual system is different from mine, though very likely it is at least equally consistent and serviceable: in short, we can find *why* we disagree – you choose to classify in one way, I in another. If the usage is loose, we can understand the temptation that leads to it, and the distinctions that it blurs: if there are 'alternative' descriptions, then the situation can be described or can be 'structured' in two ways, or perhaps it is one where, for current purposes, the two alternatives come down to the same. A disagreement as to what we should say is not to be shied off, but to be pounced upon: for the explanation of it can hardly fail to be illuminating. If we light on an electron that rotates the wrong way, that is a discovery, a portent to be followed up, not a reason for chucking physics: and, by the same token, a genuinely loose or eccentric talker is a rare specimen to be prized.

As practice in learning to handle this bogey, in learning the essential *rubrics*, we could scarcely hope for a more promising exercise than the study of excuses. Here, surely, is just the sort of situation where people will say 'almost anything', because they are so flurried, or so anxious to get off. 'It was a mistake', 'It was an accident' – how readily these can *appear* indifferent, and even be used together. Yet, a story or two, and everybody will not merely agree that they are completely different, but even discover for himself what the difference is and what each means.[4]

Then, for the Last Word. Certainly ordinary language has no claim to be the last word, if there is such a thing. It embodies, indeed, something better than the metaphysics of the Stone Age, namely, as was said, the inherited experience and acumen of many generations of men. But then, that acumen has been concentrated primarily upon the practical business of life. If a distinction works well for practical purposes in ordinary life (no mean feat, for even ordinary life is full of hard cases), then there is sure to be something in it, it will not mark nothing: yet this is likely enough to be not the best way of arranging things if our interests are more extensive or intellectual than the ordinary. And again, that experience has been derived only from the sources available to ordinary men throughout most of civilised history: it has not been fed from the resources of the microscope and its successors. And it must be added, too, that superstition and error and fantasy of all kinds do become incorporated in ordinary language and even sometimes stand up to the survival test (only, when they do, why should we not detect it?). Certainly, then, ordinary language is *not* the last word: in principle it can everywhere be supplemented and improved upon and superseded. Only remember, it *is* the *first* word.[5]

For this problem too the field of Excuses is a fruitful one. Here is matter both contentious and practically important for everybody, so that ordinary language is on its toes: yet also, on its back it has long had a bigger flea to bite it, in the shape of the law, and both again have lately attracted the attentions of yet another, and at least a healthily growing, flea, in the shape of psychology. In the law a constant stream of actual cases, more novel and more tortuous than the mere imagination could contrive, are brought up *for decision* – that is, formulas for docketing them must somehow be found. Hence it is necessary first to be careful with, but also to be brutal with, to torture, to fake, and to override, ordinary language: we cannot here evade or forget the whole affair. (In ordinary life we dismiss the puzzles that crop up about time, but we cannot do that indefinitely in physics.) Psychology likewise produces novel cases, but it also produces new methods for bringing phenomena under observation and study: moreover, unlike the law, it has an unbiased interest in the totality of them and is unpressed for decision. Hence its own special and constant need to supplement, to revise and to supersede the classifications of both ordinary life and the law. We have, then, ample material for practice in learning to handle the bogey of the Last Word, however it should be handled.

Suppose, then, that we set out to investigate excuses, what are the methods and resources initially available? Our object is to imagine the varieties of situation in which we make excuses, and to examine the expressions used in making them. If we have a lively imagination, together perhaps with an ample experience of dereliction, we shall go far, only we need system: I do not know how many of you keep a list of the kinds of fool you make of yourselves. It is advisable to use systematic aids, of which there would appear to be three at least. I list them here in order of availability to the layman.

First we may use the dictionary – quite a concise one will do, but the use must be *thorough*. Two methods suggest themselves, both a little tedious, but repaying. One is to read the book through, listing all the words that seem relevant; this does not take as long as many suppose. The other is to start with a widish selection of obviously relevant terms, and to consult the dictionary under each: it will be found that, in the explanations of the various meanings of each, a surprising number of other terms occur, which are germane though of course not often synonymous. We then look up each of *these*, bringing in more for our bag from the 'definitions' given in each case; and when we have continued for a little, it will generally be found that the family circle begins to close, until ultimately it is complete and we come only upon repetitions. This method has the advantage of grouping the terms into convenient clusters – but of course a good deal will depend upon the comprehensiveness of our initial selection.

Working the dictionary, it is interesting to find that a high percentage of the terms connected with excuses prove to be *adverbs*, a type of word which has not enjoyed so large a share of the philosophical limelight as the noun, substantive or adjective, and the verb: this is natural because, as was said, the tenor of so many excuses is that I did it but only *in a way*, not just flatly like that – i.e. the verb needs modifying. Besides adverbs, however, there are other words of all kinds, including numerous abstract nouns, 'misconception', 'accident', 'purpose', and the like, and a few verbs too, which often hold key positions for the grouping of excuses into classes at a high level ('couldn't help', 'didn't mean to', 'didn't realise', or again 'intend', and 'attempt'). In connection with the nouns another neglected class of words is prominent, namely, prepositions. Not merely does it matter considerably which preposition, often of several, is being used with a given substantive, but further the prepositions deserve study on their own account. For the question suggests itself, Why are the nouns in one group governed by 'under', in another by 'on', in yet another by 'by' or 'through' or 'from' or 'for' or 'with', and so on? It will be disappointing if there prove to be no good reasons for such groupings.

Our second sourcebook will naturally be the law. This will provide us with an immense miscellany of untoward cases, and also with a useful list of recognised pleas, together with a good deal of acute analysis of both. No one who tries this resource will long be in doubt, I think, that the common law, and in particular the law of tort, is the richest storehouse; crime and contract contribute some special additions of their own, but tort is altogether more comprehensive and more flexible. But even here, and still more with so old and hardened a branch of the law as crime, much caution is needed with the arguments of counsel and the dicta or decisions of judges: acute though these are, it has always to be remembered that, in legal cases, (1) there is the overriding requirement that a decision be reached, and a relatively black or white decision – guilty or not guilty – for the plaintiff or the defendant; (2) there is the general requirement that the charge or action and the pleadings be brought under one or another of the heads and procedures that have come in the course of history to be accepted by the courts (These, though fairly numerous, are still few and stereotyped in comparison with the accusations and defences of daily life. Moreover contentions of many kinds are beneath the law, as too trivial, or outside it, as too purely moral – for example, inconsiderateness); (3) there is the general requirement that we argue from and abide by precedents (the value of this in the law is unquestionable, but it can certainly lead to distortions of ordinary beliefs and expressions). For such reasons as these, obviously closely connected and stemming from the nature and function of the law, practising lawyers and jurists are by no means so careful as they might be to give to our ordinary expressions their ordinary meanings and applications. There is special pleading and evasion, stretching and strait-jacketing, besides the invention of technical terms, or technical senses for common terms. Nevertheless, it is a perpetual and salutary surprise to discover how much is to be learned from the law; and it is to be added that if a distinction drawn is a sound one, even though not yet recognised in law, a lawyer can be relied upon to take note of it, for it may be dangerous not to – if he does not, his opponent may.

Finally, the third sourcebook is psychology, with which I include such studies as anthropology and animal behaviour. Here I speak with even more trepidation than about the law. But this at least is clear, that some varieties of behaviour, some ways of acting or explanations of the doing of actions, are here noticed and classified which have not been observed or named by ordinary men and hallowed by ordinary language, though perhaps they often might have been so if they had been of more practical importance. There is real danger in contempt for the 'jargon' of psychology, at least when it sets out to supplement, and at least sometimes when it sets out to supplant, the language of ordinary life.

With these sources, and with the aid of the imagination, it will go hard with us if we cannot arrive at the meanings of large numbers of expressions and at the understanding and classification of large numbers of 'actions'. Then we shall comprehend clearly much that, before, we only made use of *ad hoc*. Definition, I would add, explanatory definition, should stand high among our aims: it is not enough to show how clever we are by showing how obscure everything is. Clarity, too, I know, has been said to be not enough: but perhaps it will be time to go into that when we are within measurable distance of achieving clarity on some matter.

So much for the cackle. It remains to make a few remarks, not, I am afraid, in any very coherent order, about the types of significant result to be obtained and the more general lessons to be learned from the study of Excuses.

1. *No Modification without aberration.* When it is stated that X did A, there is a temptation to suppose that given some, indeed perhaps *any*, expression modifying the verb we shall be entitled to insert either it or its opposite or negation in our statement: that is, we shall be entitled to ask, typically, 'Did X do A Mly or not Mly?' (e.g. 'Did X murder Y voluntarily or involuntarily?'), and to answer one or the other. Or as a minimum it is supposed that if X did A there must be at least *one* modifying expression that we could, justifiably and informatively, insert with the verb. In the great majority of cases of the use of the great majority of verbs ('murder' perhaps is not one of the majority) such suppositions are quite unjustified. The natural economy of language dictates that for the *standard* case covered by any normal verb – not, perhaps, a verb of omen such as 'murder', but a verb like 'eat' or 'kick' or 'croquet' – no modifying expression is required or even permissible. Only if we do the action named in some *special* way or circumstances, different from those in which such an act is naturally done (and of course both the normal and the abnormal differ according to what verb in particular is in question), is a modifying expression called for, or even in order. I sit in my chair, in the usual way – I am not in a daze or influenced by threats or the like: here, it will not do to say either that I sat in it intentionally or that I did not sit in it intentionally,[6] nor yet that I sat in it automatically or from habit or what you will. It is bedtime, I am alone, I yawn: but I do not yawn involuntarily (or voluntarily!), nor yet deliberately. To yawn in any such peculiar way is just not to just yawn.

2. *Limitation of application.* Expressions modifying verbs, typically adverbs, have limited ranges of application. That is, given any

adverb of excuse, such as 'unwittingly' or 'spontaneously' or 'impulsively', it will not be found that it makes good sense to attach it to any and every verb of 'action' in any and every context: indeed, it will often apply only to a comparatively narrow range of such verbs. Something in the lad's upturned face appealed to him, he threw a brick at it – 'spontaneously'? The interest then is to discover why some actions can be excused in a particular way but not others, particularly perhaps the latter.[7] This will largely elucidate the meaning of the excuse, and at the same time will illuminate the characteristics typical of the group of 'actions' it picks out: very often too it will throw light on some detail of the machinery of 'action' in general (see (4)), or on our standards of acceptable conduct (see (5)). It is specially important in the case of some of the terms most favoured by philosophers or jurists to realise that at least in ordinary speech (disregarding back-seepage of jargon) they are not used so universally or so dichotomistically. For example, take 'voluntarily' and 'involuntarily': we may join the army or make a gift voluntarily, we may hiccough or make a small gesture involuntarily, and the more we consider further actions which we might naturally be said to do in either of these ways, the more circumscribed and unlike each other do the two classes become, until we even doubt whether there is *any* verb with which both adverbs are equally in place. Perhaps there are some such; but at least sometimes when we may think we have found one it is an illusion, an apparent exception that really does prove the rule. I can perhaps 'break a cup' voluntarily, *if* that is done, say, as an act of self-impoverishment: and I can perhaps break another involuntarily, *if*, say, I make an involuntary movement which breaks it. Here, plainly, the two acts described each as 'breaking a cup' are really very different, and the one is similar to acts typical of the 'voluntary class, the others to acts typical of the 'involuntary' class.

3. *The importance of Negations and Opposites.* 'Voluntarily' and 'involuntarily', then, are not opposed in the obvious sort of way that they are made to be in philosophy or jurisprudence. The 'opposite', or rather 'opposites', of 'voluntarily' might be 'under constraint' of some sort, duress or obligation or influence;[8] the opposite of 'involuntarily' might be 'deliberately' or 'on purpose' or the like. Such divergences in opposites indicate that 'voluntarily' and 'involuntarily', in spite of their apparent connection, are fish from very different kettles. In general, it will pay us to take nothing for granted or as obvious about negations and opposites. It does not

pay to assume that a word must have an opposite, or one opposite, whether it is a 'positive' word like 'wilfully' or a 'negative' word like 'inadvertently'. Rather, we should be asking ourselves such questions as why there is no use for the adverb 'advertently'. For above all it will not do to assume that the 'positive' word must be around to wear the trousers; commonly enough the 'negative' (looking) word marks the (positive) abnormality, while the 'positive' word, *if* it exists, merely serves to rule out the suggestion of that abnormality. It is natural enough, in view of what was said in (1) above, for the 'positive' word not to be found at all in some cases. I do an Act A_1 (say, crush a snail) *inadvertently* if, in the course of executing by means of movements of my bodily parts some other act A_2 (say, in walking down the public path), I fail to exercise such meticulous supervision over the courses of those movements as would have been needed to ensure that they did not bring about the untoward event (here, the impact on the snail).[9] By claiming that A_1 was inadvertent we place it, where we imply it belongs, on this special level, in a class of incidental happenings which must occur in the doing of any physical act. To lift the act out of this class, we need and possess the expression 'not . . . inadvertently': 'advertently', if used for this purpose, would suggest that, if the act was not done inadvertently, then it must have been done noticing what I was doing, which is far from necessarily the case (e.g. if I did it absent-mindedly), or at least that there is *something* in common to the ways of doing all acts not done inadvertently, which is not the case. Again, there is no use for 'advertently' at the *same* level as 'inadvertently': in passing the butter I do not knock over the cream-jug, though I do (inadvertently) knock over the teacup – yet I do not by-pass the cream-jug *advertently*: for at this level, below supervision in detail, *anything* that we do is, if you like, inadvertent, though we only call it so, and indeed only call it something we have done, if there is something untoward about it.

A further point of interest in studying so-called 'negative' terms is the manner of their formation. Why are the words in one group formed with *un-* or *in-*, those in another with *-less* ('aimless', reckless', 'heedless', etc.), and those in another with *mis-* ('mistake', 'misconception', 'misjudgement', etc.)? Why care*less*ly but *in*-attentively? Perhaps care and attention, so often linked, are rather different. Here are remunerative exercises.

4. *The machinery of action.* Not merely do adverbial expressions pick out classes of actions, they also pick out the internal detail of the machinery of doing actions, or the departments into which the

business of doing actions is organised. There is for example the stage at which we have actually to *carry out* some action upon which we embark – perhaps we have to make certain bodily movements or to make a speech. In the course of actually *doing* these things (getting weaving) we have to pay (some) attention to what we are doing and to take (some) care to guard against (likely) dangers: we may need to use judgement or tact; we must exercise sufficient control over our bodily parts; and so on. Inattention, carelessness, errors of judgement, tactlessness, clumsiness, all these and others are ills (with attendant excuses) which affect one specific stage in the machinery of action, the *executive* stage, the stage where we *muff* it. But there are many other departments in the business too, each of which is to be traced and mapped through its cluster of appropriate verbs and adverbs. Obviously there are departments of intelligence and planning, of decision and resolve, and so on: but I shall mention one in particular, too often overlooked, where troubles and excuses abound. It happens to us, in military life, to be in receipt of excellent intelligence, to be also in self-conscious possession of excellent principles (the five golden rules for winning victories), and yet to hit upon a plan of action which leads to disaster. One way in which this can happen is through failure at the stage of *appreciation* of the situation, that is at the stage where we are required to cast our excellent intelligence into such a form, under such heads and with such weights attached, that our equally excellent principles can be brought to bear on it properly, in a way to yield the right answer.[10] So too in real, or rather civilian, life, in moral or practical affairs, we can know the facts and yet look at them mistakenly or perversely, or not fully realise or appreciate something, or even be under a total misconception. Many expressions of excuse indicate failure at this particularly tricky stage: even thoughtlessness, inconsiderateness, lack of imagination, are perhaps less matters of failure in intelligence or planning than might be supposed, and more matters of failure to appreciate the situation. A course of E. M. Forster and we see things differently: yet perhaps we know no more and are no cleverer.

5. *Standards of the unacceptable.* It is characteristic of excuses to be 'unacceptable': given, I suppose, almost any excuse, there will be cases of such a kind or of such gravity that 'we will not accept' it. It is interesting to detect the standards and codes we thus invoke. The extent of the supervision we exercise over the execution of any act can never be quite unlimited, and usually is expected to fall within fairly definite limits ('due care and attention') in the case of

acts of some general kind, though of course we set very different limits in different cases. We may plead that we trod on the snail inadvertently, but not on a baby – you ought to look where you are putting your great feet. Of course it *was* (*really*), if you like, inadvertence: but that word constitutes a plea, which is not going to be allowed, because of standards. And if you try it on, you will be subscribing to such dreadful standards that your last state will be worse than your first. Or again, we set different standards, and will accept different excuses, in the case of acts which are rule-governed, like spelling, and which we are expected absolutely to get right, from those we set and accept for less stereotyped actions: a wrong spelling may be a slip, but hardly an accident, a winged beater may be an accident, but hardly a slip.

6. *Combination, dissociation, and complication.* A belief in opposites and dichotomies encourages, among other things, a blindness to the combinations and dissociations of adverbs that are possible, even to such obvious facts as that we can act at once on impulse and intentionally, or that we can do an action intentionally yet for all that not deliberately, still less on purpose. We walk along the cliff, and I feel a sudden impulse to push you over, which I promptly do; I acted on impulse, yet I certainly intended to push you over, and may even have devised a little ruse to achieve it; yet even then I did not act deliberately, for I did not (stop to) ask myself whether to do it or not.

It is worth bearing in mind, too, the general rule that we must not expect to find simple labels for complicated cases. If a mistake results in an accident, it will not do to ask whether 'it' was an accident or a mistake, or to demand some briefer description of 'it'. Here the natural economy of language operates: if the words already available for simple cases suffice in combination to describe a complicated case, there will be need for special reasons before a special new word is invented for the complication. Besides, however well equipped our language, it can never be forearmed against all possible cases that may arise and call for description: fact is richer than diction.

7. *Regina v. Finney.* Often the complexity and difficulty of a case is considerable. I will quote the case of *Regina v. Finney*:[11]

Shrewsbury Assizes.   1874   12 Cox 625.
   Prisoner was indicted for the manslaughter of Thomas Watkins.
   The Prisoner was an attendant at a lunatic asylum. Being in charge of a lunatic, who was bathing, he turned on hot water into

the bath, and thereby scalded him to death. The facts appeared to be truly set forth in the statement of the prisoner made before the committing magistrate, as follows: 'I had bathed Watkins, and had loosed the bath out. *I intended putting in a clean bath*, and asked Watkins if he would get out. At this time *my attention was drawn* to the next bath by the new attendant, who was asking me a question; and *my attention was taken from the bath* where Watkins was. I put my hand down to turn water on in the bath where Thomas Watkins was. *I did not intend to turn the hot water*, and *I made a mistake in the tap. I did not know what I had done until* I heard Thomas Watkins shout out; and *I did not find my mistake out till* I saw the steam from the water. You cannot get water in this bath when they are drawing water at the other bath; but at other times it shoots out like a water gun when the other baths are not in use. . . .'

(It was proved that the lunatic had such possession of his faculties as would enable him to understand what was said to him, and to get out of the bath.)

A. Young (for Prisoner). The death *resulted from accident*. There was no such *culpable negligence* on the part of the prisoner as will support this indictment. A *culpable mistake*, or some degree of *culpable negligence*, causing death, will not support a charge of manslaughter; unless the *negligence* be so gross as to be *reckless*. (*R. v. Noakes.*)

Lush, J. To render a person liable for *neglect of duty* there must be such a degree of culpability as to amount to *gross negligence* on his part. If you accept the prisoner's own statement, you find no such amount of *negligence* as would come within this definition. It is not every little *trip or mistake* that will make a man so liable. It was the duty of the attendant not to let hot water into the bath while the patient was therein. According to the prisoner's own account, *he did not believe that* he was letting the hot water in while the deceased remained there. The lunatic was, we have heard, a man capable of getting out by himself and of understanding what was said to him. He was told to get out. A new attendant who had come on this day, was at an adjoining bath and he *took off the prisoner's attention*. Now, if the prisoner, knowing that the man was in the bath, had turned on the tap, and turned on the hot instead of the cold water, I should have said there was gross negligence; for he ought to have looked to see. But from his own account he had told the deceased to get out, and *thought he had got out*. If you think that indicates

gross *carelessness*, then you should find the prisoner guilty of
manslaughter. But if you think it *inadvertence* not amounting to
culpability – i.e. what is properly termed an *accident* – then the
prisoner is not liable.

Verdict, Not guilty.

In this case there are two morals that I will point. (1) Both
counsel and judge make very free use of a large number of terms of
excuse, using several as though they were, and even stating them to
be, indifferent or equivalent when they are not, and presenting as
alternatives those that are not. (2) It is constantly difficult to be sure
what act it is that counsel or judge is suggesting might be qualified
by what expression of excuse. The learned judge's concluding
direction is a paradigm of these faults.[12] Finney, by contrast, stands
out as an evident master of the Queen's English. He is explicit as to
each of his acts and states, mental and physical; he uses different,
and the correct, adverbs in connection with each; and he makes
no attempt to boil down.

8. *Small distinctions, and big too*. It should go without saying
that terms of excuse are not equivalent, and that it matters which
we use: we need to distinguish inadvertence not merely from (save
the mark) such things as mistake and accident, but from such nearer
neighbours as, say, aberration and absence of mind. By imagining
cases with vividness and fullness we should be able to decide in
which precise terms to describe, say, Miss Plimsoll's action in writing, so carefully, 'DAIRY' on her fine new book: we should be able
to distinguish between sheer, mere, pure, and simple mistake or inadvertence. Yet unfortunately, at least when in the grip of thought,
we fail not merely at these stiffer hurdles. We equate even – I have
seen it done – 'inadvertently' with 'automatically': as though to
say I trod on your toe inadvertently means to say I trod on it
automatically. Or we collapse succumbing to temptation into
losing control of ourselves – a bad patch, this, for telescoping.[13]

All this is not so much a *lesson* from the study of excuses as the
very object of it.

9. *The exact phrase and its place in the sentence*. It is not
enough, either, to attend simply to the 'key' word: notice must also
be taken of the full and exact form of the expression used. In considering mistakes, we have to consider seriatim 'by mistake',
'owing to a mistake', 'mistakenly', 'it was a mistake to', 'to make a
mistake in or over or about', 'to be mistaken about', and so on; in
considering purpose, we have to consider 'on', 'with the', 'for the',

etc., besides 'purposeful', 'purposeless', and the like. These varying expressions may function quite differently – and usually do, or why should we burden ourselves with more than one of them?

Care must be taken too to observe the precise position of an adverbial expression in the sentence. This should of course indicate what verb it is being used to modify: but more than that, the position can also affect the *sense* of the expression, i.e. the way in which it modifies that verb. Compare, for example:

> a_1 He clumsily trod on the snail.
> a_2 Clumsily he trod on the snail.
> b_1 He trod clumsily on the snail.
> b_2 He trod on the snail clumsily.

Here, in a_1 and a_2 we describe his treading on the creature at all as a piece of clumsiness, incidental, we imply, to his performance of some other action; but with b_1 and b_2 to tread on it is, very likely, his aim of policy, what we criticise is his execution of the feat.[14] Many adverbs, though far from all (not, for example, 'purposely'), are used in these two typically different ways.

10. *The style of performance.* With some adverbs the distinction between the two senses referred to in the last paragraph is carried a stage further. 'He ate his soup deliberately' may mean, like 'He deliberately ate his soup', that his eating his soup was a deliberate act, one perhaps that he thought would annoy somebody, as it would more commonly if he deliberately ate *my* soup, and which he decided to do; but it will often mean that he went through the performance of eating his soup in a noteworthy manner or *style* – pause after each mouthful, careful choice of point of entry for the spoon, sucking of moustaches, and so on. That is, it will mean that he ate *with* deliberation rather than *after* deliberation. The style of the performance, slow and unhurried, is understandably called 'deliberate' because each movement *has the typical look* of a deliberate act: but it is scarcely being said that the making of each motion *is* a deliberate act or that he is 'literally' deliberating. This case, then, is more extreme than that of 'clumsily', which does in both uses describe literally a manner of performing.

It is worth watching out for this secondary use when scrutinising any particular adverbial expression: when it definitely does not exist, the reason is worth inquiring into. Sometimes it is very hard to be sure whether it does exist or does not: it does, one would think, with 'carelessly', it does not with 'inadvertently', but does it or does it not with 'absent-mindedly' or 'aimlessly'? In some cases a word akin to but distinct from the primary adverb is used for this special role of describing a style of performance: we use 'purposefully' in this way, but never 'purposely'.

11. *What modifies what?* The judge in *Regina* v. *Finney* does not make clear what event is being excused in what way. 'If you think that indicates gross carelessness, then. . . . But if you think it inadvertence not amounting to culpability – i.e. what is properly called an accident – then. . . .' Apparently he means that Finney may have *turned on the hot tap* inadvertently:[15] does he mean also that the tap may have been turned accidentally, or rather that *Watkins may have been scalded* and killed accidentally? And was the carelessness in turning the tap or in thinking Watkins had got out? Many disputes as to what excuse we should properly use arise because we will not trouble to state explicitly *what* is being excused.

To do so is all the more vital because it is in principle always open to us, along various lines, to describe or refer to 'what I did' in so many different ways. This is altogether too large a theme to elaborate here. Apart from the more general and obvious problems of the use of 'tendentious' descriptive terms, there are many special problems in the particular case of 'actions'. Should we say, are we saying, that he took her money, or that he robbed her? That he knocked a ball into a hole, or that he sank a putt? That he said 'Done', or that he accepted an offer? How far, that is, are motives, intentions, and conventions to be part of the description of actions? And more especially here, what is *an* or *one* or *the* action? For we can generally split up what might be named as one action in several distinct ways, into different *stretches* or *phases* or *stages*. Stages have already been mentioned: we can dismantle the machinery of the act, and describe (and excuse) separately the intelligence, the appreciation, the planning, the decision, the execution, and so forth. Phases are rather different: we can say that he painted a picture or fought a campaign, or else we can say that first he laid on this stroke of paint and then that, first he fought this action and then that. Stretches are different again: a single term descriptive of what he did may be made to cover either a smaller or a larger stretch of events, those excluded by the narrower description being then called 'consequences' or 'results' or 'effects' or the like of his act. So here we can describe Finney's act *either* as turning on the hot tap, which he did by mistake, with the result that Watkins was scalded, *or* as scalding Watkins, which he did *not* do by mistake.

It is very evident that the problems of excuses and those of the different descriptions of actions are throughout bound up with each other.

12. *Trailing clouds of etymology.* It is these considerations that bring us up forcibly against some of the most difficult words in the whole story of Excuses, such words as 'result', 'effect', and 'consequence', or again as 'intention', 'purpose', and 'motive'. I will mention two points of method which are, experience has convinced me, indispensable aids at these levels.

One is that a word never – well, hardly ever – shakes off its etymology and its formation. In spite of all changes in and extensions of and additions to its meanings, and indeed rather pervading and governing these, there will still persist the old idea. In an *accident* something befalls; by *mistake* you take the wrong one; in *error* you stray; when you act *deliberately* you act after weighing it up (*not* after thinking out ways and means). It is worth asking ourselves whether we know the etymology of 'result' or of 'spontaneously', and worth remembering that 'unwillingly' and 'involuntarily' come from very different sources.

And the second point is connected with this. Going back into the history of a word, very often into Latin, we come back pretty commonly to pictures or *models* of how things happen or are done. These models may be fairly sophisticated and recent, as is perhaps the case with 'motive' or 'impulse', but one of the commonest and most primitive types of model is one which is apt to baffle us through its very naturalness and simplicity. We take *some very simple action*, like shoving a stone, usually as done by and viewed by oneself, and use *this*, with the features distinguishable in it, as our model in terms of which to talk about other actions and events; and we continue to do so, scarcely realising it, even when these other actions are pretty remote and perhaps much more interesting to us in their own right than the acts originally used in constructing the model ever were, and even when the model is really distorting the facts rather than helping us to observe them. In primitive cases we may get to see clearly the differences between, say, 'results', 'effects', and 'consequences', and yet discover that these differences are no longer clear, and the terms themselves no longer of real service to us, in the more complicated cases where we had been bandying them about most freely. A model must be recognised for what it is. 'Causing', I suppose, was a notion taken from a man's own experience of doing simple actions, and by primitive man every event was construed in terms of this model: every event has a cause, that is, every event is an action done by somebody – if not by a man, then by a quasi-man, a spirit. When, later, events which are *not* actions are realised to be such, we still say that they must be 'caused', and the word snares us: we are struggling to ascribe to it a new, unanthropomorphic meaning, yet constantly, in searching for its analysis, we unearth and incorporate the lineaments of the ancient model. As happened even to Hume, and consequently to Kant. Examining such a word historically, we may well find that it has been extended to cases that have by now too tenuous a relation to the model case, that it is a source of confusion and superstition.

There is too another danger in words that invoke models, half-forgotten or not. It must be remembered that there is no necessity whatsoever that the various models used in creating our vocabulary, primitive or recent, should all fit together neatly as parts into one single, total model or scheme of, for instance, the doing of actions. It is possible, and indeed highly likely, that our assortment of models will include some, or many, that are overlapping, conflicting, or more generally simply *disparate*.[16]

13. In spite of the wide and acute observation of the phenomena of action embodied in ordinary speech, modern scientists have been able, it seems to me, to reveal its inadequacy at numerous points, if only because they have had access to more comprehensive data and have studied them with more catholic and dispassionate interest than the ordinary man, or even the lawyer, has had occasion to do. I will conclude with two examples.

Observation of animal behaviour shows that regularly, when an animal is embarked on some recognisable pattern of behaviour but meets in the course of it with an insuperable obstacle, it will betake itself to energetic, but quite unrelated, activity of some wild kind, such as standing on its head. This phenomenon is called 'displacement behaviour' and is well identifiable. If now, in the light of this, we look back at ordinary human life, we see that displacement behaviour bulks quite large in it: yet we have apparently no word, or at least no clear and simple word, for it. If, when thwarted, we stand on our heads or wiggle our toes, then we are not exactly *just* standing on our heads, don't you know, in the ordinary way, yet is there any convenient adverbial expression we can insert to do the trick? 'In desperation'?

Take, again, 'compulsive' behaviour, however exactly psychologists define it, compulsive washing for example. There are of course hints in ordinary speech that we do things in this way – 'just feel I have to', 'shouldn't feel comfortable unless I did', and the like; but there is no adverbial expression satisfactorily pre-empted for it, as 'compulsively' is. This is understandable enough, since compulsive behaviour, like displacement behaviour, is not in general going to be of great practical importance.

Here I leave and commend the subject to you.

VI A plea for linguistics

C. G. New

I

One type of 'linguistic' philosophy is primarily an attempt to discriminate the uses of related expressions in what is vaguely called 'ordinary language' – that is, educated, non-technical English. The most authoritative and detailed exposition of the aims and methods of this kind of analysis is contained in J. L. Austin's celebrated paper 'A Plea for Excuses' (Chapter V above). The aims have aroused a good deal of more or less inconclusive controversy, but not much has been said about the methods. Yet it is the methods that are most obviously controversial. In fact they are open to objections that are fatal to this type of investigation as Austin conceived it. These objections are revealed by a consideration of the relationship between philosophy and linguistics. A clear distinction must be drawn between the methods of descriptive linguistics and those of philosophical analysis. Neglecting this distinction has led some philosophers to talk about philosophy as though it were linguistics and about linguistics as though it were philosophy; which they are not. Not that philosophy and linguistics have no concern with each other: in some respects at least they clearly have. Only they should not be confused.

In the following sections I shall recapitulate some of Austin's aims and then examine in detail the methods he advocates for achieving them. It will become clear that the methods are in principle unreliable; and this conclusion will be reinforced by examining some of the results that Austin reached by means of them.

In 'A Plea for Excuses', Austin restricted himself to the topic of actions and, in particular, excuses. I shall restrict my criticism in the same way. But it is clear that his explanatory and methodological remarks are meant to be applicable to other topics (aesthetics, for example) also.

II

Why study ordinary usage? Austin's answer can be summarised under three points (p. 84 above).

(i) To understand what we mean, we must examine the words we use. Language sets traps, especially for philosophers, and it is only by rigorously examining what we all ordinarily do with language that we can forearm ourselves against these traps. Forgetting, in the grip of some theory, the ordinary usage of some expression, we may easily slide into a misuse of it that leads us hopelessly astray.

(ii) Moreover, our ordinary words are themselves inadequate and arbitrary. Examining how they work will help us to realise this and to 're-look at the world without blinkers'. Some actions for instance, like heaving a brick through your neighbour's window, involve physical movements. The etymology of the word 'action', combined with our familiarity with relatively simple cases of actions which do involve physical movements, tends to suggest that all actions in the last analysis come down to making physical movements. By examining how the word 'action' is actually used in a variety of cases, we come to see that and how this tendency is misleading.

(iii) The study of ordinary usage has a positive value also. For 'our common stock of words embodies all the distinctions men have found worth drawing, and the connections they have found worth marking in the lifetimes of many generations'. We should understand these at least before we go any further. Noticing and understanding these distinctions is not merely looking at words. In examining how we use the words we do, we are also examining the 'realities we use the words to talk about'. Thus by examining the ordinary usage of the words with which we describe actions, we shall both rid ourselves of possible misconceptions and bring to light distinctions in the kinds of things and situations we use the words to talk about.

These three points constitute, very briefly, Austin's justification of this type of 'linguistic' philosophy. The brevity of my summary can only be excused by the plea that I do not want to discuss here the justifiability of Austin's aims, but only to point out what they are. It is important to notice that there are really two aims. Points (i) and (ii) declare that ordinary language must be investigated so that we shall avoid distorting it or being misled by it. Point (iii) declares that understanding ordinary language will give us a sharper awareness of distinctions in the phenomena we use the words to talk about. These two aims appear complementary; as Austin formulates them they seem to be no more than two sides of the same penny. But they can come apart, and I shall argue that the methods Austin advocates in fact force them apart, so that distinctions which are all his own are foisted on to expressions in ordinary language although they may be quite inconsistent with the actual usage of these expressions. And so far as this happens, or is likely to happen, it is clear that the first of these aims – the avoidance of misconception and error by charting actual usage – is not being fulfilled. Austin recognised of course that ordinary language is not the last word: it can in principle be supplemented and improved on everywhere. But his main contention is that it *is* the first word. We are not entitled to supplement or improve on it until we understand it. I shall argue that since Austin's method of investigating actual usage is defective, this is just what is bound to happen to anyone that adopts it. Improving after understanding ordinary usage is permissible: altering by misunderstanding it is not.

III

How then is ordinary language to be investigated? Austin's method can be summarised under a further two points (p. 85 and p. 88 above).

(i) The field of ordinary language that the philosopher investigates must be germane to some philosophical problem. This defines the scope of the inquiry. There is no philosophical interest in the study of expressions like 'grin', 'smile', 'laugh', 'chuckle', 'cackle', and 'guffaw', for instance. For these expressions have no connection with anything that has ever been called a problem of philosophy. But there *is* a philosophical interest in studying the uses of expressions like 'deliberate', 'intentional', 'accidental', 'by mistake' and 'involuntary'. For these ordinarily mark distinctions in the doing of actions which may be significant in the philosophical discussion of freedom and responsibility. Similarly, the investigation of the uses of expressions like 'elegant', 'graceful', 'pretty', 'ugly', 'dumpy', 'coarse' could conceivably yield results of some importance for aesthetics.

(ii) Having thus chosen our field, we are to go through the dictionary, listing all the words that seem relevant. When the list is complete, we can set to work discriminating the uses of these expressions and the distinctions that they mark in the phenomena. This is to be done by imagining appropriate situations and asking ourselves how they should be described – that is, by asking ourselves what precise discriminations these expressions ordinarily mark. Our imagination can be supplemented by the examination of actual legal reports, in so far, that is, as we are investigating the topic of excuses and the doing of actions. For legal reports obviously have a great deal to do with pleas and excuses. Here, however, we have to guard against the possibility that an ordinary expression may be used in an extraordinary way, under the pressure of need to reach a decision and to work from precedents.

The first step then is to examine the actual uses of the groups of words by means of which we describe and classify the doing of actions. Austin's method can be illustrated by an example. Among the expressions listed from the dictionary as relevant to the notions of 'action' and 'excuse' will be such expressions as 'voluntarily', 'deliberately', 'intentionally', 'purposely', 'wilfully'. To make clear to ourselves what distinctions these related expressions serve to mark, we try to imagine situations with a 'suitable background of story' which it would be appropriate to describe in each of these ways. We try to imagine a situation for example in which it would be right to say 'X did Y *deliberately*' but wrong to say 'X did Y *intentionally (voluntarily*, etc.)'. In this case we are examining the effect of making different substitutions for 'Mly' in the sentence frame 'X did Y Mly'. But we shall also make structural changes in the sentence whilst retaining the same words. What is the difference between saying 'X did Y *deliberately*' and 'X *deliberately* did Y'? In this case we are examining the effect of changing the frame 'X did Y Mly' to the frame 'X Mly did Y', substituting for the variable 'Mly' each of the various modifiers under consideration.[1]

The main attraction of this method as an approach to philosophy has seemed to many to be that it relies on a disciplined and systematic study of facts. Here, it seems, is an opportunity for 'field work' in philosophy. In examining ordinary usage, we are dealing with hard facts. 'Here at last we should be able to unfreeze, to loosen up and get going on agreeing about discoveries however small.' Hence Austin finds this 'an attractive subject methodologically'. But, paradoxically, it is just here that a radical objection arises.

The facts that are the subject of this field work are facts of 'ordinary language' – that is, of certain educated, non-technical English usages. It is by making clear to ourselves what distinctions are made in actual usage that we are to get going on agreeing about discoveries. Now facts of this kind must be studied empirically if they are to be studied at all. But the method Austin formulates is not empirical; it is self-consciously intuitive and frequently prescriptive. As an elucidation of actual usages, it must therefore be unreliable. Yet that is what Austin claims it is: 'It will go hard with us if we cannot arrive at the meanings of large numbers of expressions' (p. 90 above).

It is fairly easy to see how this objection arises and to appreciate its force. 'Ordinary language' (an ominously vague phrase) is for philosophical purposes that range of the English language whose lexis is the main subject of English dictionaries and whose grammar is the main subject of English grammars. How then are we to find out the meanings of expressions in ordinary language? Take the words 'deliberately', 'intentionally', 'purposely' from the example given above. We want to find out what precise distinction these expressions ordinarily mark. Often, of course, we use them synonymously; we all know that. But are there cases where each of them may describe some feature of a situation which the others do not? The only way to answer this question is to inspect ordinary language and find out. The obvious first step is to consult the dictionary. Some dictionaries are more informative than others and the unabridged *Oxford English Dictionary* (*O.E.D.*) is the most informative of all. Therefore the first step will be to consult the *O.E.D.*

Before thumbing through the pages in search of 'deliberately', however, we should look at the editor's preface. Describing how the project developed, the editors write:

It was resolved to begin at the beginning and extract anew typical quotations for the use of words. . . . The materials continued to accumulate till upwards of two million quotations had been amassed (p. iv).

In the scrutiny of 'upwards of two million quotations', it is not likely that many words will have slipped past unnoticed, nor that many uses of words will have done so either. The editors' declaration of aims reassures us further:

The aim of this dictionary is to furnish an adequate account of the meaning, origin and history of English words now in general use or known to have been in use at any time during the last seven hundred years (p. vi).

Passing to the expressions whose use we want to determine, we now look up 'deliberately', 'intentionally' and 'purposely', which involves looking up of course the adjectives of which these expressions are the adverbs. Each expression has various uses listed, each use being documented with at least one example. The glosses suggest that in some uses these expressions may be nearly synonymous. Our interest is not in semantic overlaps, however, but in the distinctive uses of each word. A closer inspection of the glosses and the passages quoted makes some differences clear. The full gloss on 'deliberately', for example (which presupposes the gloss on 'deliberate'), is:

> In a deliberate manner. 1. With careful consideration, not hastily or rashly; of set purpose. 2. Without haste, leisurely, slowly.

Seven quotations illustrate these uses.

This is pretty valuable information; but we may feel it is not enough. There are three points we might legitimately raise. First, it is possible that there are uses of 'deliberately' that the *O.E.D.* has missed. This could have come about either through change of meaning over the course of time or through the *O.E.D.*'s reliance on written rather than spoken language. There is a temptation to think of written language as speech on paper; but in fact ordinary usage in speech is often considerably different from ordinary usage in written language.

Second, the uses that the *O.E.D.* does note may not be *accurately* noted. Take the use of 'deliberately' which the dictionary glosses 'with careful consideration'. Now we can consider things in two ways: we can consider *whether* to do *x* or not; and we can consider *how* to do *x*. Possibly 'deliberately' is used normally to indicate the first of these ways of considering, but not the second. If this is so (*if*), the *O.E.D.*'s gloss is not as accurate as it might be.

Third, the *O.E.D.* sometimes notes usages accurately, but does not explain them clearly. Thus we have the two main uses of 'deliberately' noted as: '1. With careful consideration. 2. Without haste.' But it is not pointed out that whether the word is used in sense 1 or sense 2 depends on the linguistic context in which it appears. Compare these two sentences:

1. He *deliberately* trod on my toe.
2. He trod *deliberately* on my toe.

In the syntactic structure of sentence 1 'deliberately' has sense 1: in the structure of sentence 2, it has sense 2. The introduction of further words of a certain kind will, however, complicate matters. Consider now

> 1(*a*). He *very deliberately* trod on my toe.
> 2(*a*). He trod *quite deliberately* on my toe.

'Deliberately' in 1(*a*) seems now to be being used in sense 2, whilst in 2(*a*) it appears to have sense 1. It would be possible to complicate matters still further by considering how the sense of 'deliberately' also depends on the type of verb with which it is collocated. But it is enough here only to point out that the *O.E.D.* does not investigate the role of these factors in the meanings of words.

In these three ways then it is possible in principle to add to or revise the *O.E.D.*'s rich and detailed information about ordinary language. The question is how to do so. There is only one method that is reliable. First, we must have at our disposal a body of techniques that will enable us to sort out, systematise and generally handle the complicated linguistic material we are working with. Second, with the help of these techniques, we must survey texts of actual language (spoken and written) and examine the expressions we want to investigate in the context of these texts. What we are interested in is 'the ordinary meanings' of our 'ordinary expressions'. Consequently the test of our analyses and descriptions will always be whether people actually do use these expressions in the way we say they do.

This, very generally, is the method that any linguist, whether lexicographer or grammarian, must adopt. The one danger to be avoided above all is that of relying exclusively on linguistic intuitions – especially when they are self-conscious. The compilers of the *O.E.D.* did not let their intuitions decide what words mean. They looked at more than two million quotations.

Now compare the method Austin adopts in 'A Plea for Excuses'. We are to consult the dictionary, certainly; but only in order to *list* expressions. Hence 'quite a concise' dictionary will do. This suggests that the unique documentation of ordinary usage contained in the unabridged *O.E.D.* is just not relevant. But to use a dictionary just for listing words when we want to find out what they mean is about as good as using a map for listing place names when we want to find out where the places are.

The second stage, in Austin's exposition, is to imagine situations in describing which one might use some of these expressions and to ask ourselves which expression would in fact be appropriate and why. The shortcomings of this method as an inquiry into ordinary language must be obvious. It is not empirical, but self-consciously intuitive; and consequently it is likely to fall into exactly those traps of language which it is intended to expose. So far from charting the exact distinctions marked by our ordinary expressions, the most this method will establish linguistically is how a group of philosophers *think* they would describe certain (often highly imaginative) situations. This is a pretty far cry from the impartial examination of ordinary language. For all we know, these conclusions may go beyond, distort or conflict with ordinary usage (in fact they sometimes do: see section IV). But if so, this cannot be a reliable method of investigating the distinctions and connections embodied in 'our common stock of words'. What we think we do with words is not necessarily what we actually do with them.

It is important to make clear the scope of this objection, for it may seem to be exposed to an obvious rejoinder. A counter-objection to what I have been saying might take this form: Surely it is a fact that as speakers of language we operate intuitively. Why then should it be objected to Austin that he relies on intuition? We should need to make an empirical study of words in texts only if we were not already familiar with them. But this is clearly not true of the expressions ('deliberately', 'intentionally', 'purposely', etc.) whose distinctive uses Austin is exploring. For Austin's aim is only to make explicit what is already contained in our ready, intuitive use of the familiar expressions of ordinary language.

This objection is plausible but mistaken. It rests on the false assumption that all our ordinary, intuitive usages are in principle accessible to further deliberate processes of intuition – in other words, that we can always self-consciously introspect our unselfconscious intuitions.

There are of course in any language certain grammatical and lexical (as well as other) usages which any competent speaker of the language will recognise immediately. Anyone who thinks the sentence 'Dog bites man' is synonymous with the sentence 'Man bites dog' shows that he has not mastered English grammar. Now it is true that it would normally be superfluous to consult a grammar on this point. Our intuitive recognition of the semantic difference between these two sentences would not need to be checked against the facts of actual usage. But that should not obscure the fact that it is *only* because ordinary grammatical usage is as it is that these two sentences are not synonymous. Our intuitive denial of synonymity would simply be wrong if ordinary usage did not deny it too. Consequently, anyone who questioned our denial could only be refuted by an appeal to the facts of actual usage.

In the same way, but at the lexical level, anyone who could see no semantic difference between 'deliberately' and 'accidentally' – anyone who used these two words as synonyms – simply would not know what these two expressions meant in English. Again, it would normally be superfluous to consult a dictionary or check actual usage on this point. Nevertheless it is the dictionary, or, ultimately, actual 'standard' usage that we should have to appeal to if our denial that the two expressions are synonymous were to be questioned.

Usages of this kind we might call 'requirements' of a language. Anyone who claims to speak English is required amongst other things to be able to distinguish the semantic function of certain (not all) syntactic patterns and to distinguish semantic contrasts of the 'accidentally'–'deliberately' type over a tolerably wide area (certainly not all) of the lexicon of English.

On the other hand, there are grammatical and lexical usages which we should hesitate to call 'requirements' of English in this sense. Someone who claims to speak English is not required to be able to specify immediately a semantic distinction between the two sentences 'The man deliberately bit the dog' and 'The man bit the dog deliberately'. Nor is he required to be able to specify immediately a semantic distinction between the expressions 'accidentally' and 'unintentionally'. Yet these distinctions do exist and can be discriminated, even in ordinary language. We might call such usages 'options' of the language.

Now for discriminating usages which are 'requirements' of a language, it may be enough *for practical purposes* to trust our intuition. But for discriminating 'options', we need to be much more careful. And the more finely we want to distinguish usages, the more careful we need to be. Intuition may suggest; but only evidence will confirm. It is all right to imagine situations and construct intuitively-based examples; it is not all right to rely exclusively on such examples unsupported by any appeal to the independent evidence of actual texts.

Consequently, the objection I have been bringing against Austin's method is not necessarily an objection to the validity or interest of the distinctions he makes. It is an objection to the method of establishing such distinctions as *part of the meanings* of our ordinary expressions. In some cases his conclusions are in fact correct, and in others they are wrong: but in all cases they rest on *unsupported* intuition and introspection. It is clear that a method permitting such vagaries is in principle unreliable.

IV

Finding out what an expression means in a language, whether or not we are speakers of the language, is ultimately an empirical, not an intuitive, matter. Its meaning is (roughly) the ways in which it is actually used by speakers (and writers) of the language in various contexts of situation. Different groups vary in their usage, and so do different individuals: so do the same individuals at different times and in different contexts. 'Ordinary usage' is therefore usage above a certain minimum of generality that excludes 'private' – such as family and strictly idiolectal – uses. How an expression is actually used is a study which belongs to descriptive linguistics, the disciplines and techniques of which

> are directed to assist us in making statements of meaning. Every scientific worker must work out his field in accordance with the resources of his disciplines and techniques and develop them in the handling of his chosen material. The linguist studies the speaking person in the social process.[2]

In this section I want to illustrate the necessity of these disciplines and techniques for the kind of linguistic analysis that Austin undertakes in 'A Plea for Excuses'. I will mention three points where the lack of them has led Austin to torture the ordinary usages he claims to be describing.

I. *Standards of the unacceptable*. One move that Austin makes is to consider excuses that he thinks are 'unacceptable'. Linguistically, this move consists in contrasting several sentences in which an adverb (say) is collocated with different verbal phrases.[3] Sometimes these collocations produce sentences that he thinks we would reject, and he then tries to explain why we should do so. An example of this is his treatment of the adverb 'inadvertently': 'We may plead that we trod on the snail inadvertently, but not on a baby – you ought to look where you are putting your great feet' (p. 94 above).

Now consider the following exponents of the sentence frame 'I *x* inadvertently'.

12   *C. G. New*

A1. I trod on the snail inadvertently.
A2. I broke my promise inadvertently.
B1. I trod on the baby inadvertently.
B2. I he inadvertently.

Of these exponents, A1 and A2 give no trouble: A1 describes a 'physical' action, A2 describes an action that is not 'physical'. B2 infringes a grammatical rule for sentence formation in English and so is not a sentence at all. B1 does not infringe any obvious grammatical rule of English. What then (if anything) is wrong with it? Austin's suggestion is that to say B1, as an excuse for treading on the baby, is to offer an excuse that is unacceptable. The argument is that 'inadvertently' picks out an act that is done when, in the course of performing some other act, I failed to proceed with such meticulous care and attention as would have ensured the non-occurrence of the unfortunate event in question. Hence, Austin concludes, to plead that I trod on the baby inadvertently is to suggest that treading on the baby is the sort of thing that would naturally happen unless I exercised *meticulous* care and attention over the details of what I was doing. And to suggest this is to imply that I have odd views as to what requires *meticulous* care and attention in order to be avoided in the course of doing something else.

Now the distinction Austin draws here may be an interesting one in its own right, but it is not an accurate account of ordinary usage. So far as the evidence of ordinary usage goes, it is not necessary that I should have failed to exercise 'meticulous supervision' of detail before I can be truly said to have done something inadvertently. I can do something inadvertently without exercising any conscious supervision over what I am doing at all, as when I press the wrong door bell inadvertently – I simply wasn't paying attention to what I was doing. Or I can do something inadvertently simply by not realising what side-effects I am producing *even although* I am exercising meticulous supervision over the details of what I am doing. In the course of a very careful summing-up in a capital murder trial, the judge says 'I may inadvertently have misled you in one thing I said yesterday about the law'. This is not a misuse of English; but it is clear that what may have happened is that although the judge exercised meticulous supervision over what he was doing, something nevertheless may have gone wrong.

What then is wrong with B1? I am not sure whether we all do or ought to find anything wrong with it at all. For we know nothing about the context in which it is presupposed to have been uttered. This indeed is one of the dangers of constructing examples on a solely intuitive basis: we are likely to draw conclusions about the meanings of expressions that are really due to an implied context of utterance. Suppose, however, that we do all find this sentence, isolated as it is, one that we are intuitively inclined to doubt or reject. What factors should we have to consider in explaining this? There are three at least; I will only indicate them.

(*a*) *Normal situation*. People tread on snails and break promises more often than they tread on babies. This conditions our linguistic expectations. Consequently, if we are asked to complete the sentence frame 'I trod on the *x*', 'baby' is less likely to be produced than 'step', 'edge', 'pin', or even 'snail' – unless of course some particular context is supplied. Hence the sentence 'I trod on the baby' may also have the queerness which is at first thought to belong uniquely to 'I trod on the baby *inadvertently*'. Compare 'I trod on the H-bomb'.

(*b*) *Contextual association*. Possibly 'inadvertently' (except in its legal use, which resists change) is coming to be used more in certain types of context than in others. For many people it may thus develop contextual associations which would make it seem out of place, or even in bad taste, to use 'inadvertently' to describe the circumstances in which they had trodden on the baby. If 'inadvertently' is usually associated with slips like pressing the wrong door bell or taking the wrong umbrella, it may well sound positively frivolous to use it in baby-treading contexts too.

(*c*) *'Not realising'*. When I press the wrong bell inadvertently I do not realise what I am doing until it is too late. Walking down the public footpath, I may very well not realise I am about to tread on a snail, and so I may tread on it inadvertently. But how could I *help* realising I was about to tread on a baby? This indicates another reason why B1 may seem queer: we may be supplying the same sort of context as for A1. If so, what is 'unacceptable' about B1 is not that it suggests I would have had to exercise 'meticulous supervision' of detail to avoid treading on the baby, but that we do not see how anyone could have failed to *realise* that that was what he was about to do. (You don't have to be meticulous to see there is a baby there.) A few changes in the context presupposed and the queerness may diminish (suppose the lights had just fused?).

2. *'Deliberately' and 'intentionally'*. Is there a clear distinction between types of situation which can be picked out by the use of 'deliberately', contrasted with 'intentionally'? Austin says there is.

He explains the distinction in these terms: 'We walk along the cliff, and I feel a sudden impulse to push you over, which I promptly do; I acted on impulse, yet I certainly intended to push you over, and may even have devised a little ruse to achieve it; yet even then I did not act deliberately for I did not (stop to) ask myself whether to do it or not.' The suggestion is then that 'when you act deliberately you act after weighing it up (*not* after thinking out ways and means (p.94 and p. 99 above)'. On the other hand 'intentionally' covers both these cases.

Now no evidence is brought in favour of this contention about ordinary language except the wholly unsatisfactory evidence of etymology (on which see below). Going just by intuition, I myself would reject Austin's account of ordinary usage: and working the dictionary and noting actual (unselfconscious) usages of educated speakers, we find that the facts conflict with Austin's account. There are certainly cases of deliberate actions in which the agent considered whether or not to do it. But there are also cases, equally sanctioned by ordinary usage, where he had thought out ways and means: 'He laid his plans deliberately'; 'He arranged his arguments deliberately'; 'He aimed his blows deliberately'. In these sentences 'deliberately' may pick out the fact that he gave careful thought to *how* to do what he did, not to *whether* or not to do it. Lastly, there are a vast number of cases in which (as we should expect) weighing up *whether* to do *x* involves thinking out *how* it would be done. In these cases, 'He did *x* deliberately' refers to the fact that he did consider 'it' carefully, but simply does not specify what kind of consideration he gave it. How 'deliberately' is to be construed in a particular sentence therefore will depend on the lexis of the sentence, the syntax and grammar and the wider linguistic and (perhaps) extra-linguistic context. These are the factors we should have to consider if we had to translate 'He did it deliberately' into a language in whose lexicon there were separate words corresponding to the two senses of 'deliberately' in English. It may seem a pity, at any rate to some philosophers, that English does not mark this distinction clearly by means of separate words in its lexicon too. But the fact is, it does not. And would we be much better off if it did?

All this does not mean of course that there is no distinction between doing *x* deliberately and doing *x* intentionally. A glance at the unabridged *O.E.D.* will reveal quite a few differences. What I have said above is only an indication of how we should establish what ordinary usage is. And how we should not.

3. *Clouds of etymology.* One of the reasons why Austin thought the correct use of 'deliberately' was 'after weighing it up' is etymological. One point of method which he is convinced is an 'indispensable aid' is to investigate a word's etymology: 'In spite of all changes in and extensions of and additions to its meanings, and indeed rather pervading and governing these, there will still persist the old idea. In an *accident* something befalls; by *mistake* you take the wrong one; in *error* you stray; when you act *deliberately* you act after weighing it up (*not* after thinking out ways and means)' (p. 99 above). This is a very revealing mistake.

The etymology of a word may be important and interesting. But it is in principle impossible to establish the contemporary use of a word by appealing to its etymology. What uses a word once had may have affected many of the uses it has now: they cannot *tell* us what uses it has now. Past actions in the life of John Smith may have affected what John Smith is doing today. But they cannot *tell* us what John Smith is doing today. What John Smith did five years ago may make what he is doing today intelligible: but you do not establish what John Smith is doing today by asking what it would be intelligible for him to be doing, considering what he did five years ago. What uses a word had five hundred years ago may make the uses it has today intelligible: but you do not establish what uses it has today by asking what uses it would be intelligible for it to have, considering the uses it had five hundred years ago. It is clear surely that if you are trying to distinguish the uses of words by reference to their etymologies, you are not describing their *present* uses. If you do happen to get their present uses right in this way, it is not because of the words' etymology, but because its etymology happens in this case to correspond with its present use.

Austin's own examples illustrate the pitfalls of this method in practice. Take them in turn from the passage quoted above.

(i) *Accident.* The most general and widest use of this word, according to the *O.E.D.*, is 'anything that happens'. Austin prefers what he wrongly believes to be the etymology of 'accident' – 'something that befalls'. His etymology is wrong because 'befalls' is not an accurate translation of the Latin components of 'accident', 'ad'+'cadere'. The prefix 'be-' in English means (originally) 'about' or 'around' (hence 'bestir'); the nearest equivalent to Latin 'ad' is 'to' or 'towards'. So, on his own principles, Austin should have preferred 'fall to' to 'befall'.

This is a minor point. But now what about the word 'fall'? Studying its etymology, we come across Old English 'fallan', cognate with German 'fallen'. These may be derived from Latin 'fallere', to deceive. Are we to understand then that in the meaning of the word 'fall' there may be contained some idea of deception? What are we going to find when we look further into the etymology of Latin 'fallere'? Is there any limit to how far back we should trace the history of a word in pursuit of its present meaning? These facts of language plainly refute the notion that 'the old idea' persists through all changes of a word's meaning.

(ii) *'Mistake' and 'error'*. The first recorded use of 'error' in English is to describe the action of going astray; the first use of 'mistake' is a reference to taking something wrongly (*not*, as Austin puts it, 'taking the wrong one'). This shows that at that time 'mistake' and 'error' were distinguished in use in accordance with their etymology. It does not show that in contemporary ordinary usage this same distinction persists. In fact the evidence is against it. In this case, it is enough (and particularly revealing) to compare Austin's *actual* usage with the etymological uses he *prescribes*. He claims that 'by *mistake* you take the wrong one; in *error* you stray'. Earlier in the same paper occurs the sentence 'But by the way, and more negatively, a number of traditional cruces or *mistakes* in this field can be resolved or removed (p. 83 above)'. Surely what he has in mind here is a case of 'going astray', not 'taking the wrong one'? Or is there after all no difference? Certainly we cannot say that the sentence quoted is faulty by any standard of ordinary usage.

(iii) *'Deliberately'*. I have pointed out already that a survey of actual usage does not show that to do something deliberately is necessarily to do it after considering *whether* to do it, but necessarily not to do it after considering *how* to do it. Austin makes it clear that etymology has influenced him in his attempt to make a distinction here. It is interesting to see how etymology has misled him. 'Deliberately' derives from Latin 'de'+'libra', a balance. Hence Austin glosses 'deliberately' as 'after weighing it up (*not* after thinking out ways and means)'. Now if we read its etymology into the present meaning of a word in this way, it is only too likely that we shall arrive at a conclusion like Austin's. But the trouble is, it conflicts with the facts of actual usage which it is his declared aim to elucidate. The sentence 'He always planned deliberately how to achieve ends he had adopted on impulse' is a sentence in which 'deliberately' is used in the sense which Austin claims ordinary usage forbids: but no one not in the grip of an etymology would reject it. Ordinary usage makes no ruling here.

These examples should make clear how unreliable it must be to argue from a word's past to its present. Etymology is the study of the history of words, not (as 'etymology's' etymology may suggest) the study of their 'true' meanings.

V

I hope I have now demonstrated the radical defects in Austin's method of elucidating the precise meanings of our ordinary expressions. The exact distinctions and connections marked in the lexical and grammatical features of ordinary language cannot be explained by means of a purely intuitive approach, especially one that disregards the techniques available in general linguistics for the handling of the linguistic material to be explained. How disabling, lastly, is this faulty method? How damaging a criticism is this of the whole enterprise outlined in 'A Plea for Excuses'?

To answer this question, we must look again at Austin's justification of this type of analysis. In section II, I pointed out that the aims were really twofold: negatively, 'the traps that language sets us' are to be revealed and understood; positively, we are to be made aware of all the distinctions and connections embodied in ordinary usage, which are likely to be 'more sound and more subtle than any that you or I are likely to think up in our armchairs of an afternoon' (p. 84 above). These are the aims. But what Austin actually does with ordinary language is rather different. He notices a distinction between doing x after weighing it up and doing x after thinking out ways and means; and he reads this distinction into the expression 'deliberately' – in accordance with its etymology, but in defiance of its use. He imagines a situation in which someone might be said to have done y *inadvertently*; and prescribes this as the *only* legitimate usage without regard to the full range of linguistic factors involved. He distinguishes between 'error' and 'mistake', although his own usage shows this distinction is far from ordinary. The distinctions he draws are, or may be, valid. But they are not necessarily distinctions of ordinary language. The dictionary, and the etymologies of words, have thus become a sort of heuristic device for finding distinctions in a given area of discourse, whether or not the distinctions correspond to, go beyond or distort actual usage.

But does it matter? Surely what matters is whether the distinctions are real and important, not whether they are marked by gram-

matical and lexical features of English? The answer to this depends
on the importance of Austin's primary aim. This is to understand the
distinctions that we *do* mark with our ordinary expressions. Ordinary
language is 'the first word'. Unless we understand that, we are only
too likely to fall into its traps. What I have argued here is that since
his method of investigating ordinary language is unreliable, he is
only too likely to fail to understand the distinctions that ordinary
language does in fact mark; and I have indicated (only) some
places where he actually does fail. The answer to the question 'Does
it matter?' then is this: If it is important to map the exact distinctions marked in ordinary language, then the fact that they are
being inaccurately mapped is important too. If we use inaccurate
maps, we are just as likely to get lost as before.

PART THREE

The Verification of Linguistic Characterisations

This section reprints in its entirety the major engagement that was fought between Cavell on the one hand and Mates, Fodor and Katz on the other, over the justifiability of the appeal to the use of language as it is made by the philosopher. Also included is an early paper on this subject by R. M. Hare that reveals, at the very least, the concern of the philosopher with his methods. Hare's important paper is particularly valuable in that it locates the methods of the modern analytic philosopher in a mainstream that begins at least as far back as Plato. There follows a paper by Searle which restates a justification for the appeal by the philosopher to his own idiolect. The section is completed by Vendler's remarkable summary of the points at issue in the dispute and with his attempted arbitration.

VII On the verification of statements about ordinary language[1]

B. Mates

In this paper I shall discuss certain difficulties which seem to me to stand in the way of understanding or properly appreciating the work of the so-called 'ordinary language' philosophers. These difficulties concern the interpretation of the various seemingly factual statements which such philosophers make about language. I am mainly interested in the question of how one would go about verifying these statements; in so far as meaning is bound up with verification, this is also a question of their meaning. Of course, it is possible to pretend that no clarification is required at all, that the sense of assertions about the ordinary use of language is perfectly obvious, or at least sufficiently so for the purposes at hand. But I do not think that such optimism is justified. Even among those who can claim to be 'in the know' or to 'get the point' there are wide disagreements both as to the truth and as to the meaning of given assertions of the sort under consideration, and these disagreements are by themselves a basis for scepticism. When in addition it is seen that such assertions play a crucial role in the discussions which are supposed to answer, dissolve, or somehow get rid of the traditional problems of philosophy, a philosopher may perhaps be excused for looking at the matter a little more closely.

First, a parenthetical remark about terminology. As is always the case when one attempts to formulate objections to a philosophical position of scope and subtlety, there is here the problem of finding a convenient vocabulary which does not beg too many questions. I shall make use of such terms as 'analytic', 'synthetic', 'meaning', 'sense', 'denotation', in the hope that I am not thereby drawing a number of red herrings across the trail, and in the belief that if necessary I could reformulate my points without the use of these terms, though with a considerable loss of compactness. For instance, when I ask whether a given statement about ordinary language is normative or descriptive, and whether it is analytic or synthetic, I am not asking questions to which the alleged difficulties with the fringes of these terms are decisively relevant. Instead, I merely wish to know with what attitude the given statement is to be confronted; for instance, is it to be regarded as a recommendation, so that an appropriate query is 'What will be gained by following this advice?', or is it to be regarded as true or false? And if it is to be taken as true or false, does the author intend it as true by virtue of the meanings of the terms involved, or does he consider himself to have made a statement the truth-value of which depends upon matters of fact? The answers to such questions will fundamentally affect our understanding of the given statement, and they do not, so far as I can see, need to involve us in any of the philosophical tangles which are supposed to be connected with the terms 'normative' and 'analytic'. I believe that somewhat analogous comments apply to the other cases in which I make use of notorious philosophical terminology.

It will be useful to have before us some examples of the type of statement under consideration. Accordingly I quote a passage from Professor Ryle's treatment of the Freedom of the Will:

It should be noticed that while ordinary folk, magistrates, parents and teachers, generally apply the words 'voluntary' and 'involuntary' to actions in one way, philosophers often apply them in quite another way.

In their most ordinary employment 'voluntary' and 'involuntary' are used, with a few minor elasticities, as adjectives applying to actions which ought not to be done. We discuss whether someone's action was voluntary or not only when the action seems to have been his fault. . . . In the same way in ordinary life we raise questions of responsibility only when someone is charged, justly or unjustly, with an offence. It makes sense, in this use, to ask whether a boy was responsible for breaking a window, but not whether he was responsible for finishing his homework in good time. . . .

In this ordinary use, then, it is absurd to discuss whether satisfactory, correct or admirable performances are voluntary or involuntary. . . .

But philosophers, in discussing what constitutes acts voluntary or involuntary, tend to describe as voluntary not only reprehensible but also meritorious actions, not only things that are someone's fault but also things that are to his credit. The motives underlying their unwitting extension of the ordinary sense of 'voluntary' . . . will be considered later. . . .

The tangle of largely spurious problems, known as the problem of the Freedom of the Will, partly derives from this unconsciously stretched use of 'voluntary' . . . (Chapter I above).

These, then, are examples of the sort of remark I wish to consider. They may not be the best examples that could have been chosen, but they do have the not inconsiderable merit of being relatively lucid. Ryle seems here to assert that the ordinary use of the word 'voluntary' is quite different from the philosophic use. He does not mean merely that the ordinary man seldom talks philosophy. The difference between the ordinary use and the philosophic use hinges rather upon the alleged fact that the ordinary man applies the word 'voluntary' almost exclusively to actions which ought not to be done, while the philosopher stretches it to cover meritorious actions as well. Now although the question whether Ryle is right or wrong in this particular case is not essential to the point of the present paper, I will say at once (1) that I very much doubt whether as a matter of fact the ordinary man does apply the term 'voluntary' only to actions which (he thinks) ought not to be done, and (2) that even if this were shown to be the case, it would not have decisive relevance to a determination of the ordinary use of the word 'voluntary'. Some other factor, such as perhaps a disposition on the part of the ordinary man to talk more about things of which he disapproves than about things of which he approves, could by itself account for a relatively frequent application of the word 'voluntary' to disapproved actions, even if the word were simply being used in one of its dictionary senses, e.g. 'proceeding from the will or from one's own choice or full consent'. In short, at first glance it seems that Ryle's assertion about the ordinary use of the word 'voluntary' is false, and, moreover, that it is based upon doubtful evidence which would be entirely insufficient even if it were sound.

When one comes to so drastic a conclusion about an assertion seriously made, it is time to reconsider the possibility that one has not understood what was asserted. For further light we may consult an article entitled 'Ordinary Language',[2] in which Ryle attempts by means of a distinction between use and usage to indicate why empirical studies like those of the lexicographers or philologists are irrelevant to the truth of statements about the ordinary use of language. Such studies have a place in determining the *usage* of a word, he says, but not in determining the *use*. Uses are ways or techniques of doing the thing, the more or less widely prevailing practice of doing which constitutes the usage. He explains further that 'ordinary use' is to be contrasted with 'non-stock use', and that in general 'use' contrasts in these contexts with 'misuse'. Now it seems to me that Ryle fails to make good the alleged distinction between use and usage, and still less the point that through confusion in this matter philosophers have misunderstood the character of claims that the ordinary use of a word is this or that. Nevertheless, his discussion is not without significance for the matters we are considering: it appears to indicate that for him there is some sort of normative element in assertions about ordinary use. If the opposite of use is misuse, then use must be somehow right, proper, or correct. It is not easy to see how this can be applied to statements like those quoted about the word 'voluntary', but perhaps Ryle's discussion in that passage comes down to an assertion that to predicate the word 'voluntary' of praiseworthy actions is to misuse the word, presumably in some sense of 'misuse' which cannot be defined statistically. But if this is the way the wind blows, it would be instructive to have an indication of the standards or goals with reference to which the term 'misuse' is applicable. What authority deems it wrong to use the word 'voluntary' as the philosopher does? What unwelcome consequences would attend the proscribed use? Surely the point is not merely that if you use the word 'voluntary' just as the philosopher does, you may find yourself entangled in the philosophic problem of the Freedom of the Will.

Despite Ryle's own explanations, I am reluctant to believe that the expression 'ordinary use' is really a normative term for the ordinary-language philosophers. The way in which they use it seems better explained on the hypothesis that it is a rough descriptive term, employed with little definiteness of intention, and that there is in addition a *belief*, not part of the meaning of 'ordinary use', to the effect that it is somehow wrong or inadvisable, or at least dangerous, to use ordinary words in ways different from those in which the ordinary man uses them. It is further supposed, and often expressly asserted, that in daily life words function well enough and lead to no great problems. In any case, although all forms of 'nose-counting, are deprecated in these quarters, it often happens that when support is offered for an assertion that the ordinary use of a given word is thus and so, this support takes the form of an attempt to remind or convince us that the use in question is indeed quite frequent among 'ordinary folk, magistrates, parents and teachers'. In other words, the statement is taken as having a factual basis and presumably as refutable by observation of the ordinary folk, magistrates, parents and teachers.

This brings me to the question of how one might verify a statement about the ordinary use of a word or phrase, when the statement is interpreted neither as a piece of advice nor as a claim that the use is sanctioned by authority. It is necessary here to make passing mention of a point of view, or rather a dodge, which cannot be taken very seriously. This is the comfortable suggestion that the average adult has already amassed such a tremendous amount of empirical information about the use of his native language that he can depend upon his own intuition or memory and need not undertake a laborious questioning of other people, even when he is dealing with the tricky terms which are central in philosophical problems. Such an assertion is itself an empirical hypothesis, of a sort which used to be invoked in favour of armchair psychology, and it is not borne out by the facts.[3] It has been found that even relatively careful authors are often not reliable reporters of their *own* linguistic behaviour, let alone that of others. (Indeed, this is hardly surprising in view of the fact that most of the time we use language in a more or less automatic manner.) The weakness of the hypothesis is further revealed by the fact that the intuitive findings of different people, even of different experts, are often inconsistent. Thus, for example, while Ryle tells us that 'voluntary' and 'involuntary' in their ordinary use are applied only to actions which ought not to be done, his colleague Professor Austin states in another connection: '. . . for example, take "voluntarily" and "involuntarily": we may join the army or make a gift voluntarily, we may hiccough or make a small gesture involuntarily . . .' (p. 91 above). If agreement about usage cannot be reached within so restricted a sample as the class of Oxford Professors of Philosophy, what are the prospects when the sample is enlarged?

Let us now look at the question of how to verify an assertion that a given person uses a word in a given way or with a given sense. It seems to me that, roughly speaking, there are two basic approaches, which I shall call the 'extensional' and the 'intensional', though any really adequate procedure will probably have to be a combination of both. In the extensional approach one observes a reasonably large class of cases in which the subject applies the word, and then one 'sees' or 'elicits' the meaning by finding what is common to these cases. For some reason or other this method, with all of its obvious difficulties, is thought by many people to be more scientific than the intensional approach. In the latter, one asks the subject what he means by the given word or how he uses it; then one proceeds in Socratic fashion to test this first answer by confronting the subject with counter-examples and borderline cases, and so on until the subject settles down more or less permanently upon a definition or account. The difficulties with this method are also very considerable, and I hold no particular brief for it. I only wish to say that it has just as legitimate a claim to be 'right' as the extensional method has. Things become interesting when, as will often happen, the two approaches give different results. What the analyst sees in common among the cases to which the subject applies the term may have little or nothing to do with what the subject says he means by the term; and, further, the subject may in fact apply the term to cases which lack the characteristics which he himself considers essential for proper application of the term. In whatever manner these conflicts are to be resolved, I wish only to repeat that the outcome of the intensional approach is as much a characterisation of ordinary usage as the outcome of the extensional approach, assuming of course that the same subjects are involved. Thus, even if Ryle had determined that ordinary folk in fact apply the word 'voluntary' only to actions which ought not to be done, while philosophers apply it to meritorious actions as well, he would be far from establishing that philosophers and ordinary folk apply the word 'voluntary' in different ways, i.e. attach different senses to it.[4] For if he had proceeded by the intensional route he might have found that both philosophers and ordinary folk tend to give the same sort of definition or account – perhaps something similar to what one finds in the dictionary – and this would have been evidence that they use the term in the *same* sense. Both approaches may lead to interesting results, but I do not see that one is scientific and the other is not, or that one is useful and the other is not.

Now the ordinary-language philosophers, I believe, tend towards an armchair version of the extensional method, though sometimes they read the dictionary for intensional guidance before surveying the cases in which they know or suppose the term would be applied. This extensional approach appears in the quoted passage from Ryle,[5] and it may also be seen in the following quotation from J. O. Urmson's article, 'Some Questions Concerning Validity':

In his popular book, *The Nature of the Physical World*, . . . Eddington said in effect that desks were not really solid. Miss Stebbing, in her book *Philosophy and the Physicists*, [showed] that this way of putting things involved illegitimate mystification; this she did by simply pointing out that if one asked what we ordinarily mean by *solid* we immediately realise that we mean something like 'of the consistency of such things as desks'. Thus she showed conclusively that the novelty of scientific theory does not consist, as had been unfortunately suggested, in showing the inappropriateness of ordinary descriptive language.[6]

I interpret (perhaps erroneously) Urmson and Stebbing to be saying that if you look and see to which objects people regularly apply the word 'solid', you will find that by and large these objects have the consistency of such things as desks. But from this it does not follow that by 'solid' we *mean* something like 'of the consistency of such things as desks'. If you want to know what we mean by 'solid', you should in addition ask us; the answers will very likely be inconclusive, but they will be relevant. Perhaps they will tend to converge on several senses, one of which could be 'not hollow, having its interior entirely filled with matter'. If you follow out *this* strand of the ordinary use of 'solid' it will no longer appear so obvious that Eddington was using 'solid' in a new or mystifying sense when he said that desks are not really solid. Indeed, the effectiveness of Eddington's remark seems to derive from the fact that the properties which one is inclined to regard as the defining properties of solidity do not really belong to the objects to which we customarily apply the term 'solid', and the interest of this fact is in no way diminished by repeating 'Oh, but we *do* apply the word "solid" to such things as desks'. Of course we do, but we also say that by 'solid' we mean 'having its interior entirely filled with matter', or something like that. The collision is *within* ordinary usage, and not between it and scientific theory.

I should like now to mention some of the difficulties which attend the two methods I have discussed. Only when one gets down to cases do these problems appear with clarity, and in this general account I can list just a few. In connection with the extensional approach we have the problem of deciding which occurrences of the word are to be considered (especially when the word is thought to have different senses) and what are the relevant features of the objects to which the word is applied or of the situations in which it is applied. Much depends upon how these objects or situations are described (or 'thought of') in the data from which the meaning is to be 'elicited'.[7] Further, shall we describe the objects and situations in terms of the properties which they really have, or in terms of the properties which they are thought by the subject to have? (If the latter alternative is chosen, then even the extensional approach might lead to the conclusion that tables are not really solid, in the ordinary sense of 'solid'.) When it comes to seeing what is common to the various items which make up the extension, the difficulties become still worse. The objects in any collection will have infinitely many properties in common; furthermore, two words with quite different senses may happen to have the same extension or, even more likely, their extensions may happen to coincide in the domain investigated. Thus perhaps Ryle happened to consider only some part of the extension of 'voluntary act' which is also a part of the extension of 'voluntary act that ought not to be done'. On top of all these problems is the problem of determining what will justify the conclusion that a word has more than one sense or use. We shall never find a case in which it is not true that all items of the extension have *something* in common, even when on other grounds we are inclined to say that the word in question has two senses. Some principle is needed for singling out the 'real' or 'important' properties, but it is not easy to state what that would be. In view of all these matters it becomes apparent that the task of looking at the applications of a word and 'seeing' what it means is not so simple after all.

Before describing some of the difficulties attending the intensional approach I should like to add one more observation which pertains mainly to the extensional approach. We have all heard the wearying platitude that 'you can't separate' the meaning of a word from the entire context in which it occurs, including not only the actual linguistic context but also the aims, feelings, beliefs, and hopes of the speaker, the same for the listener and any bystanders, the social situation, the physical surroundings, the historical background, the rules of the game, and so on *ad infinitum*. There is no doubt some truth in this, but I fail to see how it helps one get started in an empirical investigation of language. At the very least, provisional divisions of the subject have to be made somewhere. It seems to me that there is much to be said for the well-known syntax–semantics–pragmatic division, and that often many of the factors which the ordinary-language philosophers find in common among the cases in which an expression is employed belong more to the pragmatics of the expression than to its semantics. In particular, most of the facts which are expressed by statements of the form 'He wouldn't say that unless he . . .' belong in the category of the pragmatics of the expression and should be avoided when 'eliciting' or 'seeing' the meaning. To take an example, consider all the fuss about the sentence 'I know it, but I may be wrong', which has been called everything from 'contradiction' to 'nonsense'. Perhaps it is true that ordinarily I wouldn't say 'I know it' unless I felt great confidence in what I was asserting, and it might also be true that ordinarily I wouldn't say 'I may be wrong' unless I felt only a small amount of such confidence. So that if I say 'I know it, but I may be wrong' the listener may be momentarily befuddled before he hits upon the right diagnosis of the form 'He wouldn't say that unless he . . .'. But all this does not suffice to show that 'I know it, but I may be wrong' is contradictory or nonsensical according to ordinary usage. The confidence I signify by saying 'I know it' does not have to be mentioned in giving a semantical account of the word 'know', but only in describing its pragmatics. Likewise, when I say 'I may be wrong' I do not *imply* that I have no confidence in what I have previously asserted; I only indicate it. If I do have the confidence and yet say 'I may be wrong', I have not told a falsehood, though I may indeed have misled someone. Limitation of time prevents my going further into this matter, and I only bring it up so as to be able to formulate the following: it seems to me that not only do the ordinary-language philosophers tend towards an armchair version of the extensional method, but also they are inclined to overlook the semantic–pragmatic distinction when they find what is common to the situations in which a given word is used. If, in the example concerning 'voluntary', Ryle means that the ordinary man applies the word only to actions of which he disapproves, while the philosopher applies it to approved actions as well, and that hence the philosopher uses the word in a stretched, extraordinary sense, then this would be an example of the sort of semantic-pragmatic confusion which I am here trying to describe.[8]

The intensional approach to the problem of verifying assertions about meaning or use seems to involve us in a conceptual difficulty of its own. If we are to do justice to the notions (1) that what an individual means by a word depends at least in part upon what he *wants* to mean by that word, and (2) that he may have to think awhile before he discovers what he 'really' means by a given word, we are led to consider a test which will amount to a sort of Socratic questionnaire. That is, there will have to be prodding questions aimed at drawing the subject's attention to borderline cases, counter-examples, and various awkward consequences of his first and relatively off-hand answers. If as a result of these questions he is inclined to give a different answer from the one he gave at first, we may describe the phenomenon in various ways: we can say that he has changed his mind or learned something new, or we can say that he has now managed to find a better way of expressing what he really means (and perhaps has always meant) by the word. In general, it does not seem possible to differentiate in a practical way between *finding out* what someone means by a word, and *influencing* his linguistic behaviour relative to that word. A philosopher who had been brought up on Plato might be inclined to think that when a group of persons were subjected to a Socratic interrogation their answers would at first be very diverse and later would tend to converge on one, or at most a few, definitions of the term in question. It would be interesting to know whether questionnaires could be designed which would have this effect, and also whether one could design a sort of anti-Socratic questionnaire which would tend to lead subjects to greater and greater disagreement.[9]

On the whole, it seems to me unwise, initially at least, to try to limit oneself either to the intensional or to the extensional approach. It will in practice be difficult to separate the two when one is designing a concrete test for determining the ordinary sense of a given word; they are rather to be thought of as different moments or tendencies which actual methods will combine in varying proportions. It could easily happen, however, as it has in certain well-known analogous cases, that experience would teach us to revise our conceptual framework, or at least to change our estimates of what is important and valuable.[10] It may turn out desirable to distinguish different senses of the expression 'ordinary use', corresponding to different methods of verifying statements in which this expression occurs, and one would then wish to know in which, if any, of these senses it would be true and important to say that in philosophic problems words do not have their ordinary use.

VIII Must we mean what we say?[1]

S. Cavell

That what we ordinarily say and mean may have a direct and deep control over what we can philosophically say and mean is an idea which many philosophers find oppressive. It might be argued that in part the oppression results from misunderstanding; that the new philosophy which proceeds from ordinary language is not *that* different from traditional methods of philosophising, and that the frequent attacks upon it are misdirected. But I shall not attempt to be conciliatory, both because I think the new philosophy at Oxford is critically different from traditional philosophy, and because I think it is worth trying to bring out their differences as fully as possible. There *is*, after all, something oppressive about a philosophy which seems to have uncanny information about our most personal philosophical assumptions (those, for example, about whether we can ever know for certain of the existence of the external world, or of other minds; and those we make about favourite distinctions between 'the descriptive and the normative', or between matters of fact and matters of language) and which inveterately nags us about them. Particularly oppressive when that philosophy seems so often *merely* to nag and to try no special answers to the questions which possess us – unless it be to suggest that we sit quietly in a room. Eventually, I suppose, we will have to look at that sense of oppression itself: such feelings can come from a truth about ourselves which we are holding off.

My hopes here are modest. I shall want to say why, in my opinion, some of the arguments Professor Mates brings against the Oxford philosophers he mentions are on the whole irrelevant to their main concerns. And this will require me to say something about what I take to be the significance of proceeding, in one's philosophising, from what we ordinarily say and mean. That will not be an easy thing to do without appearing alternately trivial and dogmatic. Perhaps that is only to be expected, given the depth and the intimacy of conflict between this way of proceeding in philosophy and the way I take Mates to be following. These ways of philosophy seem, like friends who have quarrelled, to be able neither to tolerate nor to ignore one another. I shall frequently be saying something one could not fail to know; and that will appear trivial. I shall also be suggesting that something we know is being overemphasised and something else not taken seriously enough; and that will appear dogmatic. But since I am committed to this dialogue, the time is past for worrying about appearances.

Mates is less concerned to dispute specific results of the Oxford philosophers than he is to question the procedures which have led these philosophers to claim them. In particular, he doubts that they have assembled the sort of evidence which their 'statements about ordinary language' require. As a basis for his scepticism. Mates produces a disagreement between two major figures of the school over the interpretation of an expression of ordinary language – a disagreement which he regards as symptomatic of the shallowness of their methods.[2] On Mates's account of it, the conflict is not likely to be settled successfully by further discussion. We are faced with two professors (of philosophy, it happens) each arguing (claiming, rather) that the way he talks is the right way and that what he intuits about language is the truth about it. But if this is what their claims amount to, it hardly seems worth a philosopher's time to try to collect evidence for them.

To evaluate the disagreement between Austin and Ryle, we may distinguish, among the statements they make about ordinary language, three types:[3] (1) There are statements which produce *instances* of what is said in a language ('We do say . . . but we don't say –'; 'We ask whether . . . but we do not ask whether –'. (2) Sometimes these instances are accompanied by *explications* – statements which make explicit what is implied when we say what statements of the first type instance us as saying ('When we say . . . we imply (suggest, say) –'; 'We don't say . . . unless we mean –'). Such statements are checked by reference to statements of the first type. (3) Finally, there are *generalisations*, to be tested by reference to statements of the first two types. Since there is no special problem here about the testing of generalisations, we will be concerned primarily with the justification of statements of the first two types and especially with the second.

Even without attempting to be more precise about these differences, the nature of the clash between Ryle and Austin becomes somewhat clearer. Notice, first of all, that the statement Mates quotes from Austin is of the first type: 'Take "voluntarily" . . .: we may . . . make a gift voluntarily . . .' – which I take to be material mode for 'We say "The gift was made voluntarily"'. (The significance of this shift of 'mode' will be discussed.) Only one of the many statements Mates quotes from Ryle is of this type, viz., 'It makes sense . . . to ask whether a boy was responsible for breaking a window, but not whether he was responsible for finishing his homework in good time . . .'. The statements of Ryle's which clash with Austin's are different: 'In their most ordinary employment "voluntary" and "involuntary" are used . . . as adjectives applying to actions which ought not to be done. We discuss whether some-one's action was voluntary or not only when the action seems to have been his fault . . . etc.' These do not produce *instances* of what we say (the way 'We say "The boy was responsible for break-ing the window"' does); they are generalisations – as the phrases 'actions which' and 'only when' show – to be tested by producing such instances.

It is true that the instance quoted from Austin does go counter to Ryle's generalisation: making a gift is not always something which ought not to be done, or something which is always someone's fault. There is clearly a clash here. But is our only intelligent course *at this point* to take a poll? Would it be dogmatic or unempirical of us to conclude simply that Ryle is wrong about this, that he has settled upon a generalisation to which an obvious counter-instance has been produced? It is, moreover, an instance which Ryle himself may well be expected to acknowledge as counter to his generalisa-tion; indeed, one which he might have produced for himself. The fact that he did not need indicate only that he was too quick to accept a generalisation, not that he is without (good) evidence for it. One of Mates's objections to Ryle can be put this way: Ryle *is* without evidence – anyway, without very good evidence – because he is not entitled to a statement of the first type (one which presents an *instance* of what we say) in the absence of experimental studies which demonstrate its occurrence in the language.

To see that this objection, taken in the general sense in which Mates urges it, is groundless, we must bear in mind the fact that these statements – statements that something is said in English – are being made by native speakers of English. Such speakers do not, in *general*, need evidence for what is said in the language; they are the source of such evidence. It is from them that the descriptive linguist takes the corpus of utterances on the basis of which he will construct a grammar of that language. To answer *some* kinds of specific questions, we will have to engage in that 'laborious questioning' Mates insists upon, and count noses; but in general, to tell what is and isn't English, and to tell whether what is said is properly used, the native speaker can rely on his own nose; if not, there would be nothing to count. No one speaker will say everything, so it may be profitable to seek out others; and sometimes you (as a native speaker) may be unsure that a form of utterance is as you say it is, or is used as you say it is used, and in that case you will have to check with another native speaker. And because attending so hard to what you say may itself make you unsure more often than is normal, it is a good policy to check more often. A good policy, but not a methodological necessity. The philosopher who proceeds from ordinary language, in his use of himself as subject in his collection of data, may be more informal than the descriptive linguist (though not more than the linguistic theorist using examples from his native speech); but there is nothing in that to make the data, in some general way, suspect.

Nor does this imply a reliance on that 'intuition or memory' which Mates (p. 125 above) finds so objectionable. In claiming to know, in general, whether we do or do not use a given expression, I am not claiming to have an infallible memory for what we say, any more than I am claiming to remember the hour when I tell you what time we have dinner on Sundays. A normal person may forget and remember certain words, or what certain words mean, in his native language, but (assuming that he has used it continuously) he does not remember the *language*. There is a world of difference between a person who speaks a language natively and one who knows the language fairly well. If I lived in Munich and knew German fairly well, I might try to intuit or guess what the German expression for a particular phenomenon is. Or I might ask my landlady; and that would probably be the extent of the laborious questioning the problem demanded. Nor does the making of either of the sorts of statement about ordinary language I have distinguished rely on a claim that '[we have] already amassed . . . a tremendous amount of empirical information about the use of [our] native language' (Mates, ibid.). That would be true if we were, say, making statements about the history of the language, or about its sound system, or about the housewife's understanding of political slogans, or about a special form in the morphology of some dialect. But for a native speaker to say what, in ordinary circumstances, is said when no such special information is needed or claimed. All that is needed is the truth of the proposition that a natural language is what native speakers of that language speak.

Ryle's generalisation, however, requires more than simple, first-level statements of instances; it also requires statements of the second type, those which contain first-level statements together with an 'explication' of them. When Ryle claims that '. . . we raise questions of responsibility only when someone is charged, justly or unjustly, with an offence', he is claiming both 'We say "The boy was responsible for breaking a window", but we do not say "The boy was responsible for finishing his homework in good time"', and also claiming 'When we say "The boy was responsible for (some action)" we imply that the action was an offence, one that ought not to have been done, one that was his fault'. I want to argue that Ryle is, in general, as entitled to statements of this second type as he is to statements of the first type; although it is just here that the particular generalisation in question misses. We know Austin's example counters Ryle's claim because we know that the statement (of the second type) 'When we say "The gift was made voluntarily" we imply that the action of making the gift was one which ought not to be done, or was someone's fault' is false. This is clearly knowledge which Mates was relying on when he produced the clash between them. I will take up statements of the second type in a moment.

Before proceeding to that, let us look at that clash a bit longer: its importance has altered considerably. What Austin says does not go fully counter to Ryle's story. It is fundamental to Austin's account to emphasise that we cannot *always* say of actions that they were voluntary, even when they obviously were not involuntary either. Although we can (sometimes) say 'The gift was made voluntarily', it is specifically not something we can say about ordinary, unremarkable cases of making gifts. Only when the action or circumstances) of making the gift is in some way unusual (instead of his usual Christmas bottle, you give the neighbourhood policeman a cheque for $1000), or extraordinarily (you leave your heirs penniless and bequeath your house to your cat), or untoward (you give your rocking horse to your new friend, but the next morning you cry to have it back), can the question whether it was voluntary intelligibly arise. Ryle has not completely neglected this: his 'actions which ought not be done' and his 'action [which] seems to have been . . . [someone's] fault' are clearly examples of actions which are abnormal, untoward, questionable; so he is right in saying that about these we (sometimes) raise the question whether they were voluntary. His error lies in characterising these actions incompletely, and in wrongly characterising those about which the question *cannot* arise. Normally, it is true, the question whether satisfactory, correct or admirable performances are voluntary does not arise; but this is because there is usually nothing about such actions to question; nothing has gone wrong.

Not seeing that the condition for applying the term 'voluntary' holds quite generally – viz., the condition that there be something (real or imagined) fishy about any performance intelligibly so characterised – Ryle construes the condition too narrowly, supposes that there must be something *morally* fishy about the performance. He had indeed sensed trouble where trouble was: the philosophical use of 'voluntary' stretches the idea of volition out of shape, beyond recognition. And his diagnosis of the trouble was sound: philosophers imagine, because of a distorted picture of the mind, that the term 'voluntary' must apply to all actions which are not involuntary (or unintentional), whereas it is only applicable where there is some specific reason to raise the question. The fact that Ryle fails to specify its applicability precisely enough no more vitiates his entire enterprise than does the fact that he indulges a mild form of the same vice he describes: he frees himself of the philosophical tic of stretching what is true of definite segments of what we do to cover *everything* we do (as epistemologists stretch doubt to cover everything we say), but not from the habit of identifying linguistic antitheses with logical contradictories:[4] in particular, he takes the question 'Voluntary or not?' to mean 'Voluntary or involuntary?', and seems to suppose that (responsible) actions which are not contemptible must be admirable, and that whatever I (responsibly) do either is my fault or else is to my credit. These antitheses miss exactly those actions about which the question 'Voluntary or not?' really has no sense, viz., those ordinary, unremarkable, natural things we do which make up most of our conduct and which are neither admirable nor contemptible; which, indeed, could only erroneously be said to go on, in general, in *any* special way.[5] Lacking firmness here, it is not surprising that Ryle's treatment leaves the subject a bit wobbly. Feeling how *enormously* wrong it is to remove 'voluntary' from *a specific* function, he fails to sense the slighter error of his own specification.[6]

I have said that the ordinary-language philosopher is also and equally entitled to statements of the second type I distinguished, which means that he is entitled not merely to say what (words) we say, but equally to say what we should mean in (by) saying them. Let us turn to statements of this type and ask what the relation is between what you explicitly say and what you imply; or, to avoid begging the question, ask how we are to account for the fact (supposing it to be a fact) that we only say or ask A ('X is voluntary', or 'Is X voluntary?') where B is the case (something is, or seems, fishy about X).[7] The philosophical problem about this arises in the following way: Philosophers who proceed from ordinary language are likely to insist that if you say A where B is not the case, you will be misusing A, or distorting its meaning. But another philosopher will not want to allow that, because it makes the relation between A and B appear to be a logical one (if A then B; and if not-B then not-A); whereas logical relations hold only between statements, not between a statement and the world: *that* relation is 'merely' conventional (or, even, causal?). So the occasion on which we (happen to?) *use* a statement cannot be considered part of its meaning or logic. The solution is then to call the latter the semantics of the expression and the former its pragmatics.

But if we can forget for a moment that the relation between A and B *cannot* be a logical one, we may come to feel how unplausible it is to *say* that it is not logical; or rather, to say that nothing *follows* about B from the utterance of A. It is unplausible because we do not accept a question like 'Did you do that voluntarily?' as appropriate about any and every action. If a person asks you whether you dress the way you do voluntarily, you will not understand him to be curious merely about your psychological processes (whether your wearing them 'proceeds from free choice . . .'); you will understand him to be implying or suggesting that your manner of dress is in some way peculiar. If it be replied to this that 'voluntary' does not *mean* 'peculiar' (or 'special' or 'fishy') and hence that the implication or suggestion is part merely of the pragmatics of the expression, not part of its *meaning* (semantics), my rejoinder is this: that reply is relevant to a different claim from the one urged here; it is worth saying *here* only if you are able to account for the *relation* between the pragmatics and the semantics of the expression. In the absence of such an account, the reply is empty. For consider: If we use Mates's formula for computing the pragmatic value of an expression – 'He wouldn't say that unless he . . .' – then in the described situation we will complete it with something like '. . . unless he thought that my way of dressing is peculiar'. Call this implication of the utterance 'pragmatic'; the fact remains that he wouldn't (couldn't) say what he did without implying what he did: he MUST MEAN that my clothes are peculiar. I am less interested now in the 'mean' than I am in the 'must'. (After all, there is bound to be some reason why a number of philosophers are tempted to call a relation logical; 'must' is logical.) But on this, the 'pragmatic' formula throws no light whatever.

What this shows is that the formula does not help us account for the element of necessity ('must') in statements whose implication we understand. But it is equally unhelpful in trying to explain the implication of a statement whose use we do *not* understand (the context in which the formula enters Mates's discussion). Imagine that I am sitting in my counting-house counting up my money. Someone who knows that I do that at this hour every day passes by and says 'You ought to do that'. What should we say about his statement? That he does not know what 'ought' means (what the dictionary says)? That he does not know how to use the word? That he does not know what obligation is? Applying the formula, we compute: 'He wouldn't say that unless he asks himself whenever he sees anyone doing anything, "Ought that person to be doing that or ought he not?" ' This may indeed account for his otherwise puzzling remark; but it does so by telling us something we did not know about *him*; it tells us nothing whatever we did not know about the words he used. Here it is *because* we know the meaning and use of 'ought' that we are forced to account in the way Mates suggests for its extraordinary occurrence. I take Mates's formula, then, to be expandable into 'Since I understand the meaning and use of his expression, he wouldn't say that unless he . . .'. Perhaps Mates would consider this a distortion and take a different expansion to be appropriate: 'He wouldn't say that unless he was using his words in a special way'. But now 'say that' has a very different force. The expanded form now means 'I know what his expression would ordinarily be used to say, but he can't wish to say that: I don't understand what he is saying'. In neither of its expansions, then, does the formula throw any light on the way an expression is being used: in the one case we already know, in the other we have yet to learn. (Another expression may be: 'He wouldn't say that unless he was using X to mean Y.' But here again, it is the semantics and pragmatics of Y which are relevant to understanding what is said, and the formula presupposes that we already understand Y.)

Our alternatives seem to be these: Either (1) we deny that there is any rational (logical, grammatical) constraint over the 'pragmatic implications' of what we say – or perhaps deny that there *are* any *implications*, on the ground that the relation in question is not deductive – so that unless what I say is flatly false or unless I explicitly contradict myself, it is pointless to suggest that what I say is

wrong or that I must mean something other than I say; or else (2)
we admit the constraint and say either (a) since all necessity is
logical, the 'pragmatic implications' of our utterance are (quasi-)
logical implications; with or without adding (b) since the 'pragmatic implications' cannot be construed in terms of deductive (or
inductive) logic, there must be some 'third sort' of logic; or we say
(c) some necessity is not logical. None of these alternatives is without its obscurities, but they are clear enough for us to see that
Mates is taking alternative (1),[8] whereas the philosopher who proceeds from ordinary language is likely to feel the need of
some form of (2). Alternative (2(a)) brings out part of the reason
behind the Oxford philosopher's insistence that he is talking logic,
while (2(b)) makes explicit the reason other philosophers are perplexed at that claim.[9]

The difference between alternatives (1) and (2) is fundamental; so
fundamental, that it is very difficult to argue. When Mates says
'Perhaps it is true that ordinarily I wouldn't say "I know it" unless
I felt great confidence in what I was asserting . . .', what he says is
not, if you like, *strictly* wrong; but it is wrong – or, what it implies
is wrong. It implies that whether I confine the formula 'I know . . .'
to statements about which I feel great confidence is *up to me*
(*rightly* up to me); so that if I say 'I know . . .' in the absence of confidence, I have not misused language, and in particular I have not
stretched the *meaning* of the word 'know'. And yet, if a child were
to say 'I know . . .' when you know the child does not *know* (is in
no position to say he knows), you may reply 'You don't really mean
(N.B.) you *know*, you only mean you believe'; or you may say 'You
oughtn't to say you *know* when you only *think* so'.

There are occasions on which it would be useful to have the
'semantic–pragmatic' distinction at hand. If, for example, a philosopher tells me that the statement 'You ought to do so-and-so'
expresses private emotion and is hortatory and hence not, strictly
speaking, meaningful, then it may be worth replying that nothing
follows about the meaning (semantics) of a statement from the way
it is used (pragmatics); and this reply may spare our having to
make up special brands of meaning. But the time for that argument is, presumably, past.[10] What needs to be argued now is that
something *does* follow from the fact that a term is used in its usual
way: it entitles you (or, using the term, you entitle others) to make
certain inferences, draw certain conclusions. (This is part of what
you say when you say that you are talking about the *logic* of
ordinary language.) *Learning what these implications are is part of*

learning the language; no less a part than learning its syntax, or learning what it is to which terms apply: they are an essential part of what we communicate when we talk. Intimate understanding is understanding which is implicit. Nor *could* everything we say (mean to communicate), in normal communication, be said explicitly[11] – otherwise the only threat to communication would be acoustical. We are, therefore, exactly as responsible for the specific implications of our utterances as we are for their explicit factual claims. And there can no more be some general procedure for securing that what one implies is appropriate than there can be for determining that what one says is true. Misnaming and misdescribing are not the only mistakes we can make in talking. Nor is lying its only immorality.

I am prepared to conclude that the philosopher who proceeds from ordinary language is entitled, without special empirical investigations, to assertions of the second sort we distinguished, viz., assertions like 'We do not say "I know . . ." unless we mean that we have great confidence . . .', and like 'When we ask whether an action is voluntary we imply that the action is fishy' (call this S). But I do not think that I have *shown* that he is entitled to them, because I have not shown what kind of assertions they are: I have not shown when such assertions should be said, and by whom, and what should be meant in saying them. It is worth trying to indicate certain complexities of the assertions, because they are easy to overlook. Something important will be learned if we realise that we do *not* know what kind of assertion S is.

When (if) you feel that S is necessarily true, that it is *a priori*, you will have to explain how a statement which is obviously not analytic *can* be true *a priori*. (That S is not analytic is what (is all) that is shown by Mates's arguments about the 'semantic–pragmatic' confusion; it is perfectly true that 'voluntary' does not *mean* (you will not find set beside it in a dictionary) 'fishy'.) When I am impressed with the necessity of statements like S, I am tempted to say that they are categorical – about the concept of an action *überhaupt*. (A normal action is neither voluntary nor involuntary, neither careful nor careless, neither expected nor unexpected, neither right nor wrong. . . .) This would account for our feeling of their necessity: they are instances (not of Formal, but) of Transcendental Logic. But this is really no explanation until we make clearer the need for the concept of an action in general.

However difficult it is to make out a case for the necessity of S, it is important that the temptation to call it *a priori* not be ignored; otherwise we will acquiesce in calling it synthetic, which would be badly misleading. Misleading (wrong) because we know what would count as a disproof of statements which are synthetic (to indicate the willingness to entertain such disproof is the point of calling a statement synthetic), but it is not clear what would count as a disproof of S. The feeling that S must be synthetic comes, of course, partly from the fact that it obviously is not (likely to be taken as) analytic. But it comes also from the ease with which S may be mistaken for the statement ' "Is X voluntary?" implies that X is fishy' (T), which does seem obviously synthetic. But S and T, though they are true together and false together, are not everywhere interchangeable; the identical state of affairs is described by both, but a person who may be entitled to say T, may not be entitled to say S. Only a native speaker of English is entitled to the statement S, whereas a linguist describing English may, though he is not a native speaker of English, be entitled to T. What entitles him to T is his having gathered a certain amount and kind of evidence in its favour. But the person entitled to S is not entitled to *that* statement for the same reason. He *needs* no evidence for it. It would be misleading to say that he *has* evidence for S, for that would suggest that he has done the sort of investigation the linguist has done, only less systematically, and this would make it seem that his claim to know S is very weakly based. And it would be equally misleading to say that he does *not* have evidence for S, because that would make it appear that there is something he still needs, and suggests that he is not yet entitled to S. But there is nothing he needs, and there is no evidence (which it makes sense, in *general*, to say) he has: the question of evidence is irrelevant.

An examination of what does entitle a person to the statement S would be required in any full account of such statements. Such an examination is out of the question here. But since I will want to claim that Mates's 'two methods' for gathering evidence in support of 'statements about ordinary language' like S are irrelevant to what entitles a person to S, and since this obviously rests on the claim that the concept of evidence is, in general, irrelevant to them altogether, let me say just this: The clue to understanding the sort of statement S is lies in appreciating the fact that 'we', while plural, is first-person. First-person *singular* forms have recently come in for a great deal of attention, and they have been shown to have very significant logical-epistemological properties. The plural form has similar, and equally significant properties but it has been, so

far as I know, neglected.[12] The claim that in general we do not
require evidence for statements in the first-person plural present
indicative, does not rest upon a claim that we cannot be wrong
about what we are doing or about what we say, but only that it
would be extraordinary if we were (often). My point about such
statements, then, is that they are sensibly questioned only where
there is some special reason for supposing what I say about what I
(we) say to be wrong; only here is the request for evidence competent. If I am wrong about what he does (they do), that may be no
great surprise; but if I am wrong about what I (we) do, that is liable,
where it is not comic, to be tragic.

Statements like T have their own complexities, and it would be
unwise even of them to say simply that they are synthetic. Let us
take another of Mates's examples: ' "I know it" is not (ordinarily)
said unless the speaker has great confidence in it' (T'). Mates
takes this as patently synthetic, a statement about matters of fact
(and there is no necessary connection among matters of fact). And so
it might be, said by a Scandinavian linguist as part of his description
of English. But if that linguist, or if a native speaker (i.e. a speaker
entitled to say 'We do not say "I know it" unless . . .') uses T' in
teaching someone to speak English, or to remind a native speaker
of something he knows but is not bearing in mind, T' sounds less
like a descriptive statement than like a rule.

Because of what seems to be the widespread idea that rules always
sort with commands and must therefore be represented as imperatives, this complementarity of rule and statement may come as
something of a shock. But that such complementarity exists can be
seen in writings which set out the rules for games or ceremonies or
languages. In *Hoyle's Rules of Games* we find statements like 'The
opponent at declarer's left makes the opening lead. . . . Declarer's
partner then lays his whole hand face up on the table, with his
trumps if any on the right. The hand so exposed is the *dummy*. . . .
The object of play is solely to win tricks, in order to fulfil or defeat
the contract'; in *Robert's Rules of Order*, the rules take the form
'The privileged motion to adjourn takes precedence of all others,
except the privileged motion "to fix the time to which to adjourn",
to which it yields' (in Section 17, headed 'To Adjourn'); taking
a grammar at random we find 'Mute stems form the nominative
singular by the addition of -s in the case of masculines and feminines.
. . . Before -s of the nominative singular, a labial mute (p, b) remains
unchanged.' These are all statements in the indicative, not the imperative, mood. (Some expressions in each of these books tell us

what we *must* do; others that we *may*. I will suggest later that a reason for this shift.) In one light, they appear to be descriptions; in another to be rules. Why should this be so? What is its significance?

The explanation of the complementarity has to do with the fact that its topic is actions. When we say how an action is done (how to act) what we say may report or describe the way we *in fact* do it (if we are entitled to say how 'we' do it, i.e. to say what we do, or say what we say) but it may also lay out a way of doing or saying something which is to be *followed*. Whether remarks like T' – remarks 'about' ordinary language, and equally about ordinary actions – are statements or rules depends upon how they are taken: if they are taken to state facts and are supposed to be believed, they are statements; if they are taken as guides and supposed to be followed, they are rules. Such expressions are no more 'in themselves' rules or (synthetic) statements than other expressions are, in themselves, postulates or conclusions or definitions or replies. We might put the relation between the two contexts of T' this way: Statements which describe a language (or a game or an institution) are rules (are binding) if you want to speak that language (play that game, accept that institution); or, rather, *when* you are speaking that language, playing that game, etc. *If it is TRUE to say '"I know it" is not used unless you have great confidence in it', then, when you are speaking English, it is WRONG (a misuse) to say 'I know it' unless you have great confidence in it.* Now the philosopher who proceeds from ordinary language assumes that he and his interlocutors are speaking from within the language, so that the question of whether you want to speak that language is pointless. Worse than pointless, because strictly the ordinary-language philosopher does not, in general, *assume* that he and his interlocutors are speaking from within a given (their native) language – any more than they speak their native language, in general, *intentionally*. The only condition relevant to such philosophising is that you speak (not this or that language, but) period.

At this point the argument has become aporetic. 'Statements about ordinary language' like S, T and T' are not analytic, *and* they are not (it would be misleading to call them) synthetic (just like that).[13] Nor do we know whether to say they are *a priori*, or whether to account for their air of necessity as a dialectical illusion, due more to the motion of our argument than to their own nature. Given our current alternatives, there is no way to classify such statements; we do not yet know what they are.

Before searching for new ways into these problems, I should perhaps justify my very heavy reliance on the idea of *context*, because on Mates's description of what a statement of context involves, it should be impossible ever to make one. Let me recall his remarks: 'We have all heard the wearying platitude that "you can't separate" the meaning of a word from the entire context in which it occurs, including not only the actual linguistic context, but also the aims, feelings, beliefs, and hopes of the speaker, the same for the listener and any bystanders, the social situation, the physical surroundings, the historical background, the rules of the game, and so on *ad infinitum*' (p. 128 above). Isn't this another of those apostrophes to the infinite which prevents philosophers from getting down to cases?[14] Of course if I have to go on about the context of 'voluntary' *ad infinitum*, I would not get very far with it. But I would claim to have characterised the context sufficiently (for the purpose at hand) by the statement that something is, or is supposed to be, fishy about the action. Giving directions for using a word is no more prodigious and unending a task than giving directions for anything else. The context in which I make a martini with vodka is no less complex than the context in which I make a statement with 'voluntary'. Say, if you like, that these actions take place in infinitely complex contexts; but then remember that you can be given directions for doing either. It may be wearying always to be asked for a story within which a puzzling remark can seriously be imagined to function; but I know no better way of maintaining that relevance, or sense of reality, which each philosopher claims for himself and claims to find lacking in another philosophy. At least it would spare us the surrealism of worries like ' "What time is it?" asserts nothing, and hence is neither true nor false; *yet* we all know what it means *well enough* to answer it';[15] or like 'If we told a person to close the door, and received the reply "Prove it!", should we not, to speak mildly, grow somewhat impatient?'[16]

In recommending that we ignore context in order to make 'provisional divisions' of a subject and get an investigation started, Mates is recommending the wrong thing for the right reason. It is true that we cannot say everything at once and that for some problems some distinction of the sort Mates has in mind may be of service. My discontent with it is that it has come to deflect investigation – I mean from questions on which Oxford philosophy trains itself. Where your concern is one of constructing artificial languages, you may explain that you mean to be considering only the syntax (and perhaps semantics) of a language, and not its pragmatics. Or where it becomes important to emphasise a distinction between (where there has come to be a distinction between) scientific and metaphysical assertion, or between factual report and moral rule, you may set out a 'theory' of scientific or factual utterance. In these cases you will be restricting concern in order to deal with certain properties of formal systems, certain problems of meaning, and to defeat certain forms of nonsense. Flat contradiction, metaphysical assertion masquerading as scientific hypothesis, mere whim under the posture of an ethical or aesthetic (or psychological or legal) judgement – these perhaps need hounding out. But the philosopher who proceeds from ordinary language is concerned less to avenge sensational crimes against the intellect than to redress its civil wrongs; to steady any imbalance, the tiniest usurpation, in the mind. This inevitably requires reintroducing ideas which have become tyrannical (e.g. existence, obligation, certainty, identity, reality, truth . . .) into specific contexts in which they function naturally. This is not a question of cutting big ideas down to size, but of giving them the exact space in which they can move without corrupting. Nor does our wish to rehabilitate rather than to deny or expel such ideas (by such sentences as 'We can never know for certain . . .'; 'The table is not real (really solid)'; 'To tell me what I ought to do is always to tell me what you want me to do' . . .) come from a sentimental altruism. It is a question of self-preservation: for who is it that the philosopher punishes when it is the mind itself which assaults the mind?

I want now to turn to two other, related, questions on which Mates finds himself at issue with the Oxford philosophers. The first concerns their tendency to introduce statements of the first sort I distinguished not with 'We do say . . .' but with 'We *can* say . . .' and 'We *can't* say . . .'. The second question concerns, at last directly, reasons for saying that we 'must' mean by our words what those words *ordinarily* mean.

Let me begin by fulfilling my promise to expand upon my remark that Austin's saying 'We may make a gift voluntarily' is 'material mode' for 'We can say "The gift was made voluntarily"'. The shift from talking about language to talking about the world occurs almost imperceptibly in the statement of Austin's which Mates quotes – almost as though he thought it did not much matter *which* he talked about. Let me recall the passage from Austin: '. . . take "voluntarily" and "involuntarily": we may join the army or make a gift voluntarily, we may hiccough or make a small gesture involuntarily.' He begins here by mentioning a pair of words, and goes on to tell us what we may in fact do. With what right? Why is it assumed that we find out what voluntary and involuntary actions *are* (and equally, of course, what inadvertent and automatic and pious, etc., actions are) by asking when we should *say* of an action that it is voluntary or inadvertent or pious, etc.?

But what is troubling about this? If you feel that finding out what something is must entail investigation of the world rather than of language, perhaps you are imagining a situation like finding out what somebody's name and address are, or what the contents of a will or a bottle are, or whether frogs eat butterflies. But now imagine that you are in your armchair reading a book of reminiscences and come across the word 'umiak'. You reach for your dictionary and look it up. Now what did you do? Find out what 'umiak' means, or find out what an umiak is? But how could we have discovered something about the world by hunting in the dictionary? If this seems surprising, perhaps it is because we forget that we learn language and learn the world *together*, that they become elaborated and distorted together, and in the same places. We may also be forgetting how elaborate a process the learning is. We tend to take what a native speaker does when he looks up a noun in a dictionary as the characteristic process of learning language. (As, in what has become a less forgivable tendency, we take naming as the fundamental source of meaning.) But it is merely the end point in the process of learning the word. When we turned to the dictionary for 'umiak' we already knew everything about the word, as it were, but its combination: we knew what a noun is and how to name an object and how to look up a word and what boats are and what an Eskimo is. We were all prepared for that umiak. What seemed like finding the world in a dictionary was really a case of bringing the world to the dictionary. We had the world with us all the time, in that armchair; but we felt the weight of it only when we felt a lack in it. Sometimes we will need to bring the dictionary to the world. That will happen when (say) we run across a small boat in Alaska of a sort we have never seen and wonder – what? What it is, or what it is called? In either case, the learning is a question of aligning language and the world.[17] What you need to learn will depend on what specifically it is you want to know; and how you can find out will depend specifically on what you already command. How we answer the question 'What is X?' will depend, therefore, on the specific case of ignorance and of knowledge.

It sometimes happens that we know everything there is to know about a situation – what all of the words in question mean, what all of the relevant facts are – and everything is in front of our eyes. And yet we feel we don't know something, don't understand something. In this situation, the question 'What is X?' is very puzzling, in exactly the way philosophy is very puzzling. We feel we want to ask the question, and yet we feel we already have the answer. (One might say we have all the *elements* of an answer.) Socrates says that in such a situation we need to remind ourselves of something. So does the philosopher who proceeds from ordinary language: we need to remind ourselves of *what we should say when.*[18] But what is the point of reminding ourselves of that? When the philosopher asks 'What should we say here?', what is meant is 'What would be the normal thing to say here?', or perhaps 'What is the most natural thing we could say here?' And the point of the question is this: answering it is sometimes the only way to tell – tell others and tell for ourselves – what the situation *is*.

Sometimes the only way to tell. But when? The nature of the Oxford philosopher's question, and the nature of his conception of philosophy, can be brought out if we turn the question upon itself, and thus remind ourselves of when it is we need to remind ourselves of what we should say when. Our question then becomes: When should we ask ourselves when we should (and should not) say 'The x is F' in order to find out what an $F(x)$ is? (For 'The x is F' read 'The action is voluntary (or pious)', or 'The statement is vague (or false)', or 'The question is misleading'.) The answer suggested is, when you have to. When you have more facts than you know how to make use of, or when you do not know what new facts would show. When, that is, you need a clear view of what you already know. When you need to do philosophy.[19] Euthyphro does not need to learn any new facts, yet he needs to learn something: you can say either that in the *Euthypho* Socrates was finding out what 'piety' means or finding out what piety is.

When the philosopher who proceeds from ordinary language tells us 'You can't say such-and-such', what he means is that you cannot say that *here* and communicate *this* situation to others, or understand it for yourself.[20] This is sometimes what he means by calling certain expressions 'misuses' of language, and also makes clear the consequences of such expressions: they break our understanding. The normativeness which Mates felt, and which is certainly present, does not lie in the ordinary-language philosopher's assertions *about* ordinary use; what is normative is exactly ordinary use itself.

The way philosophers have practised with the word 'normative' in recent years seems to me lamentable. But it is too late to avoid the word, so even though we cannot now embark on a diagnosis of the ills which caused its current use, or those which it has produced, it may be worth forewarning ourselves against the confusions most likely to distract us. The main confusions about the problem of 'normativeness' I want to mention here are these: (1) the idea that descriptive utterances are opposed to normative utterances; and (2) that prescriptive utterances are (typical) instances of normative utterances.

We have touched upon these ideas in talking about rule–statement complementarity; here we touch them at a different point. In saying here that it is a confusion to speak of some general opposition between descriptive and normative utterances, I am not thinking primarily of the plain fact that rules have counterpart (descriptive) statements, but rather of the significance of that fact, viz., that what such statements describe are *actions* (and not, e.g., the *movements* of bodies, animate or inanimate). The most characteristic fact about actions is that they can – in various specific ways – go wrong, that they can be performed incorrectly. This is not, in any restricted sense, a moral assertion, though it points the moral of intelligent activity. And it is as true of describing as it is of calculating or of promising or plotting or warning or asserting or defining. . . . These are actions which we perform, and our successful performance of them depends upon our adopting and following the ways in which the action in question is done, upon what is normative for it. Descriptive statements, then, are not opposed to ones which are normative, but in fact presuppose them: we could not do the thing we call describing if language did not provide (we had not been taught) ways normative for describing.

The other point I wish to emphasise is this: if a normative utterance is one used to create or institute rules or standards, then prescriptive utterances are not examples of normative utterances. Establishing a norm is not telling us how we *ought* to perform an action, but telling us how the action *is* done, or how it is *to be* done.[21] Contrariwise, telling us what we ought to do is not instituting a norm to cover the case, but rather presupposes the existence of such a norm, i.e. presupposes that there is something to do which it would be correct to do here. Telling us what we ought to do may involve *appeal* to a pre-existent rule or standard, but it cannot constitute the establishment of that rule or standard. We may expect the retort here that it is just the *appeal* which is the sensitive normative spot, for what we are really doing when we appeal to a rule or standard is telling somebody that they ought to adhere to it. Perhaps this will be followed by the query 'And suppose they don't accept the rule or standard to which you appeal, what then?' The retort is simply false. And to the query one may reply that this will not be the first time we have been tactless; nor can we, to avoid overstepping the bounds of relationship, follow every statement by '. . . if you accept the facts and the logic I do', nor every evaluation by '. . . if you accept the standards I do'. Such cautions will finally suggest appending to everything we say '. . . if you mean by your words what I mean by mine'. Here the pantomime of caution concludes. It is true that we sometimes appeal to standards which our interlocutor does not accept; but this does not in the least show that what we are there really doing is attempting to institute a standard (of our own). Nor does it in the least show that we are (merely) expressing our own opinion or feeling on the matter. We of course *may* express our private opinion or feeling – we normally do so where it is not clear what (or that any) rule or standard fits the case at hand and where we are therefore not willing or able to appeal to any.

The practice of appealing to a norm can be abused, as can any other of our practices. Sometimes people appeal to a rule when we deserved more intimate attention from them. Just as sometimes people tell us what we ought to do when all they mean is that they want us to. But this is as much an abuse where the context is moral as it is where the context is musical ('You ought to accent the appogiatura'), or scientific ('You ought to use a control group here'), or athletic ('You ought to save your wind on the first two laps'). Private persuasion (or personal appeal) is not the paradigm of ethical utterance, but represents the breakdown (or the transcending) of moral interaction. We can, too obviously, become morally inaccessible to one another; but to tell us that these are the moments which really constitute the moral life will only add confusion to pain.

If not, then, by saying what actions *ought* to be performed, how *do* we establish (or justify or modify or drop) rules or standards? What general answer can there be to this general question other than 'In various ways, depending on the context?' Philosophers who have imagined that the question has one answer for all cases must be trying to assimilate the members of Football Commissions, of Child

Development Research Teams, of University Committees on Entrance Requirements, of Bar Association Committees to Alter Legal Procedures, of Departments of Agriculture, of Bureaus of Standards, and of Essene Sects, all to one 'sort' of person, doing one 'sort' of thing, viz., establishing (or changing) rules and standards. Whereas the fact is that there are, in each case, different ways normative for accomplishing the particular normative tasks in question. It has in recent years been emphasised past acknowledgement that even justifications require justification. What now needs emphasising is that (successfully) justifying a statement or an action is not (cannot be) justifying its justification.[22] The assumption that the appeal to a rule or standard is only justified where that rule or standard is simultaneously established or justified can only serve to make such appeal seem hypocritical (or anyway shaky) and the attempts at such establishment or justification seem tyrannical (or anyway arbitrary).

It would be important to understand why we have been able to overlook the complementarity of rule and statement and to be content always to sort rules with imperatives. Part of the reason for this comes from a philosophically inadequate (not to say disastrous) conception of action; but this inadequacy itself will demand an elaborate accounting. There is another sort of reason for our assumption that what is binding upon us must be an imperative; one which has to do with our familiar sense of alienation from established systems of morality, perhaps accompanied by a sense of distance from God. Kant tells us that a perfectly rational being does in fact (necessarily) conform to 'the supreme principle of morality', but that we imperfectly rational creatures are necessitated *by* it, so that for us it is (always appears as) imperative. But if I understand the difference Kant sees here, it is one *within* the conduct of rational animals. So far as Kant is talking about (the logic of) action, his Categorical Imperative can be put as a Categorical Declarative (description-rule), i.e. a description of what it *is* to act morally: When we (you) act morally, we act in a way we would regard as justified universally, justified no matter who had done it. (This categorical formulation does not tell us how to determine *what was done*; neither does Kant's categorical formulation, although, by speaking of 'the' maxim of an action, it pretends to, or anyway makes it seem less problematical than it is.) Perhaps it is by now a little clearer why we are tempted to retort 'But suppose I don't *want* to be moral?'; and also why it would be irrelevant here. The Categorical Declaration does not tell you what you *ought* to do *if* you want to be moral (and hence is untouched by the feeling that no imperative can really be *categorical*, can bind us no matter what); it tells you (part of) what you in fact do when you *are* moral. It cannot – nothing a philosopher says can – ensure that you will not act immorally; but it is entirely unaffected by what you do or do not want.

I am not saying that rules do not sometimes sort with imperatives, but only denying that they always do. In the *Britannica* article (11th edition) on chess, only one paragraph of the twenty or so which describe the game is headed 'Rules', and only here are we told what we *must* do. This paragraph deals with such matters as the convention of saying 'j'adoube' when you touch a piece to straighten it. Is the difference between matters of this kind and the matter of how pieces move, a difference between penalties (which are imposed for misplay) and moves (which are accepted in order to play at all) – so that we would cheerfully say that we can play (are playing) chess without the 'j'adoube' convention, but less cheerfully that we can play without following the rule that 'the Queen moves in any direction, square or diagonal, whether forward or backward'? This would suggest that we may think of the difference between rule and imperative as one between those actions (or 'parts' of actions) which are easy (natural, normal) for us, and those we have to be encouraged to do. (What I do as a rule you may have to be made or directed to do.) We are likely to forget to say 'j'adoube', so we have to be *made* (to remember) to do it; but we do not have to be *made* to move the Queen in straight, unobstructed paths.[23] This further suggests that what is thought of as 'alienation' is something which occurs *within* moral systems; since these are profoundly haphazard accumulations, it is no surprise that we feel part of some regions of the system and feel apart from other regions.[24]

So the subject of responsibility, of obligation and commitment, opens into the set of questions having to do with differences between doing a thing wrongly or badly (strangely, ineptly, inexactly, partially . . .) and not doing the thing at all. These differences take us into a further region of the concept of an action: we have noted that there are many (specific) ways in which an action can go wrong (at least as many as the myriad excuses we are entitled to proffer when what we have done has resulted in some unhappiness); but it would be incorrect to suppose that we are *obligated* to see to it (to take precautions to ensure), *whenever* we undertake to do anything, that none of these ways will come to pass. Our obligation is to avoid doing something at a time and place or in a way which is *likely* to result in some misfortune, or to avoid being careless where it is easy to be, or to be *especially* careful where the action is dangerous or delicate, or avoid the temptation to skip a necessary step when it seems in the moment to make little difference. If for *all* excuses there were relevant obligations, then there would be no excuses and action would become intolerable. And *particular* excuse may be countered with a *specific* obligation; not even the best excuse will always get you off the hook. ('That is no excuse; you should have known that was likely to result in an accident, you ought to have paid *particular* heed here, etc.')

Without pretending to give an account of (this part of) obligation, what I think the foregoing considerations indicate is this: a statement of what we *must do* (or say) has point only in the context (against the background) of knowledge that we are in fact doing (or saying) a thing, but doing (saying it) – or running a definite risk of doing or saying it – badly, inappropriately, thoughtlessly, tactlessly, self-defeatingly, etc.; or against the background of knowledge that we are in a certain position or occupy a certain office or station, and are *behaving* or *conducting ourselves* inappropriately, thoughtlessly, self-defeatingly. . . . The same is true of statements about what we *may* do, as well as those containing other 'modal auxiliaries' – e.g. about what we *should* do, or what we *are* or *have* to do, or are *supposed* to do, and about one sense of what we *can* do; these are all intelligible only against the background of what we are doing or are in a position (one sense of 'able') to do. These 'link verbs' share the linguistic peculiarity that while they are verb-like forms they cannot stand as the main verb of a sentence. This itself would suggest that their use is not one of prescribing some new action to us, but of setting an action which is antecedently relevant to what we are doing or to what we are – setting it relevantly into the larger context of what we are doing or of what we are.[25] 'You must (are supposed, obliged, required to) move the Queen in straight paths . . .', or 'You may (can, are allowed or permitted to) move the Queen in straight paths . . .' say (assert) no more than 'You (do, in fact, always) move the Queen in straight paths . . .'; which of them you say on a given occasion depends not on any special motive or design of yours, nor upon any special mode of argument. There is no question of *going from* 'is' to 'must', but only of appreciating which of them should be said when, i.e. of appreciating the position or circumstances of the person to whom you are speaking. Whatever makes one of the statements true makes them all true, though not all appropriate.

To tell me what I must do is not the same as to tell me what I ought to do. I must move the Queen in straight paths (in case I am absent-minded and continue moving it like the Damsel, cf. n. 23). What would it mean to tell me that I *ought* to move the Queen in straight paths? 'Ought', unlike 'must', implies that there is an alternative; 'ought' implies that you can, if you choose, do otherwise. This does *not* mean merely that there is something else to do which is in your *power* ('I *can* move the Queen like the Knight; just watch!') but that there is one within your *rights*. But if I say truly and appropriately 'You must . . .', then in a perfectly good sense nothing you then do can prove me wrong. You CAN *push the little object called the Queen* in many ways, as you can *lift* it or *throw* it across the room; not all of these will be *moving the Queen.* You CAN ask, 'Was your action voluntary' and say to yourself 'All I mean to ask is whether he had a sensation of effort just before he moved', but that will not be finding out whether the action was voluntary. Again, if I have borrowed money then I *must* (under normal circumstances) pay it back (even though it is rather painful).[26] It makes sense to tell me I *ought* to pay it back only if there is a specific reason to suppose, say, that the person from whom I got the money *meant to give* it to me rather than merely *lend* it (nevertheless he needs it badly, worse than I know), or if there is a reason to pay it back tomorrow instead of next week, when the debt falls due (I'll save interest; I'll only spend it and have to make another loan). The difference here resembles that between doing a thing and doing the thing well (thoughtfully, tactfully, sensibly, graciously . . .).

This difference may be made clearer by considering one way principles differ from rules. Rules tell you what to do when you do the thing at all; principles tell you how to do the thing well, with skill or understanding. In competitive games, acting well amounts to doing the sort of thing that will win, so the principles of games recommend strategy. 'No raise should (N.B.) be given to partner's suit without at least Q-x-x, J-10-x, K-x-x, A-x-x, or any four trumps. . . .' But you could fail to adopt this and still play bridge, even play well. It is a principal strategy in Culbertson's system;[27] but another expert may have a different understanding of the game and develop principles of strategy which are equally successful. Principles go with understanding. (Having an understanding of a game is not knowing the rules; you might find a book called *Principles of Economics* or *Psychology*, but none called *Rules of Economics*, etc.) Understanding a principle involves knowing how and where to apply it. But some moves seem so immediately to be called for by the principles of strategy, that their formulations come to be thought of as rules: should we say 'The third hand plays high . . .' or 'The third hand should play high . . .'? You may, strictly speaking, be playing bridge if you flout this, but you won't be doing the sort of thing which will win (and therefore not really playing? When is not doing a thing well not really doing the thing?). All players employ maxims (which may be thought of as formulating strategies as though they were moves) in order to facilitate their play; like everything habitual or summary, maxims have their advantages and their dangers. Both the rules which constitute playing the game, and the 'rules' or maxims which contribute to playing the game well, have their analogues in ordinary moral conduct.

I think it is sometimes felt that drawing an analogy between moral conduct and games makes moral conduct seem misleadingly simple (or trivial?), because there are no rules in moral conduct corresponding to the rules about how the Queen moves in chess.[28] But this misses the point of the analogy, which is that moves and actions have to be done *correctly*; not just any movement you make will be a move, or a promise, a payment, a request. This does not mean that promising *is* (just) following rules. Yet if someone is tempted not to fulfil a promise, you may say 'Promises are kept', or 'We keep our promises (that is the sort of thing a promise is)', thus employing a rule-description – what I have called a categorical declarative. You may say 'You must keep this promise' (you are underestimating its importance; last time you forgot). This is not the same as 'You ought to keep this promise', which is only sensible where you have a reason for breaking it strong enough to allow you to do so without blame (there is a real alternative), but where you are being enjoined to make a *special* effort or sacrifice. (This is partly why 'You ought to keep promises' is so queer. It suggests that we not only always want badly to get out of fulfilling promises, but that we always have some good (anyway, prima facie) reason for not keeping them (perhaps our own severe discomfort) and that therefore we are acting *well* when we do fulfil. But we aren't, normally; neither well nor ill.) 'Ought' is like 'must' in requiring a background of action or position into which the action in question is set; and, like 'must', it does not form a command, a pure imperative. All of which shows the hopelessness of speaking, in a *general* way, about the 'normativeness' of expressions. The *Britannica* 'rules' tell us what we *must* do *in playing* chess, not what we ought to do *if* we want to play. You (must) mean (imply), in speakng English, that something about an action is fishy when you say 'The action is voluntary'; you (must) mean, when you ask a person 'Ought you to do that?', that there is some *specific* way in which what he is doing might be done more tactfully, carefully, etc. . . . Are these imperatives? Are they categorical or hypothetical? Have you in no way contradicted yourself if you flout them? (cf. n. 26).

That 'modal imperatives' ('must', 'supposed to', 'are to', 'have to' . . .) require the recognition of a background action or position into which the relevant action is placed, indicates a portentous difference between these forms of expression and pure imperatives, commands. Whether I can command depends only upon whether I have power or authority, and the only characteristics I must recognise in the object of the command are those which tell me that the object is subject to my power or authority. Employing a modal 'imperative', however, requires that I recognise the object as a *person* (someone doing something or in a certain position) to whose reasonableness (reason) I appeal in using the second person. (Compare 'Open, Sesame!' with 'You must open, Sesame'.) This is one reason that commands, pure imperatives, are not paradigms of moral utterance, but represent an alternative to such utterance.

Without pretending that my argument for it has been nearly full or clear enough, let me, by way of summary, flatly state what it is I have tried to argue about the relation between what you say and what you (must) mean, i.e. between what you (explicitly) say and what saying it implies or suggests: If 'what A (an utterance) means' is to be understood in terms of (or even as directly related to) 'what is (must be) meant in (by) saying A',[29] then the meaning of A will not be given by its analytic or definitional equivalents, or by its deductive implications. Intension is not a substitute for intention. Although we would not call the statement 'When we say we know something we imply (mean) that we have confidence, that we are in a position to say we know . . .' analytic, yet if the statement is true it is necessarily true in just this sense: if it is true, then when you ask what the statement supposes you to ask you (must) mean what the statement says you (must) mean. Necessary and not analytic: it was – apart from the parody of Kant – to summarise, and partly explain, this peculiarity that I called such statements categorial declaratives: declarative, because something is (authoritatively) made known; categorial, because in telling us what we (must) mean by asserting that (or questioning whether) x is F, they tell us what it is for an x to be F (an action to be moral, a statement

claiming knowledge to be a statement expressing knowledge, a movement to be a move).[30] Shall we say that such statements formulate
the rules or the principles of grammar – the moves or the strategie
of talking? (And is this, perhaps, to be thought of as a difference
between grammar and rhetoric? But becoming clearer about thi
will require us to see more clearly the difference between not doing
a thing well (here, saying something) and not doing the thing; and
between doing a thing badly and not doing the thing.) The significance of categorial declaratives lies in their teaching or reminding
us that the 'pragmatic implications' of our utterances are (or, if
we are feeling perverse, or tempted to speak carelessly, or chafing
under an effort of honesty, let us say *must be*) *meant*; that they
are an essential part of what we mean when we say something, of
what it is to mean something. And what we mean (intend) to say,
like what we mean (intend) to do, is something we are responsible
for.

Even with this slight rehabilitation of the notion of normativeness,
we can begin to see the special sense in which the philosopher who
proceeds from ordinary language is 'establishing a norm' in employing his second type of statement. He is certainly not *instituting*
norms, nor is he *ascertaining* norms (see note 21); but he may be
thought of as *confirming* or *proving* the existence of norms when he
reports or describes how we (how to) talk, i.e. when he says (in
statements of the second type) what is normative for utterances
instanced by statements of the first type. Confirming and proving
are other regions of establishing. I have suggested that there are
ways normative for instituting and for ascertaining norms; and so
are there for confirming or proving or reporting them, i.e. for
employing locutions like 'We can say . . .', or 'When we say . . .
we imply –'. The swift use made of them by the philosopher serves
to remind mature speakers of a language of something they know;
but they would erroneously be employed in trying to report a special
usage of one's own, and (not unrelated to this) could not be used
to change the meaning of an expression. Since saying something is
never *merely* saying something, but is saying something with a
certain tune and at a proper cue and while executing the appropriate business, the sounded utterance is only a salience of what is
going on when we talk (or the unsounded when we think); so a
statement of 'what we say' will give us only a feature of what we
need to remember. But a native speaker will normally know the rest:
learning it was part of learning the language.

Let me warn against two tempting ways to avoid the significance f this: (1) It is perfectly true that English might have developed ifferently than it has and therefore have imposed different cate- ories on the world than it does; and if so, it would have enabled us o assert, describe, question, define, promise, appeal, etc., in ways ther than we do. But using English now – to converse with others the language, or to understand the world, or to think by ourselves means knowing which forms in what contexts are normative for erforming the activities we perform by using the language. (2) It is o escape to say 'Still I can say what I like; I needn't always use ormal forms in saying what I say; I can speak in extraordinary ays, and you will perfectly well understand me.' What this calls ttention to is the fact that language provides us with ways for contains forms which are normative for) speaking in special ways, .g. for changing the meaning of a word, or for speaking, *on articular occasions,* loosely or personally, or paradoxically, cryptic- lly, metaphorically. . . . Do you wish to claim that you can speak trangely yet intelligibly – and this of course means intelligibly to ourself as well – in ways not provided in the language for speaking trangely?

t may be felt that I have not yet touched one of Mates's funda- nental criticisms. Suppose you grant all that has been said about an rdinary use being normative for what anyone says. Will you still vish to ask: 'Does it follow that the ordinary uses which are norma- ive for what professors say are the same as the ordinary uses which re normative for what butchers and bakers say?' Or perhaps: 'Is an rdinary use for a professor an *ordinary* ordinary use?' Is that a ensible question?

To determine whether it is, we must appreciate what it is to talk ogether. The philosopher, understandably, often takes the isolated nan bent silently over a book as his model for what using language s. But the primary fact of natural language is that it is something spoken, spoken together. Talking together is acting together, not making motions and noises at one another, nor transferring un- speakable messages or essences from the inside of one closed chamber to the inside of another. The difficulties of talking together are, rather, *real* ones: the activities we engage in by talking are intricate and intricately related to one another. I suppose it will be granted that the professor and the baker can talk together. Consider the most obvious complexities of co-operative activity in which they engage: there is commenting ('Nice day'); commending, persuad- ing, recommending, enumerating, comparing ('The pumpernickel is good, but the whole wheat and the rye even better'); grading, choosing, pointing ('I'll have the darker loaf there'); counting, making change, thanking; warning ('Careful of the step'); promising ('Be back next week') . . .; all this in addition to the whole new or combination of actions which comprise the machinery of talking: asserting, referring, conjoining, denying. . . . Now it may be clearer why I wish to say: if the professor and the baker did not understand each other, the professors would not understand one another either.

You may still want to ask: 'Does this mean that the professor and baker use particular words like "voluntary" and "involuntary", or "inadvertently" and "automatically", the same way? The baker may never have used these words at all.' But the question has *now* become, since it is about *specific* expressions, straightforwardly empirical. Here Mates's 'two methods' (pp. 125–6 ff.) at last become relevant. But I am at the moment less interested in determining what empirical methods would be appropriate to investigate the matter than I am in posing the following questions: What should we say if it turned out, as it certainly might, that they in fact do use the words differently? Should we, for example, say that therefore we never have a right to say that people use words in the same way without undertaking an empirical investigation; or perhaps say that therefore they speak different languages? What should make us say that they do not speak the same language? Do we really know what it would be like to embark upon an empirical investigation of the *general* question whether we (ordinarily, ever) use language the way other people do?

There is too much here to try to unravel. But here are some of the threads: The words 'inadvertently' and 'automatically', however recondite, are ordinary; there are ordinary contexts (non-technical, non-political, non-philosophical contexts) which are normative for their use. It may be that half the speakers of English do not know (or cannot say, which is not the same) what these contexts are. Some native speakers may even use them interchangeably. Suppose the baker is able to convince us that he does. Should we then say: 'So the professor has no right to say how "*we* use" "inadvertently", or to say that "when *we* use the one word we say something different from what we say when we use the other"?' Before accepting that conclusion, I should hope that the following consideration would be taken seriously: When 'inadvertently' and 'automatically' seem to be used indifferently in recounting what someone did, this may not at all show that they are being used synonymously, but only that what each of them says is separately true of the person's action. The decanter is broken and you did it. You may say (and it may be important to consider that you are already embarrassed and flustered) either 'I did it inadvertently' or 'I did it automatically'. Are you saying the same thing? Well, you automatically *grabbed the cigarette* which had fallen on the table, and inadvertently *knocked over the decanter*. Naming actions is a sensitive occupation.[31] It is easy to overlook the distinction because the two adverbs often go together in describing actions in which a sudden movement results in some mishap.

Suppose the baker does not accept this explanation, but replies: 'I use "automatically" and "inadvertently" in exactly the same way. I could just as well have said: "I grabbed the cigarette inadvertently and knocked over the decanter automatically." ' Don't we feel the temptation to reply: 'You may *say* this, but you can't say it and describe the same situation; you can't mean what you would mean if you said the other.' But suppose the baker insists he can? Will we then be prepared to say: 'Well you can't say the one and mean what *I* mean by the other?' Great care would be needed in claiming this, for it may look like I am saying 'I know what I mean and I say they are different'. But why is the baker not entitled to this argument? What I must not say is: 'I know what words mean in *my* language.' Here the argument would have pushed me to madness. It *may* turn out (depending upon just what the dialogue has been and where it was stopped) that we should say to the baker: 'If you cooked the way you talk, you would forgo special implements for different jobs, and peel, core, scrape, slice, carve, chop and saw, all with one knife. The distinction is there, in the language (as implements are there to be had), and you just impoverish what you can say by neglecting it. And there is something you aren't noticing about the world.'[32]

But to a philosopher who refuses to acknowledge the distinction we should say something more: not merely that he impoverishes what he can say about actions, but that he is a poor theorist of what it is to do something. The philosopher who asks about everything we do 'Voluntary or not?' has a poor view of action (as the philosopher who asks of everything we say 'True or false?' or 'Analytic or synthetic?' has a poor view of communication), in something like the way a man who asks the cook about every piece of food 'Was it cut or not?' has a poor view of preparing food. The cook with only one knife is in much better condition than the philosopher with only 'Voluntary or involuntary?' to use in dividing

actions, or 'True or false?' to use in hacking out meaningful statements. The cook can get on with the preparation of the meal even
if he must improvise a method here and there, and makes more of
a mess than he would with more appropriate implements. But the
philosopher can scarcely *begin* to do his work; there is no job the
philosopher has to get on with; nothing ulterior he must do with
actions (e.g. explain or predict them), or with statements (e.g.
verify them). What he wants to know is what they are, what it is to
do something and to say something. To the extent that he im-
provises a way of getting past the description and division of an
action or a statement, or leaves a mess in his account – to that
extent he leaves his own job undone. If the philosopher is trying
to get clear about what preparing a meal is and asks the cook 'Do
you cut the apple or not?', the cook may say 'Watch me!', and
then core and peel it. 'Watch me!' is what we should reply to the
philosopher who asks of our normal, ordinary actions 'Voluntary or
not?' and who asks of our ethical and aesthetic judgements 'True or
false?' Few speakers of a language utilise the full range of perception which the language provides, just as they do without so much
of the rest of their cultural heritage. Not even the philosopher will
come to possess all of his past, but to neglect it deliberately is fool-
hardy. The consequence of such neglect is that our philosophical
memory and perception become fixated upon a few accidents of
intellectual history.

I have suggested that the question of '[verifying] an assertion
that a given person uses a *word* in a given way or with a given
sense' (Mates, ibid., my emphasis) is not the same as verifying
assertions that 'We say . . .' or that 'When we say . . . we imply –'.
This means that I do not take the 'two basic approaches' which
Mates offers in the latter part of his paper to be directed to the
same question as the one represented in the title he gives to his
paper (at least on my interpretation of that question). The questions
are designed to elicit different types of information; they are
relevant (have point) at different junctures of investigation. Sometimes a question is settled by asking others (or ourselves) what we
say here, or whether we ever say such-and-such; on the basis of these
data we can make statements like ' "Voluntary" is used of an
action only where there is something (real or imagined) fishy about
it'. I take this to be a 'statement about ordinary language' (and
equally, about voluntary action). But surely it is not, under ordinary
circumstances, an assertion about how a word is used by *me* (or

'some given person'); it is a statement about how the word is used in English. Questions about how a given person is using some *word* can sensibly arise only where there is some specific reason to suppose that he is using the word in an unusual way. This point can be put the other way around: the statement 'I (or some given person) use (used) the word X in such-and-such a way' implies (depending on the situation) that you intend (intended) to be using it in a special way, or that someone else is unthinkingly misusing it, or using it misleadingly, and so on. This is another instance of the principle that actions which are normal will not tolerate any special description. In a *particular* case you may realise that words are not to be taken normally, that some want or fear or special intention of the speaker is causing an aberration in the drift of his words. A little girl who says to her brother 'You can have half my candy' may mean 'Don't take any!'; the husband who screams in fury 'Still no buttons!' may really be saying 'If I were honest, I'd do what Gauguin did'. A knave or a critic or an heiress may say 'X is good' and mean 'I want or expect or command you to like (or approve of) X'; and we, even without a special burden of malice, or of taste, or of money, may sometimes find ourselves imitating them.

Mates interprets Ryle's assertion that the ordinary use of 'voluntary' applies to actions which are disapproved to mean that 'the ordinary man applies the word only to actions of which he disapproves' (p. 129 above); this apparently involves a reference to that man's personal 'aims, feelings, beliefs, and hopes'; and these, in turn, are supposely part merely of the pragmatics (not the semantics) of a word. It is therefore a mistake, Mates concludes, to claim that the philosopher is using the word in a 'stretched, extraordinary *sense*' (ibid., my emphasis) merely on the ground that he may not happen to feel disapproving about an action he calls voluntary. The mistake, however, is to suppose that the ordinary use of a word is a function of the internal state of the speaker. (It is sometimes to emphasise that your remarks about 'use' are not remarks about such states that you want to say you are talking about the *logic* of ordinary language.) Another reason for the tenacity of the idea that a statement of what we mean when we say so-and-so (a statement of the second type) must be synthetic is that we suppose it to be *describing* the mental processes of the person talking. To gain perspective on that idea, it may be of help to consider that instead of saying to the child who said he *knew* (when we knew he had no right to say so) 'You mean you *think* so', we might have said 'You *don't* know (or "That is not what it is to know something"); you just think so'. This says neither more nor less than the formulation about what he *means*, and neither of them is a description of what is going on inside the child. They are both statements which teach him what he has a *right* to say, what knowledge is.

Mates tells us (ibid.) that his 'intensional approach' is meant, in part, 'to do justice to the notions (1) that what an individual means by a word depends at least in part upon what he wants to mean by that word, and (2) that he may have to think awhile before he discovers what he "really" means by a given word'. With respect to the first notion, I should urge that we do justice to the fact that an individual's intentions or wishes can no more produce the general meaning for a word than they can produce horses for beggars, or home runs from pop flies, or successful poems out of unsuccessful poems.[33] This may be made clearer by noticing, with respect to the second notion, that often when an individual is thinking 'what he "really" means' (in the sense of having second thoughts about something), he is not thinking what he really means by a given *word*. You have second thoughts in such cases just because you cannot make words mean what you wish (*by* wishing); it is for that reason that what you say on a given occasion may not be what you really mean. To say what you really mean you will have to say something different, change the words; or, as a special case of this, change the meaning of a word. Changing the meaning is not wishing it were different. This is further confirmed by comparing the locutions 'X means YZ' and 'I mean by X, YZ'. The former holds or fails to hold, whatever I wish to mean. And the latter, where meaning does depend on me, is performative;[34] something I am doing to the word X, not something I am wishing about it.

What these remarks come to is this: there is no such activity as my-finding-out-what-I-mean-by-a-word. But there obviously is finding-out-what-a-word-means. You do this by consulting a dictionary or a native speaker who happens to know. There is also something we may call finding-out-what-a-word-really means. This is done when you already know what the dictionary can teach you; when, for some reason or other, you are forced into philosophising. Then you begin by recollecting the various things we should say were such-and-such the case. Socrates gets his antagonists to withdraw their definitions not because they do not know what their words mean, but because they do know what they (their words) mean, and therefore know that Socrates has led them into paradox. (How could I be led into a paradox if I could mean what I wished by my words? Because I must be consistent? But how could I *be inconsistent* if words would mean what I wanted them to mean?) What they had not realised was what they were saying, or, what they were *really* saying, and so not known *what they meant*. To this extent, they had not known themselves, and not known the world. I mean, of course, the ordinary world. That may not be all there is, but it is important enough: morality is in that world, and so are force and love; so is art and a part of knowledge (the part which is about that world); and so is religion (wherever God is). Some mathematics and science, no doubt, are not. This is why you will not find out what 'number' or 'neurosis' or 'mass' or 'mass society' mean if you only listen for our ordinary uses of these terms.[35] But you will never find out what voluntary action is if you fail to see when we should say of an action that it is voluntary.

One may still feel the need to say 'Some actions *are* voluntary and some *are* involuntary. It would be convenient [for what?] to call all actions voluntary which are not involuntary. Surely I can call them anything I like? Surely what I *call* them doesn't affect what they are?' Now: how will you tell me what 'they' are?[36] What we need to ask ourselves here is: In what sort of situations does it make no difference what I call a thing? or: At what point in a dialogue does it become natural or proper for me to say 'I (you) can call it what I (you) like'? At this point it may be safe to say that the question is (has become) verbal.[37] If you really have a way of telling just what is denoted by 'all actions which are not involuntary', then you can call them anything you like.

I just tried to characterise the situation in which we ordinarily ask 'What does X mean?', and to characterise the *different* situation in which we ask 'What does X really mean?' These questions neither conflict nor substitute for one another, though philosophers often take the second as a profound version of the first – perhaps to console themselves for their lack of progress. Isn't this part of the trouble about synonymy? 'Does X *really* mean the same as Y?' is not a profound version of 'Does X mean the same as Y?' It (its occasion) is, though related to the first in obvious and devious ways, different. The same goes for the pair 'What did he do?' and 'What did he really (literally) *do*?'; and for the pair 'What do you see?' and 'What do you *really* (immediately) *see*?'; and for the pair 'Is the table solid?' and 'Is the table *really* (absolutely) solid?' Since the members of the pairs are *obviously* different, philosophers who do not see that the difference in the second members lies in their

occasions, in where and when they are posed, handsomely provide
special entities, new worlds, for them to be about. But this can only
perpetuate – it will not penetrate – a new reality.

The profoundest as well as the most superficial questions can be
understood only when they have been placed in their natural
environments. (What makes a statement or a question profound is
not its placing but its timing.) The philosopher is no more magically
equipped to remove a question from its natural environment than he
is to remove himself from any of the conditions of intelligible discourse. Or rather, he may remove himself, but his mind will not
follow. This, I hope it is clear, does not mean that the philosopher
will not eventually come to distinctions, and use words to mark
them, at places and in ways which depart from the currently
ordinary lines of thought.[38] But it does suggest that (and why) when
his recommendations come too fast, with too little attention to the
particular problem for which we have gone to him, we feel that
instead of thoughtful advice we have been handed a form letter.
Attention to the details of cases as they arise may not provide a
quick path to an all-embracing system; but at least it promises
genuine instead of spurious clarity.

Some philosophers will find this programme too confining. Philosophy, they will feel, was not always in such straits; and it will
be difficult for them to believe that the world and the mind have so
terribly altered that philosophy must relinquish old excitements to
science and to poetry. There, it may be claimed, new uses are still
invented by the profession, and while this makes the scientist and the
poet harder to understand initially, it enables them eventually to
renew and to deepen and to articulate our understanding. No
wonder the philosopher will gape at such bandwagons. But he must
sit still. Both because, where he does not wish to invent (hopes not to
invent), he is not entitled to the rewards and licences of those who
do; and because he would otherwise be running from his peculiar
task – one which has become homelier perhaps, but still quite indispensable to the mind. The 'unwelcome consequences' (Mates, p. 124
above) which may attend using words in ways which are (have
become) privately extraordinary is just that our understanding
should lose its grasp. Not only is it true that this can happen without
our being aware of it, it is often very difficult to become aware of it –
like becoming aware that we have grown pedantic or childish or
slow. The meaning of words *will*, of course, stretch and shrink, and
they will be stretched and be shrunk. One of the great responsibilities
of the philosopher lies in appreciating the natural and the normative

ways in which such things happen, so that he may make us aware of the one and capable of evaluating the other. It is a wonderful step towards understanding the abutment of language and the world when we see it to be a matter of convention. But this idea, like every other, endangers as it releases the imagination. For some will then suppose that a private meaning is not more arbitrary than one arrived at publicly, and that since language inevitably changes, there is no reason not to change it arbitrarily. Here we need to remind ourselves that ordinary language is natural language, and that its changing is natural. (It is unfortunate that artificial language has come to seem a general *alternative* to natural language;[39] it would, I suggest, be better thought of as one of its capacities.) Some philosophers, apparently, suppose that because natural language is 'constantly' changing it is too unstable to support one exact thought, let alone a clear philosophy. But this Heraclitean anxiety is unnecessary: linguistic change is itself an object of respectable study. And it misses the significance of that change. It is exactly because the language which contains a culture changes with the changes of that culture that philosophical awareness of ordinary language is illuminating; it is that which explains how the language we traverse every day can contain undiscovered treasure. To see that ordinary language is natural is to see that (perhaps even see why) it is normative for what can be said. And also to see how it is by searching definitions that Socrates can coax the mind down from self-assertion – subjective assertion and private definition – and lead it back, through the community, home. That this also renews and deepens and articulates our understanding tells us something about the mind, and provides the consolation of philosophers.

Mates, at one point in his paper, puts his doubts about the significance of the claims of ordinary language this way: 'Surely the point is not merely that if you use the word "voluntary" just as the philosopher does, you may find yourself entangled in the philosophic problem of the Freedom of the Will' (p. 124 above). Perhaps the reason he thinks this is a negligible consequence is that he hears it on analogy with the assertion 'If you use the term "space-time" just as the physicist does, you may find yourself entangled in the philosophic problem of simultaneity'. The implication is that the problem must simply be faced, not avoided. I, however, hear the remark differently: If you use alcohol just as the alcoholic does, or pleasure as the neurotic does, you may find yourself entangled in the practical problem of the freedom of the will.

IX The availability of Wittgenstein's later philosophy

S. Cavell

Epochs are in accord with themselves only if the crowd comes into these radiant confessionals which are the theatres or the arenas, and as much as possible, . . . to listen to its own confessions of cowardice and sacrifice, of hate and passion. . . . For there is no theatre which is not prophecy. Not this false divination which gives names and dates, but true prophecy, that which reveals to men these surprising truths: that the living must live, that the living must die, that autumn must follow summer, spring follow winter, that there are four elements, that there is happiness, that there are innumerable miseries, that life is a reality, that it is a dream, that man lives in peace, that man lives on blood; in short, those things they will never know.

JEAN GIRAUDOUX

In June of 1929 Wittgenstein was awarded a Ph.D. from Cambridge University, having returned to England, and to philosophy, less than a year earlier. His examiners were Russell and Moore, and for his dissertation he had submitted his *Tractatus*, published some seven or eight years earlier, written earlier than that, and now famous. The following month, he refused to read a paper ('Some Remarks on Logical Form') which he had prepared for the joint session of the Mind Association and Aristotelian Society, and which obviously goes with the ideas he had worked out in the *Tractatus*. Years later he said to Moore 'something to the effect that, when he wrote [the paper on logical form] he was getting new ideas about which he was still confused, and that he did not think it deserved any attention'.[1]

In January of 1930 he began lecturing at Cambridge about those new ideas, and in the academic session of 1933-4 he dictated a set of notes in conjunction with his lectures; during 1934–5 he dictated privately another manuscript, longer than the former, more continuously evolving and much closer in style to the *Philosophical Investigations*. These two sets of dictations – which came, because of the wrappers they were bound in, to be called, respectively, the *Blue Book* and the *Brown Book* – are now publicly available, bearing appropriately the over-title *Preliminary Studies for the "Philosophical Investigations"*.[2] But the extent to which the ideas in these pages are available, now seven years after the publication of the *Investigations*, is a matter of some question even after the appearance of the first book on the later philosophy, for none of its thought is to be found in David Pole's *The Later Philosophy of Wittgenstein*.[3]

What I find most remarkable about this book is not the modesty of its understanding nor the pretentiousness and condescension of its criticism, but the pervasive absence of any worry that some remark of Wittgenstein's may not be utterly obvious in its meaning and implications. When, on the opening page, I read '[Despite the fact that] he ... has been popularly portrayed as a kind of fanatic of subtlety if not, worse, an addict of mystification ... I shall maintain that Wittgenstein's central ideas ... are essentially simple', I was, although sceptical, impressed: that would be a large claim to enter and support in discussing any difficult thinker, but it could be very worth trying to do. About Wittgenstein the claim is doubled up. For not only is one faced with the obvious surface difficulties of the writing, one is also met by a new philosophical concept of difficulty itself: the *difficulty* of philosophising, and especially of the fruitful *criticism* of philosophy, is one of Wittgenstein's great themes (and therefore, doubtless, simple, once we can grasp it). My disappointment was, accordingly, the sharper when I had to recognise that Pole was conceiving the task of steering towards a deep simplicity to be itself an easy one. Disappointment mounted to despair as I found the famous and exciting and obscure tags of the *Investigations* not only quoted without explanation, but quoted as though they *were* explanations:

At least this much is clear, first that Wittgenstein distinguishes in some sense between the structural apparatus and the content of language and secondly that he holds that philosophers are prone to the error of seeing the one in terms of the other. We make a picture of an independently existing reality. 'We predicate of the thing what lies in the mode of presentation' (p. 37).

It would, for example, have been worthwhile to try to point to the relation of that idea – which is usually entered as summary of philosophical disorder – to the idea (cited by Pole, p. 54) that 'grammar tells us what kind of object anything is' (§ 373)[4] – which hints at what philosophy might positively accomplish and at the kind of importance it might have.

Criticism is always an affront, and its only justification lies in usefulness, in making its object available to just response. Pole's work is not useful. Where he is not misdescribing with assurance, his counters may be of the 'He says . . . , but I on the other hand say . . .' variety ('For Wittgenstein . . . an expression has as much meaning as we have given it. . . . Now as against this, I shall claim that there is always more meaning in an expression than we have given it' (pp. 83–8)) as though the issues called for the actions of a prophet or a politician, as though it were *obvious* that what Wittgenstein means by 'as much meaning' denies the possibility Pole envisages as 'more meaning', and that the issue before us is not one of criticism but of commitment. The distortion to which Wittgenstein's thought is subjected is so continuous that no one error or misemphasis seems to call, more than others, for isolated discussion. This paper therefore takes the following form. The next two sections discuss the main concepts Pole attacks in his description and interpretation of Wittgenstein's view of language; the two sections which then follow comment on positions towards 'ordinary language philosophy' which Pole shares with other critics of Wittgenstein.

RULES

The main effort of Pole's work is to expose and discredit Wittgenstein's views about language. There is no problem about what those views are:

> Broadly the thesis is that a language . . . consists of a complex set of procedures, which may also be appealed to as rules. Normative notions – rightness, validity, and we may perhaps add truth – are significant inasmuch as there exist standards which we can appeal to and principles we can invoke. But where a new move is first made, a new development takes place, clearly no such standard can be applicable; we have moved beyond existing practice. Wittgenstein, it seems, is committed to holding that no such step

can be called right or wrong; no evaluative assessment is possible (p. 55 f.).

We are to think of two factors in language; on the one hand particular moves or practices which are assessed by appeal to the rules, and on the other hand those rules themselves. Beyond these there is no further appeal; they are things we merely accept or adopt.

Where there are no rules to appeal to we can only decide; and I suppose that it is primarily on this account that this step is called a decision (p. 61).

This sounds vaguely familiar. Its Manichean conception of 'rules' reminds one of Carnap's distinction between 'internal' and 'external' questions and of the recent writing in moral philosophy which distinguishes between the assessment of individual actions and of social practices; its use of 'decision' is reminiscent of, for example, Reichenbach's 'volitional decisions' and of Stevenson's 'choice' between rational and persuasive methods of supporting moral judgements. Were Pole's description meant to apply to these views, it would merely be crude, failing to suggest their source or to depict their power. As a description of Wittgenstein it is ironically blind; it is not merely wrong, but misses the fact that Wittgenstein's ideas form a sustained and radical criticism of such views – so of course it it 'like' them.

Pole's description seems to involve these notions:

1. The correctness or incorrectness of a use of language is determined by the rules of the language, and 'determined' in two senses:
    (a) The rules form a complete system, in the sense that for every 'move' within the language it is obvious that a rule does or does not apply.
    (b) Where a rule does apply, it is obvious whether it has been followed or infringed.
2. Where no existing rules apply, you can always adopt a new rule to cover the case, but then that obviously changes the game.

This is rough enough, and what Wittgenstein says about games, rules, decisions, correctness, justification, and so forth, is difficult enough, but not sufficiently so that one must hesitate before saying that Pole has not tried to understand what Wittgenstein has most painfully wished to say about language (and meaning and understanding). For Pole's description seems, roughly, to suggest the way correctness is determined in a *constructed* language or in the simplest games of chance. That everyday language does not, in fact or in essence, depend upon such a structure and conception of rules, and yet that the absence of such a structure in no way impairs its functioning, is what the picture of language drawn in the later philosophy is about. It represents one of the major criticisms Wittgenstein enters against the *Tractatus*; it sets for him many of the great problems of the later philosophy – for example, the relations between word, sentence, and language – and forces him into new modes of investigating meaning, understanding, reference, and so forth; his new, and central, concept of 'grammar' is developed in opposition to it; it is repeated dozens of times. Whether the later Wittgenstein describes language as being roughly like a calculus with fixed rules working in that way is not a question which can seriously be discussed.

Then what are we to make of the fact that Wittgenstein constantly compares moments of speech with moves in a game? Pole makes out this much.

[the] comparison ... serves his purpose in at least two ways. It serves him first in that a game is usually a form of social activity in which different players fill different roles; secondly in that games observe rules (p. 29).

But what purpose is served by these points of comparison? Let us take the points in reverse order:

A. Where the comparison of language with games turns on their both 'observing rules', Wittgenstein invokes and invents games not as contexts in which it is just clear what 'observing rules' amounts to, but contexts in which that phenomenon can be *investigated*. In particular, the analogy with games helps us to see the following:

(i) In the various activities which may be said to proceed according to definite rules, the activity is not (and could not be) 'everywhere circumscribed by rules' (§ 68). Does this mean that the rules are 'incomplete'? It tells us something about what 'being governed by rules' is like.

(ii) 'Following a rule' is an activity we learn against the background of, and in the course of, learning innumerable other

activities – for example, obeying orders, taking and giving directions, repeating what is done or said, and so forth. The concept
of a rule does not exhaust the concepts of correctness or justification ('right' and 'wrong') and indeed the former concept
would have no meaning unless these latter concepts already had.
Like any of the activities to which it is related, a rule can always
be misinterpreted in the course, or in the name, of 'following' it.

(iii) There is a more radical sense in which rules do not 'determine' what a game is. One may explain the difference between,
say, contract and auction bridge by 'listing the rules'; but one
cannot explain what *playing a game* is by 'listing rules'. Playing
a game is 'a part of our [that is, we humans'] natural history'
(§ 25), and until one is an initiate of this human form of activity,
the human gesture of 'citing a rule' can mean nothing. And we
can learn a new game without ever learning or formulating its
rules (§ 31); not, however, without having mastered, we might
say, the concept of a game.

(iv) There is no one set of characteristics – and this is the most
obvious comparison – which everything we call 'games' shares,
hence, no characteristic called 'being determined by rules'.
Language has no essence (§ 66).

B. For Wittgenstein, 'following a rule' is just as much a 'practice'
as 'playing a game' is (§ 199). Now what are its rules? In the sense
in which 'playing chess' has rules, 'obeying a rule' has none (except,
perhaps, in a special code or calculus which sets up some order of
precedence in the application of various rules); and yet it can be
done correctly or incorrectly – which just means it can be done
or not done. And whether or not it is done is not a matter of rules
(or of opinion or feeling or wishes or intentions). It is a matter of
what Wittgenstein, in the *Blue Book* refers to as 'conventions' (p. 24),
and in the *Investigations* describes as 'forms of life' (e.g. § 23).
That is always the ultimate appeal for Wittgenstein – not rules, and
not decisions. It is what he is appealing to when he says such things
as:

If I have exhausted the justifications I have reached bedrock,
and my spade is turned. Then I am inclined to say: 'This is
simply what I do' (§ 217; cf. § 211).

What has to be accepted, the given is – so one could say – *forms
of life* (II, p. 226).

Pole hears such phrases as meaning:

That [a given language-game] is played is no more than a matter of fact; it is always conceivable that it should not have been played. It might be said that the question raised is as to whether it ought to be played, and this formulation – one that Wittgenstein does not discuss – comes nearer, I believe, to the heart of the matter.

If your heart is on your sleeve, that is. Wittgenstein does not discuss whether language games *ought* to be played, for that would amount to discussing either (1) whether human beings ought to behave like the creatures we think of as human; or (2) whether the world ought to be different from what it is. For the 'matters of fact' Wittgenstein is concerned with are what he describes in such ways as these:

What we are supplying are really remarks on the natural history of human beings; we are not contributing curiosities however, but observations which no one has doubted, but which have escaped remark only because they are always before our eyes (§ 415).

I am not saying: if such-and-such facts of nature were different people would have different concepts (in the sense of a hypothesis). But: if anyone believes that certain concepts are absolutely the correct ones, and that having different ones would mean not realising something that we realise – then let him imagine certain *very general facts of nature* to be different from what we are used to, and the formation of concepts different from the usual ones will become intelligible to him (II, p. 230; my italics).

'It is always conceivable' that, for example, the game(s) we now play with the question 'What did you say?' should not have been played. What are we conceiving if we conceive this? Perhaps that when we ask this of A, only A's father is allowed to answer, or that it is answered always by repeating the next to the last remark you made, or that it is answered by saying what you wished you had said, or perhaps that we can never remember what we just said, or perhaps simply that we have no way of asking that question. What sense does it make to suggest that one or the other of these games ought or ought not to be played? The question is: what would our lives look like, what very general facts would be different, if these conceivable alternatives were in fact operative? (There would, for example, be different ways, and purposes, for lying; a different social structure; different ways of attending to what is said; different weight put on our words; and so forth.)

Even with these hints of echoes of shadows of Wittgenstein's 'purpose' in investigating the concept of a rule, we can say this much: (1) It allows him to formulate one source of a distorted conception of language – one to which, in philosophising, we are particularly susceptible, and one which helps secure distortion in philosophical theorising:

> When we talk of language as a symbolism used in an exact calculus, that which is in our mind can be found in the sciences and in mathematics. Our ordinary use of language conforms to this standard of exactness only in rare cases. Why then do we in philosophising constantly compare our use of words with one following exact rules? The answer is that the puzzles which we try to remove always spring from just this attitude towards language (*BB*, pp. 25–6).

Or again:

> The man who is philosophically puzzled sees a law [=rule] in the way a word is used, and, trying to apply this law consistently, comes up against cases where it leads to paradoxical results (*BB*, p. 27).

(2) He wishes to indicate how inessential the 'appeal to rules' is as an explanation of language. For what has to be 'explained' is, put flatly and bleakly, this.

We learn and teach words in certain contexts, and then we are expected, and expect others, to be able to project them into further contexts.[5] Nothing ensures that this projection will take place (in particular, not the grasping of universals nor the grasping of books of rules), just as nothing ensures that we will make, and understand, the same projections. That on the whole we do is a matter of our sharing routes of interest and feeling, modes of response, senses of humour and of significance and of fulfilment, of what is outrageous, of what is similar to what else, what a rebuke, what forgiveness, of when an utterance is an assertion, when an appeal, when an explanation – all the whirl of organism Wittgenstein calls 'forms of life'. Human speech and activity, sanity and community, rest upon nothing more, but nothing less, than this. It is a vision as simple as it is difficult, and as difficult as it is (and because it is) terrifying. To attempt the work of *showing* its simplicity would be a real step in making available Wittgenstein's later philosophy.

DECISION

Having begun by miscasting the role of rules, and then taking 'decision' to be a concept complementary to the concept of a rule, Pole will not be expected to have thrown light either on the real weight (and it is not much) Wittgenstein places on the concept of decision or on Wittgenstein's account of those passages of speech in which, in Pole's words, 'a new move is first made'.

The only passage Pole actually cites (on p. 44, and again on p. 61) to support his interpretation of 'decision' is this one from the *Remarks on the Foundations of Mathematics*: 'Why should I not say: in the proof I have won through to a decision?' (II, § 27). What I take Wittgenstein to be concerned with here is the question: 'What makes a proof convincing?' Without discussing either the motives of that question or the success of his answer to it, it is clear enough that Wittgenstein takes the conviction afforded by a proof to be a function of the way it can 'be taken in', 'be followed', 'be used as a model', 'serve as a pattern or paradigm'. But what can be 'taken in', and so forth, in this way is *not something we have a choice about, not something that can be decided*. Saying that 'the problem we are faced with in mathematics is essentially to decide what new forms to fashion' (p. 44) is as sensible as saying that the problem we are faced with in composing a coda is to decide what will sound like a cadence, or that the problem faced in describing a new object is to decide what will count as a description.

What is wrong with Pole's interpretation of Wittgenstein as suggesting that the mathematician decides 'to use a certain rule' is not that it takes 'too literally what Wittgenstein says of standards or rules' (p. 60), but that it is not what Wittgenstein says. ('Deciding to use a certain rule' correctly describes a logician's decision to use, say, Universal Generalisation, which involves certain liabilities but ones he considers outweighed by other advantages.) What Wittgenstein says is that 'the expression, the result, of our being convinced is that we *accept a rule*'. We no more *decide* to accept a rule in this sense than we decide to be convinced. And we no more decide what will express our conviction here than we decide what will express our conviction about anything else – for example, that the road to New Orleans is the left one, that the development section is too long, and so forth.

Pole snaps at the word 'decision' because he fears that it denies the rationality of choice; he despises this implication of its use in recent philosophising (see p. 62). I share this concern about recent moral philosophy. But what is wrong in such discussions is not the use of the word 'decision'; it is, rather, the implications which arise from an *unexamined* use of it, a use in which the concept of choice is disengaged from its (grammatical) connections with the concepts of commitment and of responsibility. How and why this has happened is something else.[6]

Wittgenstein does speak of forms of expression which we might think of as representing 'a new move' in a shared language, to wit, those whose 'grammar has yet to be explained' (*BB*, p. 10). (Adding 'because there are no rules for its employment' adds nothing). But he no more says of such expressions that in explaining them we decide to adopt the rules which confer meaning on them than he says about the concept of decision itself what Pole wishes him to say.

Some examples Wittgenstein gives of such expressions are: 'I feel the visual image to be two inches behind the bridge of my nose' (*BB*, p. 9); 'I feel in my hand that the water is three feet under the ground' (ibid.); 'A rose has teeth in the mouth of a beast' (II, p. 222). What he says about them is this:

> We don't say that the man who tells us he feels the visual image two inches behind the bridge of his nose is telling a lie or talking nonsense. But we say that we don't understand the meaning of such a phrase. It combines well-known words but combines them in a way we don't yet understand. The grammar of [such phrases] has yet to be explained to us (*BB*, p. 10).

He does not say, and he does not mean, that there is 'no right or wrong' about the use of such expressions. The question 'Right or wrong?' has no application (yet) to such phrases, and so the statement that 'such phrases are neither right nor wrong' itself says nothing. 'Neither right nor wrong' may mean something like 'unorthodox' or 'not quite right and not quite wrong', but to use such critical expressions implies a clear sense of what would be orthodox or exactly right instances of the thing in question. Are the phrases in question unorthodox ways of saying something? What are they unorthodox ways of saying?

Pole compounds critical confusion by taking the irrelevance of the question 'Right or wrong?' to mean that 'no evaluative assessment is possible'. (If it did mean that, then we should have made no evaluative assessment of a poem when we have found it trite or incoherent or wanting a summary stanza, nor of a decision when we have shown it thoughtless or heartless or spineless. Pole's insistence on right and wrong as the touchstones of assessment represents another attempt to meet an academic distrust of morality by an academic moralism. The positions are made for one another.) Is it no assessment of a phrase to say that its grammar has yet to be explained? But that is a very particular assessment, a new category of criticism. And there is no suggestion from Wittgenstein that *any* explanation will be acceptable. He calls one explanation of the diviner's statement a 'perfectly good' one (*BB*, p. 10).

Such phrases are not the only ones in which our failure to understand is attributable to our failure to understand grammar; they are only the most dramatic or obvious ones. Once we see that the grammar of an expression sometimes *needs* explaining, and realise that we all know how to provide perfectly good explanations, we may be more accessible to the request to investigate the grammar of an expression whose meaning seems obvious and ask ourselves how it *is* to be explained.

Such an investigation will doubtless be reminiscent of procedures which have long been part of the familiar texture of analytical philosophising; in particular, it sounds something like asking for the verification of a statement – and indeed Pole suggests (p. 96) that it is not, at bottom, importantly different in its criticism of metaphysics; and it sounds like Russell's asking for the 'real [that is, logical] form of a proposition' – and, of course, the Wittgenstein of the *Tractatus* had also asked for that. A profitable way, I think, to approach the thought of the later Wittgenstein is to see how his questions about grammar differ from these (and other) more familiar questions. The sorts of differences I have in mind may perhaps be suggested this way: (1) It is true that an explanation of the grammar of an assertion can be asked for by asking 'How would you verify that?' But first, where that is what the question asks for, it is not to be assumed that the question itself makes good sense; in particular it is not sensible unless there is some doubt about how that assertion is conceived to be verified, and it therefore leads to no theory of meaning at all (cf. §353). Second, it is not the only way in which an explanation of grammar can be requested; it is equally indicative of our failure to understand the grammar of an assertion if we cannot answer such questions as: 'How would you teach someone what that says?'; 'How would you hint at its truth?'; 'What is it like to wonder whether it is true?' (2) In the *Tractatus* Wittgenstein, if I understand, was asking: 'Why is the logical form of a proposition its real form?' But in the later philosophy he answers, in effect: 'It is not.' And he goes on to ask: 'Why do we (did I) think it was?'; and 'What does tell us the real form (= grammar) of a proposition?'

It is part of the accomplishment of Pole's critical study of Wittgenstein that it omits any examination of the twin concepts of 'grammar' and of 'criteria'. For what Wittgenstein means when he says that philosophy really is descriptive is that it is descriptive of 'our grammar', of 'the criteria we have' in understanding one another, knowing the world, and possessing ourselves. Grammar is what language games are meant to reveal; it is because of this that they provide new ways of investigating concepts, and of criticising traditional philosophy. All this, it should go without saying, is difficult to be clear about (Wittgenstein's own difficulty is not wilful); but it is what any effort to understand Wittgenstein must direct itself towards.

THE RELEVANCE OF THE APPEAL TO EVERYDAY LANGUAGE

Two of Pole's claims seem to be shared by many philosophers whom Wittgenstein offends, and it would be of use to do something towards making them seem less matters for common cause than for joined investigation. The claims I have in mind concern these two questions: (1) In what sense, or to what extent, does an appeal to 'our everyday use' of an expression represent a mode of criticising the use of that expression in philosophical contexts? (2) What sort of knowledge is the knowledge we have (or claim) of 'how we ordinarily use' an expression? The present section is concerned with the first of these questions, the following with the second.

Pole says, or implies, that Wittgenstein regards ordinary language as 'sacrosanct', that he speaks in the name of nothing higher than the 'status quo' and that he 'has forbidden philosophers to tamper with [our ordinary expressions]' (p. 57). Other philosophers, with very different motives from Pole's, have received the same impression, and their impatience has not been stilled by Wittgenstein's having said that a reform of ordinary language for particular purposes, an improvement in our terminology designed to prevent misunderstandings in practice, is perfectly possible. But these are not the cases we have to do with (§ 132).

for they persist in reading Wittgenstein's appeal to our everyday use of expressions as though his effort consisted in scorning the speech of his charwoman out of solicitude towards that of his Nanny.

It takes two to give an impression; if this is a distortion of Wittgenstein's thought, it is a distortion of *something*. Of what? Pole's reference for his claim about what Wittgenstein 'forbids' is to a passage which begins this way:

Philosophy may in no way interfere with the actual use of language; it can in the end only describe it (§ 124).

There is a frame of mind in which this may appear as something intolerably confining.[7] Then one will hear Wittgenstein's statement as though it meant either that philosophy ought not to change it (in which case Wittgenstein will be accused of an intellectual, even social conservatism) or that the actual use of language may in no way be changed (in which case Wittgenstein will be accused of lacking imagination or a sufficient appreciation of scientific advance). What the statement means is that, though of course there are any number of ways of changing ordinary language, philosophising does not change it. That charge cannot be evaded by making it sound like a Nanny bleating 'ou-ou-ought'.

And yet it is a very perplexing indictment which Wittgenstein has entered. Why does Wittgenstein think it is one? Why do philosophers respond to it as though it were? Have they claimed to be, or thought of themselves as, changing or interfering with language?

The force of the indictment can best be seen in considering the ancient recognition that a philosophical thesis may, or may seem to, conflict with a 'belief' which we take to be the common possession of common men, together with the equally ancient claim on the part of philosophers that in this conflict philosophy's position is superior to that common possession; that, for example, such claims as 'We know that there are material objects', 'We directly see them'. 'We know that other persons are sentient', all of which are believed by the vulgar, have been discovered by philosophers to lack rational justification.

But the *nature* of this discovery and the *kind* of conflict involved are problems as constant as epistemology itself. Their most recent guise is perhaps brought out if we can say this much: There would be no sense of such a discovery[8] unless there were a sense of conflict with 'what we all formerly believed', and there would, in turn, be no sense of conflict unless the philosopher's words meant (or were used as meaning) what they ordinarily meant. And don't they?

The ordinary language philosopher will say 'They don't; the philosopher is "misusing words" or "changing their meanings"; the philosopher has been careless, hasty, even wily[9] in his use of language.' The defender of the tradition may reply: 'Of course they don't; the philosopher uses technical terms, or terms with special senses, in order to free himself from the vagueness and imprecision of ordinary language and thereby to assess the beliefs it expresses.' Neither of these replies is very satisfactory. The former is, if not too unclear altogether to be taken seriously as an explanation of disorder, plainly incredible. I do not see how it can with good conscience be denied that ordinary-language philosophers (for example, Austin and Ryle) have found and made trouble for traditional philosophy. But the understanding of the trouble, and so an assessment of its seriousness or permanence, is a project of a different order. And I know of no effort of theirs at this task which carries anything like that immediate conviction which is so large a part of the power of their remarks when they are working within an investigation of ordinary language itself.

On the other hand, someone who imagines that he is defending the tradition by maintaining its right and need to introduce technical terms (or, as Pole suggests, to invent special philosophical language games – on, for example, pp. 96–7) probably has in mind the philosopher's use of such terms as 'sense data', 'analytic', 'transcendental unity of apperception', 'idea', 'universal', 'existential quantifier' – terms which no ordinary-language philosopher would criticise on the ground that they are not ordinary. But is the word 'seeing' in the statement 'We never directly see material objects' *meant* to be technical? Is 'private' in 'My sensations are private'? Are any of the words in such a statement as 'We can never know what another person is experiencing'? Are such statements used in some special language game? The assumption, shared by our ordinary-language critic and our defender of the tradition, that such words are not meant in their ordinary senses, destroys the point (not to say the meaning) of such statements. For on that assumption we cannot account for the way they seem to conflict with something we all (seem to, would say that we) believe; it therefore fails to account for what makes them seem to be discoveries or, we might say, fails to suggest what the hitherto unnoticed fact is which philosophy has discovered. Why would Descartes have professed 'astonishment' at his 'realisation' that he might be dreaming if he had not meant to be denying or questioning what anyone who said 'I believe, for example, that I am seated before the fire', and the like, would mean? And what cause, otherwise, would there have been for Hume to despair of his sceptical conclusions, regarding them as a 'malady which can never radically be cured' (*Treatise*, 1 (iv) 2), were they not sceptical about (or, as he puts it, 'contrary' to) 'such opinions as we . . . embrace by a kind of instinct or natural impulse'?

It may be objected to this that scientific theories, however technical their language, have no trouble conflicting with common beliefs. But it is of crucial importance that neither Hume nor the Descartes of the *Meditations*, nor indeed anyone in that continuous line of classical epistemologists from Descartes and Locke to Moore and Price, seems to be conducting scientific investigations. In particular, they do not set out a collection of more or less abstruse facts and puzzling phenomena which they undertake to explain theoretically. Their method is uniformly what Hume describes as 'profound and intense *reflection*' from which, he says, 'sceptical doubt arises *naturally*' (op. cit.; my italics). They all begin from what seem to be facts of such obviousness that no one could fail to recognise them ('We all believe that there are material objects which continue to exist when they are unperceived'), employ examples of the homeliest extraction ('We should all say that I am now holding an envelope in my hand, and that we all see it') and considerations whose import anyone can grasp who can speak ('But no two of us see exactly the same thing'; 'But there is much that I can doubt'). (Wittgenstein's originality does not come from his having said that philosophy's problems concern something we all already know.) That such facts and examples and considerations 'naturally' lead to scepticism is the phenomenon concerning us here. What the relation may be between this way of coming into conflict with common belief, and science's way, is a fascinating question and one, so far as I know, as yet unexamined.

Perhaps this can now be said: If, in the non-scientific (sceptical) conflict with common belief, words are in some way deprived of their normal functioning, a conceptualisation of this distortion will have to account for this pair of facts: that the philosopher's words must (or must seem to) be used in their normal way, otherwise they would not conflict with what should ordinarily be meant in using them; and that the philosopher's words cannot be used in (quite) their normal way, otherwise the ordinary facts, examples, and considerations he adduces would not yield a general sceptical conclusion.

It is such a pair of facts, I suggest, that Wittgenstein is responding to when he says of philosophical (he calls them 'metaphysical') expressions that (roughly) they are 'used apart from their normal language game', that their 'grammar is misunderstood', that they 'flout the common criteria used in connection with these expressions'. Such assertions do not say that the philosopher has 'changed the meaning of his words' (what meaning do they now have?). Nor are they met, if any truth is caught by them, by saying that the words are being used in special senses, for none of Wittgenstein's critical assertions would be true of technical terms. They represent new categories of criticism.

Wittgenstein is, then, denying that in the (apparent) conflict between philosophy and the common 'beliefs' (assumptions?) of ordinary men, philosophy's position is superior. This does not mean, however, that he is defending common beliefs against philosophy. That 'there are material objects' or that 'other persons are sentient' are not propositions which Wittgenstein supposed to be open either to belief or to disbelief. They seem to be ordinary 'beliefs' only when the philosopher undertakes to 'doubt' them. I am not saying that this is obviously not real doubt, but merely suggesting that it is not obvious that it is, and that it is completely unobvious, if it is not real doubt, what kind of experience it is and why it represents itself as doubt.

Nor is Wittgenstein saying that philosophy's position is inferior to that of common men. Perhaps one could say that he wishes to show that, in its conflict with 'what we all believe', the philosopher has no position at all, his conclusions are not false (and not meaningless), but, one could say, not *believable* – that is, they do not create the stability of conviction expressed in propositions which are subject (grammatically) to belief. (That was agonisingly acknowledged, as is familiar to us, by Hume, who wanted, but confessed failure in trying to find, an explanation of it. When he left his study he forgot, as he knew and hoped he would, the sceptical conclusions of his reflections. But what kind of 'belief' is it whose convincingness fades as soon as we are not explicitly attending to the considerations which led us to it?) For Wittgenstein, philosophy comes to grief not in denying what we all know to be true, but in its effort to escape those human forms of life which alone provide the coherence of our expression. He wishes an acknowledgement of human limitation which does not leave us chafed by our own skin, by a sense of powerlessness to penetrate beyond the human conditions of knowledge. The limitations of knowledge are no longer barriers to a more perfect apprehension, but conditions of knowledge *überhaupt*, of anything we should call 'knowledge'. The resemblance to Kant is obvious, and I will say another word about it below.

THE KNOWLEDGE OF OUR LANGUAGE

How can we come to such an acknowledgement of limitation? Wittgenstein's answer is: 'What we do is to bring words back from their metaphysical to their everyday use' (§ 116). I have, in effect, asked: why does that help? And my suggestion, essentially, was: it shows us that we did not know what we were saying, what we were doing to ourselves. But now I want to ask: how do we accomplish the task of bringing words back home? How do we known when we have done it?

Well, how does the logician know that (a) 'Nobody is in the auditorium' must be transcribed differently from (b) 'Peabody is in the auditorium'? By intuition? Careful empirical studies? Perhaps he will say: 'But obviously we do not want the same sorts of inferences to be drawn from (a) as from (b), in particular not the inference that somebody is in the auditorium.' But how does he know *that*? However he knows it – and he does – that is how Wittgenstein knows that the grammar of, say 'pointing to an object' is different from the grammar of 'pointing to a colour' (*BB*, p. 80; § 33). Failing an awareness of that difference we take the obvious difference between them to be a function of some special experience which accompanies the act of pointing. How does Wittgenstein know that? The way Russell (and we) know that if you do not catch the difference in logical form between 'Pegasus does not exist' and 'Whirlaway does not whinny', you will take the obvious difference between them to indicate the presence of some special realm of being which accompanies the ordinary world.

But what kind of knowledge is this? What kind of knowledge is the knowledge of what we ordinarily mean in using an expression, or the knowledge of the particular circumstances in which an expression is actually used? Pole has this to say:

Consider the great purpose of all this – this descriptive setting forth of language-games. It is to bring us to see that some particular move which we took for a move in the game has no proper place in it. Such a move is to be shown as failing to connect with the rest of the pattern. Wittgenstein compares it to a wheel spinning idly, disengaged from the machine it should belong to. Here we have a luminous metaphor – and yet no more than a metaphor. For there can be no way of testing whether this or that linguistic wheel has failed to engage, except to grasp the pattern in each case; to arrive at some sort of insight into that unique set of relations which it professes but fails to form a part of (p. 81).

This is thought to show that if we

once allow that it might be right to reject a proposition or mode of speech because the pattern has no place for it, ... it must follow that it must sometimes be right to accept others on the same ground – that the pattern requires them. There is no inherent difficulty in the notion. . . . Yet here we have a way of seeing language that the whole bent of Wittgenstein's thought was opposed to (p. 82).

If I understand what Pole is getting at (he gives no examples, here or elsewhere), he has been even less impressed by Wittgenstein's conception of language than we have seen. It is not the 'bent' of Wittgenstein's thought that is opposed to the idea that the 'requirement of the pattern' justifies the use we make of an expression, but the straight thrust of his whole teaching: 'The more narrowly we examine actual language, the sharper becomes the conflict between it and our requirement. (For the crystalline purity of logic was, of course, not a *result of investigation*: it was a requirement' (§ 107).) 'A *picture* [= pattern?] held us captive. And we could not get outside it, for it lay in our language and language seemed to repeat it to us inexorably' (§ 115). Not only is there 'no inherent difficulty in the notion' of 'grasping a pattern', the difficulty is to get ourselves not to take our feelings of what is called for or what must be appropriate, at face value.

Other philosophers have taken the knowledge of everyday language, since it is obviously knowledge of 'matters of fact', to be straightforwardly empirical, requiring the observations and verifications which we are told that any empirical judgement requires. Such philosophers find the appeal to what we should ordinarily

say and mean, when this appeal is not backed by scientific collection of 'our' utterances, archaically precious, while philosophers
dependent upon that appeal will find the invitation to science at this
point cheaply *moderne*. This conflict is not a side issue in the general
conflict between Wittgenstein (together with, at this point, 'ordinary
language philosophy') and traditional philosophy; it is itself an
instance, an expression, of that conflict, and one therefore which we
will not suppose it will be simple to resolve. Wittgenstein does not
speak very explicitly about the knowledge we have of our language,
but when we see what kind of claim this knowledge involves, we
realise that its investigation lies at the heart of the later philosophy
as a whole. I shall try to suggest what I mean by that.

Neither Wittgenstein nor the ordinary-language philosopher,
when he asks 'What should we say (would we call) . . . ?', is asking
just any question about the use of language. He is, in particular, not
predicting what will be said in certain circumstances, not, for example, asking how often a word will be used nor what the most
effective slogan will be for a particular purpose. (Those questions
can, of course, be asked; and their answers will indeed require
ordinary empirical methods for collecting sociological data.) He is
asking something which can be answered by remembering what is
said and meant, or by trying out his own response to an imagined
situation. Answers arrived at in such ways will not tell you everything, but why assume that they are meant to tell you what only the
collection of new data can tell you? The problems of philosophy are
not solved by '[hunting] out new facts; it is, rather, of the essence
of our investigation that we do not seek to learn anything *new* by it.
We want to *understand* something that is already in plain view.
For *this* is what we seem in some sense not to understand' (§ 89).

What do such answers look like? They will be facts about what
we call (how we conceive, what the concept is, what counts as), for
example, a piece of wax, the same piece of wax, seeing something,
not really seeing something, not seeing all of something, following,
finding, losing, returning, choosing, intending, wishing, pointing to
something, and so on. And we could say that what such answers are
meant to provide us with is not more knowledge of matters of fact,
but the knowledge of what would count as various 'matters of fact'.
Is this empirical knowledge? Is it *a priori*? It is a knowledge of what
Wittgenstein means by grammar – the knowledge Kant calls 'transcendental'.

And here I make a remark which the reader must bear well in

mind, as it extends its influence over all that follows. Not every kind of knowledge *a priori* should be called transcendental, but that only by which we know that – and how – certain representations (intuitions or concepts) can be employed or are possible purely *a priori*. The term 'transcendental', that is to say, signifies such knowledge as concerns the *a priori* possibility of knowledge, or its *a priori* employment.

(*Critique of Pure Reason*, trans. N. Kemp Smith, p. 96).

That is not the clearest remark ever made, but I should think that no one who lacked sympathy with the problem Kant was writing about would undertake to make sense of Wittgenstein's saying:

Our investigation . . . is directed not towards phenomena, but, as one might say, towards the 'possibilities' of phenomena (§ 90).

As the 'transcendental clue to the discovery of all pure concepts of the understanding' (*Critique*, pp. 105 ff.) Kant uses the idea that 'there arise precisely the same number of pure concepts of the understanding in general, as . . . there have been found to be logical functions in all possible judgements' (p. 113). Wittgenstein follows the remark quoted above with the words: 'We remind ourselves, that is to say, of the *kind of statement* that we make about phenomena. . . . Our investigation is therefore a grammatical one' (§ 90). And where Kant speaks of 'transcendental illusion' – the illusion that we know what transcends the conditions of possible knowledge – Wittgenstein speaks of the illusions produced by our employing words in the absence of the (any) language game which provides their comprehensible employment (cf. § 96). ('The results of philosophy are the uncovering of one or another piece of plain nonsense and of bumps that the understanding has got by running its head up against the limits of language' (§ 119).)

If his similarity to Kant is seen, the differences light up the nature of the problems Wittgenstein sets himself. For Wittgenstein it would be an illusion not only that we do know things-in-themselves, but equally an illusion that we do not (crudely, because the concept of 'knowing something as it really is' is being used without a clear sense, apart from its ordinary-language game). So problems emerge which can be articulated as: 'Why do we feel we cannot know something in a situation in which there is nothing it makes sense to say we do not know?'; 'What is the nature of this illusion?'; 'What makes us dissatisfied with our knowledge as a whole?'; 'What is the nature and power of a "conceptualisation of the world"?'; 'Why do we conceptualise the world as we do?'; 'What would alternative conceptualisations look like?'; 'How might they be arrived at?' It was, I suggest, because he wanted answers to such questions that he said 'It did not matter whether his results were true or not: what mattered was that "a method had been found"' (Moore, 'Wittgenstein's Lectures', *Mind*, LXIV (1955) p. 26).

And he also said: 'There is not *a* philosophical method, though there are indeed methods, like different therapies' (§ 133). The sorts of thing he means by 'methods' are, I take it, '[imagining or considering] a language-game for which [a given] account is really valid' (for example, § 2, § 48); 'finding and inventing intermediate cases' (§ 122); '[inventing] fictitious natural history,' (II, p. 230); investigating one expression by investigating a grammatically related expression, for example, the grammar of 'meaning' by that of 'explanation of the meaning' (*BB*, pp. 1, 24); and so on. But in all of these methods part of what is necessary is that we respond to questions like 'What would we say if . . . ?' or 'But is anyone going to call . . . ?' To suppose that what is then being asked for is a prediction of what will be said, and a prediction for which we have slim evidence, would be as sensible as responding to the request 'Suppose you have three apples and I give you three more. How many will you have?' by saying 'How can I answer with confidence? I might drop one and have five, or inherit an orchard and have thousands.'

What is being asked for? If it is accepted that 'a language' (a natural language) is what the native speakers of a language speak, and that speaking a language is a matter of practical mastery, then such questions as 'What should we say if . . . ?' or 'In what circumstances would we call . . . ?' asked of someone who has mastered the language (for example, oneself) is a request for the person to say something about himself, describe what he does. So the different methods are methods for acquiring self-knowledge; as – for different (but related) purposes and in response to different (but related) problems – are the methods of 'free' association, dream analysis, investigation of verbal and behavioural slips, noting and analysing 'transferred' feeling, and so forth. Perhaps more shocking, and certainly more important, than any of Freud's or Wittgenstein's particular conclusions is their discovery that knowing oneself is something for which there are methods – something, therefore, that can be taught (though not in obvious ways) and practised.

Someone may wish to object: 'But such claims as "We say . . .",

"We are not going to call ...", and so forth, are not merely claims about what *I* say and mean and do, but about what *others* say and mean and do as well. And how can I speak for others on the basis of knowledge about myself?' The question is: why are some claims about myself expressed in the form '*We* ...'? About what can I speak for others on the basis of what I have learned about myself? (This is worth comparing with the question: about what can I speak for others on the basis of what I decide to do? When you vote, you speak for yourself; when you are voted in, you speak for others.) Then suppose it is asked: 'But how do I know others speak as I do?' About some things I know they do not; I have some knowledge of my idiosyncracy. But if the question means 'How do I know at all that others speak as I do?' then the answer is, I do not. I may find out that the most common concept is not used by us in the same way. And one of Wittgenstein's questions is: what would it be like to find this out?[10] At one place he says:

> One human being can be a complete enigma to another. We learn this when we come into a strange country with entirely strange traditions; and, what is more, even given a mastery of the country's language. We do not *understand* the people. (And not because of not knowing what they are saying to themselves.) We cannot find our feet with them (II, p. 223).

In German the last sentence employs an idiom which literally says: 'We cannot find ourselves in them.' We, who can speak for one another, find that we cannot speak for them. In part, of course, we find this out in finding out that we cannot speak *to* them. If speaking *for* someone else seems to be a mysterious process, that may be because speaking *to* someone does not seem mysterious enough.

If the little I have said makes plausible the idea that the question 'How do we know what we say (intended to say, wish to say)?' is one aspect of the general question 'What is the nature of self-knowledge?' then we will realise that Wittgenstein has not first 'accepted' or 'adopted' a method and then accepted its results, for the nature of self-knowledge – and therewith the nature of the self – is one of the great subjects of the *Investigations* as a whole.

It is also one of the hardest regions of the *Investigations* to settle with any comfort. One reason for that, I think, is that so astonishingly little exploring of the nature of self-knowledge has been attempted in philosophical writing since Bacon and Locke and Descartes prepared the habitation of the new science. Classical epistemology has concentrated on the knowledge of objects (and, of course, of mathematics), not on the knowledge of persons. That is, surely, one of the striking facts of modern philosophy as a whole, and its history will not be understood until some accounting of that fact is rendered.[11] In a smart attack on the new philosophy, Russell suggests that its unconcern with the methods and results of modern science betrays its alienation from the original and continuing source of philosophical inspiration: 'Philosophers from Thales onward have tried to understand the world' (*My Philosophical Development* (New York, 1959) p. 230). But philosophers from Socrates onward have (sometimes) also tried to understand themselves, and found in that both the method and goal of philosophising. It is a little absurd to go on insisting that physics provides us with knowledge of the world which is of the highest excellence. Surely the problems we face now are not the same ones for which Bacon and Galileo caught their chills. Our intellectual problems (to say no more) are set by the very success of those deeds, by the plain fact that the measures which soak up knowledge of the world leave us dryly ignorant of ourselves. Our problem is not that we lack adequate methods for acquiring knowledge of nature, but that we are unable to prevent our best ideas – including our ideas about our knowledge of nature – from becoming ideologised. Our incapacity here results not from the supposed fact that ordinary language is vague; to say so is an excuse for not recognising that (and when) we speak vaguely, imprecisely, thoughtlessly, unjustly, in the absence of feeling, and so forth.

Since Wittgenstein's investigations of self-knowledge and of the knowledge of others depend upon his concept of 'criteria', it is worth noting that although Pole ventures a discussion of Wittgenstein's ideas about 'inner experience', he prudently withholds any opinion about the role of 'criteria' in those ideas. He does suggest that Wittgenstein supposed words to have meaning 'in the complete absence of conscious feeling' (p. 88), as though Wittgenstein supposed the users of language to be anaesthetised; and he finds Wittgenstein supposing that experiential elements play no part' in determining the way language is used (p. 88; cf. p. 86), whereas what Wittgenstein says is, in these terms, that what is experiential in the use of a word is not an element, not one identifiable recurrence whose presence ensures the meaning of a word and whose absence deprives it of meaning. If that were the case, how could we ever assess our feelings, recognise them to be inappropriate to what we say? Feelings (like intentions and hopes and wishes, though not in the same way) are expressed in speech and in conduct generally;

and the (actual, empirical) problem of the knowledge of oneself and of others is set by the multiple and subtle distortions of their expression. Here, what we do not know comprises not our ignorance but our alienation.

Since Wittgenstein does fuller justice to the role of feeling in speech and conduct than any other philosopher within the Anglo-American academic tradition, it is disheartening to find his thought so out of reach. Pole extends the line of those who, shocked at the way academic reasoning is embarrassed by the presence of feeling – its wish to remove feeling to the 'emotive' accompaniments of discourse, out of the reach of intellectual assessment – counter by taking feelings too much at face value and so suffer the traditional penalty of the sentimentalist, that one stops taking his feelings seriously. Other philosophers, I believe, are under the impression that Wittgenstein denies that we can know what we think and feel, and even that we can know ourselves. This extraordinary idea comes, no doubt, from such remarks of Wittgenstein's as: 'I can know what someone else is thinking, not what I am thinking' (II, p. 222); 'It cannot be said of me at all (except perhaps as a joke) that I *know* I am in pain' (§ 246). But the 'can' and 'cannot' in these remarks are grammatical; they mean 'it makes no sense to say these things' (in the way we think it does); it would, therefore, equally make no sense to say of me that I do not know what I am thinking, or that I do not know I am in pain. The implication is not that I cannot know myself, but that knowing oneself – though radically different from the way we know others – is not a matter of cognising (classically, 'intuiting') mental acts and particular sensations.

X The availability of what we say[1]

J. Fodor and J. J. Katz

But now, as we conclude, methinks I hear some objector, demanding with an air of pleasantry, and ridicule – 'Is there no speaking then without all this trouble? Do we not talk, everyone of us, as well unlearned as learned; as well poor Peasants, as Profound Philosophers?' We may answer by interrogating on our own part – Do not those same poor Peasants use the Lever and the Wedge, and many other Instruments, with much habitual readiness? And yet have they any conception of those Geometrical Principles, from which those Machines derive their Efficacy and Force? And is the Ignorance of these Peasants a reason for others to remain ignorant; or to render the Subject a less becoming Inquiry? Think of Animals, and Vegetables, that occur every day – of Time, of Place, and of Motion – of Light, of Colours, and of Gravitation – of our very Senses and Intellect, by which we perceive everything else – That they are, we all know, and are perfectly satisfied – What they are, is a Subject of much obscurity and doubt. Were we to reject this last Question, because we are certain of the first, we should banish all Philosophy at once out of the world.

JAMES HARRIS

In two recent articles, 'Must We Mean What We Say?' and 'The Availability of Wittgenstein's Later Philosophy'[2] (to which we shall refer as M and A, respectively), Professor Stanley Cavell has set forth his position on the relation between the claims Oxford philosophers make about ordinary-language and the methods and results of empirical investigations of ordinary language. These articles are important because they represent a viewpoint that is widely held by current philosophers – widely held but rarely made explicit. Cavell is surely right when he says that the conflict about the nature of our knowledge of ordinary language 'is not a side issue in the general conflict between Wittgenstein (together with, at this point "ordinary language philosophy") and traditional philosophy; it is itself an instance, an expression of that conflict' (A, p. 184 above). The position Cavell advocates in M and A seems to us, however, to be mistaken in every significant respect and to be pernicious both for an adequate understanding of ordinary-language philosophy and for an adequate understanding of ordinary language. In the present paper, we seek to establish that this is in fact the case.

In A, Cavell's main concern is to expose the inadequacies of David Pole's treatment of Wittgenstein's views on language. In the course of the exposé – especially in the section entitled 'The Knowledge of Our Language' – Cavell presents the substance of his conclusions about how we know about our native language. But since in A the exposé takes precedence over the exposition, we find little there in the way of argumentation for these conclusions. The arguments are found in M. M consists of an extensive investigation of the availability of our knowledge of our language, and we shall concern ourselves primarily (but not exclusively) with M.

Cavell begins by distinguishing three types of statements philosophers make about ordinary language:

(1) There are statements which produce *instances* of what is said in a language ('We do say ... but we don't say –'; 'We ask whether ... but we do not ask whether –'). (2) Sometimes these instances are accompanied by *explications* – statements which make explicit what is implied when we say what statements of the first type instance us as saying ('When we say ... we imply [suggest, say] –'; 'We don't say ... unless we mean –'). Such statements are checked by reference to statements of the first type. (3) Finally, there are *generalisations*, to be tested by reference to statements of the first two types (M, p. 132 above).

Cavell concerns himself with the question of the justification of statements of types 1 and 2 exclusively. Since the justification of type 3 statements is entirely a question of the degree to which they receive support from statements of types 1 and 2, it need not be considered independently.

Cavell selects as a paradigmatic example of a type 1 statement Austin's remark 'Take "voluntarily" ...: we ... may make a gift voluntarily.' This Cavell takes to be material mode for 'We say "The gift was made voluntarily"'. As a case of a type 2 statement,

Cavell chooses Ryle's remark 'In their most ordinary employment "voluntary" and "involuntary" are used ... as adjectives applying to actions which ought not to be done. We discuss whether someone's action was voluntary or not only when the action seems to have been his fault (M, p. 133 above).'[3]

Cavell recognises that these statements of Austin's and Ryle's go counter to one another: that there is a disagreement here that needs to be resolved. The basic question Cavell raises and seeks to answer is whether there is any reasonable sense in which such disagreements as this one are empirical. The position which Cavell evolves, and which we shall seek to refute, is that such disagreements are in *no* reasonable sense empirical.

According to Cavell, though Ryle is wrong about the use of 'voluntary', he is not wrong in the way that a scientist is when the scientist asserts a false hypothesis. That Ryle is wrong is, on Cavell's view, a fact for which we do not need and could not have empirical evidence. It is through an investigation of the character of Ryle's error that Cavell approaches the general question of the relation between empirical studies of language and the claims ordinary-language philosophers make about language.

Against the contention that Ryle is not entitled to his generalisation about 'voluntary' because it is unsupported by empirical evidence (or because it conflicts with empirical evidence), Cavell replies:

> We must bear in mind the fact that these statements – statements that something is said in English – are being made by native speakers of English. Such speakers do not, in *general*, need evidence for what is said in the language; they are the source of such evidence. It is from them that the descriptive linguist takes the corpus of utterances on the basis of which he will construct a grammar of that language ... but, in general, to tell what is and isn't English, and to tell whether what said is properly used, the native speaker can rely on his own nose; if not, there would be nothing to count (M, p. 133 above).

Thus Cavell argues that Ryle and other native speakers are entitled, without appeal to empirical evidence, to whatever type 1 statements they require to support their type 2 statements, since type 1 statements are not relevantly confirmed or disconfirmed by empirical evidence. As Cavell puts it, 'for a native speaker to say what, in ordinary circumstances, is said when, no special information is needed or claimed. All that is needed is the truth of the proposition that a natural language is what native speakers of that language speak (M, p. 134 above).'

This argument of Cavell's is, however, a *non sequitur*. Cavell argues from the premiss that a native speaker is the *source* of the linguist's empirical evidence for the description of a natural language, to the conclusion that the native speaker's statements about his language cannot, in turn, be in need of empirical evidence for their support. What Cavell misses is the distinction between what a native speaker says (the utterances he produces in the course of speaking) and what he says *about* what he and other native speakers say (the metalinguistic comments he makes when the reflective mood is upon him). There can be no doubt but that most (though definitely not all) of the utterances of a native speaker are utterances of the speaker's language. *This* truth *is* guaranteed by the truism that a natural language is what a native speaker of that language speaks. However, the statements that a native speaker makes about his language, his metalinguistic claims, need not be true in order for the linguist to have noses to count. What Cavell has failed to show is precisely that the possibility of an empirical description of a natural language presupposes the truth of the metalinguistic claims of its speakers.[4]

Cavell does admit that there are some questions about a natural language which require empirical evidence to answer them: these include questions about the history of a language, the sound system, and special forms in the morphology of a dialect (M, p. 134 above). But to distinguish all of these as areas of linguistics to which empirical evidence is relevant, while setting grammar and semantics apart as areas to which empirical evidence is not, is simply to make a distinction without a relevant difference. An argument might be given for classifying the history of a language and the study of special forms in the morphology of a dialect as areas about which the native speaker who is philologically naïve can say little. But clearly such an argument would be impossible in the case of the sound system, since the native speaker knows the sound system of his language in exactly the same way that he knows its syntax and semantics.[5] Thus, Cavell's statement that the native speaker's claims about the sound system of his language are empirical is inconsistent with what Cavell says about the native speaker's claims about the grammar and semantics of his language. Conversely, any argument showing that the native speaker has special licence to statements about the syntax and semantics would show also that he is similarly licensed to statements of the analogous form about the sound system.

But this constitutes a *reductio ad absurdum* of such an argument because, *inter alia*, it entails that a native speaker of English could never be wrong (or at least could not very often be wrong) about how he pronounces (we pronounce) an English word (or spells one?).

Cavell's explanation of how Ryle went wrong, even if it is wholly correct, fails to show that Ryle's mistake is not an out-and-out empirical error. Cavell's point is that Ryle specifies too narrowly the condition for applying the term 'voluntary', On Ryle's account, 'voluntary' can be applied only to 'action [which] seems to have been . . . [someone's] fault' (M, p. 135 above). But, as Cavell notes, such actions are only special cases of actions properly called voluntary. Giving the neighbourhood policeman a thousand dollars for Christmas instead of his usual bottle may be intelligibly described as voluntary, though no moral issue need be involved. Thus, Cavell concludes that the proper application of 'voluntary' is subject to the condition 'that there be something (real or imagined) fishy about any performance intelligibly so characterised (M, p. 136 above)' and that Ryle's mistake is to have formulated the condition in such a way as to leave out a large class of voluntary actions. But this explanation does not show Ryle's mistake to be non-empirical, because many empirical mistakes are of just this form. Consider a biologist who asserts the generalisation that all reproduction is sexual. He leaves out a large class of cases of reproduction, as, for example, fission, budding, and fragmentation. Thus, the biologist, like Ryle, errs by construing a condition too narrowly. The biologist takes the condition for the term 'reproduction' to be the production of offspring by sexually distinct parents. Since such uncircumspect generalisation is a typical pattern of error in empirical science, Cavell's explanation cannot by itself free Ryle from the onus of empirical error.

In order to show that the philosopher who proceeds from ordinary language is entitled without empirical investigation to assertions of type 2, Cavell says we have to explain three things: what kind of assertions type 2 assertions are; when they should be said, and by whom; and what should be meant in saying them (M, p. 140 above). In particular, Cavell wishes to derive from the answers to these questions the principle that when a type 2 statement is true it is necessarily true.

Cavell holds that type 2 statements are not analytic. Since, however, he wishes to argue that they are not empirical either, he ascribes to them the status of truths of 'Transcendental Logic'. In order to justify conferring this status upon them, type 2 state-

ments must be distinguished from certain merely empirical statements which are remarkably similar to them. First, there are assertions like: 'When we ask whether an action is voluntary we imply
that the action is fishy (M, p. 140 above).' This is simply a type 2
statement (call it S). Second, there are assertions like: ' "Is X
voluntary?" implies that X is fishy (M, p. 141 above).' For reasons
that will be made clear presently, this is not a type 2 statement but
merely an empirical one (call it T). Concerning the relation between
assertions like S and T, Cavell says the following:

> Though they are true together and false together, [they] are not
> everywhere interchangeable; the identical state of affairs is des-
> cribed by both, but a person who may be entitled to say T may not
> be entitled to say S. Only a native speaker of English is entitled to
> the statement S, whereas a linguist describing English may, though
> he is not a native speaker of English, be entitled to T. What entitles
> him to T is his having gathered a certain amount and kind of
> evidence in its favour. But the person entitled to S is not entitled to
> *that* statement for the same reason. He *needs* no evidence for it. It
> would be misleading to say that he *has* evidence for S, for that
> would suggest that he has done the sort of investigation the
> linguist has done, only less systematically and this would make it
> seem that his claim to know S is very weakly based. And it would
> be equally misleading to say that he does *not* have evidence for
> S because that would make it appear that there is something he
> still needs, and suggests that he is not yet entitled to S. But there
> is nothing he needs, and there is no evidence (which it makes
> sense, in general, to say) he has: the question of evidence is
> irrelevant (M, p. 141 above).

Since this is Cavell's main argument for claiming that native
speakers need no empirical evidence for statements like S, we must
examine it in detail.

Cavell's first mistake is to suppose that, granting that S and T are
true together and false together, anything whatever follows just
from the fact that S and T are not everywhere interchangeable. In
particular, none of the differences in status that Cavell finds between
S and T follow. No two morphemically distinct linguistic forms are
everywhere interchangeable preserving all properties of context, *not
even two synonymous versions of S*. Since Cavell conspicuously fails
to specify the properties of the context which must be preserved in
such substitution (fails to answer the question: interchangeable pre-

serving what?), what he says about S and T is literally applicable to every pair of morphemically distinct English forms. Consider the following two (synonymous) versions of S: (S) when we ask whether an action is voluntary we imply that the action is fishy; and (S′) when we ask whether an action is voluntary we imply the action is fishy. Even S and S′ are not interchangeable preserving every property of every context. For example, they are not interchangeable preserving truth or meaning in the context 'contains the word "that" ', nor are they interchangeable preserving truth, meaning, or non-oddity in the context 'contains more words than S′.' Thus, given only the information that two linguistic forms are not everywhere interchangeable, the *only* inference that can be drawn is that they are distinct in content or arrangement of morphemes. Furthermore, it is difficult to conceive of a property of contexts such that the failure to preserve that property when S and T are interchanged could be sufficient grounds for claiming that, though T is empirical, S is a truth of transcendental logic.

Cavell's second mistake consists of an outright contradiction. Cavell says that S and T are true together and false together, that is that $[(S \supset T)$ and $(T \supset S)]$. He also says that T is a statement to which someone is entitled only if he has the appropriate empirical evidence, that is that T is subject to empirical confirmation and disconfirmation. Finally, he says that S is a statement to which the question of evidence is wholly irrelevant, that is that S is not subject to empirical confirmation or disconfirmation. However, $[(S \supset T)$ and $(T \supset S)]$ implies both $(\sim T \equiv \sim S)$ and $(T \equiv S)$. From this it follows that any evidence which disconfirms T *ipso facto* disconfirms S and that any evidence which confirms T likewise confirms S.

Thus, Cavell is simply wrong when he says 'it is not clear what would count as a disproof of S' (M, p. 141 above). In particular, sufficient evidence for a disproof of T would constitute a disproof of S. If we discover, as we do, that speakers of English say such things as 'he joined the army voluntarily'[6] (that is, he was not conscripted), then, since no implication of fishiness is involved, S and T are both shown to be false.

It should be said at this point that we recognise that in making statements of types 1 or 2 the speaker of English may rarely need actually to conduct an empirical investigation of his own speech or that of other English speakers. But nothing follows from this either about the confirmability or disconfirmability of such statements or about their logical status. What is in question here is whether *in principle* there could be a case in which a type 1 or 2 statement, asserted by a native speaker, is empirically confirmed or disconfirmed. Cavell's position is the most extreme one. By taking such statements as necessary truths of transcendental logic, he precludes the possibility that any empirical evidence could ever be relevant to their confirmation or disconfirmation. Perhaps Cavell has failed to notice in this connection that there are indefinitely many statements which are clearly empirical but which, like statements of types 1 and 2, one normally does not need empirical evidence obtained by special investigation to assert. Consider the following: 'My name is not Stanley Cavell', 'I remember the good old days', 'Our family lives in Massachusetts', 'I own a hi-fi set', and so forth.

At the next step in his discussion, Cavell retreats from his former extreme position. Where he had previously contended that 'the question of evidence is irrelevant [to establishing the truth of statements like S]', he now argues:

> The claim that in general we do not require evidence for statements in the first-person plural present indicative, does not rest upon a claim that we cannot be wrong about what we are doing or about what we say, but only that it would be extraordinary if we were (often). My point about such statements, then, is that they are sensibly questioned only where there is some special reason for supposing what I say about what I (we) say to be wrong; only here is the request for evidence competent (M, p. 142 above).

Cavell's first mistake here is that of supposing that type 2 statements (or for that matter type 1 statements) are sensibly questioned *only* when there is a special reason for thinking that they may be false. Clearly, we often question statements, and sometimes demand evidence for them, because we know of no reason why they should be true. Accepting Cavell's condition on questioning statements and requesting evidence for them would make credulity a virtue and philosophy a vice.

Cavell's second mistake is that of maintaining that, assuming it would be extraordinary if we were often wrong about what we say, it is not competent to request evidence for such statements. If we are only usually right, then we are sometimes wrong. But then it is *always* competent to request evidence to show that *this* is not one of those times. Whether in any particular case a statement is in fact questioned and evidence demanded is a matter of the positive utility of being right and the negative utility of being wrong. But what

Cavell's view entails is that, even if one's life depended on deciding correctly whether to accept a type 2 statement, it would not be competent to question or demand evidence for the statement unless one had a special reason for supposing it to be false. In such circumstances, then, on Cavell's view, only the suicidal are competent.

Cavell's third mistake is to hold that we are not, in fact, often wrong about what we say about our language. What has gone wrong here is that Cavell has failed to recognise an important aspect of his own distinction between type 1 and type 2 statements. He is surely correct in maintaining that we are not often wrong when we make type 1 statements. This is not very surprising. Type 1 statements are, after all, no more than reports of rather simple and familiar facts about the speech habits of one's language community. But Cavell is surely wrong in maintaining that we are not often mistaken when we make type 2 statements, and this is not very surprising either. Type 2 statements are, in effect, a kind of theory; they are an abstract representation of the contextual features which determine whether a word is appropriately used. Referring to the literature of ordinary-language philosophy on such words as 'true', 'good', 'necessary', 'voluntary', 'mental', 'intentional', and so forth, will show that even sophisticated speakers are often wrong about type 2 statements.[7] It is far more difficult to be right about the conditions for using a word appropriately than it is to be right about the instances supporting claims about such conditions because statements of the former kind are explanations of the patterns of usage instanced by statements of the latter kind. Fallibility is the price paid for saying something interesting.

The case in which empirical evidence is most clearly relevant to evaluating what we say about our language is the one where two native speakers disagree about the truth of a type 1 or type 2 statement. But, curiously enough, Cavell fails to tell us how, on his account, such a disagreement could be decided without an appeal to empirical evidence. Consider a type 2 conflict where one native speaker asserts 'When we ask whether an action is voluntary we imply that the action is fishy', and another asserts 'When we ask whether an action is voluntary we do not imply that the action is fishy'. It does no good to argue that in such a case we should look to see which assertion is best supported by statements of type 1, since the same kind of conflict can arise there too: One native speaker asserts 'We say X but we don't say Y' and the other asserts 'We say Y but we don't say X'. One would suppose that, since each of the conflicting statements is in the first-person plural present indicative and since the 'we' occuring in them clearly refers to speakers of English in general,[8] only an empirical investigation of what speakers of English actually say could decide who is correct in such a disagreement. Since Cavell never considers a conflict of this kind, it is unclear how he would avoid this conclusion.

At the one point in M where the crucial question of a disagreement between native speakers about what we say might have arisen, Cavell skirts the problem entirely. 'Suppose', asks Cavell, '[a] baker is able to convince us that he does [use the words "inadvertently" and "automatically" interchangeably]. Should we then say "So [a] professor has no right to say how "*we* use" "inadvertently"; or to say that "when *we* use the one word we say something different from what we say when we use the other"?' (M, p. 158 above). Notice that these questions can be taken in two ways. First, they may be taken as asking what kind of information about the speech of the butcher, the candlestick-maker, and other English speakers the professor requires if he is to show that the baker's use of 'inadvertently' and 'automatically' is idiosyncratic. If Cavell had taken these questions in this way, he would have been obliged to show that the kind of information the professor requires to support his 'we' statements is not empirical in character. But Cavell does not take these questions in this way. Rather, he takes them to ask: if we already know (how we know we are not told) that the baker's use is idiosyncratic, does the fact that such idiosyncratic uses exist entail that the professor has no right to his 'we' statements? Cavell concludes that it does not, but it should be noticed that on this interpretation these questions are completely irrelevant to the essential problem of how one adjudicates a clash between native speakers.

Cavell is right when he argues that there is no sense in which the existence of idiosyncratic English uses precludes 'we' statements like the professor's; but he is right for the wrong reasons, and this is of considerable philosophical importance. The reason the professor is entitled to his 'we' statement, the baker's use to the contrary notwithstanding, is simply that the professor's statement is about standard (normal, common) English while the baker's use diverges idiosyncratically from the standard. The existence of three-legged dogs does not prevent the biologist from correctly asserting that dogs are quadrupeds. There could be no empirical generalisation if it were not possible to ignore unsystematic individual variations.[9] But this is not the argument Cavell gives. What he says is '[we can say to the baker] the distinction is there, in the language (as implements are there to be had), and you just impoverish what you can say by neglecting it. And there is something you aren't noticing about the world (M, p. 159 above).' It is clear why Cavell wants this argument: it is philosophically unimpressive to say to your opponent 'What you have just said diverges from standard English',[10] but it is most impressive to say to him 'What you have just said shows that there is something you are not noticing about the world'. And it is also impressive, though less so, to say 'If you don't make the distinction you just impoverish what you can say'. But the former argument is mistaken, and the latter is one to which we are not entitled merely on the grounds that someone uses as synonyms two words that are not interchangeable in English.

What is wrong with the latter argument is this: from the fact that a speaker does not mark a distinction using the words standardly employed to mark it, it does not follow that what he *can* say is thereby impoverished. There are expressions E_1 and E_2 which can be constructed in English such that E_1 is synonymous with the standard meaning of inadvertently' and E_2 is synonymous with the standard meaning of 'automatically'. Thus, the baker can say anything we can say about cases of inadvertent or automatic acts by using E_1 and E_2 where we use 'inadvertently' and 'automatically'. Of course, for the baker E_1 and E_2 will not be used interchangeably, nor will he realise that E_1 is synonymous in standard English with 'inadvertently' and that E_2 is synonymous in standard English with 'automatically'. Thus, on this account, the baker regards 'inadvertently' and 'automatically' as referring indiscriminately to the members of the set of acts which are either inadvertent or automatic in the standard sense, and he regards E_1 and E_2 as referring respectively to members of two mutually exclusive and exhaustive proper subsets of that set.[11]

There are two objections to Cavell's claim that if the baker uses 'inadvertently' and 'automatically' interchangeably, he fails to notice something about the world. First, it is simply false that we have distinct non-synonymous words for each distinction we notice. There are, for example, indefinitely many distinctions we make among shapes, colours, sizes, textures, sounds, and so forth, for which we have no individuating words. Hence, from the fact that we do not have distinct words to mark a distinction, nothing follows about whether or not we notice that distinction.

Second, even if it were the case that each and every distinction which speakers of English notice is marked by a pair of English words, Cavell's argument would fare no better. From the fact that the baker fails to make a distinction marked in English, Cavell could conclude that the baker fails to notice something about the world only at the price of complete triviality. To obtain a philosophically significant criticism of the baker, Cavell's argument requires a further assumption, namely that English is a philosophically privileged language with respect to the distinctions it codes. For there exist natural languages which code distinctions not coded in English, and there exist natural languages which do not code distinctions that are coded in English. The Eskimo-Aleut languages distinguish a wide variety of grades and types of what English speakers just call 'snow'; conversely, Shona (a language of Rhodesia) and Bassa (a language of Liberia) fail to code some of the colour distinctions coded in English.[12] Given these facts, we must ask: if the baker is missing something about the world just because he fails to draw a distinction coded in English, in what sense is the speaker of standard English *not* missing something about the world because he fails to draw a distinction coded by Eskimo-Aleut? Either Cavell says the English speaker is missing something about the world, or he says the English speaker is not. In the former case, the charge against the baker is completely trivialised because, then, *all* English speakers are missing every distinction coded in other languages but not in English. (The charge against the baker becomes vacuous when it is noticed that the speakers of all languages are also missing every distinction which could be, but is not as yet, coded in some language, that is, an infinite number of distinctions.) Cavell can avoid this trivialisation of his argument only by adopting the latter alternative, but this involves assuming that English is a privileged language, that is, that English codes all and only the distinctions that ought to be coded. But surely Cavell could not justify this assumption if only because, *inter alia*, it implies that Shona and Bassa speakers, simply by virtue of not speaking English, are missing distinctions they ought to draw and that Eskimos, simply by virtue of not speaking English, are drawing distinctions they ought to miss.

Obviously, none of these criticisms of Cavell's argument are intended to show that the baker, in using 'inadvertently' and 'automatically' interchangeably, may not be guilty of a philosophically significant error. What these criticisms do show is that one cannot establish that a philosophically significant error has been made *simply* by showing that someone has failed to draw a distinction coded in English. Moral: showing that one ought to draw a distinction is not something that can be done just by appealing to the way speakers in fact talk. This takes doing philosophy.

This mistake of inferring 'ought' statements about distinctions from 'is' statements about what speakers say deserves the name 'the Natural Language Fallacy'. The general philosophical importance of this fallacy is this: once the natural language fallacy has been recognised, it becomes necessary to raise seriously the question of the utility of appealing to what we ordinarily say as a means of resolving philosophical disagreements.

The conclusion at which Cavell arrives in A on the basis of the arguments from M that we have been considering is stated as follows:

> If it is accepted that 'a language' (a natural language) is what the native speakers of a language speak, and that speaking a language is a matter of practical mastery, then such questions as 'What should we say if...?' or 'In what circumstances would we call...?' asked of someone who has mastered the language (for example, oneself) is a request for the person to say something about himself, describe what he does. So the different methods are methods for acquiring self-knowledge: as – for different (but related) purposes and in response to different (but related) problems – the methods of 'free' association, dream analysis, investigation of verbal and behavioural slips, noting and analysing 'transferred' feeling, and so forth (A, p. 186 above).

From this it is apparent that underlying Cavell's whole position is a misconception about the availability of our knowledge of our language skills. It is obvious, but not worth arguing, that the knowledge we gain in correctly describing our language is in *some* sense self-knowledge. But this has no implications for the methods we can employ in discovering such knowledge, since the knowledge we gain in correctly describing human physiology is also in *that* sense self-knowledge. What is worth arguing is that anything we learn about ourselves when we describe the language we speak is also something we learn about every other speaker of standard English *qua* speaker of standard English. Conversely, anything we can learn about English by studying our own speech, we can in principle learn by studying the speech of speakers other than ourselves. This is what it means to say that we are studying English rather than the speech pathology and idiosyncracies of English speakers. Put it another way: any facet of a speaker's use of English that is not shared by other speakers is *ipso facto* not relevant to a description of English. It is perhaps Cavell's failure to grasp this principle that has led him to suppose that some special privilege accrues to statements we make about our language in the first-person plural present indicative.

We said at the outset that the position Cavell advocates is pernicious both for an adequate understanding of ordinary language and for an adequate understanding of ordinary-language philosophy. The first follows from Cavell's refusal to treat empirical questions with empirical methods. If we deny that the truth of our statements about our language must be established by the usual empirical means, we fail even to raise the question of what empirical constraints are relevant to adjudicating the adequacy of a putative description of a natural language. Clearly, answering this question must be the first step in the elaboration of any such description.[13]

That Cavell's position blocks an adequate understanding of ordinary-language philosophy follows from the fact that the Oxford philosopher, when he discusses the use of words, *is* pursuing an empirical investigation, and *is not* uncovering truths of transcendental logic. This, of course, does not mean that he goes about with pen and paper recording what people say, when they say it, how frequently it is said, and so on. That is a caricature of what the empirical investigation of language is like, though it seems to be the only conception Cavell entertains as an alternative to his viewpoint.[14] Rather, to say that the Oxford philosopher engages in empirical investigation is to say that his claims about English should be subject to the same modes of confirmation and disconfirmation that linguists accept.

What has until now distinguished the Oxford philosopher from the linguist is primarily a difference of focus. The linguist has traditionally been concerned with problems of phonology, phonemics, morphology, and syntax, while the Oxford philosopher has devoted himself almost exclusively to problems about meaning. What has distinguished some Oxford philosophers is their ingenuity at discovering recondite facts about how English speakers use their language. But methods of confirmation and disconfirmation distinguish neither the philosopher from the linguist nor the philosopher himself.

XI What we say

Richard Henson

Several years ago Professor Stanley Cavell (see Chapter VIII above) defended a view as to the status of a claim made by a native speaker about how he and his fellow native speakers talk – a view which has the welcome consequence that what 'ordinary language philosophers' say about their language does not require them to leave their armchairs. This view has recently been attacked by Jerry A. Fodor and Jerrold J. Katz (see Chapter X above). I shall not attempt a full summary of Cavell's paper or a full defence: I do not agree with all of it that I think I understand. But the arguments put forth by Fodor and Katz, while clearly and persuasively stated, seem to me to be often mistaken or inconclusive. I shall state their major arguments in the order in which they occur, numbering them consecutively throughout.

Cavell was concerned to show that Professor Benson Mates had been wrong about the methods necessary for determining 'what we say'; and he was faced with a case, discussed by Mates, which saw Ryle and Austin making incompatible claims about our use of 'voluntary' and 'voluntarily'. Ryle had said, with certain qualifications, that we apply these words only to actions which seem to be someone's fault (see Chapter I above). Austin, on the other hand, had remarked that 'we may join the army or make a gift voluntarily...' (see Chapter V above). Cavell agrees that Austin's examples show that Ryle was mistaken. The main point at issue, though, is the logical, or epistemic, character of certain statements which one makes about his own language, and in particular whether one needs empirical evidence for such statements. Cavell writes:

> ... native speakers of English ... do not, in *general*, need evidence for what is said in the language; they are the source of such evidence. It is from them that the descriptive linguist takes the corpus of utterances on the basis of which he will construct a grammar of that language ... but in general, to tell what is and isn't English, and to tell whether what is said is properly used, the

native speaker can rely on his own nose; if not, there would be nothing to count (M, pp. 133–4 above).

Here Fodor and Katz offer two criticisms:
(1) What Cavell misses is the distinction between what a native speaker says ... and what he says *about* what he and other native speakers say.

... What Cavell has failed to show is precisely that the possibility of an empirical description of a natural language presupposes the truth of the metalinguistic claims of its speakers (W, p. 193 above).[1]

(2) In respect to the kind of knowledge one has of his own language, Fodor and Katz assert that there is no difference between its grammar and semantics on the one hand and its sound system on the other.

... any arguments showing that the native speaker has special licence to statements about the syntax and semantics would show also that he is similarly licensed to statements of the analogous form about the sound system. But this constitutes a *reductio ad absurdum* of such an argument because, *inter alia*, it entails that a native speaker of English could never be wrong (or at least could not very often be wrong) about how he pronounces (we pronounce) an English word (or spells one?) (W, pp. 193–4 above).

Point (1) represents the view of Fodor and Katz on the general issue at stake in their paper and mine. Some of our metalinguistic remarks are indisputably wrong; but I postpone general discussion of which ones, and how, and what to make of it. As to (2), it seems evident that on certain questions concerning the sound system, a native speaker should prove nearly infallible, and on others not.[2, 3]

In Cavell's paper, a good deal hinges on the similarities and differences between two kinds of statements, typified by S: 'When we ask whether an action is voluntary we imply that the action is fishy', and T: ' "Is X voluntary?" implies that X is fishy.'

... though they are true together and false together, [they] are not everywhere interchangeable; the identical state of affairs is described by both, but a person who may be entitled to say T, may not be entitled to say S. Only a native speaker of English is entitled to the statement S, whereas a linguist describing English may, though he is not a native speaker of English, be entitled to T. What entitles him to T is his having gathered a certain amount and kind of evidence in its favour. But the person entitled to S is not entitled to *that* statement for the same reason. He *needs* no evidence for it. It would be misleading to say that he *has* evidence for S, for that would suggest that he has done the sort of investigation the linguist has done, only less systematically, and this would make it seem that his claim to know S is very weakly based. And it would be equally misleading to say that he does *not* have evidence for S, because that would make it appear that there is something he still needs, and suggests that he is not yet entitled to S. But there is nothing he needs, and there is no evidence (which it makes sense, in *general*, to say) he has: the question of evidence is irrelevant (M, p. 141 above; quoted on W, p. 195).

In his claim that statements S and T, though 'true together and false together', are not everywhere interchangeable and not epistemically justified in the same way, Fodor and Katz claim that Cavell makes two mistakes:

(3) His first is 'to suppose that, granting that S and T are true together and false together, anything whatever follows just from the fact that S and T are not everywhere interchangeable. . . . No two morphemically distinct linguistic forms are everywhere interchangeable preserving all properties of context, *not even two synonomous versions of S*' (W, p. 195 above).

(4) His second mistake 'consists of an outright contradiction', in that he (i) grants that S and T are 'true together and false together', i.e. that they are (as Fodor and Katz choose to put it) materially equivalent; (ii) says that T is subject to empirical confirmation and disconfirmation; (iii) says that empirical evidence is irrelevant to S. But from their material equivalence it follows that 'any evidence which disconfirms T *ipso facto* disconfirms S and that any evidence which confirms T likewise confirms S' (W, p. 196 above).

Point (3) is an *ignoratio elenchi*. The very passage which Fodor and Katz quote shows that Cavell does not claim that the important differences between S and T can be *inferred* from the fact that S and T are not everywhere interchangeable.

What Fodor and Katz intend in (4) is partly right and partly wrong. From the fact that two statements are materially equivalent it does not in general follow that what confirms or disconfirms one does the same for the other: what disconfirms 'a Russian invented the telephone' does not disconfirm 'Raphael designed St Mark's

Cathedral', although these are materially equivalent; and both are equivalent to 'three times three is twelve', to whose truth-value *no* empirical evidence is relevant. (I was so bewitched by Fodor and Katz on first reading that I needed my colleague, David W. Bennett, to point out this feature of confirmation and material equivalence to me.)

But this is perhaps unfair to Fodor and Katz: their argument is marred by the fact that they choose to represent Cavell's description of propositions like S and T as 'true together and false together' in terms of material equivalence, while in fact neither Cavell nor they were concerned with propositions which are connected in so weak a fashion. The letters 'S' and 'T' are not variables in this discussion, but names – although they represent, informally speaking, any pair of an indefinitely large class of pairs of expressions any of which could have served in the discussion just as well as S and T. It is presumably this latter fact which tempts Cavell to speak of them as true together and false together – for strictly speaking, S and T must each be either true or false, not swinging hand in hand from truth to falsity and back. Very well: let us grant that Fodor and Katz are thinking of pairs of expressions such that, within each pair, the members are not just materially equivalent, but are related as S and T are: i.e. are so related that they not only do, but must, have the same truth-value. Granted that they may not have intended to lay down a general principle about confirmation and mutual entailment – granted, that is, that they were not obliged to consider anything except the propositions S and T – I suggest that if Cavell is indeed guilty of a contradiction, then other pairs of expressions related as S and T are would generate a contradiction if the same things were said about them as he says about S and T; and I want to dispel the illusion that (4) is decisive by sketching a nearly parallel case in which a similar argument will be seen to fail. I apologise for the excessive familiarity of what I shall say about the parallel case.

Let U be my utterance 'My tooth aches'. Let V be someone else's utterance (on the same occasion) 'Henson's tooth aches'. I take it that U and V are 'true together and false together' – i.e. that depending on the occasion of utterance, U will be sometimes true and sometimes false, and that V will always have the same truth-value as U. Fodor might have some evidence in favour of V; it would *ipso facto* be evidence (for Fodor) that I was telling the truth in saying U. But it would be evidence *for Fodor*, and for Katz and for any other similarly situated observer; I am *not* similarly situated. I submit that the entire passage which I have quoted above (from

M, p. 206 above) would be perfectly correct if Cavell were speaking of U and V instead of S and T (and if other concomitant variations were introduced – reading 'person with a toothache' for 'native speaker', 'dentist' for 'linguist', etc.).

So much should help to dispel the illusion that (4) is decisive; it remains to show (i) that Cavell was right in what he said about S and T, not just that I am right about what could be said on similar lines about U and V; (ii) *how* the persuasive schema of (4) is mistaken. The former task must be attempted *ambulando*. The latter task then: the crucial weakness of that schema is in its omission of the fact that what confirms or disconfirms a given proposition depends in part upon the situation of the person to whom the 'evidence' is presented. In saying this I am not confusing confirmation with success in getting someone to believe something. What is (for you) good evidence that I have a toothache is not just as a matter of fact irrelevant to the strength of my belief, because I have already made up my mind or have enough evidence without it – I have *no* evidence, rather than too much of it to pay any more attention, and I am logically debarred from treating that 'evidence' as evidence *for me*. Similarly, in some cases I know something simply because I remember doing it, or seeing it, and what is genuine evidence for you that it happened is entirely irrelevant for me. Indeed, memory is fallible: *sometimes* I need evidence to corroborate what I (at least seem to) remember; but sometimes I do not. (See discussion of point (6) below.)

Now Fodor and Katz are right, in part: if T is proven to be false, and if S entails T, S is false; if T is proven to be true, and if T entails S, S is true. Similar things could be said of V and U; but it does not follow that evidence confirming V is evidence for *me* that my utterance, U, is true or probably so. Thus also for T and S.

So much, I am confident, is consistent with Cavell's view – but it includes a weighty concession to his critics. Neither Cavell nor they seem to me to be entirely right. When a native speaker says something like S, he does not normally say it on the basis of empirical evidence, much or little; but what if something like T should (at least seem to) be disconfirmed by empirical evidence? (I will henceforth use 'S_n' and 'T_n' as variables, representing any pair of statements related as S and T are.) There are several cases to consider:

(i) S_n (and thus T_n) may in fact be true, even though some evidence is uncovered which seems to count against them. This case is worth noticing only because it is worth remembering that disconfirmation is generally inconclusive.

(ii) The speaker may be ignorant of features of dialects other than his own, so that what he says about what 'we' say will be incompatible in those respects with T_n unless T_n is restricted to that speaker's dialect. This case does not, I think, vitiate Cavell's argument: I know of no case in which differences of dialect have led to an S-like claim's being mistaken in a philosophically interesting way. *The Concept of Mind* is not weakened by Ryle's failure to notice such expressions as '... the pore gentleman was mental.... For an 'ole hour, 'e went on something chronic.' (A sample of 'ordinary language' cited by Bertrand Russell.)[4] In the unlikely case that differences between dialects of the same language turn out not to be intertranslatable, and to have some conceptual significance, this would be of great interest: but even this would not tend to show that information from a user of one of those linguistic-conceptual systems about his own system is mistaken.

(iii) It may happen that T_n is decisively shown to be false by the evidence which a linguist gathers. Could such evidence induce the native speaker to withdraw his S_n? Well, what is to count here as empirical evidence? When one does withdraw such a claim, it is often because someone has offered him a case of a certain description and asked him whether he (or 'we' or 'one') would be willing to ask or say so-and-so about it. Suppose, for instance, that I have noticed that to say 'Jones is a capable fellow' is to say something good of him, to say that he can generally be expected to succeed at things at which he, and probably other people, want him to succeed. And suppose I say 'We don't say that something is capable of something, unless we regard that something as good. We say *'liable* to err', but *"capable* of success".' My generalisation is of course false. Someone might get me to see that it is false by asking 'What about "I think he's capable of murder"?' Presented with this suggestion, I might very well modify my initial claim. Now have I been presented with *evidence* against that claim? I have not necessarily, on this occasion, (*a*) observed someone using (as distinct from raising a question about the use of) the expression, (*b*) been given any research reports on its use, (*c*) looked it up in Fowler, (*d*) remembered myself or another using it.[5] Presented with the example, I have realised that that is a perfectly proper use of the word, such as I or any other native speaker might employ (see M, p. 133, above, first new paragraph). An outsider might have as evidence against my initial generalisation either the fact that native speakers do use the phrase 'capable of murder' with some frequency, or the fact that they report to him that they would be quite willing to use it, that it does not sound odd, etc. But *I* did not weigh any such evidence in coming to realise that I had been mistaken: I did not count my own nose.

A harder case remains. (iv) Suppose I have uttered S (or some sentence S_n) and am presented with statistical data against T (or T_n). Well, what shape is this evidence supposed to be in? Does it take the form 'On such-and-such occasions, native speakers were found to discuss the question whether certain actions were voluntary but did not consider the action in question in any way fishy'? If so, I might be quite unmoved by the data, and sensibly so: I might wonder how the investigator was sure the actions were not considered fishy, who (the investigator?) introduced the word 'voluntary', and so on. Or do the data take the form of more detailed specification of the circumstances of utterance of 'voluntary'? In this case, they might serve me exactly as well as – *and in the same way as* – the examples that someone might present for my consideration in connection with the previous case, e.g. the phrase 'capable of murder'. Suppose, though, that the data gained by other people from close observation of the speech of my language community do in fact conflict with some statement S_n, and suppose that the specific counter-examples are described to me in full – suppose then that I do not budge, that I still claim that they are improper or do not make sense.

Now the fact that this is logically possible does not establish that it happens; and a more careful treatment of this whole problem would include detailed analyses of several kinds of cases in which it seems to or does happen. But I reluctantly concede that it probably does. If so, this a serious weakness in my position; the most serious, I hope, because it seems very serious indeed. I offer for consideration two relevant facts and an argument; I shall discuss the matter further in connection with point (7) below. One fact is that some people simply speak more carefully than others, and some have a keener ear for the linguistic proprieties. I do not see the significance of this fact clearly enough to know whom it helps; but it is a fact. Another fact is that when philosophers are discussing and especially when they are arguing about the use of an expression, they are likely to be in a peculiarly bad condition for getting it right, and this for at least two reasons: they let their philosophical prejudices get in the way, and they suffer from sheer excess of concentration. Compare the distortion of one's normal perceptions which may occur when one stares at a familiar object – or repeats a familiar word over and over – until it becomes strange. Perhaps our trouble here comes from the fact that in such cases, as in arguments about what we say, the usual background fades away, with resultant distortion in that which is at the centre of attention.[6] But I confess peculiar dissatisfaction with what I have been saying. Does it reduce to the assertion that when such a conflict between native speakers occurs, it is because either (a) they lack sufficient erudition and/or are not paying close attention to what they are saying, or (b) they are too sophisticated and/or are paying too close attention? (I do not have a handy index of optimum sophistication and/or closeness of attention.)

The argument bearing on the point (as promised in the preceding paragraph) is this: in order to *understand* and thus in order to evaluate evidence against any statement S_n which I might make, I should of course have to rely on my knowledge of the language in which it is presented to me; and that language might be my own and could not be a language which I know better than 'my own'. (This is tautological.) If S_n concerned a locution with which I am sufficiently familiar, then evidence which counted against my S_n might strike so deeply at my confidence in my knowledge of my own language that it would be simply impossible for me to accept: it would count as strongly against my understanding the sentences in which it (the evidence) was formulated as against my original claim.[7]

Cavell had said that it would be extraordinary if we were often wrong in statements about what we say, made in the first-person plural present indicative; 'they are sensibly questioned only where there is some special reason for supposing what I say about what I (we) say to be wrong; only here is the request for evidence competent' (M, p. 142 above). In this connection, Fodor and Katz accuse Cavell of several mistakes.

(5) He says that type 2 statements[8] can be sensibly questioned only where we have special reason to think them false, whereas Fodor and Katz point out that 'we often question statements, and sometimes demand evidence for them, because we know of no reason why they should be true' (W, p. 197 above).

(6) They add:

If we are only usually right, then we are sometimes wrong. But then it is *always* competent to request evidence to show that *this* is not one of those times. Whether in any particular case a statement is in fact questioned and evidence demanded is a matter of the positive utility of being right and the negative utility of being wrong (W, p. 197 above).

(What Fodor and Katz presumably mean here is 'Whether in any particular case a statement *ought* to be questioned. . .').

(7) He holds that we are not often wrong in what we say about our own language; Fodor and Katz grant this for type 1 statements but not for type 2 statements, since a type 2 statement is 'a kind of theory . . . an abstract representation of the contextual features which determine whether a word is appropriately used' (W, p. 198 above). Fodor and Katz claim that even the literature of the ordinary-language philosophers is rich in disagreements on type 2 statements – witness Ryle and Austin on 'voluntary'. They remark that Cavell does not discuss cases in which there is a flat disagreement on such a statement; and they claim that such disagreements cannot be resolved by reference to the relevant type 1 assertions, 'since the same kind of conflict can arise there too' (W, p. 198 above).

Point (7) is the one which has great weight; I shall deal first with (5) and (6), which I think have little. As to (5), when I make a type 1 (or even a type 2) statement, I can hardly be in the position of having no reason to think that it is true: I am a component of the 'we' whose practice I am reporting, and I have learned the practice from other members of that group. Point (6) seems weak, even outside the realm of the special kind of knowledge under discussion. I am sometimes wrong in my computations in elementary arithmetic; does it follow that I may now be wrong in saying three and four are seven, or that it is 'competent' to require special investigation in this case? I am sometimes mistaken in matching a given person with a given name; does it follow that I can now sensibly raise the question whether my own name is Richard, or my daughter's Elizabeth? My general objection to Fodor and Katz here may be put as follows: from the fact that one is sometimes mistaken in his assertions about members of a class of entities K, it does not follow that he may on just any occasion be mistaken in just any assertion about some member k of that class. For k may belong to a more or less clearly delimited subclass of K, concerning which subclass he is never mistaken, or never mistaken without there being, on the occasion of his mistake, special features which prompt doubt. (In delirium or amnesia, perhaps I *would* be mistaken about or ignorant of my daughter's name.)

The seventh point is the crucial one. Some consideration of the claim that a type 2 statement is a 'theory' will help us see an important difference which Cavell seems to me to slight, though he is clearly not oblivious to it. The difference in question is between (i) generalising as to what we mean when we say so-and-so, and

(ii) recognising cases *described in some detail* as ones in which, if one said so-and-so, he would be taken to mean or not to mean such-and-such. Utterances of both these kinds are generalisations; the former are more general, in that they abstract from the more or less detailed sketch of circumstances which distinguishes the latter. Since an account of circumstances can be indefinitely detailed, there is perhaps no difference in principle between the two kinds of utterances; but there is more difference in their epistemic status than one might expect from the difference in generality. The former kind is indeed, as Fodor and Katz claim, 'a kind of theory', and of course one might over-generalise about it. The latter, if theory at all, is theory of a very special kind.

Suppose someone asks me whether, when I count, I say 'five' before 'six', or vice versa. If I take the question seriously at all, I suppose I could resolve it right there by counting past six, and finding which I did. Am I then *theorising* about my own practice? Well, I don't say to myself 'First I say "one"; then I say "two" . . .' – I just *say* 'One, two . . .'. This makes for an enormous difference between the status of my report on how I count and the status of my report, say, on how I tie my shoelaces. The latter action is perfectly familiar, but to my fingers rather than to my tongue. If I had to describe it, I should do it either through an effort of imagination or by actually tying them and reporting my actions step by step; but either way, the action described would be different from the act of describing it. But if asked how I count, I do not (need not) perform two different actions at all.

I shall turn in a moment to some of the relevant respects in which counting is an atypical use of language. But what I have tried to bring out is that in some circumstances we tell (or show) how we would perform some linguistic act simply by doing it. And when we are presented with a suitably detailed sketch of a situation and asked what we would say, or what we would imply, suggest, or whatnot, in saying it, we are very close to that kind of case. Thus the vast difference between *this* sort of question about how we talk, and questions about what is *generally* meant by the use of a given expression. It is a familiar fact that we can generalise after candid and careful reflection and be wrong, even when the materials which should have shown us that we were wrong are in some sense accessible to us, (sometimes) in memory. 'I don't believe I have ever known of a star football player who was also an outstanding middle-distance runner.' 'But how about Ollie Matson?' Of course: once reminded, I realise that I know, and in some sense have known all

along, that Matson was both a star football player and an outstanding quarter-miler, thus an outstanding middle-distance runner.
No research was needed to persuade me that my remark was wrong,
no expert testimony; simply a reminder. I do not mean to suggest
that this item of knowledge, temporarily unaccessible to me, was
not empirical; I am trying rather to bring out the fact that we
sometimes generalise incorrectly even when the knowledge we need
to show our mistake is all but immediately available – available,
so to speak, for the asking. It is abundantly clear that the same sort
of thing happens when we make type 2 statements. The moral is that
the proper cure for such mistakes in type 2 assertions is through
'assembling reminders' consisting of detailed accounts of cases
(see note 6).

We are hardly through with the question what kind of theory a
type 2 statement is, however. Even in the case of counting, one might
claim that I must make several empirical assumptions before I can
get much good out of it. For the question was not just 'Will you on
this occasion say "five" before "six"?' but '*Do* you (regularly)
say ...?' Am I not then *assuming* that what I did on that occasion
was typical of my general practice? And is it not an empirical
question whether my practice accords with that of my fellow native
counters?

But how seriously can such questions be taken? Sometimes they
can be seriously raised – with a child who has not yet quite
mastered counting, with a person suspected to be suffering from
aphasia.... But a community in which people counted idiosyncratically – in which each man, in counting, 'had his little ways' –
would be a community in which *counting* did not take place.
(Can you play chess without the *moves*?) It is an empirical question
whether we do have such a practice, but this is not the issue. It is an
empirical question whether, on a given occasion, I am in some
pathological state which prevents me from counting properly. But
we are not here concerned with pathological counters; nor are
philosophers of ordinary language concerned with pathological
speakers.

Counting, though, is a use of language which is peculiarly
favourable to my views. It lacks borderline cases, eccentricities which
are only perhaps errors, etc. It is almost unique in that there is, at
each step in the process, exactly one right number and so (except
for minor elasticities, as between 'one hundred and one' and 'one
hundred one') exactly one right word or phrase to use. A similar
situation prevails in respect to certain religious and legal formulae;

but for the most part, there will be several different ways of saying whatever one wants to say in a given situation; and occasionally there may be no standard way of saying it. But still, though the rules are vastly more complex and flexible, these other uses of language are governed by rules, and the meaningfulness of an expression *consists in* its conformity to those rules.

The familiar 'game' analogy will be useful for exposition. One who plays a game which is moderately complex and highly organised must know the rules and a good deal of its strategy and tactics. There may be *some* rules with which he is unacquainted, although of course such ignorance tends to put him at a disadvantage. There are also likely to be occasional situations not covered by the rules, such that only ambiguous (if any) guidance to player and official can be gained from the rules. But (in the moderately complex and highly organised games to which these remarks are limited) it must be very rare that a player is ignorant how or whether a rule applies to a given situation. Otherwise, he would simply be unable to play the game, and his incapacities would quickly become evident to the other players. One who plays the game often and fairly well knows and can say how 'we' play it and does not need to take surveys or (except in especially out-of-the-way cases) consult the rule-book. What a beginner, or any outsider, learns as he comes to the game is empirical in character; the rules might have been different, and of course there are official bodies which make certain changes in the rules of many games. But we are talking about an experienced player of the game and the epistemic status of his reports on how it is played.

The analogy to our uses of language seems to me to be close, differing however in at least these respects: (1) The rules of a (complex, highly organised) game are likely to be more strict and inflexible and comprehensive than the rules of language, deliberately designed to cover any situation the rule-makers can envision. Innovation is often possible in language without prior notice, so to speak, but in the rules of games it bespeaks bullying or chicanery. In this regard, the game analogy perhaps makes my case look better than it deserves; but in the following two respects, the analogy makes my case look weaker than it deserves. For the rules of most of our 'language games' differ from those of other games also in that (ii) the 'rule-books' for language are not used in the same way as those for games; in particular, a dictionary or a grammar is to be tested by its fidelity to the practice of the speakers, instead of violations being authoritatively established as such by the fact that a player has gone against the rule-book, as in a game. And (iii) many of the rules of games impose what might be called 'external impediments' to a player's achievement of his goals, which, of course, are also normally specified in the rule-book. (Given that the object of a football player is, at a given moment, to score a touchdown, and granting that some of the rules specify what is to count as a touchdown, there are other rules which prohibit certain kinds of blocking by his team-mates, prohibit him from throwing a second forward pass in a single play, prohibit him from 'hurdling' a defender, and so on. I call these 'external' impediments, because they could be changed without reconstituting the game, without affecting its basic objectives or strategy. And of course such rules are changed from time to time, often to maintain an interesting balance between attack and defence in the game. But generally speaking the rules of language are not of this sort; one does not normally try to achieve certain things in the use of language, feeling its rules as impediments; it would not often make sense to *wish that the rules were different*, or that one could suspend them, so that one could achieve one's ends more readily – as it often would in a game. It is exactly through fidelity to these rules that one does achieve what he does, in most uses of language; it is through the common understanding of the rules that it becomes clear to one's listener what moves in the *language* game are being made.)

These differences – (ii) and (iii) – between the role of rules in such games as football and in our use of language, seem to me to tell strongly in favour of my position. From (ii), we see more clearly that the 'native player' of a language-game is normally one of the collective arbiters of correctness, superior to any rule-book; from (iii), we can perhaps see more clearly that in the mastery of a language, one's knowledge of the common rules is not necessary merely for engaging in the activity properly, or elegantly, or efficiently, but for his engaging in it – making and appreciating its moves – at all. (Much of what I have said would be mistaken if one interpreted, e.g., frightening or amusing people as 'uses of language' in this context. These and many other things can sometimes be done without following any linguistic rules at all. See – of course – Austin's *How to do Things with Words* (Oxford, 1962).)

Fodor and Katz next offer a battery of criticisms of what Cavell says about a case in which there appears to be a significant difference between the ways in which a pair of native speakers speak. Cavell asks us to suppose that we become convinced that someone (a baker) uses the words 'inadvertently' and 'automatically' interchangeably:

he claims that this does not prevent someone else (a professor) from saying that when 'we' use the one word, we mean something different from what we mean when we use the other; and the professor is entitled also to say to the baker 'the distinction is there, in the language (as implements are there to be had), and you just impoverish what you can say by neglecting it. And there is something you aren't noticing about the world' (M, p. 159 above).

Fodor and Katz point out that Cavell assumes without argument that the case is one in which the baker's use is idiosyncratic, i.e. that we already know that there is a difference in meaning between this pair of words. Cavell's discussion of it cannot be expected to throw light, then, on the difficult questions we have just been discussing, concerning the possibility of conflict between native speakers, or between the reports of one of them and the results of empirical study of their practice. But they offer a doubtful argument against Cavell's claim that the baker's speech must be impoverished.

(8) It may be the case that English contains expressions exactly synonymous with 'automatic' and 'inadvertent' – indeed, they claim that 'there are' such expressions 'which can be constructed in English' (W, p. 200 above). (I find this claim puzzling: *are* there such expressions, or is it only that they can be 'constructed'?) But if there are such expressions, they say, the baker may of course use them to mark the distinction(s) which others mark by using 'inadvertent' and automatic'; so his speech is not necessarily impoverished.

Well, one who misses a distinction between such a pair of words *may* notice, nevertheless, the difference(s) which they mark; and he *might* be able to 'construct' some other expression to mark the difference in question. (A Bushman who lacks words for numbers over five *might* be able to tell that five groups of four dingoes total fewer dingoes than three groups of seven.) But at what stage of discourse will the baker's rectification prove effective? When he speaks to other people? How easily will they find out (*a*) that he does not distinguish between the meanings of the two words, and (*b*) which of them he uses as the other one ought to be used (supposing, that is, that he does use *one* of them correctly and the other one like it)? And – a far harder question – what about the impoverishment of his understanding of what others say? He will not 'translate' what they say into his own idiom, because he does not realise that translation is necessary. The baker's insensitivity may not lead *him* into any philosophical difficulty, because he may not engage in philosophical debate; but the remarks of Fodor and Katz suggest that they may be thinking of meaning as a private mental activity. If it were that, one could mean what he chose to mean by his words, or perhaps one could simply *mean*, without bothering to use words; although he could still not simply *understand*, without listening to and discriminating the words of others. But if we are disabused of that error, it is hard to avoid the conclusion that the baker's speech and especially his comprehension of the speech of others is seriously impoverished.

As to Cavell's allegation that the baker fails to notice something about the world, Fodor and Katz offer two objections:

> (9) First, it is simply false that we have distinct non-synonymous words for each distinction we notice. . . . Hence, from the fact that we do not have distinct words to mark a distinction, nothing follows about whether or not we notice that distinction (W, p. 200 above).

And (10), even if it were true that the baker is failing to notice a distinction marked by this pair of English words, this is philosophically unimportant unless we assume that English 'is a philosophically privileged language with respect to the distinctions it codes' (W, p. 201 above). Many natural languages code distinctions which English does not, and *vice versa*; and there are innumerable differences which could be but are not coded by any natural language. If it were the case – as they have argued it is not – that a speaker necessarily misses whatever distinctions are not coded in his (perhaps partly idiosyncratic) lexicon, then Fodor and Katz point out that every speaker of any natural language would be missing not only every distinction coded by other languages and not his own, but also the innumerable differences which are not marked by *any* natural language. The accusation that the baker is not noticing something about the world is thus 'completely trivialised' (W, p. 201 above). It does not follow from all this, according to our authors, that the baker *cannot* be making some philosophically significant mistake in his idiosyncratic use of these words.

> What these criticisms do show is that one cannot establish that a philosophically significant error has been made *simply* by showing that someone has failed to draw a distinction coded in English. Moral: showing that one ought to draw a distinction is not something that can be done just by appealing to the way speakers in fact talk. This takes doing philosophy.

This mistake of inferring 'ought' statements about distinctions from 'is' statements about what speakers say deserves the name 'the natural language fallacy'. The general philosophical importance of this fallacy is this: once the natural language fallacy has been recognised, it becomes necessary to raise seriously the question of the utility of appealing to what we ordinarily say as a means of resolving philosophical disagreements (W, pp. 201–2 above).

Fodor and Katz are of course right that we notice many differences not 'coded' by pairs of words in our language, and that many other languages code some of these and miss some of the differences which are coded in English. They are presumably well aware of the fact (and this is perhaps what they allude to in their remark about 'constructing' expressions) that the lack of a single word in one natural language which is exactly synonymous with a single word of another by no means establishes that the speakers of the former cannot notice or give expression to the concept carried by that word in the latter. (See their references, note 12 above.)

But two considerations occur to me in favour of Cavell's remark that the baker would be missing something 'about the world'.

(i) In reply to the charge that Cavell's argument is 'trivialised', let us suppose that someone reproaches me for being a teacher when I might make substantially more money, say, in real estate; I reply 'You reproach me for not making a few thousand dollars more a year? How trivial that would be in comparison with the billions of dollars I should still not be making – not to mention the francs, piastres, pesos, and the untapped wealth which no one is yet making.' I acknowledge that the analogy is not quite fair and the reply partly (perhaps 40 per cent) facetious. Consider then any scientist who abandons a research project because what he can hope to learn is as nothing to what he will still be ignorant of. In short, to notice something worth noticing is to do something worth doing, even though one cannot notice everything worth noticing.

(ii) What I said in connection with the 'impoverishment' charge applies to the argument I have numbered (9) above. Here I add only that Fodor and Katz may be right that 'from that fact that we do not have distinct words to mark a distinction, nothing follows about whether or not we notice that distinction', although I should agree with Roger Brown[9] that the presence of a lexical clue in a given language (e.g. a word for a particular kind of snow) probably increases the 'cognitive availability' of whatever that word characterises (e.g. the difference between that kind of snow and other kinds). But where there *is* a distinct lexical clue provided by the vernacular and a native speaker fails to distinguish between the relevant expressions, it seems a plausible assumption that he *is* failing to notice the difference. That Bushman whose language has no numbers above five cannot be assumed to be incapable of telling the difference between a pack of eight dingoes and a pack of twenty; but if one of us (whose language contains the words for five and twenty and lots of other numbers) never used different number-words for different-sized packs over five, there might be reason for suspicion.

The real importance of the issues discussed in the last few paragraphs presumably lies in their bearing on 'the natural language fallacy': but our authors' enunciation of the fallacy is so brief that I am (almost) at a loss what to say about it. I take it that they might be paraphrased thus: it is a mistake to think that the distinctions which are in fact coded by a given natural language are the ones, and the only ones, which one ought to notice. (This is not the only sense which their words might be given: I hope they do not mean 'What a word does mean is irrelevant to what it should (be used to) mean'.) If I interpret them correctly, they are clearly right in one part of this conjoint claim: but neither Cavell nor anyone else has said that such distinctions are the *only* ones which one ought to notice. (See – if this requires any support – Cavell's first paragraph on p. 164 above.) But I am at a loss to see what reason could be given for denying that one ought to notice the distinctions which *are* coded in one's own language. To say they are coded in the language is to say that they are marked in the linguistic practice of those who speak the language, not just recorded in a lexicon which may be obsolete or pedantically over-refined, or whatnot. Of course one does not on every occasion want to make every distinction for which the language offers scope (if indeed that is a coherent suggestion). But in using a natural language, we are not obliged thus to use it to the hilt, so to speak: and to use it correctly, we must mark the distinctions coded by such parts of it as we are using.

Finally, Fodor and Katz consider Cavell's remark that

such questions as 'What should we say if . . .?' or 'In what circumstances would we call . . .?', asked of someone who has mastered the language . . . is a request for the person to say something about himself, describe what he does. So the different methods [of determining how we talk] are methods for acquiring self-knowledge . . . (A, p. 186 above).[10]

(11) Granting that the knowledge in question is 'in *some* sense self-knowledge', Fodor and Katz remark that 'this has no implications for the methods we can employ in discovering such knowledge, since the knowledge we gain in correctly describing human physiology is also in *that* sense self-knowledge' (W, p. 202 above). And in a most telling passage:

> (12) any facet of a speaker's use of English that is not shared by other speakers is *ipso facto* not relevant to a description of English. It is perhaps Cavell's failure to grasp this principle that has led him to suppose that some special privilege accrues to statements we make about our language in the first-person plural present indicative (W, pp. 202–3 above).

In the last quotation but one, Cavell speaks of the respondent as being asked to 'describe what he does', and this language seems appropriate. Speaking is something we *do*, not something which happens to us or in us; we sometimes choose our words deliberately, and we seldom say what we say unintentionally. None of us is today so innocent as to think that the concept of intentional action is easy to characterise, or that what we do intentionally is *ipso facto* easy to report accurately or even honestly; but I cannot take seriously the suggestion that it is 'inaccessible' in the degree and manner in which the facts of physiology are.

What I have said above, about counting and the rules of games, is the rest of my answer to point (11) and most of my answer to (12). I have admitted that our use of words is very seldom as strictly uniform as our use of the numerals in counting; but it must also be admitted that to speak a language just is to speak it, with very minor aberrations, as the other members of the linguistic community speak it. The problem of dialect is certainly important here, not only in that some speakers will be familiar with special technical vocabularies unknown to others, but also in that people at one level of education will use correctly words which people at a different level will sometimes use incorrectly. But it cannot be too heavily stressed that it is not this kind of difficulty about 'how to talk' that contributes to philosophical error. If a native speaker says 'When we call something "precious", we mean . . .' it is possible that he will be unfamiliar with the sense of the word in which a drama critic describes a performance as 'perhaps somewhat precious'. But this is simply not the kind of problem that causes trouble for philosophers, whatever it may do for lexicographers. The disagreement over 'voluntary' did not arise from this sort of ignorance; and no extravagant erudition distinguishes the users of such words as 'know', 'see', 'good', 'prove', 'true', 'think', 'mean', 'explain', or 'faith'. Our use of such words could not, in general, be any more idiomatic than our practice of making change or keeping score in a game. I am looking at one side of the coin which Fodor and Katz see from the other side when they say that 'any facet of a speaker's use of English that is not shared by other speakers is *ipso facto* not relevant to a description of English'. Fair enough; and my side of the coin reads something like 'One who moves his knight like a bishop is not accepted as a chess player'. (Inscriptions on coins must be brief and unqualified; some of my qualifications and explanations are in preceding parts of the paper. A large question which I have not tried to answer except partially and negatively is: What deviations from the common linguistic practice are philosophically significant? I shall try to deal with this question in another place.)

How important is this dispute about the epistemic status of our knowledge of our own language for the 'ordinary language philosophy'? None of the parties to this discussion has suggested that we cannot by *any* means find out what we say, or what we mean in saying it; and is this not enough to enable the ordinary-language philosophy to bear whatever burdens it must? We can answer only tentatively pending a full account of the nature of those burdens; but I am inclined to agree with Mates, Cavell, Fodor, and Katz that the present dispute is of great importance.

Cavell has done much to bring out this importance, in passages not discussed by Fodor and Katz or by me. More should be said about this than he said or than I shall attempt here. For the present: the 'oppressive' effect of the ordinary-language philosophy which Cavell mentions (M, p. 131 above) comes partly from the fact that, with exceptions and qualifications which have been dealt with here only partially and skimpily (I have said nothing about poetic deviations, for instance), it tells us that we must mean what we say, i.e. what *is meant* by one who utters the words we utter.[11] (I do not pause to argue this now familiar point here.) Any private intention of meaning such-and-such in using a form of words which is not accepted in the practice of the community as an appropriate bearer of that meaning is irrelevant to what is meant. But such an account of meaning can be true only if our knowledge of what we say and what we mean in saying it is – except in very special cases – immune to refutation by empirical evidence about how we talk.

XII Philosophical discoveries[1]

R. M. Hare

I

There are two groups of philosophers in the world at present who
often get across one another. I will call them respectively 'analysts'
and 'metaphysicians', though this is strictly speaking inaccurate –
for the analysts are in fact often studying the same old problems of
metaphysics in their own way and with sharper tools, and the metaphysicians of an older style have no exclusive or proprietary right to
the inheritance of Plato and Aristotle who started the business. Now
metaphysicians often complain of analysts that, instead of doing
ontology, studying *being qua being* (or, for that matter, *qua* anything
else), they study only *words*. My purpose in this paper is to diagnose
one (though only one) of the uneasinesses which lie at the back of
this common complaint (a complaint which analysts of all kinds,
and not only those of the 'ordinary-language' variety, have to
answer). The source of the uneasiness seems to be this: there are
some things in philosophy of which we want to say that we *know*
that they are so – or even that we can *discover* or *come to know*
that they are so – as contrasted with merely deciding arbitrarily that
they are to be so; and yet we do not seem to know that these things
are so by any observation of empirical fact. I refer to such things as
that an object cannot both have and not have the same quality.
These things used to be described as metaphysical truths; now it is
more customary, at any rate among analysts, to express them meta-
linguistically, for example by saying that propositions of the form
'*p* and not *p*' are analytically false. An analyst who says this is
bound to go on to say what he means by such expressions as
'analytically false'; and the account which he gives will usually be
of the following general sort: to say that a proposition is analytically
false is to say that it is false in virtue of the meaning or use which
we give to the words used to express it, and of nothing else. But this
way of speaking is not likely to mollify the metaphysician; indeed,
he might be pardoned if he said that it made matters worse. For
if philosophical statements are statements about how words are

actually used by a certain set of people, then their truth will be contingent – whereas what philosophers seem to be after are necessary truths: but if they are expressions of a certain philosopher's *decision* to use words in a certain way, then it seems inappropriate to speak of our *knowing* that they are true. The first of these alternatives would seem to make the findings of philosophy contingent upon linguistic practices which might be other than they are; the second would seem to turn philosophy into the making of fiats or conventions about how a particular writer or group of writers is going to use terms – and this does not sound as if it would provide answers to the kind of questions that people used to be interested in, like 'Can an object both have and not have the same quality, and if not why not?' This is why to speak about 'decisions' (Henle, op. cit., pp. 753 ff.) or about 'rules' which are 'neither true nor false' (Körner, op. cit., pp. 760 ff.) will hardly assuage the metaphysician's legitimate anxiety, although both of these terms are likely to figure in any successful elucidation of the problem.

It is worth pointing out that this dilemma which faces the analyst derives, historically, from what used to be a principal tenet of the analytical movement in its early days – the view that all meaningful statements are either analytic (in the sense of analytically true or false) or else empirical. From this view it seems to follow that the statements of the philosopher must be either empirical or analytic; otherwise we can only call them meaningless, or else not really statements at all but some other kind of talk. Many analysts failed to see the difficulty of their position because of a confusion which it is easy to make. It is easy to suppose that the proposition that such and such another proposition is analytically true, or false (the proposition of the analyst), is itself analytic, and therefore fits readily into one of the approved categories of meaningful discourse. But though it may *perhaps* be true, it is not *obviously* true that to say 'Propositions of the form "*p* and not *p*" are analytically false' is to make an analytically true statement; for is not this a statement about how the words 'and not' are used? And is it analytically true that they are used in this way? There are conflicting temptations to call the statement analytic, and empirical, and neither. The early analysts therefore ought to have felt more misgivings than most of them did feel about the status of their own activities; and this might have made them more sympathetic towards the metaphysicians, whose activities are of just the same dubious character (neither clearly empirical nor clearly analytic).

This is not to say that the matter has not been widely discussed since that time; and indeed there are certain well-known simple remedies for the perplexity. But I am not convinced that the disease is yet fully understood; and until it is, metaphysicians and analysts will remain at cross-purposes. It is a pity that the early analysts, in general, tended to follow the lead, not of Wittgenstein, but of Carnap. Wittgenstein was moved by doubts on this point among others to describe his own propositions as 'nonsensical' (*Tractatus*, 6.54); but Carnap wrote '[Wittgenstein] seems to me to be inconsistent in what he does. He tells us that one cannot state philosophical propositions and that whereof one cannot speak, thereof one must be silent; and then instead of keeping silent, he writes a whole philosophical book' (*Philosophy and Logical Syntax*, p. 37), thus indicating that he did not take Wittgenstein's misgivings as seriously as he should have. At any rate, the time has surely come when analysts and metaphysicians ought to co-operate in attacking this problem, which touches them both so nearly.

Once it is realised that the propositions of the analyst are not obviously analytic, a great many other possibilities suggest themselves. Are they, for example, empirical, as Professor Braithwaite has recently affirmed?[2] Or are some of them analytic and some empirical? Or are they sometimes ambiguous, so that the writer has no clear idea which of these two things (if either) they are? Or are they, not statements at all, but resolves, stipulations or rules? Or, lastly, are they (to use an old label which has little if any explanatory force) synthetic *a priori*? These possibilities all require to be investigated.

This paper is intended to serve only as a prolegomenon to such an investigation. It takes the form of an analogy. If we could find a type of situation in which the same sort of difficulty arises, but in a much clearer and simpler form, we might shed some light on the main problem. In choosing a much simpler model, we run the risk of oversimplification; but this is a risk which has to be taken if we are to make any progress at all. If we are careful to notice the differences, as well as the similarities, between the model and that of which it is a model, we shall be in less danger of misleading ourselves.

The suggestion which I am going tentatively to put forward might be described as a demythologised version of Plato's doctrine of *anamnesis*. Plato says that finding out the definition of a concept is like remembering or recalling. If this is correct, some of the difficulties of describing the process are accounted for. To remember (whether a fact, or how to do something) is not (or at any rate not obviously) to make an empirical discovery; yet it is not to make a decision either. So there may be here a way of escaping from the analyst's dilemma.

II

Suppose that we are sitting at dinner and discussing how a certain dance is danced. Let us suppose that the dance in question is one requiring the participation of a number of people – say one of the Scottish reels. And let us suppose that we have a dispute about what happens at a particular point in the dance; and that, in order to settle it, we decide to dance the dance after dinner and find out. We have to imagine that there is among us a sufficiency of people who know, or say they know, how to dance the dance – in the sense of 'know' in which one may *know* how to do something without being able to *say* how it is done.

When the dance reaches the disputed point everybody may dance as he thinks the dance should go; or they may all agree to dance according to the way that one party to the dispute says it should go. Whichever of these two courses they adopt, there are several things which may, in theory, happen. The first is chaos – people bumping into one another so that it becomes impossible, as we should say, for the dance to proceed. The second is that there is no chaos, but a dance is danced which, though unchaotic, is not the dance which they were trying to dance – not, for example, the dance called 'the eightsome reel'. The third possibility is that the dance proceeds correctly. The difficulty is to say how we tell these three eventualities from one another, and whether the difference is empirical. It may be thought that, whether empirical or not, the difference is obvious; but I do not find it so.

It might be denied that there is any empirical difference between the first eventuality (chaos) and the second (wrong dance). For, it might be said, we could have a dance which consisted in people bumping into one another. In Michael Tippett's opera *The Midsummer Marriage* the character called the He-Ancient is asked reproachfully by a modern why his dancers never dance a new dance: in reply, he says 'I will show you a new dance' and immediately trips one of the dancers up, so that he falls on the ground and bruises himself. The implication of this manoeuvre is the Platonic one that innovations always lead to chaos – that there is only one right way of dancing (the one that we have learnt from our elders and betters) and that all deviations from this are just wrong. But whether or not we accept this implication, the example perhaps shows that we *could* call *any* series of movements a dance. If, however, we started to call it a dance, we should have to stop calling it chaos. The terms 'dance' and 'chaos' mutually exclude one another; but although we cannot call any series of movements *both* chaos *and* dance, we can call any series of movements *either* chaos *or* dance; so the problem of distinguishing dance from chaos remains.

The first and second eventualities (chaos and wrong dance) are alike in this, that, whether or not we can say that *any* series of movements is *a* dance, we cannot say that *any* series of movements is *the* dance (viz. the eightsome reel) about the correct way of dancing which we were arguing. It might therefore be claimed that, although it may be difficult to say what counts as *a* dance, and thus distinguish between the first and second eventualities, we can at least distinguish easily between either of them and the third (right dance). And so we can, *in theory*; for obviously both the wrong dance, and chaos or no dance at all, are distinct from the right dance. That is to say, the terms of my classification of things that might happen make it analytic to say that these three things that might happen are different things. But all distinctions are not empirical distinctions (for example evaluative distinctions are not); and the question is rather, How, empirically (if it is done empirically) do we tell, of these three logically distinct happenings, which has happened? And how, in particular, do we tell whether the third thing has happened (whether the dance has been danced correctly)?

III

Let us first consider one thing that might be said. It might be said: 'The dance has been danced correctly if what has been danced is the dance *called* the eightsome reel.' On this suggestion, all we have to know is how the expression 'eightsome reel' is used; then we shall be able to recognise whether what has been danced *is* an eightsome reel. This seems to me to be true; but it will be obvious why I cannot rest content with this answer to the problem. For I am using the dance analogy in an attempt to elucidate the nature of the discovery called 'discovering the use of words'; and therefore

I obviously cannot, in solving the problems raised within the analogy, appeal to our knowledge of the use of the expression 'eightsome reel'. For this would not be in the least illuminating; the trouble is that we do not know whether the knowing how the expression 'eightsome reel' is used is knowing something empirical. We shall therefore have to go a longer way round.

It may help if we ask, What does one have to assume if one is to be sure that they have danced the right dance? Let us first introduce some restrictions into our analogy in order to make the dance-situation more like the language-situation which it is intended to illustrate. Let us suppose that the dance is a traditional one which those of the company who can dance it have all learnt in their early years; let us suppose that they cannot remember the circumstances in which they learnt the dance; nothing of their early dancing-lessons remains in their memory except: how to dance the dance. And let us further suppose that there are no books that we can consult to see if they have correctly danced the dance – or, if there are books, that they are not authoritative.

What, then, in such a situation, do we have to rely on in order to be sure that we have really established correctly what is the right way to dance the eightsome reel? Suppose that someone is detailed to put down precisely what happens in the dance that the dancers actually dance – what movements they make when. We then look at his description of the dance and, under certain conditions, say 'Well then, *that* is how the eightsome reel is danced'. But what are these conditions?

We have to rely first of all upon the accuracy of the observer. We have to be sure that he has correctly put down what actually happened in the dance. And to put down correctly what one actually sees happening is, it must be admitted, empirical observation and description. But what else do we have to rely on? There are, it seems to me, at least two other requirements. As Henle correctly observes (I do not know why he thinks I would disagree), we cannot 'discover the rules of a ballroom dance simply by doing it' (op. cit., p. 753). The first requirement is that the dance which is being danced is indeed the eightsome reel; the second is that it is being danced right. These are not the same; for one may dance the eightsome reel but dance it wrong. Though the distinction between dancing a dance and dancing it right is not essential to my argument, it is in many contexts a crucial one (and with games, even more crucial than with dances; it must, e.g., be possible to play poker but, while playing it, cheat). Even Körner, who on p. 759

of his paper objects to the distinction, uses it himself on p. 762, where he says 'If it [*sc.* a performance of a dance] is relevant but uncharacteristic, it is incorrect'. For both these requirements, we have to rely on the *memory* of the dancers; and, as I have said, to remember something is not (or at any rate not obviously) to make an empirical discovery.

IV

The sort of situation which I have been describing is different from the situation in which an anthropologist observes and describes the dances of a primitive tribe. This, it might be said, *is* an empirical inquiry. The anthropologist observes the behaviour of the members of the tribe, and *he* selects for study certain parts of this behaviour, namely those parts which, by reason of certain similarities, *he* classifies as dances. And within the class of dances, *he* selects certain particular patterns of behaviour and names them by names of particular dances – names which *he* (it may be arbitrarily or for purely mnemonic reasons) chooses. Here we have nothing which is not included in the characteristic activities of the empirical scientist; we have the observation of similarities in the pattern of events, and the choosing of words to mark these similarities.

In the situation which I have been discussing, however, there are elements which there could not be in a purely anthropological inquiry. If a party of anthropologists sat down to dinner before starting their study of a particular dance, they could not fall into the sort of argument that I have imagined. Nor could they fall into it *after* starting the study of the dance. This sort of argument can arise only between people who, first of all, know how to dance the dance in question or to recognise a performance of it, but secondly are unable to say how it is danced. In the case of the anthropologists the first condition is not fulfilled. This difference between the two cases brings certain consequences with it. The anthropologists could not, as the people in my example do, know *what* dance it is that they are disputing about. In my example, the disputants know that what they are disputing about is how *the eightsome reel* is danced. They are able to say this because they have learnt to dance a certain dance, and can still dance it, and know that if they dance it it will be distinctively different from a great many other dances which, perhaps, they can also dance. The anthropologists, on the other hand, have not learnt to dance the dance which they are going to see danced after dinner; and therefore, even if they have decided to *call* the dance that they are to see danced 'dance no. 23', this name is for them as yet unattached to any disposition of theirs to recognise the dance when it is danced. The anthropologists will not be able to say, when a particular point in the dance is reached, 'Yes, *that's* how it goes'. They will just put down what happens and add it to their records. But the people in my example, when they say 'eightsome reel', are not using an arbitrary symbol for *whatever* they are going to observe; the name 'eightsome reel' has for them already a determinate meaning, though they cannot as yet say what this meaning is. It is in this same way that a logician knows, before he sets out to investigate the logical properties of the concept of negation, *what* concept he is going to investigate.

The second consequence is that, when my dancers have put down in words the way a dance is danced, the words that they put down will have a peculiar character. It will not be a correct description of their remarks to say that they have just put down how a particular set of dancers danced on a particular occasion; for what has been put down is not: how a particular set of dancers *did* dance on a particular occasion, but: how *the* eightsome reel *is* danced. It is implied that if *any* dancers dance like *this* they are dancing an eightsome reel correctly. Thus what has been put down has the character of universality – one of the two positive marks of the *a priori* noted by Kant (we have already seen that what has been put down has the negative characteristic which Kant mentioned, that of not being empirical). What about the other positive mark? Is what we have put down (if we are the dancers) *necessarily* true? Is it necessarily true that the eightsome reel is danced in the way that we have put down?

What we have put down is 'The eightsome reel is danced in the following manner, viz. . . .' followed by a complete description of the steps and successive positions of the dancers. We may feel inclined to say that this statement is necessarily true. For, when we have danced the dance, and recognised it as an eightsome reel correctly danced, we may feel inclined to say that, if it had been danced differently, we *could* not have called it, correctly, an eightsome reel (or at any rate not a correct performance of one); and that, on the other hand, danced as it was, we could not have denied that it was an eightsome reel. The statement which we have put down seems as necessary as the statement 'A square is a rectangle with equal sides'. I do not wish my meaning to be mistaken at this point. I am not maintaining that there is any temptation to say that the statement 'The dance which we have just danced is an eightsome reel' is a necessary statement; for there is no more reason to call this necessary than there is in the case of any other singular statement of fact. The statement which I am saying is necessary is 'The eightsome reel is danced as follows, viz. . . .' followed by a complete description.

We may, then, feel inclined to say that this statement, since it has all the qualifications, is an *a priori* statement. But there is also a temptation to say that it is synthetic. For consider again for a moment the situation as it was before we began to dance. Then we already knew how to dance the eightsome reel, and so for us the term 'eightsome reel' had already a determinate meaning; and it would be plausible to say that, since we knew the meaning of 'eightsome reel' already before we started dancing, anything that we subsequently discovered could not be something attributable to the meaning of the term 'eightsome reel'; and therefore that it could not be something analytic; and therefore that it must be something synthetic. Have we not, after all, *discovered* something about how the eightsome reel is danced?

There is thus a very strong temptation to say that the statement 'The eightsome reel is danced in the following way, viz. . . .' followed by a complete description, is, when made by people in the situation which I have described, a synthetic *a priori* statement. Perhaps this temptation ought to be resisted, for it bears a very strong resemblance to the reasons which made Kant say that 'Seven plus five equals twelve' is a synthetic *a priori* statement. Yet the existence of the temptation should be noted. Certainly to call this statement 'synthetic *a priori*' would be odd; for similar grounds could be given for considering all statements about how words are used as synthetic *a priori* statements. If, which I have seen no reason to believe, there is a class of synthetic *a priori* statements, it can hardly be as large as this. Probably what has to be done with the term 'synthetic *a priori*' is to recognise that it has been used to cover a good many different kinds of statement, and that the reasons for applying it to them differ in the different cases. It is, in fact, an ambiguous label which does not even accurately distinguish a class of statements, let alone explain their character. What would explain this would be to understand the natures of the situations (as I said, not all of the same kind) in which we feel inclined to use the term; and this is what I am now trying, in one particular case, to do.

V

The peculiar characteristics of the situation which I have been discussing, like the analogous characteristics of the language-situation which I am trying to illuminate, all arise from the fact (on which Professor Ryle has laid so much stress) that we can know something (e.g. how to dance the eightsome reel or use a word) without being able yet to say what we know. Professor Henle has objected to the extension of Ryle's distinction to the language-situation. 'This distinction is no longer clear', he says, 'when one comes to language, and it is by no means apparent that one can always know how to use a word without being able to say how it is used' (op. cit., p. 750). But, although I do not claim that the distinction is entirely clear in any field, in language it is perhaps clearer than elsewhere. To say how a term is used we have, normally, to *mention* the term inside quotation marks, and to *use*, in speaking of the quoted sentence or statement in which it occurs, some logician's term as 'means the same as' or 'is analytic'. In saying how a term is used, we do not have to use it; and therefore we may know fully how to use it in all contexts without being able to say how it is used. For example, a child may have learnt the use of 'father', and use it correctly, but not be able to say how it is used because he has not learnt the use of 'mean' or any equivalent expression. Henle seems to confuse being able to 'decide on logical grounds' that a statement is true with being able to say 'the statement is logically true'. A person who did not know the use of the expression 'logically true' could do the former but not the latter.

Besides noticing that the dance-situation has the characteristics which I have described, we should also be alive to certain dangers. There is first the danger of thinking that it could not have been the case that the eightsome reel was danced in some quite different way. It is, of course, a contingent fact, arising out of historical causes with which I at any rate am unacquainted, that the dance called 'the eightsome reel' has the form it has and not some other form. If it had some different form, what my dancers would have learnt in their childhood would have been different,

and what they would have learnt to call 'the eightsome reel' would
have been different too; yet the statement 'the eightsome reel is
danced in the following manner, etc.' would have had just the
same characteristics as I have mentioned (though the 'etc.' would
stand for some different description of steps and movements).

Next, there is the danger of thinking that if *anthropologists*
were observing the dance, and had been told that the dance which
they were to observe was called 'the eightsome reel', *they*, in reporting their observations, would be making the same kind of
statement – namely a non-empirical, universally necessary statement which at the same time we are tempted to call synthetic.
They would not be making this sort of statement at all, but an
ordinary empirical statement to the effect that the Scots have a
dance which they dance in a certain manner and call 'the eightsome reel'.

VI

There is also a third thing which we must notice. If a completely
explicit definition were once given of the term 'eightsome reel', it
would have to consist of a specification of what constitutes a
correct performance of this dance. To give such a definition is to
give what is often called a 'rule' for the performance of the dance.
Now if we already have such a definition, then statements like
'The eightsome reel is danced in the following way, viz. . . .',
followed by a specification of the steps, will be seen to be analytic,
provided only that we understand 'is danced' in the sense of 'is
correctly danced'. It might therefore be said that, once the definition is given, there remains no problem – no proposition whose status
defies classification. Similarly, if we were to *invent* a dance and
give it explicit rules of performance, there would be no problem.
But in this latter case there would be no *discovery* either. It is
because, in my problem-case, we do not *start off* by having a
definition, yet do start off by having a determinate meaning for
the term 'eightsome reel', that the puzzle arises. It is the *passage to*
the definition that the mystery creeps in – in the passage (to use
Aristotle's terms) from the ἡμῖν γνώριμον to the ἁπλῶς γνώριμον.[3]
What we have to start with is not a definition, but the mere ability
to recognise instances of correct performances of the dance; what
we have at the end is the codification in a definition of what we
know. So what we have at the end is different from what we have

at the beginning, and it sounds sensible to speak of our *discovering* the definition – just as those who first defined the circle as the locus of a point equidistant, etc., thought that they had discovered something about the circle, namely what later came to be called its essence. We see here how definitions came to be treated as synthetic statements; and, since the real or essential definition (the prototype of all synthetic *a priori* statements) is one of the most characteristic constituents of metaphysical thinking, this explains a great deal about the origins of metaphysics.

Briefly, there are two statements whose status is unproblematical, both expressed in the same words. There is first the anthropologist's statement that the eightsome reel (meaning 'a certain dance to which the Scots give that name') is (as a matter of observed fact) danced in a certain manner. This is a plain empirical statement. Secondly, there is the statement such as might be found in a book of dancing instructions – the statement that the eightsome reel is danced (meaning 'is correctly danced') in a certain manner. This statement is analytic, since by 'eightsome reel' the writer *means* 'the dance which is (correctly) danced in the manner described'. Should we then say that the appearance of there being a third, mysterious, metaphysical, synthetic *a priori* statement about the dance, somehow intermediate between these two, is the result merely of a confusion between them, a confusion arising easily from the fact that they are expressed in the same words? This, it seems to me, would be a mistake. For how do we *get* to the second, analytic statement? Only via the definition or rule; but if the definition is not a mere empirical description, then there is, on this view, nothing left for it to be but a stipulative definition, the result of a decision. So there will be again no such thing as discovering how the eightsome reel is danced. There will only be something which might be described as 'inventing the eightsome reel'. It is preferable, therefore, to say that there is a third kind of statement, intermediate between the first and the second, which forms, as it were, the transition to the second – we settle down in the comfortable analyticity of the second only after we have discovered that this definition of the term 'eightsome reel', and no other, is the one that accords with our pre-existing but unformulated idea of how the dance should be danced. And this discovery seems to be neither a mere decision, nor a mere piece of observation. But, since I am still very perplexed by this problem, I do not rule out the possibility that, were I to become clearer about it, I should see that there is no third alternative.

Before I conclude this section of my paper, and go on to describe more complicated kinds of dances which resemble talking even more closely, I have two remarks to make. The first is that, unless *some* people knew how to dance dances, anthropologists could not observe empirically how dances are danced; and that therefore there could not be empirical statements about dances unless there were at least the possibility of the kind of non-empirical statement that I have been characterising. The situation is like that with regard to moral judgements; unless *some* people make genuine evaluative moral judgements, there is no possibility of other people making what have been called 'inverted commas' moral judgements, i.e. explicit or implicit descriptions of the moral judgements that the first set of people make.[4] So, if philosophical analysis resembles the description of dances in the respects to which I have drawn attention, empirical statements about the use of words cannot be made unless there is at least the possibility of these other, non-empirical statements about the use of words. This perhaps explains the odd fact that analytical inquiries seem often to start by collecting empirical data about word-uses, but to end with apparently *a priori* conclusions.[5]

The second remark is that I have nothing to say in this paper which sheds any direct light on the question (often confused with the one which I am discussing) – the question of the distinction between logic and philology. The features which I am trying to pick out are features as well of philological as of logical discoveries, and this makes them more, not less, perplexing.

VII

I will now draw attention to some differences between the comparatively simple dance-situation which I have been discussing so far and the language-situation which is the subject of this paper. Talking is an infinitely more complex activity than dancing. It is as if there were innumerable different kinds of steps in dancing, and a dancer could choose at any moment (as is to a limited extent the case in ballroom dancing) to make any one of these steps. Talking is in this respect more like ballroom dancing than like reels – there is a variety of different things one can do, and if one's partner knows how to dance, she reacts appropriately; but to do *some* things results in treading on one's partner's toes, or bumping into other couples and such further obstacles as there may be, how-ever well she knows how to dance. Nevertheless there are a great many things which one can do; and not all of them are laid down as permissible in rules which have been accepted before we do them. There can be innovations in dancing and in speech – and some of the innovations are understood even though they are innovations.

Both dancing and talking can become forms of creative art. There are kinds of dancing and of talking in which the performer is bound by no rules except those which he cares to make up as he goes along. Some poetry is like this; and so is 'creative tap-dancing' (the title of a book which once came into my hands). The most creative artists, however, are constrained to talk or dance *solo*. It is not about these highest flights of talking and dancing that I wish to speak, but about those more humdrum activities which require the co-operation of more than one person, and in which, therefore, the other people involved have to know a good deal about what sort of thing to expect one to do, and what they are expected to do in answer. It is in this sense that I am speaking of 'knowing how to dance' and 'knowing how to talk'.

What makes co-operation possible in both these activities is that the speaker or dancer should not do things which make the other people say 'We don't know what to make of this'. That is to say, he must not do things which cannot be easily related to the unformulated rules of speaking or dancing which everybody knows who has learnt to perform these activities. The fact that these rules are unformulated means that to learn to formulate them is to make some sort of discovery – a discovery which, as I have said, cannot be described without qualification as an empirical one. If a person in speaking or dancing does something of which we say 'We don't know what to make of this', there are only two ways of re-establishing that *rapport* between us which makes these co-operative activities possible: either he must explain to us what we *are* to make of what he has done; or else he must stop doing it and do something more orthodox. He must either teach us his new way of dancing or talking, or go on dancing or talking in our old way. I should like to emphasise that I am not against what Körner calls 'replacement-analysis'; the last chapter of my *The Language of Morals* is evidence of this. But we need to be very sure that we understand the functioning of the term that is being replaced before we claim that a new gadget will do the old job better.

It might be said, dancing is not like talking, because dancing is a gratuitous activity, and talking a purposeful one; therefore there are things which can go wrong in talking that cannot go wrong in dancing – things which prevent the purposes of talking being realised. This I do not wish to deny; though the existence of this difference does not mean that there are not also the similarities to which I have been drawing attention. And the difference is in any case not absolute. Some talking is gratuitous; and some dancing is purposeful. When dancing in a crowded ballroom, we have at least the purpose of avoiding obstacles, human and inanimate. If we imagine these obstacles multiplied so that our dance-floor becomes more like its analogue, that elusive entity which we call 'the world', dancing becomes very like talking. And all dance-floors have at least a floor and boundaries of some kind; so no kind of dancing is *completely* gratuitous; all dancers have the purpose of not impinging painfully against whatever it is limits their dance-floor (unless there are penitential dances which consist in bruising oneself against the walls – but this too, would be a purpose). And there are some markedly purposeful activities which, though not called dances, are like dances in the features to which I have drawn attention – for example, the pulling up of anchors (old style).

This analogy points to a way of thinking about our use of language which is a valuable corrective to the more orthodox representational view, in which 'facts', 'qualities', and other dubious entities flit like untrustworthy diplomats between language and the world. We do not need these intermediaries; there are just people in given situations trying to understand one another. Logic, in one of the many senses of that word, is learning to formulate the rules that enable us to make something of what people say. Its method is to identify and describe the various sorts of things that people say (the various dances and their steps) such as predication, conjunction, disjunction, negation, counting, adding, promising, commanding, commending – need I ever stop? In doing this it has to rely on our knowledge, as yet unformulated, of how to do these things – things of which we may not even know the names, and which indeed may not *have* names till the logician invents them; but which are, nevertheless, distinct and waiting to be given names. Since this knowledge is knowledge of something that we have learnt, it has, as I have said, many of the characteristics of memory – though it would be incorrect, strictly speaking, to say that we *remember* how to use a certain word;

Plato's term 'recall' (ἀναμιμνήσκεσθαι) is, perhaps, more apt. As in the case of memory, however, we know, without being, in many cases, able to give further evidence, that we have got it right. And often the only test we can perform is: trying it out again. In most cases there comes a point at which we are satisfied that we have got the thing right (in the case of speaking, that we have formulated correctly what we know). Of course, the fact that we are satisfied does not show that we are not wrong; but if once satisfied, we remain satisfied until we discover, or are shown, some cause for dissatisfaction.

VIII

Meno, in the Platonic dialogue named after him, is asked by Socrates what goodness is (a question much more closely akin than is commonly allowed to the question, How and for what purposes is the word 'good' used?). Being a young man of a sophistical turn of mind, Meno says 'But Socrates, how are you going to look for something, when you don't in the least know what it is? . . . Or even if you do hit upon it, how are you going to know that this is *it*, without having previous knowledge of what *it* is?'[6] In more modern terms, if we do not already know the use of the word 'good' (or, in slightly less fashionable language, its analysis), how, when some account of its use (some analysis) is suggested, shall we know whether it is the correct account? Yet (as Socrates goes on to point out) if we knew already, we should not have asked the question in the first place. So philosophy either cannot begin, or cannot reach a conclusion.

It will be noticed that my dancers could be put in the same paradoxical position. If they know already how the dance is danced, what can they be arguing about? But if they do not know already, how will they know, when they have danced the dance, whether they have danced it correctly? The solution to the paradox lies in distinguishing between knowing how to dance a dance and being able to say how it is danced. Before the inquiry begins, they are able to do the former, but not the latter; after the inquiry is over they can do the latter, and they know that they are right because all along they could do the former. And it is the same with the analysis of concepts. We know how to use a certain expression, but are unable to say how it is used (λογὸν διδόναι, give an analysis or definition, formulate in words the use of the expression). Then we try to do the latter; and we know we have succeeded when we have found an analysis which is in accordance with our hitherto unformulated knowledge of how to use the word. And finding out whether it *is* in accordance involves talking (dialectic), just as finding out whether the account of the dance is right involves dancing.

Dialectic, like dancing, is typically a co-operative activity. It consists in trying out the proposed account of the use of a word by using the word in accordance with it, and seeing what happens. It is an experiment with words, though not, as we have seen, an altogether empirical experiment. In the same way, we might dance the dance according to someone's account of how it is danced, and see if we can say afterwards whether what we have danced is the dance that we were arguing about (e.g. the eightsome reel) or at least *a* dance, or whether it is no dance at all. There is no space here to give many examples of dialectic; but I will give the most famous of all.[7] It is a destructive use of the technique, resulting in the *rejection* of a suggested analysis. An account of the use of the word 'right' is being tried out which says that 'right' means the same as 'consisting in speaking the truth and giving back anything that one has received from anyone'. The analysis is tried out by 'dancing' a certain statement, viz. 'It is always right to give a madman back his weapons which he entrusted to us when sane'. But the dance has clearly gone wrong; for this statement is certainly not (as the proposed definition would make it) analytic, since to deny it, as most people would, is not to contradict oneself. So the analysis has to be rejected.

Plato was right in implying that in recognising that such a proposition is not analytic we are relying on our memories. It is an example of the perceptive genius of that great logician, that in spite of being altogether at sea concerning the *source* of our philosophical knowledge; and in spite of the fact that his use of the material mode of speech misled him as to the *status* of the analyses he was looking for – that in spite of all this he spotted the very close logical analogies between philosophical discoveries and remembering. He was wrong in supposing that we are remembering something that we learnt in a former life – just as more recent mythologists have been wrong in thinking that we are discerning the structure of some entities called 'facts'. What we are actually remembering is what we learnt on our mother's knees, and cannot remember learning.

Provisionally, then, we might agree with the metaphysicians

that philosophy has to contain statements which are neither empirical statements about the way words are actually used, nor yet
expressions of decisions about how they are to be used; but we
should refuse to infer from this that these statements are about some
non-empirical order of being. The philosopher elucidates (not by
mere observation) the nature of something which exists before the
elucidation begins (for example, there is such an operation as
negation before the philosopher investigates it; the philosopher no
more invents negation than Aristotle made man rational). He
neither creates the objects of his inquiry, nor receives them as
mere data of experience; yet for all that, to say that there is such
an operation as negation is no more mysterious than to say that
there is such a dance as the eightsome reel. But even that is quite
mysterious enough.

XIII The verification of linguistic characterisations

J. R. Searle

How do I know the sorts of things about language that I claim to know? Even assuming that I do not need to back my intuitions by appeal to criteria of certain sorts, still if they are to be shown to be valid must they not be backed by something? What sorts of explanation, or account, or justification could I offer for the claim that such and such a string of words is a sentence or that 'oculist' means eye doctor or that it is analytically true that women are females? How, in short, are such claims to be verified? These questions acquire a particular urgency if they are taken as expressions of the following underlying question: 'It is not the case that all such knowledge, if really valid, must be based on an empirical scrutiny of human linguistic behaviour?' How could one know such things unless one had done a really exhaustive statistical survey of the verbal behaviour of English speakers and thus discovered how they in fact used words? Pending such a survey, is not all such talk mere pre-scientific speculation?

As a step towards answering these challenges, I wish to make and develop the following suggestion. Speaking a language is engaging in a (highly complex) rule-governed form of behaviour. To learn and master a language is (*inter alia*) to learn and to have mastered these rules. This is a familiar view in philosophy and linguistics, but its consequences are not always fully realised. Its consequence, for the present discussion, is that when I, speaking as a native speaker, make linguistic characterisations of the kind exemplified above, I am not reporting the behaviour of a group but describing aspects of my mastery of a rule-governed skill. And – this is also important – since the linguistic characterisations, if made in the same language as the elements characterised, are themselves utterances in accordance with the rules, such characterisations are manifestations of that mastery.[1]

By reflecting on linguistic elements I can offer linguistic characterisations which do not record particular utterances but have a general character, deriving from the fact that the elements are governed by rules. The 'justification' I have for my linguistic intuitions as expressed in my linguistic characterisations is simply that I am a native speaker of a certain dialect of English and consequently have mastered the rules of that dialect, which mastery is both partially described by and manifested in my linguistic characterisations of elements of that dialect. The only answer that I can give to the question, how do you know? (e.g. that 'Women are female' is analytic), is to give other linguistic characterisations ('woman' means adult human female) or, if pushed by the insistent how-do-you-know question beyond linguistic characterisations altogether, to say 'I speak English'.

It is possible (equals not self-contradictory) that other people in what I suppose to be my dialect group have internalised different rules and consequently my linguistic characterisations would not match theirs. But it is not possible that my linguistic characterisations of my own speech, of the kind exemplified above, are false statistical generalisations from insufficient empirical data, for they are not statistical, nor other kinds of empirical generalisations, at all. That my idiolect matches a given dialect group is indeed an empirical hypothesis (for which I have a lifetime of 'evidence'), but the truth that in my idiolect 'oculist' means eye doctor is not refuted by evidence concerning the behaviour of others (though, if I find that my rules do not match those of others, I shall alter my rules to conform). In short, the possibility of my coming to know and being able to state such facts as are recorded in linguistic characterisations of the kind we have been considering without following certain orthodox paradigms of empirical verification is to be explained by the following. My knowledge of how to speak the language involves a mastery of a system of rules which renders my use of the elements of that language regular and systematic. By reflecting on my use of the elements of the language I can come to know the facts recorded in linguistic characterisations. And those characterisations can have a generality which goes beyond this or that instance of the use of the elements in question, even though the characterisations are not based on a large or even statistically interesting sample of the occurrences of the elements, because the rules guarantee generality.

An analogy: I know that in baseball after hitting the ball fair, the batter runs in the direction of first base, and not in the direction, say, of third base or the left field grandstand. Now what sort of knowledge is this? On what is it based? How is it possible? Notice that it is a general claim and not confined to this or that instance of base-running behaviour. I have never done or even seen a study of base-runner behaviour, and I have never looked the matter up in a book. Furthermore, I know that if the book, even if it were a rule book, said anything to the contrary it would be mistaken or describing a different game or some such. My knowledge is based on knowing how to play baseball, which is *inter alia* having internalised a set of rules. I wish to suggest that my knowledge of linguistic characterisations is of a similar kind.

If this is correct, then the answer to the philosopher's question 'What would we say if . . . ?' is not a prediction about future verbal behaviour but a hypothetical statement of intention within a system of rules, where mastery of the rules dictates the answer (provided, of course, that both the rules and the question are determinate enough to dictate an answer, conditions which are by no means always satisfied).

On this account there is nothing infallible about linguistic characterisations; speakers' intuitions are notoriously fallible. It is not always easy to characterise one's skills, and the fact that in these cases the skill is involved in giving the characterisation does not serve to simplify matters.[2] There is also the general difficulty in correctly formulating knowledge that one has prior to and independent of any formulation; of converting *knowing how* into *knowing that*. We all know in one important sense what 'cause', 'intend', and 'mean' mean, but it is not easy to *state* exactly what they mean. The mistakes we make and the mistakes I shall make in linguistic characterisations in the course of this work[3] will be due to such things as not considering enough examples or misdescribing the examples considered, not to mention carelessness, insensitivity, and obtuseness; but, to repeat, they will not be due to over-hasty generalisation from insufficient empirical data concerning the verbal behaviour of groups, for there will be no such generalisation nor such data.

We need to distinguish between (a) talking, (b) characterising talk, and (c) explaining talk – the difference between, e.g., (a) 'That's an apple', (b) ' "Apple" is a noun', and (c) 'The rule for indefinite article preceding a noun beginning with a vowel requires an 'n' as in "an apple" '. (b) and (c) are linguistic characterisations and explanations respectively. I have been emphasising that the ability to do (a) is what underlies and, indeed, what explains the possibility of knowledge of certain kinds of statements of kind (*b*). It is the data of kind (*a*) as recorded in statements of kind (*b*) which are explained by explanations of kind (*c*). The philosophical controversies over (b) statements have prompted me to this discussion of their epistemological status. But (*c*) statements have raised no such controversial dust, and I shall say nothing about them save that they are subject to the usual (vaguely expressed and difficult to explicate) constraints on any explanation whether in the exact sciences or elsewhere. Like all explanations, to be any good, they must account for the data, they must not be inconsistent with other data, and they must have such other vaguely defined features as simplicity, generality, and testability.

So, in our era of extremely sophisticated methodologies, the methodology of this book must seem naïvely simple. I am a native speaker of a language. I wish to offer certain characterisations and explanations of my use of elements of that language. The hypothesis on which I am proceeding is that my use of linguistic elements is underlain by certain rules. I shall therefore offer linguistic characterisations and then explain the data in those characterisations by formulating the underlying rules.

This method, as I have been emphasising, places a heavy reliance on the intuitions of the native speaker. But everything I have ever read in the philosophy of language, even work by the most behaviouristic and empirical of authors, relies similarly on the intuitions of the speaker. Indeed, it is hard to see how it could be otherwise since a serious demand that I justify my intuition that 'bachelor' means unmarried man, if consistent, would also involve the demand that I justify my intuition that a given occurrence of 'bachelor' means the same as another occurrence of 'bachelor'. Such intuitions can indeed be justified, but only by falling back on other intuitions.

XIV Summary: Linguistics and the *a priori*

Z. Vendler

1. The best way to show that a thing can be done is to do it: according to the old maxim, *valet illatio ab esse ad posse*. (It is legitimate to infer from existence to possibility.) In the following pages I shall draw several philosophical conclusions on the basis of various applications of structural linguistics. Yet, as appears from a good number of oral and written exchanges, there is a strong current of opinion challenging the possibility of such a move. Moreover, and this gives me pause, the opposing voices are not restricted to philosophers who are sceptical towards any kind of linguistic approach, nor even to those who regard appeals to ordinary language with suspicion. Indeed, the new wave of attack has been launched by authors belonging to or influenced by the Oxford School and by followers of the later Wittgenstein – by philosophers, in other words, who are very much concerned with ordinary language. Gilbert Ryle, for instance, in his 'Ordinary Language' and more explicitly in 'Use, Usage and Meaning', seems to imply that the results of linguistic science have no utility on the level of philosophical analysis (Chapters II and III above). And Stanley Cavell, in his 'Must We Mean What We Say?' and 'The Availability of Wittgenstein's Later Philosophy', makes the same claim even more forcefully that Ryle, and from a strictly Wittgensteinian point of view (Chapters VIII and IX above). This reluctance of philosophers of ordinary language to use the science of that language as a tool in their labours needs to be understood, explained, and if possible overcome, before I, and other people working along similar lines, can be sure of not being deluded in our efforts.

2. This need, at least to my mind, has not been sufficiently answered in the capable papers by William P. Alston (Chapter XVI below) and by Jerry A. Fodor and J. J. Katz (Chapters X above and XV below). In the first place I do not think that these

authors sufficiently appreciate the difficulties arising out of the claim that philosophical statements are *a priori*. This is what Fodor and Katz write:

> That Cavell's position blocks an adequate understanding of ordinary-language philosophy follows from the fact that the Oxford philosopher, when he discusses the use of words, *is* pursuing an empirical investigation, and *is not* uncovering truths of transcendental logic. . . . What has until now distinguished the Oxford philosopher from the linguist is primarily a difference of focus. The linguist has traditionally been concerned with problems of phonology, phonemics, morphology, and syntax, while the Oxford philosopher has devoted himself almost exclusively to problems about meaning. What has distinguished some Oxford philosophers is their ingenuity at discovering recondite facts about how English speakers use their language. But methods of confirmation and disconfirmation distinguish neither the philosopher from the linguist nor the philosopher himself (p. 203 above).

What emerges from this text is the idea that the Oxford philosopher is nothing but an ingenious amateur linguist exploring certain hitherto neglected features of our language. No doubt, philosophers of ordinary language may, and very often do, give linguistic facts in support of their conclusions. But these conclusions do not fall within the domain of linguistic science: they are philosophical conclusions and the authors who draw them are doing philosophy and not linguistics.

If the assumption of Fodor and Katz were right, then scientific linguistics would tend to replace linguistic philosophy. Alston, though more cautious than Fodor and Katz, foresees exactly such a development:

> Even though the analysis of language in purely formal terms does not itself give the philosopher the result he needs for his purposes, it might well separate out classes that the philosopher would find it profitable to examine in his own way. That is, the class distinctions the linguist discovers by formal procedures might parallel important conceptual distinctions, and the presentation of such formal results might provide the philosopher with hints for such distinctions. . . . And, of course, if and when semantics is developed and integrated into structural lin-

guistics along with grammar, the differences between the two sorts of inquiry in methods and status of conclusions, though not in ultimate aim, may well be reduced to the vanishing point (pp. 295–6 below).

Here again I would like to deny that the 'methods and status of conclusions' of linguistics and philosophy can ever be the same. True, the philosopher may use linguistic data, found by himself or borrowed from the expert, but he will go beyond these in establishing conclusions of an entirely different logical status.

3.   There are two other suggestions touching upon the relation of linguistics and philosophy put forward by Fodor and Katz. In their article 'What is Wrong with the Philosophy of Language?' they propose that 'the philosophy of language should be considered as nothing other than the philosophy of linguistics: a discipline analogous in every respect to the philosophy of psychology, the philosophy of mathematics, the philosophy of physics, etc.' (p. 280 below). This would amount to a mere terminological suggestion (though even so a misleading one) were it not for the fact that the authors keep regarding positivists like Carnap and ordinary-language philosophers like Ryle as philosophers of language who went about their task in a wrong way. Consequently, what is wrong with their philosophy is that they did not do something different from what they were actually doing. Fortunately, at least Katz recognises the error of this position in a later work.[1] He proposes instead the view that the philosophy of language is an investigation of conceptual knowledge based upon the general theory of language, which is 'the theory in descriptive linguistics that represents the facts about linguistic structure common to all natural languages'.[2] Although I am more sympathetic towards this view, it still appears to me too narrow, since, as I believe and hope to show, even the linguistic data giving the structure of a particular natural language are a fruitful source of genuine philosophical insight.

4.   Katz's hesitation about the nature of the philosophy of language is indicative of a serious conceptual confusion that pervades most recent studies, anthologies, and textbooks in the field. I think I am justified in pausing for a moment to mark off some of the distinct ingredients from the multifarious content of the catch-all phrase, philosophy of language. First of all, there is indeed, or at

least there should be, *a philosophy of linguistics*. This comprises philosophical reflections on such linguistic universals as meaning, synonymy, paraphrase, syntax, and translation, and a study of the logical status and verification of linguistic theories. Accordingly, the philosophy of linguistics is one of the special branches of the philosophy of science, like the philosophy of physics, of psychology, and so on. This discipline would be quite distinct from another, which I would prefer to call *linguistic philosophy*. This would comprise conceptual investigations of any kind based upon the structure and functioning of natural or artificial languages. Examples of this kind of study could range from Aristotle's reflections on being to Russell's theory of descriptions and Ryle's work on mental concepts. The catch-all phrase, *philosophy of language*, could be retained to label the remainder of the original domain, still containing more or less philosophical works on the nature of language, its relation to reality, and so forth. Whorf's *Language, Thought and Reality*,[3] and perhaps Wittgenstein's *Tractatus*, would remain in this category. It is possible that the science of linguistics and the philosophy of linguistics may jointly come to replace the philosophy of language – in much the same way as the physical sciences, together with the philosophy of science, have replaced, to a large extent, the cosmological speculations of the past. Linguistic philosophy, on the other hand, can only gain by an increased understanding of how language works, but will never be absorbed by linguistics plus its philosophy. In the light of these distinctions, it will be obvious that the main part of this book[4] falls squarely into the realm of linguistic philosophy.

5. In the passage quoted above, Alston seems to imply that the philosophically interesting results of linguistics have been hitherto confined to grammar. This, I think, is a fair statement of the situation as it is. For, although the first attempts towards the formulation of a semantic theory have been made by Paul Ziff[5] and by Fodor and Katz,[6] we are not even at the beginning of the enormous empirical work that could produce semantic data in a scientific sense.

The fact that linguistic science cannot, thus far, give us semantic data, and that consequently we still have to rely on intuition in semantic matters, is certainly part of the reason why people like Ryle and Cavell do not see much hope in linguistics for philosophy. For, after all, they are primarily concerned with semantic problems: questions about what certain words mean.

Take the standard illustration used in the Cavell versus Fodor and Katz controversy about the relevance of linguistics to philosophy.[7] Ryle had claimed that the philosophically important word *voluntarily* is used only in connection with actions that seem to have been someone's fault. Austin denied this by pointing out that one can make a gift voluntarily. Then Cavell strikes a middle course by suggesting that at least there must be 'something fishy' about the performance thus characterised. Finally Fodor and Katz reject this, referring to the possibility of joining the army voluntarily, in which case nothing fishy need be involved. Now who is right? More important, what can, or rather what does, linguistic science offer us here? The answer is simple: beyond a hope, nothing. Even the best dictionaries are notoriously wrong about philosophically important words. No wonder, then, that Ryle and Cavell remain sceptical.

What they overlook, however, is that another part of linguistics, namely syntax, is in better shape. Owing to some advances made in the last decade or so, which really amount to a breakthrough, we now have a fairly elaborate and quite powerful grammar of the English language, which, even if not complete and unified, is very serviceable in handling individual problems.[8] If, therefore, one raises the question whether linguistics is relevant to philosophy, one cannot, in fairness, answer it by showing that an embryonic branch of linguistics, semantics, fails in this respect. But, then, does syntax have anything to offer the philosopher who is interested in conceptual problems? Yes, it does. This is so because the meaning of a word is to a large extent – but, of course, by no means entirely – a function of its syntactic constraints. To mention the most obvious example: that a word is a noun, verb, adjective, or adverb is nothing but a piece of syntactic information indicating the role of the word in sentence structures. And, surely, knowing its grammatical category is the first step in understanding the meaning of the word. But fortunately, as we shall see, syntax does not stop here: there are a great many other things it can tell us pertinent to the meaning of words. Some of these things, moreover, bear upon lively issues of contemporary philosophy, issues about which even the most prominent linguistic philosophers have been sorely mistaken precisely because their otherwise excellent intuition was not aided by the grammatical insight obtainable by means of structural and transformational linguistics.

6.   I am aware that a mere appeal to the practical impotence of

semantics is not sufficient to explain the reluctance that some
people, like Ryle and Cavell, feel towards admitting linguists to
the pastures of philosophy. They also produce arguments, and persuasive ones at that, to show that the results of linguistics cannot
possibly support philosophical conclusions. If these arguments are
sound, then no matter how many illustrations I may produce, I
still must labour under an illusion – for just as it is true that *contra
factum non valet argumentum* (An argument carries no weight
against a fact), it is also true that *contra argumentum bonum non
existit factum* (Against a good argument there is no opposing fact).
I shall now survey these arguments. In doing so I shall not restrict
myself to the reasons offered by Ryle and Cavell, but shall broaden
and strengthen them in such a way as to express some qualms of
authors who also oppose ordinary-language philosophy in general.

The first objection is a formidable one. It may run as follows:
the results of linguistics are empirical generalisations and, as
such, express contingent facts. Philosophical statements, on the
other hand, are not empirical generalisations and cannot be supported by such. Therefore, no linguistic result can amount to a
philosophical assertion, nor can it support one. The first premiss
of this argument is taken for granted by the linguists themselves,
and Fodor and Katz, following Noam Chomsky, lay great stress
upon the similarity of linguistics to other empirical sciences. The
hypothetico-deductive superstructure employed in modern linguistics only reinforces this analogy. The second premiss, concerning
the *a priori* nature of philosophy, may be debated in some quarters,
but it is generally upheld by my opponents and I am willing to
debate the issue on their own ground. It is interesting to note that
the very words of the chief defender of the purity of philosophy
are summoned to make the point clear. What philosophers are
interested in, says Cavell, is the *a priori*, based upon the 'categorical
declaratives' of the native speaker (pp. 140 ff. above). R. M.
Hare is tempted to speak of synthetic *a priori* propositions in a
similar context (Chapter XII above). The philosopher, to quote
Wittgenstein himself, 'is directed not towards phenomena, but, as
one might say, towards the '*possibilities*' of phenomena'.[9] His
syntax is 'logical' syntax, his logic, for Cavell again, is 'transcendental', not merely formal or semantic (pp. 140 ff. above). And
the grammar he wants to explore is 'depth'-grammar:[10] 'It is a
knowledge of what Wittgenstein means by grammar – the knowledge Kant calls "transcendental"' (p. 184 above). In Ryle's
terminology: 'The Rules of Logical Syntax . . . belong not to a

Language or Languages, but to Speech' (p. 60 above). This tendency to take shelter under the mantle of Kant against the foray of linguists into the fields of philosophy is quite understandable as we evoke the spectre that caused the alarm, the phantom arising out of the work of some over-zealous champions of 'linguistics for philosophy'. Can philosophical problems ever be solved by interviewing native informants, recording conversations, and committing a written corpus to the care of a computer? . . .

But then, is the argument valid? It is not. And the really interesting thing is not that it is invalid in spite of the premisses' being true, but that people like Cavell do not realise its invalidity in spite of clearly seeing the point that makes it so. I shall soon restate that point myself.

7. Before doing so, however, I must mention two other arguments, which, no doubt, are connected with the first. One of these is as old as the rise of contemporary linguistic philosophy. From the very beginning, philosophers of ordinary language tried to protect themselves against the charge that no genuine philosophical problem can be handled on the basis of the peculiarities of a particular language. Quite recently, however, Tsu-lin Mei has shown that a good many of the linguistic reasons P. F. Strawson uses to support his conclusions in 'Proper Names' and *Individuals* fail in Chinese,[11] and I myself have been reminded by H. H. Dubs that some of the arguments in my paper 'Verbs and Times' could not be conducted in Chinese.[12] Chinese being somewhat inaccessible to most of us, I select a more familiar example to illustrate the point. Since Ryle's discussion in *The Concept of Mind*, some obviously philosophical conclusions have been drawn from the fact that certain crucial verbs like *know, believe,* or *love,* unlike, say, *run, study,* or *think,* have no continuous tenses. While I can say that I am studying geometry, I cannot say that I am knowing geometry. For this and similar reasons, philosophers have concluded that while studying and the like are actions or processes, knowing and the like are states or dispositions. The trouble, however, is that this distinction cannot be made in German or French – or, indeed, in most of the Indo-germanic languages. And how should one know that other arguments of this kind will hold in languages other than English? What shall we say then? That, for instance, knowing is not a process in English? But what sort of a philosophical thesis is this? Or shall we do comparative linguistics before making a philosophical claim? What we definitely should not do is to say what Ryle does in

'Ordinary Language': 'Hume's question was not about the word
"cause"; it was about the *use* of "cause". It was just as much
about the *use* of "Ursache". For the use of "cause" is the same
as the use of "Ursache", though "cause" is not the same word as
"Ursache"' (p. 45 above). This is an incredible claim. How does
Ryle know, without an exhaustive study of both languages, that
the use of *Ursache* is the same as that of *cause*? How, moreover,
can two words ever have the same use in two different languages
that do not show a one-to-one correlation of morphemes and syntactic structures? Anyway, in so far as Ryle's claim is understandable it is obviously false: the word *cause* is both a noun and a
verb. *Ursache*, on the other hand, is never a verb. And this, I
say, is quite a difference in use. As for Hume, I shall have the opportunity to show that his use of *cause* has very little to do with
the normal English use of that word.[13] To him, as to Locke before
him, and to most philosophers in their tradition, tables and chairs
would be caused by the carpenter. Yet the sentence 'This chair is
caused by Jones' is very odd, to say the least. Now the plot really
thickens. Is the philosopher interested in Hume's use of the word
cause? Then he should take up a Hume concordance, if there is
one. Is he interested in the way English speakers at large use the
word *cause*? Then he should start the enormous empirical study
that the task requires. Or does he aim at finding a common de-
nominator of *cause*, *Ursache*, *causa*, αἰτία or ἀρχή (which one?) and
so on, which would commit him to the still more formidable task of
a comparative linguistic study. But I have to remind the reader that
our philosopher is unwilling to do any of these empirical studies.
His results are *a priori*; his syntax is logical syntax; his grammar is
depth-grammar.

8.   This leads us to the third argument, involving the 'categorical
declaratives' of Cavell's 'native speaker' (Chapters VIII and IX
above). Cavell presents the argument in the framework and in the
phraseology of the later Wittgenstein. The result is a somewhat
'mystical' doctrine about what philosophical inquiry ought to be.
If we pare away the trimmings of mysticism, we are left with something like the following. The philosopher is a native speaker with a
mastery of his language, arguing with himself or with other native
speakers. Having a mastery of the language means that the speaker
does not need evidence for statements (categorical declaratives) of
the following sort: 'In those circumstances *we* would say . . .' or
'Such a thing *we* would call . . .'. 'He is asking something which

can be answered by remembering what is said and meant, or by trying out his own response to an imagined situation' (p. 184 above). Since the language is *our* language, we will find out things about ourselves, or, rather, we will remind ourselves of certain things about the way *we* think, things we overlooked or got confused. Cavell quotes Wittgenstein: 'It is of the essence of our investigation that we do not seek to learn anything *new* by it. We want to *understand* something that is already in plain view.'[14] But what if *I* discover that *you* would talk differently? Well, then *this* is the discovery; the insight making me realise that 'one human being can be a complete enigma to another', that 'We do not *understand* the people', that 'Wir können uns nicht in Sie finden' ('We cannot find ourselves in them').[15] The result of philosophy is self-knowledge: knowledge of *our*selves, and knowledge of *my*self, who may be different from *others*. Then what can all the results of linguistics tell me about the way I think? How can it help me to overcome the confusions in my thinking? Whatever one may think of the method of the *Investigations*, Cavell's interpretation seems to be a faithful and instructive rendering of Wittgenstein's thought. I would be the last person to underrate Wittgenstein's method. I do not think, however, that it makes linguistic data irrelevant, provided their role in philosophical reasoning is properly understood.

9.   The fundamental consideration on the basis of which I want to defend linguistics as a philosophical tool and to refute the three arguments just presented is not at all original. It is, in fact, a commonplace these days to compare language with games or with other, shall we say, rule-governed forms of behaviour. The role of language-games is central in the *Investigations*, and analogies to chess, bridge, and even the eightsome reel abound in the literature[16] (Chapter XII above). The point of the analogy is fairly clear. The use of language, like the playing of a game, presupposes certain norms to which the speaker, or the player as such, has to adhere, but from which he can deviate at will. He can, in other words, be correct or incorrect, right or wrong, in what he does. This is quite different from other aspects of human behaviour, or from the processes of nature. True, they too are governed by certain laws, but if deviations occur, these deviations remain aspects of human behaviour, remain processes of nature. So that any variance with the law is not a shortcoming of nature, but a shortcoming of the law. The perihelion motion of Mercury deviated from Newton's laws, con-

sequently these laws had to be amended and Mercury could not be blamed for violating the rule. If, however, I play chess and suddenly start moving a Pawn backward, then I am to be blamed for violating the rule and not the rule for failing to account for my move. For, after all, my move was not really a move; it is the rule that determines what counts as a move. There is no need to pursue the chess analogy any further; its application to language is quite familiar.

Yet I want to make a couple of remarks that bear upon the analogy. First, I would like to point out that chess is not a very fortunate example, inasmuch as it is a strictly codified and highly exact game. Language, on the other hand, is certainly not. Nobody knows better than professional linguists the flexibility of linguistic rules and their tolerance with respect to factors of time, region, variety of discourse, and individual style. Yet, in spite of this, language remains a rule-governed activity in the sense that the native speaker, in all his freedom, still maintains that he is speaking the language; that is to say, he will permit other speakers to use the same expressions: if something is understandable *from* him, it is understandable *to* him. In a similar way, in the playing of a game with loose rules, like war games or hide-and-seek, a participant may resort to some unexpected stratagem, but, if he does so in good faith, that is, in the spirit of innovation and not of cheating, he will accord the same freedom to his partners. Kant's idea of the moral agent legislating in acting is a paradigm of what I want to say here. One can even formulate the 'categorical imperative' of all games: do whatever you would permit others to do in the same game. And for language: say whatever you would accept from other speakers of the same language. Then we see that language can remain rule-governed in the strictest sense, even with loose or changing rules. A given set of rules, like the ones we find in grammar books, may fall short in comprehension, may vary in space and time, but the regulative idea of the rule has to remain sovereign. But, and this is to anticipate, we should remind ourselves of Kant's warning that regulative ideas do not yield synthetic *a priori* propositions.

The second consideration I wish to offer concerns a radical difference between language and games like chess, bridge, or hide-and-seek. Whereas talking about chess does not consist in making chess moves, in order to talk about language, or about anything, I must use language. Moreover, in describing what goes on in a chess game I have the option of using or not using chess terminology; in other words, my description of what happens might be entirely un-affected by the conceptual framework shaped by the rules of the game. Think of a person who is ignorant of board game. He would, to use Miss Anscombe's terminology,[17] stick to 'brute facts': pieces of ivory being moved about on a chequered slab of wood. And his description, in a sense, would be complete. The conceptual frame-work of chess is, we might say, an optional one; we can take it or leave it. With language, the case is different. No matter how 'I brutalise' the facts, even if I view talk as the production of noises in certain situations, these facts, themselves, will be framed and stated in the same 'full-blown' language – will be affected, that is, by all the rules and conventions that make language what it is. Even while regarding my language as something contingent, even while envisioning alternatives such as other languages, or language-games, my 'regarding' and 'envisioning' will be by means of concepts crystallised out of the very matrix I wish to view 'objectively'. The attempt to get 'out' of language, the desire for 'brute facts' un-tainted by it is, as Cavell puts it, a form of the 'transcendental illusion' (p. 185 above).

Imagine a chess player who is unable to look at the game at the level of brute facts. Yet he realises the contingent nature of the rules. So he might say: 'But it could be otherwise; Pawns might move backward too; Kings might be lost and the game carried on to final extermination', and so on. But he still speaks of Kings and Pawns and moves. And there are no such things as these without the existing rules of chess.

Users of language are like this chess player. Only the situation is radically worse: for it is conceivable that our player might learn how to escape from his mental restriction, but it is inconceivable that we can ever say anything, ask or wonder about anything, without our 'bond', which, of course, is not a fetter at all, but the organ of the mind. To conclude, the conceptual framework im-posed upon us by the rules of game can be cast away and we can still talk intelligently, but the conceptual framework imposed upon us by language cannot be left behind, under penalty of our being reduced to a Cratylus wagging his fingers.[18] Needless to say, the possibility of continuing the discussion in German or Chinese does not help matters. It is no 'liberation' but a mere change of masters.

10. This last point looms large as we begin to examine certain propositions warranted by rule-governed activities. Suppose that

while watching a game of chess I see two Pawns of the same colour standing in the same column. Then I say: 'One of them must have taken an opposing piece in a previous move.' How do I know this? It is sufficient to say that in all chess games we ever witnessed this correlation held? No, *given the rules of the game*, the relation holds *a priori*; the contrary is not something unusual or unlikely: it is inconceivable. Nor is this an analytic connection in the Kantian sense of the term: any given position on the board is perfectly comprehensible without historical data (think of chess puzzles). One might never realise the connection, but once it is noticed, one sees that it cannot be otherwise. So here we have a small example of what can be called a synthetic *a priori* judgement. No matter how trivial such an example may be, the question it makes us to ask, How are such judgements possible?, is anything but trivial. It is, as we remember, the *transzendentale Hauptfrage* (the great transcendental question) itself. And, on the grounds of the given example, we can suggest an answer. The rules of chess invest certain natural objects and processes with a new character and as a result certain natural relationships of these entities necessarily acquire a new value. Thus, seen through the conceptual framework constituted by the rules of the game, two contingent historical states of affairs appear to be necessarily connected. Moreover, obviously almost any 'game', or, in a larger context, almost any rule-governed activity, will be the source of such propositions. And this domain may range so far as to include mathematics or the rules governing the synthesis of the manifold of experience. Remember that to Kant the understanding is 'the faculty of rules'.[19]

Now we see the importance of the point previously made. While it is up to us whether or not we want to play chess, and a matter of free choice whether or not we talk in chess terms, we cannot discard the conventions of language at will and still continue to ask questions and raise problems, philosophical or otherwise. Mute philosophers cannot exist. If so, then the *a priori* truths that this 'game' yields will not be trivial ones, but will be the supreme and unavoidable laws of all discourse and of all conceptual thought – laws, in other words, that the philosopher is required to discover and formulate. The word 'discovery' should not frighten us here: this is not a discovery of something new; it is the realisation of something we 'knew', in a sense, all along, but never had the opportunity or the need to reflect upon. Is the chess connection mentioned above something new to a chess-player? Most likely not. Or we might get an answer like 'I never thought of it, but I should have known it had anybody every asked me'. In a similar way, the philosophical 'discovery', for instance, that one cannot know that *p* without *p* being the case, is not a new fact we have to assimilate, but the realisation of a connection we knew all along in using the verb correctly. And yet, as the history of philosophy shows, we need to be reminded of it lest we go astray.

Unfortunately, not all *a priori* truths arising out of chess or out of language, are so easy to discern. Can you checkmate a lone King with a Knight and Bishop alone? You can, and this is an *a priori* truth. Yet it takes an expert to show you why. But then you will see it for yourself, much the same way as you see the truth of a theorem of geometry that has just been proved for you. Chess, as I said, is a strictly codified and, compared with language, a relatively simple game. It stands to reason, therefore, that certain truths that arise out of the very structure of language may remain hidden to the native speaker, not only because of the remoteness of their connection with the linguistic rules, but simply because some of these rules themselves remained unnoticed by the speaker. The philosopher, therefore, who is interested in connections of this nature, should welcome any help that the linguist, the professional codifier of language, can offer him.

11. But the linguist is an empirical scientist, and his results are contingent statements, while the philosopher is interested in *a priori* truths. We are back to the first objection I mentioned above. Now, however, we can deal with it.

Suppose the game of chess has not yet been codified; people, as some actually do, learn to play by watching games. Imagine, then, that a devoted observer wants to save others the labour by setting down the rules of the game. After watching a good number of games he says 'So the game is played this way', and then he gives the rules. This, no doubt, is an empirical study and its results are contingent statements. For there is no necessity about *these* being the rules. One can imagine other games played on the same board, with the same bits of ivory. Yet this empirical task is a peculiar one. The observer has to be selective in what he takes into consideration. Not all features of the players' behaviour will be relevant, nor even everything they do on the board. For one thing, they may make illegitimate moves. But then these will be objected to and corrected. To be sure about what really belongs to the game, the observer may ask the players or test them: 'Can you do this?' 'Is it all right to move that piece this way?' and so forth. In other words he will appeal not only to what they do, but also to what they know about the game. Accordingly, his results will not be mere empirical generalisations about what certain people do in certain circumstances, but they will codify what chess players regard as permissible moves in the game. A set of rules may be said to *describe* a game but only inasmuch as it *prescribes* how the game should be played. Rules are prescriptive descriptions.

Some of the rules are constitutive ones. For instance, Pawns will be defined by giving their original positions and their possibilities of movement. Pieces that conform to these specifications are Pawns in the game, no matter what they look like. That these are the rules determining the role of the piece called 'Pawn' is, I repeat, a contingent fact. But suppose that our codifier then goes on to assert that consequently no two Pawns of the same colour can be found in the same column without one's having had captured an opposite piece. This is no longer a contingent statement but a necessary truth, since the terminology of the assertion ('Pawn', 'opposite piece', etc.) is chess terminology, understandable only in the context of the game – that is, within the conceptual framework created by the constitutive rules. And, in this framework, the proposition in question is a necessary truth. Adding the hypothetical 'in the game of chess' would be redundant, unless one had an alternative game in mind with the same terms but different interpretations. Barring this possibility, the statement is categorically true. Accordingly, there is a radical difference between the empirical task of finding the rules constitutive of the conceptual framework, and the investigation into the *a priori* correlations that obtain within that framework. I shall call the statements resulting from the former task *external* statements, and those issuing from the latter *internal* statements. Then it is clear that in spite of the logical difference between these two kinds, the external statements will be highly relevant to the establishment of the internal ones. How can you see or show that such a statement is true without implicitly, or, in more involved cases, also explicitly invoking the rules? What will be irrelevant is the fact that the rules are themselves contingent, and can be arrived at empirically.

12. The linguist's work is very similar to that of our chess codifier. He too is doing empirical research in order to discover contingent facts about a given language. And, once more, this empirical research will be of a peculiarly selective type, since the results he aims at will be rules that discriminate between correct and in-

correct performances. So he is not a mere observer: he will ask questions about what is right and wrong in order to elicit what the native speakers know about their language. His findings will not be 'brute' generalisations about vocal noises made by a tribe of the species *Homo sapiens* but a set of rules, formulated by him according to the methodological requirements of simplicity, consistency, and comprehensiveness, that account for acceptable utterances of a given language. To repeat the paradoxical phrase, he will end up with prescriptive descriptions.

Yet the statement of such rules will remain contingent; there is no *a priori* necessity about *these* being the semantic and syntactic rules of a language, say English, that is, the one used by the native inhabitants of England, the United States, and so forth. After all, there are languages with very different structures. Accordingly, a statement such as 'The verb-phrase *to know that p* is used in English correctly only if *p* is true' records a contingent fact. One can imagine a language-game in which that phrase would be synonymous with *to believe firmly that p*. Another example: the linguist might conclude 'In English the verb *to cause*, with a few clearly definable exceptions, cannot take genuine nouns, but only nominalised sentences for verb object'.[20] This, too, will be a contingent fact, rather in the domain of syntax than in that of semantics. But then the linguist, or the philosopher, may go on and say things like 'Therefore we cannot know something that is false', or 'Therefore table and chairs, horses and cows, cannot be caused, while disturbances or revolutions can'. These truths are by no means contingent: here the speaker is not talking about certain features of the English language, but is talking about knowledge and causation. He does not mention the verbs *to know* or *to cause*, he uses them. He does not give rules constituting the conceptual framework of the language, but, talking in that very framework, expresses a truth necessitated by it. Thus, while it is possible to envision different constraints on the use of the phoneme sequence *know* or *cause*, it is impossible to grasp what knowing something false or causing a horse would be like. In much the same way, while it is possible to imagine different rules governing the moves of the piece called 'Bishop', it is impossible to imagine a checkmate of a lone King achieved by a King and a Bishop alone. The first half of these two sentences envisions a somewhat different language or game from what we actually have, while the second half invites us to think something impossible in the language or the game we in fact do have.

In connection with the chess example, I remarked that adding 'in chess' to internal statements would be redundant unless we needed it to exclude other games with the same terminology but different rules. In the language case, it would not only be redundant but outright silly to add a similar clause to internal statements and to say, for instance, 'One cannot know something false in English', or 'Spinsters are not married in English'. The reason for this difference is easy to see. Talking about Kings, Pawns, and Bishops is not the same thing as playing chess, so there is a possibility of these names having a different meaning in some other game. In saying, however, 'One cannot know something false', I am talking English, so the possibility of interpreting the phoneme sequences according to the rules of some other language does not arise. To say things like 'Having a mistress was a respectable thing in Old English but not in current English' is to make a bad joke. And to say 'History is a science in German (*Wissenschaft*) but not in French (*science*)' is not even that. It is just confusion. To conclude, a statement such as 'One cannot know something false' is not true in English or for English; it is absolutely and categorically true.

13. In view of these reflections the first two objections mentioned above seem to evaporate. A few words will be sufficient to give formal answers.

Linguistics, as I have emphasised, is an empirical science and its findings, the rules of a language, are contingent truths. Yet this is only half of the story. We have to add that a rule, as such, has a normative as well as a descriptive function: it describes the *correct* performance. It is in this normative aspect that the rule becomes a constitutive principle of the conceptual framework of a language. Now some philosophical statements are nothing but expressions of necessary connections emerging within this conceptual framework. In supporting them, if need be, we appeal to the rule as a normative principle and not as an empirical generalisation. Yet the fact remains that it takes an empirical study, albeit of a special kind, to determine what these normative principles are. Thus an argument may run as follows: 'One cannot know something false, because in English the verb-phrase *to know that p* is used correctly only in case *p* is true, and this might be verified by interviewing informants, or by other suitable methods.' Granted that we have to shift logical gears a couple of times in the course of the argument; yet, in the light of what we said, these shifts are characteristic of any discourse involving games and other rule-governed activities.

This, I think, answers the first objection, and shows that linguistic data cannot be denied philosophical interest merely on the ground that they are empirical. This, of course, does not show that the native speaker ever needs linguistic data in his philosophical reflections, which is the point of the third objection.

14.   Before taking that up, however, I want to answer the second objection involving the diversity of languages. Here, again, the answer has already been given. Internal statements, like the ones quoted about knowledge and causality, are unconditionally true and not only with respect to a given language, although, of course, they are formulated in a given language. 'But', you ask, 'could I not say the same thing, if, for instance, I were talking Chinese?' My reply is: I do not understand the phrase 'the same thing' in the sentence. But I can give a kinder answer too: think of the ways in which we try to understand what the Classic Greeks meant by παιδεία or what the Germans mean by *Weltanschauung*. In such a way a foreigner, with a language radically different from English, might try to understand what we mean by *to know*. And, if he is successful, then he too will see that one cannot know something erroneously, precisely because he has succeeded in reconstructing in his own language a conceptual model sufficiently similar to the linguistic environment of the English word. This is like showing in Riemannian geometry that the internal angles of a Euclidean triangle must total 180°. It is difficult but not impossible. Wittgenstein's policy shows full awareness of the situation: he did not prohibit the translation of his work, but insisted that the original text should accompany the translation. Take the key word, *game*, from the *Investigations*. It is *Spiel* in the original. And this word has a much broader application than *game*. Think of *Schauspiel* (theatre play) or *Festspiel* (festival). If we realise this, then we are less tempted to object to Wittgenstein's claim that there is no common characteristic to all games, by citing some such thing as competition. *Game* might connote competition, *Spiel* does not. *Game* seems to be the best translation, yet not good enough. So we have to make adjustments till we are able to follow what the author meant. One more illustration. In Hungarian, as in many other languages, the use of the copula is more restricted than in English, German, Latin, or Greek, so there is no close translation for the verb *to be*. Shall we conclude, then, that Hungarians cannot understand Aristotle? Not at all; they can, but it takes some effort at the beginning. Accordingly, if you like to put it that way, a

statement like 'One cannot know something erroneously' is true in all languages provided it is well translated. But, as we woefully see, this is a tautology. To conclude, the philosopher must realise that the only way of arriving at conclusions that are necessarily true is to explore the necessary truths embedded in some actual language or other. For, to repeat, the regulative idea of language or thought *as such* is sterile in this respect.

15. This, however, does not mean that we are trapped in the conceptual network of our native language. We may, and often do, realise that a part of that network is inadequate for some reason or other. Once upon a time a family of concepts relating to witchcraft may have been embedded in the English language. People at that time may have understood what is meant by casting a spell or being possessed by the devil, and their philosophers may have enounced some necessary truths about such states. It happened, however, that the development of science gradually appropriated the domain of application of the concepts involved, and the language of witchcraft, overshadowed by a more powerful branch, slowly withered away through disuse. Examples of similar developments could be given, ranging from harmless survivors like 'the rising of the sun' to the radical reappraisal of our concept of time necessitated by the theory of relativity. In this way, concepts borrowed from the latest growth of science may coexist side by side with petrified relics of past theories. We have no reason to think that the conceptual framework of a natural language has to be consistent in all details. In ordinary discourse we muddle through somehow, and the scientist operates with his carefully sharpened conceptual tools, often ignoring the rest. The philosopher, on the other hand, whose stock-in-trade is concepts, cannot fail to notice a variety of infelicities, confusions, and paradoxes. No wonder, then, that he will be inclined to suggest amendments and restrictions, or to propose artificial substitutes. He is perfectly entitled to do so, provided he realises that in making his suggestions and proposals he is still speaking a natural language, so that the very sense and relevance of what he offers depends upon the understanding of that language as it is. He who wants to rebuild the ship has to know more about it than one who merely sails it.

16. During the last few years a fascinating doctrine has been developed by Chomsky and his associates.[21] They claim that humans are born with an innate device of language acquisition,

which predisposes a child to the rapid learning of any natural language, inasmuch as all such languages exhibit the same basic features. In addition to the psychological evidence, they can appeal to the fact, usually taken for granted but really surprising, that all natural languages are intertranslatable with far less difficulty than one would expect. Again, all natural languages are subject to the linguist's study, that is to say, are describable in terms of the same linguistic universals. As we mentioned above, the linguist engages in an empirical investigation of a very special sort: he wants to find out the rules of a *language*. He knows what to expect, and his expectations do not fail: he finds phonemes and morphemes, sentences, constituent structures, and transformational relations. Of course, all these facts could perhaps be explained by assuming a common origin of all languages. However this may be, it seems to be true that all human languages share some basic features. The important question, for our present purposes, is the following: do we have to restrict philosophically relevant aspects of a language to those shared by all languages, as Katz, for instance, suggests? In view of what I said before, I see no necessity to do so. Philosophical statements mirroring some idiosyncratic aspect of a particular language are no less true than the ones corresponding to some common feature. The difference is that assertions of the former kind will be more difficult to translate than assertions of the latter kind. We can nourish the hope that philosophical statements of importance will belong to the second type. Indeed, even the finer points made by the Oxford philosophers can be translated, without much difficulty, into other languages.[22]

17. I return finally to the third objection and face Cavell's 'native speaker'. Sure enough, such a person does not ordinarily need any evidence, from the linguist or from anybody else, in order to be able to talk correctly. Normally he knows, without semantic or syntactic data, what he should call a certain thing or what he would say in certain circumstances. Moreover, the native speaker is quite capable of realising some philosophically interesting features of his language. Indeed, as far as I know, it was philosophers, and not linguists, who first pointed out the restriction governing the use of *to know* mentioned above. And, admittedly, the work of people like Austin or Ryle makes profitable reading for linguists as well. Yet, unfortunately, the 'game' of language is a very involved one, and its system of rules is more complex than we think. And the philosophical pay dirt is by no means confined to

the surface. With due respect to Wittgenstein, many features of our language are apt to remain hidden from us, and some of these are no less important philosophically than the ones we can locate merely by recalling what we would or would not say given such and such. We must not forget, of course, that Wittgenstein and his followers were primarily concerned with semantic problems, and, as I mentioned at the beginning, in purely semantic matters the linguist has practically no advantage over the educated layman with a good sense for words. I have yet to meet a linguist who could match Austin in discerning fine shades of meaning. It is in the domain of syntax, of the structure of language, that the difference begins to show. A competent speaker may be as well equipped as any linguist to discriminate, for instance, between *unintentionally* and *unwittingly*, because the grammar of these words is roughly the same; if, on the other hand, the difference is also a function of grammar, then the linguist will have a definite advantage over the uninstructed speaker.

The crucial differences in meaning between words like *cause* and *make*, *effect* and *result*, *fact* and *event*, *good* and *yellow*, are given by syntax. In many of these cases, moreover, we have to operate on a quite sophisticated level of syntax, including transformational grammar, to account for the differences. True, the philosopher might find some indications in simply reflecting upon 'what can be said' and 'what cannot be said', but, as appears from concrete examples, this method can be as misleading as helpful. Only in the light of a grammatical theory will the pieces fall into a coherent pattern. In a word, the facts of language do not always lie open to plain view; sometimes they are quite hidden from us. And the philosopher, native speaker though he be, needs all the help he can get to obtain the clarity and insight into the working of the language that he needs in order to arrive at his philosophical conclusions.[23]

Locke, Hume, and their successors were native speakers of English, yet they never realised that persons or objects cannot be caused, while events, processes, and states of affairs can be, obviously because they did not notice the fact that the verb of *to cause* normally has to be a nominalised sentence. So explosions, revolutions, and the rising of the temperature can be caused, but people, horses, or chairs cannot. 'But', you object, 'fires or hurricanes can, and these words are not nominalised sentences.' True, but then the linguist will show you that these words belong to a small class of nouns that behave *as if* they were nominalised sentences; they can, for instance, take verbs like *occur, last, take place*, and adjectives like *sudden, gradual, prolonged* – which is not true of ordinary nouns like *man, horse,* and *rock*. These linguistic facts, then, will enable the philosopher to arrive at a more satisfactory view of causation.

If you say that the empiricists were not really interested in the concepts of ordinary language, then I mention G. E. Moore, who certainly was. Yet he compares *good* with *yellow*, says that they both denote simple and unanalysable qualities, obviously overlooking the enormous differences between them. The temptation to assimilate *good* to *yellow*, simply because they are both adjectives, is quickly overcome as soon as we reflect upon the fact that while a person can be good *at* something, and a thing can be good *for* something, nothing or nobody can be yellow at or for anything; that while a good thief can be a bad citizen, a yellow rose cannot be a non-yellow flower, and so on. That, in other words, while *good* is essentially attributed to a thing with respect to what it does or what can be done with it, *yellow* is not.

Finally, Austin himself tends to assimilate facts to events on the basis of 'what one can say' – for instance that the collapse of the Germans can be called both a fact and an event. In this case, as far as I can see, only transformational grammar can show that 'the collapse of the Germans' is an ambiguous phrase that can be interpreted either in the sense of an imperfectly or in the sense of a perfectly nominalised sentence. What I mean is this. The phrase 'the collapse of the Germans' may be taken to mean 'that the Germans collapsed', in which case the collapse of the Germans can be unlikely or surprising, can be mentioned or denied. In this sense, the collapse of the Germans is a fact. In the other sense, however, in which that collapse can be observed and followed, in which it can occur or take place, in which it can be slow, fast, or gradual, it is not a fact but an event. Indeed, the same sequence of words may identify both a fact and an event; but from this it does not follow that some facts are events, if that sequence of words is structurally ambiguous. Yet Austin, a master of English prose, misses this point because he simply follows 'what can be said' in a situation in which this happens to be misleading.

Linguistics is helpful in analytic philosophy even for the native speaker. And its empirical source need not sully the transcendental purity of philosophical thought.

PART FOUR

Syntactic and Semantic Theory

In this final section there are three important papers which attempt to relate significant developments in linguistic theory to the work of the philosopher. The paper by Fodor is at least in part a discussion of the notion of linguistic acceptability, a notion that is of current concern.

XV What's wrong with the philosophy of language?

J. Fodor and J. J. Katz

The unsuitability of the positivist's view of natural language has led many philosophers to reject this approach and to turn instead to a careful study of the details of a natural language. But the approach known as ordinary-language philosophy has been rightly criticised by the positivists as lacking in systematicity and theoretical orientation. One must agree with the positivist's charge against the ordinary-language philosopher that any account of a natural language which fails to provide a specification of its formal structure is *ipso facto* unsatisfactory. For it is upon this structure that the generative principles which determine the syntactic and semantic characteristics of a natural language depend. These principles determine how each and every sentence of the language is structured and how sentences and expressions are understood. It is his failure to appreciate the significance of the systematic character of the compositional features of languages which accounts for the ordinary-language philosopher's disregard of the study of sentences and sentential structure.

Ryle, for example, dismisses the study of sentences as *a priori* not within the scope of a philosophical analysis of language, on the grounds that sentences do not have uses and that uses are what philosophers study. In a recent article Ryle even claims that sentences are not part of language, but only of speech (Chapter II and III above). This is a rather curious move, since the most characteristic feature of language is its ability to make available an infinity of sentences from which a speaker can choose appropriate and wholly novel ones to use when the need arises. That is to say, what qualifies one as a fluent speaker of a language is not the ability to imitate previously encountered utterances, but rather the ability to extrapolate from them and thus freely to produce and understand utterances never before encountered. This feature, however, must rely upon mechanisms which are recursive, and hence it cannot be reduced to any properties of the (necessarily finite) lexicon of the language. Furthermore, it is clear that since what we learn when we learn a language is precisely how to produce and understand new sentences, such learning must be explained as the assimilation of these recursive mechanisms.

The closest ordinary-language philosophy has come to providing a theory of language which might explain these phenomena is the so-called 'use theory of meaning'. What all variants of this theory have in common is the programme of providing a careful characterisation of the use of each philosophically interesting word in the language. It must be noticed, however, that even if such a programme were successfully carried through for every word in the language, it would fail to explain how new utterances are produced and understood. A solution to the problem of explicating the compositional mechanisms in language requires not only that we be able to characterise the meaning of the words of the language but also that we be able to describe the function which determines the meaning of a sentence on the basis of the meanings of its components. Without attention to the syntactic and semantic structures of the language, the problem of novel utterance cannot be solved, since the meaning of a sentence is partly determined by these structures.

A characterisation of the use of a word is a description of the way it is employed by speakers. We may regard such a description as the dictionary entry for the word, thus using the notion 'dictionary entry' as a cover term for whatever type of characterisation a use theory employs for describing uses. Thus, we may regard the ultimate aim of a use theory of meaning as that of writing a dictionary which provides the correct entry for each word in the language. But even to achieve this aim would be to fall far short of a semantic theory.

It is of course true that a good dictionary *intelligently applied by a fluent speaker of the language* enables him to characterise the meaning of every sentence of the language. But the skills the fluent speaker exercises in using a dictionary to understand sentences constitute an implicit theory of the syntactic and semantic structure of the language, and it is such a theory which ordinary-language philosophy fails to consider. What is needed is a reconstruction of these skills, for it is quite clear that they involve not only non-lexical facts about the language, but, more significantly, the organising principles of the language. Anyone who learns a foreign language discovers that to know a language is to know more than correct dictionary entries for its words. No matter how good a dictionary is, it can tell us nothing about these skills, since they are concerned with relating the meaning of a sentence to the meaning of the words appearing in it.

The failure of ordinary-language philosophy to consider this problem would be excusable were it easy to solve. But, in fact, it is exceedingly difficult. There are several reasons for this, of which we will mention only the most obvious here. At very best, a dictionary can enumerate the uses of a word and provide a small number of diagnostic sentences as examples of each use. In order to extrapolate beyond these few diagnostic sentences and determine the meaning of each of the infinitely many sentences of the language, we require at least the following: First, a complete grammar of the language. Second, a characterisation of the semantic import of grammatical forms, e.g. a way of distinguishing when adjective–noun constructions have the import of property attributions as in the expressions 'blue vase' and 'foolish virgin' and when they do not, as in the expressions 'utter jerk' and 'a certain smile'. Third, in all cases where the dictionary provides more than one entry for a given word (and usually it will provide many more than one) it will be necessary to have a procedure for deciding *which* entry characterises an occurrence of the word in a given sentence. Simply consulting a good English dictionary on the word 'play' will convince the reader of the need for such a procedure. The difficulty of satisfying these three preconditions is, then, a measure of the difficulty of the problem of relating the meanings of words to the meanings of sentences.

However, it is conceivable that the use theory of meaning in one or another of its variants might prove revealing at the lexical level even though it failed to explicate the compositional mechanisms of the language. To prove revealing at this level a theory must at least provide a basis for a unique assignment of semantic properties to lexical items. A theory is vacuous if it is unable to provide a way to determine when two lexical items exhibit the same semantic property and when they do not.

This point has been appreciated in connection with theories of meaning based upon notions of 'real essence' and 'mental ideas'. Philosophers have correctly insisted that theories of meaning founded on either of these notions are wholly uninformative because there is no way to determine when two expressions express the same mental idea or denote the same real essence. But many

philosophers have failed to appreciate the significance and scope of
this requirement.

Considered abstractly, a theory about a class of entities is a system
of statements which exhibits and explains the characteristics and
interrelations of those entities. It does this by employing theoretical
concepts which articulate those of their properties and relations
relevant to such systematisation. Thus, a theory may be regarded as
having two essential components: a basis consisting of theoretical
concepts and a function which establishes a systematisation of the
characteristics and interrelations among the entities. This function
determines the cases in which a pair of entities receive the same
theoretical characterisation and the cases in which they receive
distinct characterisations. Therefore, in theories of meaning, to
require that it be determined when linguistic entities receive the
same theoretical characterisation and when they do not, is just to
require that there be a specification of the manner in which the
theoretical concepts are connected with the phenomena. Hence, this
requirement applies to all theories of meaning; for if it is not satisfied, then there is no connection between the concepts and the
phenomena. Thus no theory.

But, unfortunately, none of the variants of the use theory of
meaning fare better than 'real essence' or 'mental idea' theories.
For by this requirement the use theory must answer the following
questions: 'Under what conditions do two words have the same
use?', 'When do the uses of a pair of words differ?', 'What
determines when a word has more than one use?', 'How is the use
of a word distinguished from misuses of that word?', and so on. But
since all such questions are left wholly unanswered by any use
theory of meaning so far proposed, one is justified in concluding
that no use *theory* of meaning exists. What we have instead is no
more than a recommendation that questions of meaning are to be
handled as questions about the use of expressions.

It may be replied by the use theorist that our requirement is to
be satisfied by reference to rules of language: two expressions have
the same use when their employment is governed by the same rules,
and not otherwise. The programme implicit in this reply seems
appealing in that it appears to focus on the significance of structural
regularities in the language, but the reply itself is unconvincing
because we are uninformed as to both the form and content of such
rules. No one has ever adequately described what a rule of language
is, though we are presented with a plethora of analogies for what a
rule of language is *like*. Depending upon which ordinary-language

analyst one reads, one is informed that a rule of language is like a recipe, or a rule of grammar, or a rule of logic, or a rule of a game, or a dance instruction, or perhaps a moral imperative. With such a variety already in vogue, one might as well compare a rule of language to a rule of thumb. Clearly, there is no basis for deciding which of these analogies is most profitably used to interpret the notion 'rule of language'. Moreover, no analogy can explicate itself. In particular, even an illuminating analogy cannot itself tell *why* it is illuminating. In the case of these putative analogies for rules of language, one would like to know what *precisely* are the features of rules of language which license the analogy. One would also like to know the respects in which rules of language are idiosyncratic; that is, the respects in which talking a language is neither like baking a cake, nor like playing a game or dancing a dance. If someone says that the flow of electricity is like the flow of water, he succinctly summarises a number of truths about electricity, but also he suggests a number of things which are false. For example, that puncturing a wire will cause the electricity to drip out. But we know this is false only because we know the laws of electricity. *What this shows is simply that we would know how to choose an analogy which is revealing and not misleading only if we know exactly what a rule of language is.*

A variant of the use theory of meaning which says that sentences are classified by reference to the speech acts a speaker may perform by uttering the sentence under appropriate circumstances is open to the same sort of objections. The requirement discussed above demands, in the case of such a theory, that there be some general and systematic way of telling when two occurrences of a sentence instance the same speech act and when they are associated with distinct speech acts. It seems clear, however, that no examination of the syntactic and semantic characteristics of the utterance can *per se* determine the speech act with which the utterance is associated. The same utterance will be associated with a given speech act under certain environmental conditions but not under others. For example, if I utter 'A travelling salesman was looking for a place to spend the night', then, depending upon the environmental conditions, I may be making an assertion, starting a joke, referring to a joke, giving an example, providing an explanation, quoting, informing, talking to myself, damaging my reputation, and so forth. But the environmental conditions which determine which, if any, of these acts I am performing can clearly not be discovered by merely examining the utterance. And since there is no way, and very likely could be no way, to systematise such conditions, the speech-act theory does not satisfy the requirement that we be able to determine, given that certain conditions obtain, which speech acts are associated with an utterance occurring under those conditions.

Even in the case of the so-called *explicit performatives* (roughly, verbs *that can* appear in the context 'I hereby . . .'),[1] it is clear that an utterance of the appropriate sentence type does not invariably constitute a performance of the sort normally associated with the verb. The conditions under which an apparent performance 'misfires' are themselves environmental. Hence, we are presented with the same problem encountered above. For example, if I utter the sentence 'I hereby promise to marry her', I may be starting a joke, giving an example, quoting, talking to myself, reciting a randomly chosen sentence, making an honest woman of her, and so forth. Which of these I am doing, as well as or instead of promising, depends on contextual factors which the theory of explicit performatives, like the general theory of speech acts, does not systematise to any extent whatever.

The notion of use has proved an exceedingly difficult one in terms of which to frame a theory, partly because of an undetected ambiguity. There *is* a sense in which it is true that the meaning of a word or expression is determined by its use. The actual use of a word or expression by speakers, i.e. the combinations into which the word or expression enters in sentences and the situations in which it is uttered, constitutes the data for any theory which hopes to answer questions about meaning. But to suppose that this fact lends support to what is usually called the use theory of meaning is to commit what we shall refer to as 'the Use–Use Fallacy'.

In the sense in which it is true that 'meaning is dependent on use', all that this slogan claims is that semantic investigation must be responsible to empirical constraints framed in terms of the facts of linguistic behaviour. However, the claim that questions of meaning should be *replaced* by questions about use has clearly never been intended in this sense, for then it would have been evident that the insistence upon the study of use does not amount to a theory of meaning, but only to a specification of the data relevant to such a theory. Once we are clear about the use–use fallacy, we see that there is no use *theory* of meaning.

Lacking a theory of meaning which would serve theoretically to characterise basic semantic concepts, to settle whether two uses of an expression are the same or different, to delineate deviations from the regularities in the language, and to provide some means for evaluating proposed solutions to philosophical problems arising in connection with the employment of language, the ordinary-language philosopher is increasingly forced to resort to his linguistic intuitions. It may be claimed that in so far as an analysis of language is relevant to solving philosophical problems, all the information required is available by virtue of the fact that the investigator is a fluent speaker of the language.[2] In particular, the ordinary-language philosopher may claim that he is able to detect intuitively cases of linguistic oddity, and that what is relevant to the solution of a philosophical problem is precisely information about what it would be odd to say. Thus, it is held that what is required in the practice of philosophy is that we avoid using words in ways in which we would not ordinarily use them, but it is also held that we can generally tell by using our linguistic intuition when a word is used in an extraordinary way.

Granted that it is often intuitively clear when a given use is odd, it is equally clear that the mere knowledge *that* a use is odd is insufficient either for philosophical purposes, or for a theory of language.

Simply knowing that a use is odd is insufficient for philosophical purposes because a use may be odd for any one of a number of different reasons, many of which are completely non-vicious. Consider the following utterances, all of which are odd for different reasons:

1. I just swallowed my nose.
2. I will show you fear in a handful of dust.
3. This lovely red rose is a red rose.
4. Physical objects do not exist.
5. I have just been decapitated.
6. Pain is the stimulation of C-fibres.

These utterances do not, of course, exhaust all the types of linguistic oddity, but even from this short list it seems clear that some of the things that can make an utterance odd are not such as to make that utterance philosophically objectionable. Hence, *if* a philosopher claims that an utterance is odd and *claims no more*, he has brought no effective criticism against an argument in which that utterance plays an essential role. Thus, accused of having used language oddly, the metaphysician who replies 'So what?' replies correctly. What is needed is a theory which tells us what oddity is, and indicates which kinds of oddity are philosophically objectionable and why.

But we do not wish to claim that an adequate theory of meaning will explicate oddity in such a way that every utterance which a theoretically unsophisticated speaker would call odd is so counted by the theory. Rather, it may be expected that it will reconstruct only those intuitions of oddity which are provoked by violations of semantic regularities of the language. Thus, for example, (1) and (3) would not be characterised as violations of the semantic regularities governing the language since they elicit intuitions of oddity for reasons having nothing whatever to do with the structure of the language; i.e. (1) is odd because the fact it describes is so extremely unlikely and (3) is odd because it is too obviously true. For these reasons such cases are not philosophically objectionable. Furthermore, there are cases when the oddity of an *utterance*, as opposed to an utterance type, depends upon features of its context. Thus, it would be odd to say 'Goodbye!' on first arriving at a gathering or to say 'Two tickets to Mars, please!', given our current state of technology. Similarly, where the context is a context of sentences in a discourse, its features may make an otherwise normal sentence appear odd. For example, imagine reading a book on calculus and in the middle of a discussion of the integration of rational functions coming across the sentence 'Bring me a hot pastrami on rye bread!' This type of oddity differs from that exhibited by the previous examples and it is conceivable that a special theory will be needed to · deal with it. What these arguments show is that the claim that an utterance is odd is not, by itself, a revealing claim. Philosophical arguments based upon this claim thus often go astray. Witness the following case study:

> The last argument I shall consider on the subject of mind–body identity is a widely used linguistic argument. . . . Consider the sentence:
>
> (1) Pain *is identical with* stimulation of C-fibres. The sentence is deviant (so the argument runs, though not in this terminology): there is no statement that it could be used to make in a normal context. Therefore, if a philosopher advances it as a thesis he must be giving the words a new meaning, rather than expressing any sort of discovery. For example . . . one might begin to say 'I have stimulated C-fibres' instead of 'I have a pain', etc. But then one would *merely* be giving the expression 'has stimulated C-fibres' the new meaning 'is in pain'. The contention is that as long as the words keep their present meanings, (1) is unintelligible.

I agree that the sentence (1) is a 'deviant' sentence in present-day English. I do *not* agree that (1) can never become a normal, non-deviant sentence unless the words change their present meanings.

The point, in a nutshell, is that what is 'deviant' depends very much on context, including the state of our knowledge, and with the development of new scientific theories it is constantly occurring that sentences that did not previously 'have a use', that were previously 'deviant', acquire a use – not because the words acquire *new* meanings, but because the old meanings, as fixed by the core of stock uses, *determine* a new use given the new context.[3]

What this example shows is that there can be agreement about the oddity of an utterance, but disagreement about the significance of its oddity. It is this latter sort of disagreement that we need to be able to resolve if the notion of oddity is to play an important role in philosophical polemics.

Furthermore, if it is true that the mere fact that we can tell intuitively when an utterance is odd is insufficient for philosophical purposes, it is equally true that it is inadequate for the purposes of a theory of language. This follows immediately if one accepts the claim that the goal of a theory of language must be at least to make explicit the generative principles that structure sentences. But even if one rejects this claim, the consequences of relying upon intuition alone to decide questions of oddity is that there is then no way to extrapolate one's decisions. Each decision must be handled by a new appeal to intuition, each sentence being treated as though it were unrelated to the rest of the language. But then we have no theory whatever. All we have is overworked intuition. It is in this way that the ordinary-language philosopher's reliance upon linguistic intuition may have been responsible for his failure to develop an adequate theory of language.[4]

Let us consider in its most general form the question of the role of appeal to intuition in the study of language.

The goal of a theory of a particular language must be the explication of the abilities and skills involved in the linguistic performance of a fluent native speaker. The question asked is: 'What skills and abilities have been assimilated by someone who has learned the language?' To answer this question the theorist attempts to develop systems which aim at matching the various facets of the behaviour of fluent speakers by reconstructing the mechanisms underlying linguistic communication and formulating these mechanisms and their interrelations in a systematic manner. Each part of the theory of a natural language – phonology, morphology, syntax, and semantics – seeks to uncover and explicitly state the rules underlying certain of the linguistic skills and abilities of speakers. Phonology and morphology mark the sound and word distinctions of the speaker in terms of formal features of a system of representation. Syntax provides a reconstruction of the rules by which speakers are able to recognise and produce grammatically well-formed strings of words. Semantics seeks to reconstruct the mechanisms which enable the speaker to use sentences under appropriate conditions and to understand sentences used by others.

Just as the performance of a fluent speaker is the result of the interplay of diverse abilities which combine and supplement each other, so the system which the parts of a theory of a natural language comprise seeks to explain the interplay of the speaker's abilities. In this way, the contribution of each separate set of abilities can be assessed, the complexity of linguistic phenomena reduced to manageable proportions, and the interrelations between specific abilities reconstructed in terms of the network of connections established between each of the parts of the system. Hence, the adequacy of any part of such a theory, or of the theory as a whole, is to be judged primarily by how well its rules accomplish the task of reconstruction. Thus, all other things being equal, the more closely a linguistic theory matches the performance of speakers, the more satisfactory it is.

One of the main dangers encountered in the construction of the rules of such a theory is that they may be formulated so as to be workable only when an appeal is made to 'linguistic intuition'. By this is meant that in order for the rules to serve their intended purpose, it is necessary that a fluent speaker exercise his linguistic skill to guide their application. This, then, constitutes a vicious circularity. The rules are supposed to reconstruct the speaker's abilities and yet they are unable to perform their function without the speaker employing these abilities to apply them. As much of the abilities and skills of the speaker as are required for the application of such rules, this much at least the rules fail to reconstruct.

This, however, is not meant to imply that the appeal to intuition plays no role in theory construction in the study of language. The intuitions of fluent speakers determine the data for which a linguistic theory must account. For example, the native speaker intuitively recognises a difference in structure between 'Think of an example of such cases', and these words in reverse order. Such intuitions establish sets of clear cases, on the one hand of grammatically well-formed strings of words, and on the other of ungrammatical strings. Clear cases, intuitively determined, provide the empirical constraints on the construction of a grammar. The appeal to linguistic intuition is question-begging when intuitions replace well-defined theoretical constructs in an articulated system or when intuitions are permitted to determine the application of rules. Intuition in its proper role is indispensable to the study of language, but misused it vitiates such a study.

In effect, then, part of the charge we have to bring against ordinary-language analysis is that it is aprioristic. Lacking a theory to characterise such key notions as 'use', 'misuse', 'speech act', and 'rule of language', a resort is made to the intuitions of the speaker (who, as often as not, is also the theorist). But one's intuitions – even if one's intuitions about one's own speech habits – are by no means infallible. One can be wrong about 'what one would say' since the utterances one has produced during one's lifetime constitute a corpus which is *itself* amenable to analysis in a manner differing in no essential respect from that of any other sample corpus drawn from the language. Just as the intuitions of speakers provide constraints upon a theory of a language, so a developed theory may correct and supplement the intuitions of speakers. On the other hand, if one has no theory, when questions of justification arise in connection with the adequacy of specific analyses of the use of expressions, the appeal to intuition, defended on *a priori* grounds, prevents an objective evaluation of the degree to which the analysis fits the verbal behaviour of speakers.

It cannot be surprising, then, that the usual methods of ordinary-language analysis often yield solutions for philosophical problems which are as controversial as classical solutions. Uncontroversial solutions will be forthcoming to the extent that one can make explicit the empirical and theoretical requirements that a putative analysis must satisfy in order to be a revealing representation of the verbal habits of speakers. Unless it is decided what criteria an analysis must satisfy, our inability to decide between competitive solutions to philosophical problems simply reflects our inability to decide between competitive linguistic *analyses*.

II

The situation in philosophy of language today is reminiscent of that in psychology near the end of the last century. In the latter case apriority led to sterility and conceptual confusion until the empirical constraints upon psychological theory were made explicit. In succeeding years, philosophical psychology came to take its proper role, viz. the analysis of the concepts, theories, and methodology of scientific psychology. The general tenor of the above criticisms of current schools in the philosophy of language suggests that there is more here than a *superficial* resemblance. What we suggest is that these situations are actually parallel. This parallelism, in turn, suggests that what is needed is a theory of language developed on the basis of empirical methods. Given such a theory, the philosophy of language comes to take its proper role as the analysis of the concepts and methodology of that theory. In so far as current linguistics provides an empirical theory of language, the philosophy of language should be construed as nothing other than the philosophy of linguistics: a discipline analogous in every respect to the philosophy of psychology, the philosophy of mathematics, the philosophy of physics, etc.[5]

At the beginning of the present paper we remarked that it is perhaps because of the lack of viable alternative to positivist and ordinary-language theories of language, of an acceptable *tertium quid*, that the shortcomings of both positions have not led to their abandonment. The view of philosophy of language we have suggested above, that it is the analytic study of the concepts, theories, and methodology of empirical linguistics, provides such an alternative if linguistics can offer a satisfactory theory of language. In the remaining part of this paper we shall try to establish that there exists a *tertium quid* by showing that linguistics does provide at least the framework for such a theory.

The theory of language implicit in current work in linguistics deals with problems that have traditionally concerned philosophers of language, but it does so without falling victim either to the positivist's preconceptions about the structure of language, and his lack of empirical controls, or to the ordinary-language philosopher's illicit appeal to intuitive judgements and his consequent unsystematic orientation. It thus provides a real alternative to theories of language found in positivism and ordinary-language philosophy, though it shares the concern with formalisation characteristic of the one and the attention to details of usage characteristic of the other.

III

Empirical linguistics takes the most general problem of the study of language to be that of accounting for the fluent speaker's ability to produce freely and understand readily all utterances of his language, including wholly novel ones.[6] To explicate this ability, linguists construct a system of description which seeks to capture the regularities of the language used by speakers to produce and interpret sentences. The descriptive system which represents these regularities must include recursive rules since, as we have remarked before, the set of sentences of a language is infinite.[7] Such a system of description is a genuine scientific theory. A scientific theory systematically and economically interconnects a wide variety of observable events by representing them in terms of laws stated with theoretical concepts. It affords predictions of new events by deducing them from laws and explains why certain events occur by reference to the underlying structures it exhibits. In the case of a theory of language, verbal behaviour of speakers constitutes the observable events to be systematised by the theory. 'Verbal behaviour' is construed to include: perceptual discriminations, verbal productions, intuitions of oddity, judgements regarding similarity and difference in structure or meaning, etc. The theoretical concepts in terms of which the laws are stated are such constructs as phoneme, morpheme, word, etc., and the laws are the rules which represent the regularities of the language.

To think of a theory of a language in this way is immediately to postulate empirical constraints upon its construction. The theory is, *inter alia*, a predictive device: *what* it predicts is that some strings of words will be acceptable to speakers as sentences of their language, and that others will not ('Let us choose an example' but not 'Example an choose us let'). Similarly, it predicts that *if* certain utterances in fact occur, the speaker will interpret them in one way and not another and that certain utterances will be interpreted in several ways ('Failing students may be kindest' must be so represented as to bear more than one interpretation). Again, it predicts that certain utterances occur non-deviantly in some contexts but deviantly in others ('Here is a pretty red apple' must be so represented as to occur non-deviantly only in cases where the context determines the presence of an apple). In general, as is usually the case with fruitful empirical theories, possibilities for testing the theory proliferate as the theory develops.

Of particular interest to philosophers are the parts of a theory of language which are concerned with syntax and semantics. The former deals with that part of the general problem of the production and understanding of linguistic forms that involves grammatical structure. What a speaker does when he understands or produces an utterance must include at least the implicit analysing of its syntactic structure. It is this ability that a theory of syntax seeks to explicate. That is, it seeks to answer such questions as 'What are the basic construction types of the language?', 'What units are available in the language for sentence composition?', 'How may they be related to one another?', 'How are sentences formally related to other sentences?', and so forth. A semantic theory takes the solution to the general problem of production and understanding a step further. It seeks to account for the speaker's ability to assign interpretations to sentences on the basis of his knowledge of the meanings of their parts, to recognise semantic relations between pairs of words, expressions, or sentences, etc.

In the explanation of linguistic skills, the development of a theory of semantics requires the prior elaboration of a theory of syntax. This does not mean that semantics is necessarily conceived of as a system for interpreting a previously articulated syntactic structure, but only that the solution of problems in semantics requires syntactic information. One way to see this is the following: Let us suppose for the moment that a semantic theory is concerned in part with stating the conditions of truth and reference for arbitrary sentences of the language. Then consider such syntactically ambiguous sentences as 'Failing students may be kindest'. Ambiguous sentences must be so construed as to be paired with separate sets of truth conditions. The previous example is a sentence which is true in cases *either* where it is sometimes kindest to students to fail them, *or* where students who are in fact failing are sometimes the kindest students. But notice that the disjunction of the relevant truth conditions is based upon the syntactical form of the sentence, so that the rule which says that sentences of this form must be paired with disjoint conditions must make explicit reference to their grammatical features.

This point may be further generalised as follows: wherever a semantic theory seeks to assign meaning interpretations to sentences, it seems reasonable to suppose that it will treat *complex* sentences by resolving them into their constituent parts and making the relevant assignments part by part.[8] But the very task of resolving a complex sentence into its components presupposes that the underlying compositional structure of the sentence has been marked by grammatical analysis.

Finally, even on the weakest conception of a semantic theory it is required that such a theory assign meaning to the words and expressions of the language under study. But even in this case a knowledge of the grammatical structure of the language is necessary to make these assignments. For usually the meaning of a word or expression varies depending upon its grammatical role in context. Compare 'He papers the tables' and 'He tables the papers', or 'He peoples the houses' and 'He houses the people.'.

Such considerations require philosophers to pay more attention to grammar in their theorising about language than they have usually been willing to do. This will be found especially profitable because grammarians have developed a powerful new system of grammatical description which is directly relevant not only to the development of a semantic theory, but also to standard philosophical problems.

XVI Philosophical analysis and structural linguistics

W. P. Alston

In the course of this century philosophical analysis has increasingly turned from the material to the formal mode. In both their meta-philosophical pronouncements and their first-hand philosophical practice analytical philosophers have been increasingly moving away from talking in terms of the description, dissection, or analysis of extra-linguistic ideas, concepts, or meanings, and more and more tending to talk in terms of uses of words, the 'grammar' of our language, or the rules governing our use of linguistic expressions. It has not escaped the notice of friend and foe alike that, as this latter style becomes firmly entrenched, the enterprise of analytical philosophy comes to bear a striking similarity to such traditional linguistic disciplines as lexicography and grammar. This observation has evoked a variety of reactions. Critics of this form of analytic philosophy have taken these similarities to be a reflection of the triviality or lack of philosophical significance of such researches, while the practitioners of this style have often striven to distinguish their work from 'mere lexicography' or 'school grammar'. On the other hand, some philosophers of late, particularly those heavily influenced by the linguistic work of Zelig Harris and Noam Chomsky, have hailed contemporary structural linguistics as a saviour which will lead analytical philosophy out of the wilderness into the promised land of scientific precision and certitude.

The question as to just what connections, and lacks thereof, there are between philosophical analysis and linguistics is a tangled one, partly because of the great diversity of what goes on under the name of philosophical analysis and partly because of the fact that linguistics is in a stage of rapid development. In this paper I propose to make a contribution to the problem by taking an example of philosophical analysis that might seem to be quite similar to what contemporary linguists do, and trying to determine how deep the similarity goes and what differences if any are being masked.

The type of philosophical analysis under consideration will be sufficiently indicated by the example, but, as for linguistics, I should say that I am restricting my attention to what would be called 'structural linguistics' in this country today (not that this indicates any *precise* boundaries).

Let us get under way by considering the following passage from Gilbert Ryle's *The Concept of Mind*.[1]

There is another class of episodic words which, for our purposes, merit special attention, namely the class of episodic words which I have elsewhere labelled 'achievement words' . . . .

The verbs with which we ordinarily express these gettings and keepings are active verbs, such as 'win', 'unearth', 'find', 'cure', 'convince', 'prove', 'cheat', 'unlock', 'safeguard' and 'conceal'; and this grammatical fact has tended to make people, with the exception of Aristotle, oblivious to the differences of logical behaviour between verbs of this class and other verbs of activity or process. The differences, for example, between kicking and scoring, treating and healing, hunting and finding, clutching and holding fast, listening and hearing, looking and seeing, travelling and arriving, have been construed, if they have been noticed at all, as differences between co-ordinate species of activity or process, when in fact the differences are of quite another kind. . . .

One big difference between the logical force of a task and that of a corresponding achievement verb is that in applying an achievement verb we are asserting that some state of affairs obtains over and above that which consists in the performance, if any, of the subservient task activity. . . . They are not acts, exertions, operations or performances, but, with reservations for purely lucky achievements, the fact that certain acts, operations, exertions or performances have had certain results.

This is why we can significantly say that someone has aimed in vain or successfully, but not that he has hit the target in vain or successfully; that he has treated his patient assiduously or unassiduously, but not that he has cured him assiduously or unassiduously; that he scanned the hedgerow slowly or rapidly, systematically or haphazardly but not that he saw the nest slowly or rapidly, systematically or haphazardly. Adverbs proper to task verbs are not generally proper to achievement verbs; in particular, heed adverbs like 'carefully', 'attentively', studiously', 'vigilantly', 'conscientiously', and 'pertinaciously' cannot be used to qualify such cognitive verbs as 'discover', 'prove', 'solve', 'detect', or 'see', any more than they can qualify such verbs as 'arrive', 'repair', 'buy' or 'conquer'.

... They do not stand for perplexingly undetectable actions or reactions, any more than 'win' stands for a perplexingly undetectable bit of running, or 'unlock' for an unreported bit of key-turning. The reason why I cannot catch myself seeing or deducing is that these verbs are of the wrong type to complete the phrase 'catch myself'.... The questions 'What are you doing?' and 'What was he undergoing?' cannot be answered by 'seeing', 'concluding', or 'checkmating'....

The distinction between task verbs and achievement verbs or 'try' verbs and 'got it' verbs frees us from another theoretical nuisance. It has long been realised that verbs like 'know', 'discover', 'solve', 'prove', 'perceive', 'see' and 'observe' (at least in certain standard uses of 'observe') are in an important way incapable of being qualified by adverbs like 'erroneously' and 'incorrectly'. Automatically construing these and kindred verbs as standing for special kinds of operations or experiences, some epistemologists have felt themselves obliged to postulate that people possess certain special inquiry procedures in following which they are subject to no risk of error....

Clearly, Ryle is trying to make a philosophical point by pointing out certain features of the use of certain words. He thinks that once we see that words like 'see', 'prove', and 'know' function in the way he sums up by calling them 'achievement verbs', we will no longer feel a necessity to postulate mysterious and undetectable activities of seeing, proving, and knowing.[2] And, of course, he thinks of this in turn as one step in getting away from traditional mind–body dualism. What I want to do is to compare the linguistic points that Ryle is making for this purpose with analogous points that a structural linguist does, or might, make. In the course of this comparison I would like to make a start towards answering the following questions: (1) What important differences, if any, are there between what Ryle says here about 'see', 'know', etc., and what a linguist might say about them? (2) What similarities and differences are there between the data to which Ryle and the linguist appeal? In the course of attempting to answer these questions I shall consider some ways in which the concepts and/or methods of structural linguistics might be of help to the philosopher.

I

Let us begin with (2). In supporting his conclusion that 'see', 'prove', etc., are achievement verbs and therefore do not denote any sort of activity or process Ryle appeals to two sorts of facts, or supposed facts. First there are facts about what is entailed by an application of a given word ('in applying an achievement verb we are asserting that some state of affairs obtains over and above that which consists in the performance, if any, of the subservient task activity'). This could equivalently be put in terms of the conditions for correct application of the term; Ryle could have said instead that an achievement verb can only be applied correctly if some state of affairs obtains over and above. . . . Second, there are facts about what can and cannot be said; sometimes qualifications like 'significantly', 'intelligibly', and 'make sense' are added ('we can significantly say that someone has aimed in vain or successfully, but not that he has hit the target in vain or successfully; . . . that he scanned the hedgerow slowly or rapidly, systematically or haphazardly, but not that he saw the nest slowly or rapidly, systematically or haphazardly'). Now if we ask whether data of these sorts play an important role in the work of structural linguists, we shall first have to decide (*a*) what stand we are going to take on the vexed question of whether the grammatical structure of a language can be determined without raising such semantic questions as what linguistic units have meaning and whether two linguistic units have the same or different meaning, and (*b*) whether we are going to consider semantics to be part of structural linguistics. As for (*b*), I am simply going to rule semantics out of consideration without more ado, on the grounds that it is insufficiently developed at present to give much point to asking about its possible contributions to philosophy. As for (*a*), I am going to side with those (like Harris and Chomsky) who maintain that the grammatical structure of a language can be specified without first having settled any semantic questions. I choose this position largely because of the fact that on the other view there is an obvious coincidence between the sorts of facts appealed to by the two groups, whereas on the Harris–Chomsky view the relationship is more complicated and more in need of careful discussion. (Of course a necessary condition of my proceeding in this way is that I think there is some chance that this position is correct.)

Without even attempting to go into the difficult question of the boundary between grammar and semantics, it is clear that state-

ments about entailments and about the conditions under which a
word is correctly applied to something belong to semantics if anything does, and so would not be appealed to in grammatical investigations by the linguists we are considering. What they will use as a
basis are facts about what is and is not said in the language (the
constitution of the 'corpus') and facts about whether one utterance
is or is not the same as another utterance. Now it looks as if facts
of the first sort are the same as the first sort of facts appealed to by
Ryle. But things are not so simple. There are many reasons for a
given combination of words (or morphemes) not being uttered.
Of course neither Ryle nor, e.g., Harris would be interested in
determining just which combinations have as a matter of fact been
uttered; they are both interested in what *can* be said. But there are
various reasons why a given combination cannot or would not be
uttered (especially if we restrict our attention to what can or would
be uttered on a given occasion, and it is always on a given occasion
that a given test is carried out). It may be because it is radically
defective grammatically (horse the when already), because it doesn't
make sense (He saw the nest systematically), because it is self-
contradictory (I live north of the north pole), because it is so obviously absurd (President Kennedy was born yesterday), because it is
obscene, rude, or unseemly. It is incumbent on one who bases
important conclusions on considerations as to what can and cannot
be said to specify just what sort of possibility and impossibility he has
in mind. Clearly both Ryle and the structural linguist would want
to filter out the last two groups, on the grounds that here the
impossibility is not based on something in the language. But as for
the others, the situation is not so clear, partly because of the difficulty of drawing the line between grammar and semantics. It is
obvious that if a grammarian is testing his tentative grammatical
rules by determining whether all and only combinations that can
be uttered in the language would be contructed in accordance with
those rules, it must be the ability to occur without ungrammatical-
ness that is in question. And it is equally obvious that a philosopher
like Ryle is constantly appealing to what can or cannot be said
significantly. But before we can be sure that two different types of
possibility of occurrence are involved here, we shall have to get
clear as to what grammaticalness is and what significance is, and I
would suppose that a definitive answer to these questions awaits the
development of an adequate metatheory of grammar and semantics,
which in turn awaits further developments in grammar and semantics themselves. Chomsky[3] says that 'Colourless green ideas sleep

furiously', though nonsensical, is grammatical, while 'Furiously sleep ideas green colourless' is ungrammatical as well. But it may be that a more subtle grammar would show the former to be grammatically defective, e.g. by setting up formally defined classes of 'abstract' nouns like 'idea') and 'concrete' verbs (like 'sleep') and introducing syntactical rules that restrict their combination. And if achievement verbs can be set up as a grammatical form-class (see below), then 'He saw the nest systematically' would be exhibited as ungrammatical as well as non-significant. It might even be suggested that all supposed non-significant but grammatical sentences could be shown to be special types of ungrammatical sentences, though this seems to me to be too extreme. In any event, as long as we are working with the terms 'grammatical' and 'significant' in a completely undigested state, it will be impossible to show that Ryle and Chomsky are appealing to different sorts of linguistic possibility and impossibility. But it does seems plausible to suppose that they are not quite the same.

But even if linguists and philosophers do not appeal to exactly the same data, it might be that philosophers can learn something from the way linguists deal with analogous data. Various philosophers have expressed considerable dissatisfaction with statements made by philosophers like Ryle about what can and cannot be said. The more serious objections have to do with the absence of any empirical evidence for such claims and the difficulty of distinguishing between different kinds of impossibility, such as those mentioned in the last paragraph. The embattled philosopher might well expect to get some guidance on these matters from the structural linguist, who considers himself to be an empirical scientist. One would expect that linguists would have worked out some reliable empirical tests for the possibility or impossibility of occurrence of some combination of elements in a given language. But such expectations would be frustrated. Many linguists work with a quite naïve conception of a 'corpus', which presumably contains, e.g., any samples of speech one might happen to pick up with a tape recorder or other recording device, human or non-human. This would presumably include all sorts of slips, misuses, drunken ravings, etc. A man who is setting out to give a complete description of the language may ignore these problems in practice if the 'corpus' is sufficently large, for if he can find a set of elements and a set of rules for their combination which is not too unwieldy and which fits almost all the utterances in the corpus, he can dismiss the residue as misuses (though it will still be desirable to have some sort of independent test of the hypothesis that they are misuses). But a philosopher is not concerned to give a complete description of a language; he wants to concentrate on certain terms that are crucial for certain philosophical problems. Hence he does not have the above kind of device for washing out misuses, and it is important for him to be quite accurate on each individual claim as to what can and can't be said. And on this point he can expect no help from contemporary linguistics.

II

I now turn to a consideration of the character of Ryle's thesis, vis-à-vis analogous theses a structural linguist might conceivably put forward, though in order to get at the important points it will be useful to raise further questions about the character of his data. It is not surprising that one cannot get at the nature of the theory and the nature of the data in complete independence of each other. Let us state Ryle's thesis as follows: certain verbs, such as 'find', 'score', 'see', 'know', and 'prove', fall into a class, which we may term 'achievement verbs', that is distinguished from other classes of verbs by such facts as that none of its members admit the present continuous tense (one cannot say 'I am knowing that the Giants won the pennant') and that none of them can be used with certain adverbs, 'successfully', 'unsuccessfully', 'assiduously', etc. So stated, the thesis seems quite similar to attempts by linguists to separate out a certain class of elements of morpheme size or larger, in terms of their distribution relative to other elements. In fact, in A. A. Hill's *Introduction to Linguistic Structures*,[4] we have a quite analogous class demarcated, termed by him 'habitual verbs' on the grounds that the so-called habitual present tense (I swim often) is the only one they have, the present continuous tense not being available. In his rather sketchy treatment this is the only criterion he considers.

Just how close to linguists is Ryle in what he is doing here? (In terms of the sort of linguistics we are considering, this is equivalent to asking 'Is the distinction between achievement verbs and task verbs a grammatical distinction?') He himself is given to drawing, or attempting to draw, a sharp distinction between what he and other philosophers do by way of bringing out category distinctions and features of the use of words and what linguists do. In his essay 'Categories', he says: 'category-propositions are semantic propositions. This does not imply that they are of the same types as the propositions of philologists, grammarians or lexicographers. There are not English category-propositions as opposed to German ones, or Occidental as opposed to Oriental.'[5] And in his essay 'Ordinary Language', he tries to get at this difference by maintaining that those who philosophise in this style are dealing not with words but with uses that one or another word may happen to have:

> Hume's question was not about the word 'cause'; it was about the *use* of 'cause'. It was just as much about the *use* of 'Ursache', though 'cause' is not the same word as 'Ursache'. Hume's question was not a question about a bit of the English language in any way in which it was not a question about a bit of the German language. The job done with the English word 'cause' is not an English job, or a continental job.[6]

Ryle then goes on to claim that the term 'usage' is the appropriate term for marking the fact that a certain word in a certain language has the particular use that 'cause' and 'Ursache' share. In these terms he argues that philosophers are properly concerned with use, not with usage (pp. 48–53 above); i.e. with bringing out the features of a certain job one can do with one word or another, not with claims to the effect that a certain word in a certain language is in fact employed to do this job.

I am quite sure that Ryle cannot dissociate himself from grammarians, lexicographers, etc., in just this way. If we take these passages at their face value, he seems to be saying that, contrary to appearances, in *The Concept of Mind* he is not setting out to tell us anything about the English words 'see', 'know', 'prove', etc. Of course, the sentence 'Hume's question was not about the word 'cause'; it was about the *use* of "cause"' admits of more than one interpretation. It might simply mean that Hume was not concerned with the phonetic or phonemic constitution of the word 'cause' or with its past history, but with the way(s) in which it is now employed. But if that is all that is meant, it would obviously afford no basis at all for distinguishing what Hume and Ryle are doing from what grammarians and lexicographers do. If what Ryle says is to provide such a differentiation, we shall have to interpret him as maintaining that what he is concerned with is, e.g., a way of using verbs to denote not 'acts, exertions, operations or performances, but . . . the fact that certain acts, operations, exertions or performances have had certain results' and that he makes reference to particular English words like 'win', 'find', 'cure, 'see', 'prove', etc., only as one device, among many others he might have used instead, to direct our attention to that sort of use. Once our attention is so directed, these words are of no more interest, just as once we have arrived at our destination we no longer need concern ourselves with the particular signpost which, as it happened, guided us there. This would have the further implication that it would make no essential difference to Ryle's enterprise if he were quite mistaken in what he says, or appears to be saying, about 'know', 'see', etc. – if, e.g., contrary to what he says, or appears to be saying, one could say significantly 'I assiduously know that the Giants won the pennant' or 'At this moment I am knowing that the Giants won the pennant', Of course being in error on such points might result in Ryle's failing to get our attention directed to the use in which he is interested, but if it didn't then the error would make no difference. But if we look closely at what Ryle is trying to do, we see that this account of his enterprise simply does not fit. Ryle is trying to direct our attention to this sort of use of words, in order to relieve certain philosophical discomforts or 'conceptual cramps' into which he thinks people have got in reflecting on knowledge and perception (in the course of their employment of the words 'know' and 'see' or equivalent terms in other languages). But this means that Ryle has to be correct in what he says about the English words 'know' and 'see' if his remarks about this way of using words is to have any relevance to those problems. (Words in other languages come in only *qua* being equivalent to 'know' and 'see', so these latter constitute the keystone. More on this in a moment.) If 'I am now knowing that . . .' makes perfectly good sense, then whether or not the achievement way of using verbs exists as an abstract possibility or as exemplified by other verbs, pointing this out can have no bearing on the problem of what it is to know something, nor can it have any efficacy in clearing up puzzles and dilemmas into which we fall in thinking about knowledge.

To be sure, there is a point in what Ryle is saying in the passages just quoted, and it deserves to be extricated from the confusions in which it is embedded. Hume's discussion of causation and Ryle's discussion of knowledge are not relevant only to English-speaking philosophers, and this means that in some sense they are not concerned exclusively with the English words 'cause' and 'know'. But this is far from showing that they are not essentially concerned to say something about the way in which these particular words are used, or that it is not essential that what they say be true of these particular words. The point is that these discussions have relevance beyond the English-speaking community to the extent that there are words and/or larger units in other languages which have the sorts of uses the English words 'know' and 'cause' have and which figure, or might figure, in a like way in the generation of philosophical puzzles and paradoxes. But Ryle has to get straight as to how the English word 'know' is used, or he will not have any results, an analogue of which might be specified for various other languages. So, far from this wider relevance showing that Ryle does not have to concern himself with facts as to how 'know' is in fact employed, it is rather the case that accuracy with respect to the use of 'know' is an indispensable basis for that wider relevance. Ryle must at the very least be right about 'know'. If there are analogous points to be made for other languages, so much the better.

This means that at this point there is a distinction between what Ryle is doing and what a linguist might be doing. If a linguist is describing English, then the non-existence of parallels in all other languages, or even any other language, to a certain form-class he demarcates or a certain syntactical construction he analyses does nothing to detract from the value or significance of his results. (I am not saying that linguists cannot or do not have an interest in 'linguistic universals'. I am saying merely that linguists can and do set out to specify the structure of a given language; and it is this aspect of linguistics on which I am concentrating at the moment.) But if it turned out that although what Ryle says about 'win', 'cure', 'see', etc., were correct, there were no achievement verbs in any other languages, then he and we would feel that his results had much less philosophical significance than had been claimed for them, or perhaps even no philosophical significance at all. This difference can be brought out by the fact that when *The Concept of Mind* is translated, as by Professor Rossi-Landi into Italian, the English words Ryle is examining are themselves replaced by Italian equivalents; and if this had been impossible then it would not have been worth while carrying out the translations. But if Hill's book on the structure of English were translated into Italian, the English words whose behaviour he is describing would be left in English. This shows that it is true to say that Hill is specifically concerned with the English word 'see' in a way in which Ryle is not. But, as already indicated, this has to do with the import the thesis about 'see' is taken to have and the uses to which it is put, rather than the character of the thesis itself or the sorts of considerations that are relevant in testing it.

III

Nevertheless there are some important differences between the character of Ryle's thesis about 'see', etc., and the sort of thesis that would be put forward by the somewhat idealised linguist we are using as a foil. These can be brought out by considering the way in which structural linguistics aspires to be 'formal'. As used here, 'formal' restricts criteria for the presence of a kind of element and for the permissibility of combinations to publicly observable characteristics of speech sounds and their patterning.[7] Thus in specifying a class of elements or in specifying rules for their combination in formal manner, one cannot take into account meaning, what is referred to, or what would be said if a certain sequence were uttered. Ryle's account of achievement verbs fails to be 'formal' in two ways. First, instead of proceeding formally by specifying the other elements (themselves formally defined) with which a given word can or cannot be conjoined in certain configurations, Ryle makes his points in terms of our ability or inability to say something or to answer a given question in a certain way, where 'say something' and 'answer a question' are not formal concepts in the required sense. Thus he says 'we can significantly say that someone has aimed in vain or successfully, but not that he has hit the target in vain or successfully', instead of putting it formally in terms of the possibility of occurrence of the sequence 'he has hit the target successfully'. And he says 'The questions "What are you doing?" and "What was he undergoing?" cannot be answered by "seeing", "concluding", or "checkmating"', instead of saying something formal about what units can follow the sequence 'What are you doing?' Even where he encloses adverbs and verbs in quotes, what he says is that the adverbs 'cannot be used to qualify such cognitive verbs as . . .', and 'qualify' is hardly a formal term. Of course it may be that all Ryle's points could be translated into the formal mode, or, less strongly, that points could be made in the formal mode which in some sense correspond to them. But even if this is possible, it would not be a simple matter. In trying to convert Ryle's second point, e.g., into the formal mode, we would run into the difficulty that whether or not a given sequence, e.g. 'Concluding . . .', could occur after another, e.g. 'What are you doing?', would certainly depend on whether the first was uttered by way of asking a question and if so whether the second was uttered as an answer to that question. And it does not readily appear how these conditions could be stated in formal terms.

Ryle also falls short of being purely formal by virtue of the fact that it is of considerable importance to him that the class in question be named in one way or another. Or rather it is not the name that is so important (one might find a term just as apt for Ryle's purposes as 'achievement'); it is the characterisation that lies behind the name (these verbs denote not special performances but the outcomes of otherwise denoted performances). If Ryle is going to apply his account of achievement to traditional philosophical problems about perception and knowledge, he must get to this sort of character- isation. But it is clear that this goes beyond formal matters. Even though a linguist might label a class he has specified by purely formal criteria as 'mass nouns', 'habitual verbs', or 'quality ad- jectives', he has no right to draw on any of the implications or connotations of these labels, so long as he is being purely formal.

These considerations indicate important differences between Rylean philosophical analysis and the analysis of a language under- taken by a structural linguist, and the existence of these differences will certainly prevent any straightforward assimilation of the two enterprises or any simple transfer of methods from the one to the other. But it by no means follows that the procedures and results of structural linguistics are of no value to the analytical philosopher. Even though the analysis of language in purely formal terms does not itself give the philosopher the results he needs for his purposes, it might well separate out classes that the philosopher would find it profitable to examine in his own way. That is, the class distinctions the linguist discovers by formal procedures might parallel important conceptual distinctions, and the presentation of such formal results might provide the philosopher with hints for such distinctions. Thus the distinction of classes of adjectives that Hill has carried out, or at least begun, in terms of the formal criterion of obligatory order[8] might reflect conceptual distinctions between sorts of properties that would be philosophically important. We have something of this sort actually worked out in J. O. Urmson's essay 'Parenthetical Verbs',[9] where first the class of verbs is demarcated in terms of such formal considerations as flexibility of position in a sentence, and then the distinctive features of the concepts expressed by such verbs are explored. In this way structural linguistics might be of real impor- tance to philosophy. And, of course, if and when semantics is developed and integrated into structural linguistics along with grammar, the differences between the two sorts of inquiry in methods and status of conclusions, though not in ultimate aim, may well be reduced to the vanishing point.

XVII On knowing what we would say

J. Fodor

Philosophers, philosophising, sometimes ask themselves or their colleagues questions of the form 'What would we say if ...?' where the blank is filled by a description, more or less circumstantial, of a state of affairs in which some philosophically interesting word might get used, and where 'we' are supposed to be fluent and judicious speakers of English with no philosophical axes to grind. I want to distinguish two quite different kinds of case in which philosophers seek answers to questions about what we would say, and to argue that in one of them there is no reason to suppose the answers they get are trustworthy.

To describe a language is to formulate the rules which are internalised by speakers when they learn the language and applied in speaking and understanding it. The data for such a description derive from observation of particular speech episodes: incidents of talking in which the speaker's knowledge of the rules of his language is exercised. Very often philosophers ask what we would say as a means of obtaining such data. That is, they describe situations in which they think the word *might* be used (that is, situations in which a putative linguistic rule predicts that the word *could* be used without oddity) and then ask themselves or their informants what they would say about such situations. It would be equally effective, though less practical, actually to bring about the situation in question and see what the informant *does* say. In indefinitely many cases, either or both of these techniques might be employed.

For example, a philosopher interested in the use(s) of the word 'responsible' might ask such questions as these: 'My brakes fail and I go through a red light and hit a child. Am I responsible for the death of the child? What if I had known my brakes to be bad and had not bothered to have them fixed? What if at the moment my brakes failed, the car skidded on ice, so that I would have hit the child even if the brakes had worked? ...' and so on through a series of questions designed to elicit the relation between responsibility, forethought, control over the events, and so forth. Notice that the hypothetical air of these questions is inessential and perhaps misleading, for the informant's answer is useful only in so far as it is a reliable index of what he would say if the situation described were actualised. The posing of the question is an indirect way of determining in which situations speakers willingly invoke notions of responsibility and in which ones they do not. Generalisation is accomplished and insight into the structure of the language gained when we can formulate a rule which correctly extrapolates common features of observed situations in which the word 'responsible' is used, thus permitting us to predict how 'responsible' would be used in indefinitely many situations not yet observed.[1]

It is perfectly reasonable to ask: how good are speakers at answering the kind of questions instanced in the last paragraph? An answer would be forthcoming were we to check what speakers say they would say about problematic situations against what they in fact *do* say when such situations arise. The wise philosopher tests his own and his informant's intuitions against discourses produced in circumstances less academic than the philosophy seminar and the philosophy journal. We do not always say what we say that we would say.[2]

That we are at best imperfect observers of our own behaviour is a commonplace. But this is only to say that the degree of reliability of the informant is as much a subject for empirical investigation as the rules of the language the informant speaks. It is not to say that there is any *general* reason to distrust the speaker's intuitions in the sorts of cases we have been considering. On the contrary, it seems reasonable to suppose that the speaker's knowledge of his language provides him with some basis for claims about what he would say in novel situations. In any event, we run no serious risk in making this supposition since if it is false we can find out that it is by comparing the speaker's claims with the linguistic facts.

There are, however, cases in which the intuitions of speakers about what they would say are to be distrusted on *a priori* grounds; cases in which it is unreasonable to suppose that a knowledge of what he would say is implicit in the speaker's mastery of his language. It is such cases that I wish to explore in this paper.

In one or another form, the following doctrine has considerable currency among philosophers. Of the features which regularly characterise the occasions upon which a word is used, some must be attributable to the meaning of that word. Such features are definitive or 'criterial' in that their presence is a necessary condition of the proper use of the word. If F is such a feature relative to the word w, then 'If w is properly used, then F' is held to be an analytic, or quasi-logical or necessary truth.

'Occasion' and 'feature' must not be taken too seriously, and 'analytic', 'necessary', 'quasi-logical', and so forth are notoriously little more than the names of problems. (I do not wish even to suggest that they are names of the same problem.) In the sense of these terms intended here, it is a feature of occasions on which I correctly refer to someone as 'the brother of x' that I am referring to a male, and *that* statement is analytic, necessary, or quasi-logical. When a feature is related to occurrences of a word in this way, I shall say that that feature is 'logically characteristic' of the occurrence of the word. This is, of course, just another name.

Associated with the logically characteristic features of occurrences of a word there will often be features which we may call 'empirically characteristic'. A feature F' is empirically characteristic of the occurrences of w if:

1. There is some feature F which is logically characteristic of the occurrences of w; and
2. 'If F' then generally F' expresses a true empirical generalisation or a law of nature.

Put briefly, it is supposed that there often exist empirical correlates of logically characteristic features of words. I shall say that such correlates are empirically characteristic of the occurrences of words.

Empirically characteristic features of occurrences of words are sometimes considered to be symptomatic of logically characteristic features. 'I cannot see what sort of animal it is, but I can see that it is clothed.' It is, then, a good bet that it is human since humans are clothed much of the time and other sorts of animals hardly ever. The features which are logically characteristic of occurrences of 'human' are correlated with the empirically characteristic feature 'being clothed'. Being clothed is not criterial for being human, but it is a reasonably reliable correlate of the features which *are* criterial. One way of formulating the difference between logically and empirically characteristic features of the occurrences of a word is this: questions of reliability can be raised in the latter case but not in the former. (This is, however, a point of no more than verbal interest since the 'can' in the preceding sentence is the 'can' of logic. Hence this formulation presupposes the distinction it is intended to explicate.)

Given that one accepts some version of this view, the following philosophical problem arises: how to distinguish between features which are logically characteristic of occurrences of *w* and features which are (only) empirically characteristic but perfectly reliable – that is, between 'criteria' on the one hand and, on the other, 'symptoms' which obtain when and only when the relevant criteria do.

That it is likely to be difficult to discover a *general* solution for this problem follows from this: it is clear that no observational datum can by itself suffice to distinguish between perfect reliability and logical characteristicness since, by definition, an empirically characteristic feature of the occurrences of a word is not perfectly reliable unless it obtains on each occasion upon which the word is properly used – that is, on each occasion on which the logically characteristic features of the occurrences of the word obtain. If a feature is perfectly reliable, then *ex hypothesi* we shall never observe a case in which the word is properly used where that feature does not obtain. But since this is also true of criterial features of the use of a word, it follows that we cannot distinguish between perfectly reliable empirical correlates and criteria on the basis of observation alone.

Faced with this difficulty, philosophers have often adopted the following strategy: if *F* is a feature that you know to be perfectly correlated with regular occurrences of *w* but which you suspect may not be logically characteristic of occurrences of *w*, ask your informant *whether he would be willing to use w even in the absence of F*. If so, then *F* must be only empirically characteristic of *w*, since something could count as a regular occurrence of *w* from which *F* is absent. If not, then *F* must be logically characteristic of *w*, since nothing could count as a regular occurrence of *w* from which *F* is absent.

It is very important to much recent philosophising that this strategy should prove capable of vindication. Since no philosopher has ever proposed a tenable theory of the distinction between logical characteristicness and perfect reliability, the appeal to the informant's intuitions about what he would say must carry the whole burden of that distinction. Moreover, in this sort of case the appeal to the intuition of the informant is not subject to direct empirical check since, as we have seen, no observation can reveal a situation in which a word is properly used and a perfectly reliable empirically characteristic feature fails to obtain. Hence, there is in principle no way of directly verifying what an informant says about what he would say in such a situation. That is, there is no way of comparing what the informant says he would say with what he in fact says since, *ex hypothesi*, the situations under discussion never in fact arise.[3]

To put the matter briefly: had we a theory of the distinction between empirical reliability and logical characteristicness, the fact that we cannot observationally verify the speaker's claims about what he would say should a certain feature fail to obtain would be relatively unimportant. For the speaker's claims about what he would say could be viewed as confirmed or disconfirmed depending upon their degree of consonance with the predictions of the theory, just as, in grammar, the speaker's claims about well-formedness are accepted, in part, on the grounds that they conform fairly well with syntactic theories which we have independent reasons for accepting. Conversely, had we a way of observationally checking the speaker's claims, we should not feel the lack of a theory so deeply, since we could assess the reliability of the speaker's claims about what he would say by the usual observational methods. These claims, in so far as they *were* reliable, would in turn support a distinction between empirical and logical characteristicness. In the present case, however, we do not have a theory, and the terms of the problem preclude observational verification of the speaker's claims since, *ex hypothesi*, they are claims about what he would say in situations which never arise. Hence, if there is any reason whatever to suppose that the speaker's intuitions are not to be trusted in this sort of case, that an ability to answer this sort of what-would-we-say question is not implicit in a speaker's mastery of his native language, then the philosopher's claim that a certain feature of the occurrence of a word is logically characteristic, rather than merely empirically reliable, would appear to have no evidential support whatever.

Let us consider a few examples of how the appeal to intuition is supposed to operate to distinguish criteria from symptoms; then we shall be ready to summarise the differences between the two types of what-would-we-say question which we have been attempting to distinguish and to argue for the claim that the intuitions of speakers are not to be trusted in the second sort of case, however trustworthy they may prove in the first.

A philosopher interested in determining the logically characteristic features of occurrences of 'know' might require the following of his informant: 'Suppose a man were capable of correctly answering any problem in elementary number theory but claimed neither to be able to state how he arrived at his solutions nor ever to have been taught any mathematics. Would you say that he knows number theory?' If the informant's answer is negative, then it would appear that explicit access to the rules employed in computation is a logically necessary condition upon knowledge of such things as number theory. If the informant's answer is affirmative, then it is only a psychological fact that people who know number theory are able to articulate their knowledge.

Or a philosopher interested in dreams might ask the following sort of question: 'Suppose we observe a sleeper to have passed a restless night; we have seen him toss and turn and heard him mutter and cry out in his sleep. Upon awakening (and thereafter) he firmly and sincerely claims not to have dreamed. Would you say that he has dreamed and forgotten his dream or that he has not dreamed at all?' Or, conversely: 'A man passes what, to casual observation, appears to be a quiet night. Moreover, E.E.G. readings show no alteration of slow waves, his eye movements during sleep are not patterned, and he exhibits no change in G.S.R., perspiration, and so forth. Nevertheless, upon awakening, the subject reports terrible nightmares and anxiety dreams. Assuming that you know the subject's report to be sincere, would you say that the subject did, in fact, dream?' According to the strategy currently under investigation, if speakers claim that they would say in the second case that the subject had dreamed and in the first case that he had not, then it must follow that what is logically characteristic of occasions upon which we say of someone that he dreamed is a positive dream report. That is, the relation between 'S dreamed' and 'Upon awakening S feels inclined to say that he dreamed' is a logical relation, while the relation between 'S dreamed' and 'S exhibited alteration of slow waves during sleep' is at best a symptomatic relation, though the symptom is, *ex hypothesi*, perfectly reliable in this case.

It must be clear that the essential point about these examples is their counterfactuality. It is our belief that the situations they envisage do not normally occur – and hence are not typical of the situations in which the words involved are used – which makes them examples of the second sort of what-would-we-say question. We may, then, put the difference between the two sorts of situations about which such questions get asked in the following way. In the first kind of case, we are concerned with what speakers would say about quite normal, though perhaps hypothetical, situations. Although we may not know whether any speaker has ever actually encountered the state of affairs described, we know of no reason why such states of affairs should not occur. The situations described are normal ones in the sense that no feature known to be regularly correlated with occurrences of the word is supposed to fail to obtain. In the second kind of case, however, the situation we ask our informant to characterise is one which has been chosen precisely because it is the sort that we know either does not arise or arises only atypically. This is essential to our reason for asking the second sort of what-would-we-say question: namely, to test whether a feature which we know obtains in all *normal* cases of occurrences of a word does so by virtue of the meaning of the word. We hope to eliminate from our list of logically characteristic features any upon which an informant's willingness to use a word does not depend. The employment of essentially counterfactual questions purports to make it possible to do so even in the case of features which, in fact, always obtain when a word is used correctly.

What distinguishes the second sort of what-would-we-say question from the first is that in the former we are interested in what the informant would say in situations which we believe to be anomalous. Such situations are contrived so that all the merely empirical features of the use of a word are stripped away, revealing, so it is supposed, those features which are determined by the meaning of the word alone. It is essential to an understanding of the argument in the rest of this paper to see that the anomalous character of the situations described in the second sort of what-would-we-say question is no accident. Rather, it is essential if the answer to such questions is to provide the basis for a distinction between logically and empirically characteristic features of occurrences of words.

I hold that there is no reason to suppose that what-would-we-say questions of the second sort are answerable on the basis of our knowledge of our language. Put slightly differently, there is no reason to trust our intuitions about what we would say in situations in which some of our relatively secure beliefs have proved false; the ability to answer questions about what we would say in such circumstances is not implicit in our mastery of the rules of our language. The question put is: 'What would you say if you turned out to be mistaken in believing that a certain set of features (namely, the ones which obtain when w can be used correctly) are invariably correlated?' I shall argue that there is no reason to suppose that a knowledge of, say, English equips us to answer such questions.[4]

Before stating the argument, let me block two possible mis-understandings. First, I am not claiming that English speakers are unreliable in their answers to the second sort of what-would-we-say questions in the sense that they would disagree among themselves about what answers to give. The question of how much consensus obtains among English speakers about what they would say in anomalous situations is simply an empirical question which could be answered by simply empirical techniques. I am arguing not that the speaker's answer must be unreliable, but rather that it must be irresponsible; his knowledge of his language does not provide grounds for an answer and thus his answer could not be a source of information about his language. (I do not wish to deny that some sort of non-linguistic information may be available to speakers which serves as a basis for answers to the second sort of what-would-we-say question and hence accounts for whatever consensus exists as to the answers such questions should receive. But the existence of such non-linguistic information could not justify the philosophic appeal to the intuitions of the speaker *qua* speaker as a technique for distinguishing criteria from symptoms.)

Second, I am not arguing that the speaker is incapable of imag-ining or conceiving a situation in which some of his beliefs about the correlations among features regularly associated with occur-rences of words prove false. 'Imagine' and 'conceive' are, so far as I can tell, technical terms in philosophy such that any situation which can be described consistently is *ipso facto* imaginable or conceivable. In this sense of these terms it follows immediately (though not helpfully) that any feature of the occurrences of a word which is not logically characteristic of such occurrences can be imagined not to obtain. Whether this would also be true in some less technical sense of 'imagine' or 'conceive' I do not care to inquire. I do not *think* that I can imagine, say, a world in which nothing exists but sounds, but I am not sure that I cannot and I would not wish to have an important argument rest upon this point.

I hold that there is no reason to trust the intuitions of speakers about what they would say should their current beliefs prove seriously false. That is, I hold that there is no reason to believe such intuitions to be *linguistic* intuitions and hence that there is no basis for an appeal to the speaker *qua* speaker. The reason is this: to ask what we would say should certain of our current beliefs prove false involves asking what new beliefs we would then adopt. But to answer this question we would now have to be able to predict what theories would be devised and accepted were our current theories to prove untenable.[5] Clearly, however, it is unreasonable to attempt to predict what theories would be accepted if our current theories were abandoned and, *a fortiori*, it is unreasonable to attempt to make such predictions on the basis of an appeal to our current linguistic intuitions. Hence, if it is right to claim that to ask the second sort of what-would-we-say question is tantamount to asking what beliefs we would adopt should our current beliefs prove false, then it must follow that the strategy of employing such questions to distinguish between logically and empirically characteristic features of words is an unreasonable strategy and one which ought to be abandoned.

That we cannot in general answer the second sort of what-would-we-say question without knowing what beliefs we would adopt should our current beliefs prove false follows from this: to suppose that a perfectly reliable feature fails to obtain is, by definition, to suppose that a proposition which we now believe to express a law of nature or a true empirical generalisation is false. However, the discovery that such a proposition is false may, in turn, require the abandonment of other beliefs and, in the extreme case, of whole theories. Since there is no general way to determine how many of our beliefs may need to be altered as the result of such a discovery (since, that is, the set of beliefs that it would be reasonable to abandon should the belief that P prove false need not be coextensive with the set of beliefs formally incompatible with not P), there can be no general way to determine how much of our way of talking such a discovery may require use to revise.

Against this the following might be argued. 'It is true that we cannot now say what beliefs we should adopt if our current beliefs proved false. We cannot, for example, predict what we would say should dream reports prove not to be correlated with the results of observations of E.E.G., G.S.R., eye movements, muscle tone, gross movements during sleep, and so forth, or should these prove not to be correlated with one another. What we should doubtless do in such a case is cast about for a new theory of the relation between central and molar events, and what such a theoretical revision of the foundations of psychology might require us to say about dreams cannot now be known. This is, however, all thoroughly beside the point. For, though we cannot now predict what ways of talking we would adopt if our current beliefs broke down, we *can* now say that if we were to adopt *certain* ways of talking (that is, those which involve the abandonment of logically characteristic features of the word in question) then that would constitute a change of meaning. But the fact that we cannot now assert with certainty that no changes in our beliefs could lead us to change the meanings of words cannot be a reason for doubting the reliability of speakers' intuitions about when they would use a word, given its present meaning.'

There is another way of stating the argument. Suppose English speakers claim they would never say of S that he had dreamed unless upon awakening he felt inclined to report a dream. This claim may be understood in either of two ways. In the first place, it may be understood to show that no experimental or theoretical considerations could ever lead a rational individual to hold both that S had dreamed and that S had not felt inclined upon awakening to say he had dreamed. So understood, the claim would appear to involve a prediction as to what sort of view of dreams we would take were certain correlations to fail which are currently believed to obtain. And it seems reasonable to ask how the speaker's knowledge of his *language* could conceivably afford a basis for such a prediction. The claim could, however, also be understood in another way. It could be understood to show that no experimental or theoretical considerations could ever lead a rational individual to hold both that S had dreamed and that S had not felt inclined to say he had dreamed *unless the meaning of the word 'dream' had been changed*. And it does not seem implausible that *this* claim should be one to which the speaker is entitled just on the basis of his knowledge of his language.

This argument in effect poses a dilemma. It admits that the intuitions of speakers could not afford grounds for predictions about what beliefs we would adopt should our current beliefs prove false. In so doing, it tacitly admits that the intuitions of speakers might sometimes themselves prove false in the literal sense that it might be the case that features which are intuitively logically characteristic of the use of a word (that is, features whose failure to obtain would, according to speakers, provide sufficient grounds for not using the word) could be abandoned without abandoning the word in question. But, according to this argument, such cases would be cases in which changes in our beliefs have led us to change the meaning of a word. Hence they do not provide arguments against the reliability of intuition; what they show instead is that what seems to be unreliable intuition is really unacknowledged equivocation. It appears, then, that the speaker's intuitions *could not be fallible*; for either the speaker is literally right about what we would say or, if he is literally wrong, this shows only that the meaning of some word has been changed. That the argument should arrive at so curious a conclusion is itself grounds for supposing that something has gone wrong.

What is wrong with the argument is that it presupposed some technique for determining change of meaning that is independent of an appeal to speakers' intuitions about what we would say. Given such a technique, we could define a logically characteristic feature as one the alteration of which would involve a change of meaning, and we could add that the intuitions of speakers are trustworthy whenever the features which are intuitively unalterable are in fact the logically characteristic ones. Lacking such a technique, however, we must go the other way around and say that a change of meaning occurs just in case a logically characteristic feature is abandoned, where a logically characteristic feature is simply one the abandonment of which is not intuitively acceptable to speakers. This, however, makes the isolation of change of meaning rest upon precisely the same appeal to intuition which provides support for the distinction between criterial and symptomatic features. Hence, it would be circular to attempt to defend the soundness of such institutions by claiming that a change of meaning is the inevitable consequence of their violation.

In short, it is perhaps true that though the intuitions of speakers are inadequate to determine what beliefs we should adopt were our current beliefs to prove false, they are adequate to determine when a change in our beliefs would involve a change in the meaning of some word. But to *show* this, one must have some way of demonstrating change of meaning which does not itself rely for its support solely upon the intuitions of speakers. And though there is no logical or methodological implausibility in the assumption that there could be a theory of change of meaning which we have reason to believe true, independent of appeal to intuition, it seems clear that no such theory is currently available.

Once we abandon the notion that the speaker's claims about his linguistic behaviour have some special freedom from disconfirmation, methodological probity requires that we attempt to discover in which cases such claims are likely to prove trustworthy and in which cases they are not. I have argued that there can be no general objection to reliance upon the speaker's intuitions in cases where such intuitions are, at least in principle, capable of theoretical or observational confirmation. Philosophers, however, often want to know what we would say if certain propositions widely believed to be true should prove false. In these cases, observational confirmation of the speaker's claims is precluded by the terms of the question, and theoretical confirmation would presuppose a characterisation of the distinction between logical and empirical relations which does not rely solely upon an appeal to the intuitions of speaker. Such a characterisation has not been forthcoming.

The speaker's intuitions are to be trusted when, and only when, we have good reason to believe that they derive from his mastery of his language. It would, however, seem implausible to maintain that the speaker's supposed knowledge of what he would say, were certain of his beliefs to prove false, could be ascribable to his linguistic competence. Indeed, it seems implausible to maintain that the speaker *has* such knowledge. It is notorious that the disconfirmation of any of our more firmly entrenched beliefs may be an occasion for considerable conceptual revision and that neither the direction of such revision nor its impact upon our ways of talking is likely to be predictable ahead of time.

It may still be claimed that the speaker's intuitions suffice to determine when a revision in our ways of talking is tantamount to a change in the meaning of some word. I do not deny that this is so, but I deny that it is a claim to which we are entitled without argument. (And it is worth noticing that the cases in which we are hard put to make an intuitively correct decision between criteria and symptoms are invariably precisely the cases in which our intuitions about change of meaning are uncertain.) A demonstration that speakers' intuitions are adequate to determine change of meaning would involve the construction of a criterion for meaning change which is not itself wholly dependent upon appeals to the speaker's intuitions. I do not know of any philosopher who has ever proposed such a criterion.

Notes

Editor's Introduction

1. Noam Chomsky, *Cartesian Linguistics* (New York, 1966) and John Davy, 'The Chomsky Revolution', *The Observer Review*, 10 Aug 1969.

2. J. J. Katz, *The Philosophy of Language* (New York, 1966) ch. 1.

3. Some recent work touching on this problem will be found in the volume edited by Borst in this series (*The Mind–Brain Identity Theory*).

4. See J. O. Urmson, 'Some Questions Concerning Validity,' in A. G. N. Flew (ed.), *Essays in Conceptual Analysis* (London, 1956).

5. See K. S. Donnellan, 'The Paradigm Case Argument', in Paul Edwards (ed.), *The Encyclopaedia of Philosophy* (New York, 1967) for a fuller discussion and bibliography.

6. Discussions which have a bearing on this subject are to be found in H. Putnam, 'Dreaming and Depth Grammar', in R. Butler (ed.), *Analytical Philosophy* (Oxford, 1962) and H. Putnam, 'Brains and Behaviour', in R. Butler (ed.), *Analytical Philosophy*, Second Series (Oxford, 1965).

7. If these conditionings are *not* different in kind, then it is not obvious that the meaning of the word is altered when these are added to the list of conditions under which an action is not free.

8. ' "So you are saying that human agreement decides what is true and what is false?" It is what human beings *say* that it is true and false; and they agree in the *language* they use. This is not agreement in opinions but in forms of life.' L. Wittgenstein, *Philosophical Investigations* (Oxford, 1963) para. 242.

9. See Max Black, *Language and Philosophy* (Ithaca, N.Y., 1969) ch. 1.

10. See the companion volume in this series by W. D. Hudson (*The Is–Ought Question*).

11. For some explorations in this territory, see J. L. Austin, *How to do Things with Words* (Oxford, 1962).

12. See also Katz, *The Philosophy of Language*.

13. These methods are reported on in J. O. Urmson, 'J. L. Austin', *Journal of Philosophy*, LXII (1965), reprinted in R. Rorty, *The Linguistic Turn* (Chicago, 1967).

14. These paradoxes were first put into print by Lewis Carroll, 'What the Tortoise Said to Achilles', *Mind*, IV (1895). See also G. Ryle, 'If, So and Because', in Max Black (ed.), *Philosophical Analysis* (Englewood Cliffs, N.J., 1963).

15. Compare the remarks on the difference between inadvertence and the accidental in Cavell (Chapter VIII).

16. It is rare for the language under investigation to be completely unknown; see W. V. O. Quine, *Word and Object* (Cambridge, Mass., 1960) ch. 2. The whole of that chapter is germane to the present discussion.

17. For a further discussion, see K. L. Pike, *Phonemics: A Technique for Reducing Languages to Writing* (Ann Arbor, 1947).

18. I shall discuss the philosophical relevance of a syntactic analysis in a later section.

19. Quine, *Word and Object*, pp. 28, 29.

20. See ibid., ch. 2, para. 9.

21. I hope to explore this matter in a later collection.

22. See R. Quirk and J. Svartvik, *Investigating Linguistic Acceptability* (The Hague, 1966).

23. See Wittgenstein, *Philosophical Investigations*, para. 126.

24. See Quirk and Svartvik, *Investigating Linguistic Acceptability*.

25. And theoretical linguistics, in which they are often raised, is at least in part a philosophical discipline.

26. The more positive remarks made by Austin need not be accepted without question; see J. L. Austin and G. E. M. Anscombe, 'Pretending', *Proceedings of the Aristotelian Society*, supp. vol. xxxii (1958).

27. *Philosophical Investigations*, para. 129.

28. An important contribution, in the spirit of G. E. Moore, is to be found in N. Malcolm, *Knowledge and Certainty* (Englewood Cliffs, N.J. 1963).

29. L. Wittgenstein, *Tractatus Logico-Philosophicus* (London, 1923) para. 2 4.0031.

30. 'Systematically Misleading Expressions', in A. G. N. Flew (ed.), *Logic and Language*, First Series (Oxford, 1951).

31. 'Is Existence a Predicate?', in A. G. N. Flew (ed.), *Logic and Language*, Second Series (Oxford, 1953).

32. This has been argued in a recent paper by P. F. Strawson, 'Grammar and Philosophy', *Proceedings of the Aristotelian Society* (1969–70).

33. In lieu of further extracts and discussion the following list of seminal works may be found helpful: Katz, *The Philosophy of Language*; J. J. Katz and J. A. Fodor, 'The Structure of Semantic Theory', in Fodor and Katz, *The Structure of Language* (Englewood Cliffs, N.J., 1964); J. J. Katz, 'The Relevance of Linguistics to Philosophy', *Journal of Philosophy*, lxii (1965), revised and expanded in Rorty, *The Linguistic Turn*; J. J. Katz, 'Semantic Theory and the Meaning of "Good"', *Journal of Philosophy*, lxi (1964). See also Ziff's *Semantic Analysis* (mentioned in Bibliography below). The Fodor and Katz semantic theory has been criticised by D. Bolinge in 'The Atomisation of Meaning', *Language*, xli (1965).

Chapter I

1. See ch. iii, s. 4, of *The Concept of Mind*.
2. See ibid., ch. v.

Chapter IV

1. This paper was originally commissioned by the *Philosophical Quarterly* (*PQ*) as a cross between a survey of work of a certain sort published since the end of the Second World War and an *apologia pro philosophia nostra contra murmurantes*. Hence it was to a quite exceptional degree both polemical in tone and burdened with footnotes. For this reprinting the tone has been softened and the burden lightened a little. But the former is considerably sharper and the latter very much heavier than they would be if I had been writing now and for this present purpose.

2. See J. L. Austin's classic 'Other Minds', in A. G. N. Flew (ed.), *Logic and Language*, Second Series, and also s. iii of S. E. Toulmin's 'Probability', in A. G. N. Flew (ed.), *Essays in Conceptual Analysis* (London, 1956). I shall use *LL* i and ii as abbreviations for *Logic and Language*, First and Second Series (Oxford, 1951, 1953), respectively.

3. 'God created personnel in his own image' (Sir Alan Herbert).

4. Cf. L. J. Cohen, 'Are Philosophical Theses Relative to Language?', *Analysis* (1949).

5. G. Ryle, 'Ordinary Language', *Philosophical Review* (1953) (in part reprinted in Chapter II above).

6. *PQ* (1952) p. 2 (top).

7. *Utilitarianism*, Everyman ed., p. 32 (bottom): Mill argues from this morphological analogy, explicitly, though even here it is doubtful if this was more than the occasion for a mistake, the true cause of which was the quest for a 'scientific ethics'.

8. See *Proceedings of the Aristotelian Society* (*P.A.S.*), supp. vol. XXVII (1953) pp. 42–3, 47–8, for a recent example of this howler and its criticism.

9. T. D. Weldon, *The Vocabulary of Politics* (Harmondsworth, 1953) p. 107.

10. *Critique of Practical Reasons*, trans. T. K. Abbott, p. 150.

11. For some of the many more worthy attractions, see D. F. Pears, 'Universals', in *LL* ii. For Aristotle's battle against the temptations of this idiom, in which he had to express his definition of goodness, see the early chapters of *Nicomachean Ethics*, bk i.

12. This point was originally made by Sayce, and reiterated by Russell, *Analysis of Mind*, p. 212.

13. See articles by D. D. Lee mentioned below, though her interpretation of Trobiand thought is disputed.

14. See *Republic*, 596 a6–8, for a suggestive admission: 'We have been in the habit, if you remember, of positing a Form, wherever we use the same name in many instances, one Form for each many.'

15. Cf. the language games of Wittgenstein, imaginary truncated languages used as diagrams in *Philosophical Investigations*, and the Newspeak of George Orwell's *1984*, Appendix.

16. See *LL* ii, p. 3; to the references given there in the second note can be added D. D. Lee in *Psychosomatic Medicine*, XIII (1950) and in the *Journal of Philosophy* (1949).

17. *PQ* (1952) p. 12.
18. Ibid., p. 2.
19. To the point here would be references given by P. L. Heath, ibid., p. 2 n.
20. See Sir Alan Herbert's *What a Word!*, Sir Ernest Gowers's *Plain Words* and *A.B.C. of Plain Words*, etc.
21. This point is developed by F. Waismann in his 'Analytic–Synthetic', and stressed to a point at which some might complain that it encouraged anarchic Humpty-Dumptyism (*Analysis* (1950) pp. x ff.).
22. On the analogous difficulty of knowing in advance the 'logical breaking strains of concepts', see Ryle's Inaugural, *Philosophical Arguments* (Oxford, 1945).
23. See the *Philosophical Investigations*, especially *ab init.*, for his own account of the reasons for this maxim.
24. See M. Weitz, 'Oxford Philosophy', *Philosophical Review* (1953) and *P.A.S.*, supp. vol. XVIII (1939), for Austin's first characteristic publication.
25. *PQ* (1952) p. 5 (top).
26. 'How to Talk', *P.A.S.* (1952–3) p. 227.
27. For some subtle and very important examples of a sensitivity to ordinary usage, see G. J. Warnock's *Berkeley* (Harmondsworth, 1953) esp. chs 7–10.
28. *PQ* (1952) p. 6.
29. Ibid.
30. *Inquiry Concerning Human Understanding*, s. viii, pt i.
31. His views had been substantially anticipated: by Hobbes, *Leviathan*, ch. xxi, and in his 'Of Liberty and Necessity', and no doubt by many others long before.
32. See *LL* II, pp. 5–6, for an attack on this once popular misdescription of philosophical problems; Ryle, *Concept of Mind*, p. 71 (top), lapses by writing 'largely spurious problems'.
33. Kant, *Critique of Practical Reason,* trans. T. K. Abbott, p. 188.
34. Hume, *Inquiry Concerning the Principles of Morals*, App. iv.
35. *PQ* (1952) p. 1.
36. *P.A.S.*, supp. vol. xxv (1951).
37. *Mind* (1953).
38. *LL* I.
39. Kant, *Critique of Practical Reason*, trans. T. K. Abbott, p. 190.
40. See Waismann, 'Language Strata', in *LL* II, and Ryle, 'Ordinary Language', for suggestions about this clustering.
41. Not that such adaptation or invention may not be called for: see P. D. Nowell-Smith in *The Rationalist Annual* (1954) for suggestions designed to accommodate the discoveries of psychoanalysis.
42. *Mind* (1949); and incorporated with additions and improvements into *The Language of Morals* (Oxford, 1952).
43. *PQ* (1952) pp. 2 and 3.
44. *LL* I, p. 9.
45. Compare *PQ* (1952) pp. 2 and 3, with *LL* I, p. 9, of which it purports to be a criticism.

46. *LL* II, 8–9, on 'the unwitting allies of a revolution of destruction'.

47. 'Ordinary Language', loc. cit.

48. Ryle, ibid.

49. Though there has been a long tradition of this *sort* of thing, e.g. Leibniz's *characteristica universalis* and similar ideas in his century. Nowadays it is usually a matter of an overestimation of the philosophic value of the techniques of symbolic logic, found in the Vienna Circle, in Russell, and today particularly prevalent in the U.S.A.

50. By J. O. Urmson in 'Some Questions Concerning Validity', in Flew (ed.), *Essays in Conceptual Analysis*.

51. Compare R. M. Hare, *The Language of Morals,* with S. E. Toulmin, *The Place of Reason in Ethics,* and see Hare and J. Mackie on the latter in *PQ* (1951) and *AJP* (1951) respectively. T. D. Weldon in *The Vocabulary of Politics,* pp. 42–3, gives a crisp example of the false move involved. I have tried to say something myself about it in 'The Justification of Punishment', *Philosophy* (1954).

Chapter V

1. This use has little to do with the more down-to-earth occurrences of 'action' in ordinary speech.

2. Another well-flogged horse in these stakes is Blame. At least two things seem confused together under this term. Sometimes when I blame X for doing A, say for breaking the vase, it is a question simply or mainly of my disapproval of A, breaking the vase, which unquestionably X did: but sometimes it is, rather, a question simply or mainly of how far I think X responsible for A, which unquestionably was bad. Hence if somebody says he blames me for something, I may answer by giving a *justification,* so that he will cease to disapprove of what I did, or else by giving an *excuse,* so that he will cease to hold me, at least entirely and in every way, responsible for doing it.

3. All of which was seen and claimed by Socrates, when he first betook himself to the Way of Words.

4. You have a donkey, so have I, and they graze in the same field. The day comes when I conceive a dislike for mine. I go to shoot it, draw a bead on it, fire: the brute falls in its tracks. I inspect the victim, and find to my horror that it is *your* donkey. I appear on your doorstep with the remains and say – what? 'I say, old sport, I'm awfully sorry, etc., I've shot your donkey *by accident*'? Or '*by mistake*'? Then again, I go to shoot my donkey as before, draw a bead on it, fire – but as I do so, the beasts move and to my horror yours falls. Again the scene on the doorstep — what do I say? 'By mistake'? Or 'by accident'?

5. And forget, for once and for a while, that other curious question 'Is it true?' May we?

6. Caveat or hedge: of course we can say 'I did *not* sit in it "intention-

ally"' as a way simply of repudiating the suggestion that I sat in it intentionally.

7. For we are sometimes not so good at observing what we *can't* say as what we can, yet the first is pretty regularly the more revealing.

8. But remember, when I sign a cheque in the normal way, I do *not* do so *either* 'voluntarily' *or* 'under constraint'.

9. Or analogously: I do an act A_1 (say, divulge my age, or imply that you are a liar) *inadvertently* if, in the course of executing by the use of some medium of communication some other act A_2 (say, reminiscing about my war service), I fail to exercise such meticulous supervision over the choice and arrangement of the signs as would be needed to ensure that. . . . It is interesting to note how such adverbs lead parallel lives, one in connection with physical actions ('doing') and the other in connection with acts of communication ('saying'), or sometimes also in connection with acts of 'thinking' ('inadvertently assumed').

10. We know all about how to do quadratics; we know all the needful facts about pipes, cisterns, hours and plumbers; yet we reach the answer '$3\frac{3}{4}$ men'. We have failed to cast our facts correctly into mathematical form.

11. A somewhat distressing favourite in the class that Hart used to conduct with me in the years soon after war. The italics are mine.

12. Not but what he probably manages to convey his meaning somehow or other. Judges seem to acquire a knack of conveying meaning, and even carrying conviction, through the use of a pithy Anglo-Saxon which sometimes has literally no meaning at all. Wishing to distinguish the case of shooting at a post in the belief that it was an enemy, as *not* an 'attempt', from the case of picking an empty pocket in the belief that money was in it, which *is* an 'attempt', the judge explains that in shooting at the post 'the man is never on the thing at all'.

13. Plato, I suppose, and after him Aristotle, fastened this confusion upon us, as bad in its day and way as the later, grotesque, confusion of moral weakness with weakness of will. I am very partial to ice cream, and a bombe is served divided into segments corresponding one to one with the persons at High Table: I am tempted to help myself to two segments and do so, thus succumbing to temptation and even conceivably (but why necessarily?) going against my principles. But do I lose control of myself? Do I raven, do I snatch the morsels from the dish and wolf them down, impervious to the consternation of my colleagues? Not a bit of it. We often succumb to temptation with calm and even with finesse.

14. As a matter of fact, most of these examples *can* be understood the other way, especially if we allow ourselves inflections of the voice, or commas, or contexts. a_2 might be a poetic inversion for b_2; b_1, perhaps with commas round the 'clumsily', might be used for a_1; and so on. Still, the two senses are clearly enough distinguishable.

15. What Finney says is different: he says he 'made a mistake in the tap'. This is the basic use of 'mistake', where we simply, and not necessarily accountably, take the wrong one. Finney here attempts to account for his mistake, by saying that his attention was distracted. But suppose the order

is 'Right turn' and I turn left: no doubt the sergeant will insinuate that my attention was distracted, or that I cannot distinguish my right from my left – but it was not and I can; this was a simple, pure mistake. As often happens. Neither I nor the sergeant will suggest that there was any accident, or any inadvertence either. If Finney had turned the hot tap inadvertently, then it would have been knocked, say, in reaching for the cold tap – a different story.

16. This is by way of a general warning in philosophy. It seems to be too readily assumed that if we can only discover the true meanings of each of a cluster of key terms, usually historic terms, that we use in some particular field (as, for example, 'right', 'good', and the rest in morals), then it must without question transpire that each will fit into place in some single, interlocking, consistent, conceptual scheme. Not only is there no reason to assume this, but all historical probability is against it, especially in the case of a language derived from such various civilisations as ours is. We may cheerfully use, and with weight, terms which are not so much head-on incompatible as simply disparate, which just do not fit in or even on. Just as we cheerfully subscribe to, or have the grace to be torn between, simply disparate ideals – why *must* there be a conceivable amalgam, the Good Life for Man?

Chapter VI

1. Compare Austin's syntactic variations on the theme 'He clumsily trod on the snail', p. 97 above.
2. J. R. Firth, *Papers in Linguistics, 1934–1951* (Oxford, 1957) p. 190.
3. On the notion of collocation, see ibid. and A. McIntosh, 'Patterns and Ranges', *Language*, xxxvii 3(i) (1961).

Chapter VII

1. This paper and the one that succeeds it, by Professor Cavell, were read as parts of a symposium at a meeting of the American Philosophical Association, Pacific Coast Division, on 19 December 1957.
2. See Chapter II above in which certain relevant sections of this article are reprinted.
3. I do not deny that the armchair method is adequate for many purposes. Perhaps it is adequate even for deciding the correctness or incorrectness of statements like those of Ryle about 'voluntary'. I would not trust it, however, to decide such a question as whether the ordinary use of 'inadvertently' is the same as that of 'automatically' (as applied to actions) (cf. Chapter V above). Of course, even in these cases I do not propose to dispense with it, but only to add to it.
4. Note Ryle's use of the word 'sense' in the passage quoted.

5. i.e. he tries to show that the philosophic sense is different from the ordinary sense, using as evidence information that the philosophic extension is different from the ordinary extension.

6. J. O. Urmson, 'Some Questions Concerning Validity', in A. G. N. Flew (ed.), *Essays in Conceptual Analysis* (London, 1956).

7. e.g. in Ryle's case they could be described or taken as actions which ought not to be done, or as actions proceeding from the will or from the individual's own choice or full consent, or in any of a number of other ways.

8. Consider the sentence 'Jones disapproves of playing golf on Sunday'. In this sentence the word 'Jones' occurs directly, while the expression 'playing golf on Sunday' occurs obliquely. Thus, the truth-value of the given sentence may be reversed when the expression 'playing golf on Sunday' is replaced by an expression having the same denotation but different sense. Now since I use the word 'property' in such a way as to satisfy Leibniz's Law (in the form: if A is the same as B, then any property of A is a property of B, I regard the given sentence as expressing a property of Jones but not as expressing a property of the act of playing golf on Sunday. Consequently I am led to hold that although the properties of an act will in general be relevant to the semantics of any expression referring to that act, the approval or disapproval of an act by someone does not constitute one of its properties.

9. If the latter were possible, it would obviously be awkward to interpret the Socratic method as a method of *finding out* what the subject means, as against *teaching* him something new.

10. Thus, the concept of 'definiteness of intention', introduced by Professor Arne Naess (cf. 'Toward a Theory of Interpretation and Preciseness', in L. Linsky, *Semantics and the Philosophy of Language* (Urbana, Ill., 1952) pp. 256 ff.), seems to have a devastating relevance to many of the characteristic assertions of the ordinary-language philosophers.

Chapter VIII

1. This is a later, greatly expanded, version of the paper read as part of the symposium mentioned in Mates's first note. Since writing the relevant portions of this paper, I have seen three articles which make points or employ arguments similar to those I am concerned with: R. M. Hare, 'Are Discoveries about the Uses of Words Empirical?', *Journal of Philosophy* (Nov 1957); G. E. M. Anscombe, 'On Brute Facts', *Analysis* (Jan 1958); S. Hampshire and H. L. A. Hart, 'Decision, Intention and Certainty,' *Mind* (Jan 1958). But it would have lengthened an already lengthy paper to have tried to bring out more specifically than will be obvious to anyone reading them their relevance to what I have said.

2. I am too conscious of differences in the practices of Oxford philosophers to be happy about referring, in this general way, to a school. But nothing in my remarks depends on the existence of such a school – beyond

the fact that certain problems are common to the philosophers mentioned, and that similar questions enter into their attempts to deal with them. It is with these questions (I mean, of course, with what I understand them to be) that I am concerned.

3. Perhaps I should say 'ideal' types. The statements do not come labelled in the discourse of such philosophers, but I am going to have to trust that my placing of statements into these types will not seem to distort them.

4. The harmfulness of this habit is brought out in Austin's 'A Plea for Excuses' (Chapter V above).

5. Austin's discovery (for our time and place, anyway) of normal action is, I think, important enough to bear the philosophical weight he puts upon it – holding the clue to the riddle of Freedom (cf. 'Excuses', p. 83 above). A case can also be made out – as I try to do in a paper I hope soon to publish – that it was failure to recognise such action which produced some of the notorious paradoxes of classical Utilitarianism: what neither the Utilitarians nor their critics seem to have seen clearly and constantly is that about unquestionable (normal, natural) action no question is (can be) raised; in particular not the question whether the action ought or ought not to have been done. The point is a logical one: to raise a question about an action is to put the action in question. It is partly the failure to appreciate this which makes the classical moralists (appear?) so moralistic, allows them to suppose that the moral question is *always* appropriate (except, of course, where the action is unfree (caused?)). But this is no better than the assumption that the moral question is *never* appropriate (because we are never *really* free). Such mechanical moralism has got all the punishment it deserves in the recent mechanical anti-moralism, which it must have helped inspire.

6. At the same time, Ryle leaves 'involuntary' as stretched as ever when he allows himself to speak of 'the involuntariness of [someone's] late arrival' p. 42 above).

7. I realise that the point is controversial and that in putting so much emphasis on it I may be doing some injustice to the point of view I am trying to defend. There may be considerations which would lead one to be more temperate in making the point; but against the point of view Mates is adopting, it seems to me to demand all the attention it can get.

8. As is most clearly shown where he says (p. 129 above) '. . . When I say "I may be wrong" I do not *imply* that I have no confidence in what I have previously asserted; I only indicate it'. Why 'only'? Were he willing to say '. . . but I do (inevitably) indicate it', there may be no argument.

9. Alternative (2(*b*)) has been taken – for different, but not unrelated, reasons – in the writings of John Wisdom (e.g. 'Gods', in *Logic and Language*, First Series, ed. A. G. N. Flew (Oxford, 1951) p. 196), and in S. Toulmin's *The Place of Reason in Ethics* (Cambridge, 1950) p. 83, and in S. Hampshire's 'Fallacies in Moral Philosophy', *Mind* (Oct 1949) pp. 470–471.

10. It was essentially the argument with which the pragmatists attempted to subdue emotive 'meaning'. See John Dewey's 'Ethical Subject-

Matter and Language', *Journal of Philosophy* (1945) pp. 701–12.

11. I think of this as a law of communication; but it would be important and instructive to look for apparent counter-instances. When *couldn't* what is said be misunderstood? My suggestion is, only when nothing is implied, i.e. when everything you say is said explicitly. (Should we add, or when all of the implications of what is asserted can be made explicit *in a certain way*, e.g. by the methods of formal logic? It may be along such lines that utterances in logical form come to seem the ideal of understandable utterances, that here you can communicate *only* what you say, or else *more* than you say without endangering understanding. But we might think of formal logic not as the guarantor of understanding but as a substitute for it. (Cf. W. V. O. Quine, 'Mr Strawson on Logical Theory', *Mind* (Oct 1953) pp. 444–5.) Then we can express this 'law of communication' this way: What needs understanding can be misunderstood.) But when *is* everything said explicitly? When the statement is about sense-data rather than 'physical' objects? When it is about the 'physical' movements I make rather than the (non-physical?) actions I perform? Perhaps the opponents of the Quest for Certainty (whose passion seems to have atrophied into a fear of the word 'certain') have embarked upon a Quest for Explicitness. Strawson's notion of *presupposing* is relevant here, since explicitness and presupposition vary inversely. See his 'On Referring', *Mind* (1950), reprinted in *Essays in Conceptual Analysis*, ed. A. G. N. Flew (London, 1956).

12. An examination of such forms is part of a more extended study on which I am now working.

13. If it still seems that statements like S and T *must* be synthetic, perhaps it will help to realise that anyway they are not *just some more* synthetic statements about voluntary action, on a par with a statement to the effect that somebody does (indeed) dress the way he does voluntarily. It may be true that if the world were different *enough*, the statements would be false; but that amounts to saying that if 'voluntary' meant something other than it does, the statements would not mean what they do – which is not surprising. The statements in question are more closely related to such a statement as 'The future will resemble the past': this is not a (not just another prediction, on a par with statements about whether it will rain. Russell's chicken (who was fed every day throughout its life but ultimately had its neck wrung) was so well fed that he neglected to consider what was happening to other chickens. Even if he had considered this, he would doubtless still have had his neck wrung; but at least he wouldn't have been outsmarted. He could have avoided *that* indignity because he was wrong only about one thing; as Russell very properly says, '. . . in spite of frequent repetitions there sometimes is a failure at the last' (*Problems of Philosophy*, p. 102, original edition). But if the future were not (in the *general* sense needed) 'like' the past, this would not be *a* failure. The future may wring our minds, but by that very act it would have given up trying to outsmart us.

14. A complaint Austin voiced in the course of his William James Lectures, on Performatives, at Harvard in the spring term of 1955, later

published as *How to do Things with Words* (Oxford, 1962).

15. John Hospers, *Introduction to Philosophical Analysis* (Englewood Cliffs, N.J., 1953).

16. Charles Stevenson, *Ethics and Language* (New Haven, 1944) p. 26.

17. For modern instruction in the complexities of this question, see Austin's and P. F. Strawson's contributions to the symposium 'Truth', *Proceedings of the Aristotelian Society*, supp. vol. xxiv (1950); D. Pears, 'Universals' and 'Incompatibilities of Colours', both in *Logic and Language*, Second Series, ed. A. G. N. Flew (Oxford, 1953); W. V. O. Quine, 'Two Dogmas of Empiricism', *Philosophical Review* (1951), reprinted in *From a Logical Point of View* (Cambridge, Mass., 1953); John Wisdom, papers collected in *Philosophy and Psycho-Analysis* (Oxford, 1953), especially 'Philosophical Perplexity', 'Metaphysics and Verification', and 'Philosophy, Metaphysics and Psycho-Analysis'.

18. The emphasised formula is Austin's (p. 84 above). Notice that the 'should' cannot simply be replaced by 'ought to', nor yet, I believe, simply replaced by 'would'. It will not, that is, yield its secrets to the question 'Descriptive or normative?'

19. This is part of the view of philosophy most consistently represented in and by the writings of John Wisdom. It derives from Wittgenstein.

20. Of course you can *say* (the words) 'When I ask whether an action is voluntary I do not imply that I think something is special about the action'. You can say this, but then you may have difficulty showing the relevance of *this* 'voluntary' to what people are worrying about when they ask whether a person's action was voluntary or whether our actions are ever voluntary. We might regard the Oxford philosopher's insistence upon ordinary language as an attempt to overcome (what has become) the self-imposed irrelevance of so much philosophy. In this they are continuing – while at the same time their results are undermining – the tradition of British Empiricism: being gifted pupils, they seem to accept and to assassinate with the same gesture.

21. This latter distinction appears in two senses of the expression 'establishing a rule or standard'. In one it means finding what is in fact standard in certain instances. In the other it means founding what is to be standard for certain instances. 'Settle' and 'determine' have senses comparable to those of 'establish'.

22. It is perfectly possible to maintain that *any* 'justifications' we offer for our conduct are now so obviously empty and grotesquely inappropriate that nothing we used to call a justification is any longer acceptable, and that the *immediate* questions which face us concern the ultimate ground of justification itself. We have heard about, if we have not seen, the breaking down of convention, the fission of traditional values. But it is not a Continental dread at the realisation that our standards have no ultimate justification which lends to so much British and American moral philosophising its hysterical quality. (Such philosophy has been able to take the death of God in its stride.) That quality comes, rather, from the assumption that the question of justifying cases is on a par with (appropriate in the same context as) the question of justifying norms.

23. Though in another context we might have. Imagine that before chess was introduced into our culture, another game – call it Quest – had been popular with us. In that game, played on a board with sixty-four squares, and like chess in other respects, the piece called the Damsel had a fickle way of moving: its first move, and every odd move afterwards, followed the rule for the Queen in chess; its even moves followed the rule for the Knight. It may be supposed that when people began to play Quest, it often happened that a game had to be stopped upon remembering that several moves earlier a Queen was permitted a Knight's move. The rule for the Queen's move might then have been formulated in some such way as: You must move the Queen in straight, unobstructed paths. . . .

24. Perhaps this difference provides a way of accounting for our tendency sometimes to think of laws as rules and at other times to think of them as commands. This may (in part) depend upon where we – i.e. where our normal actions – stand (or where we imagine them to stand) with respect to the law or system of laws in question. It may also be significant that when you are describing a system of laws, you are likely to think of yourself as external to the system.

25. But this requires a great deal of work. We must have a better description of the 'class' and the function of 'modal auxiliaries', and we need an understanding of what makes something we do 'another' action and what makes it 'part' of an action in progress.

26. 'Must' retains its logical force here. Kant may not have provided an analysis sufficient to sustain his saying that 'a deposit of money must be handed back because if the recipient appropriated it, it would no longer be a deposit'; but Bergson too hastily concludes that Kant's explanation of this in terms of 'logical contradiction' is 'obviously juggling with words'. (See Bergson's *The Two Sources of Morality and Religion* (New York, 1935) p. 77.) The difference between your *depositing* and simply *handing* over some money has in part to do with what you mean or intend to be doing – and with what you *can* mean or intend by doing what you do in the way you do it in that particular historical context. We may, following a suggestion of H. P. Grice's (in 'Meaning', *Philosophical Review* (July 1957)), think of the actions of depositing and of accepting a deposit as complicated 'utterances': you intend that what you do shall be understood. Then it will not seem so extraordinary to say that a later 'utterance' (viz., appropriating the entrusted money) contradicts a former one (viz., accepting a deposit).

27. Cited in *Hoyle's Rules of Games*, ed. Morehead and Mott-Smith (New York, 1949).

28. Some philosophers who employ the notion of a rule have given the impression that there are. What I am trying to argue is that there aren't, but that the analogy is still a good one. One of the claims made for the concept of a rule is that it illuminates the notion of justification; and critics of the concept argue that it fails in this and that therefore the concept is unilluminating in the attempt to understand moral conduct. I think both of these claims are improper, resulting in part from the failure to appreciate differences (1) between rules and principles, and (2) between

performing an action and making some movements. The concept of rule does illuminate the concept of *action*, but not that of *justified* action. Where there is a question about what I do and I cite a rule in my favour, what I do is to *explain* my action, make clear *what* I was doing, not to justify it, say that what I did was well or rightly done. Where my action is in accord with the relevant rules, it needs no justification. Nor can it receive any: I cannot *justify* moving the Queen in straight, unobstructed paths. See John Rawls's study of this subject, 'Two Concepts of Rules', *Philosophical Review* (Jan 1955). My unhappiness with the way in which the analogy is drawn does not diminish my respect for this paper. For a criticism (based, I think, on a misunderstanding) of the view, see H. J. McCloskey, 'An Examination of Restricted Utilitarianism', *Philosophical Review* (Oct 1957).

29. Such an understanding of meaning is provided in Grice, op. cit., but I do not think he would be happy about the use I wish to put it to. A conversation we had was too brief for me to be sure about this, but not too brief for me to have added, as a result of it, one or two qualifications or clarifications of what I had said, e.g. the third point of note 32, note 33, and the independent clause to which the present note is attached.

30. If truth consists in saying of what is that it is, then (*this* sense or source of) necessary truth consists in saying of what is *what* it is. The question 'Are these matters of language or matters of fact?' would betray the obsession I have tried to calm. I do not claim that this explanation of necessity holds for all statements which seem to us necessary and not analytic, but at best for those whose topic is actions and which therefore display a rule-description complementarity.

31. Austin's work on Excuses provides a way of coming to master this immensely important idea. The way I have put the point here is due directly to it.

32. Three points about this conclusion need emphasising: (1) It was reached where the difference concerned isolated *words*; where, that is, the shared *language* was left intact. (2) The tasks to be performed (scraping; chopping; excusing a familiar and not very serious mishap) were such as to allow execution, if more or less crude, with a general or common implement. (3) The question was over the meaning of a word in general, not over its meaning (what it was used to mean) on a particular occasion; there was, I am assuming, no reason to treat the word's use on this occasion as a special one.

Wittgenstein's role in combating the idea of privacy (whether of the meaning of what is said or of what is done), and in emphasising the *functions* of language, scarcely needs to be mentioned. It might be worth pointing out that both of these teachings are fundamental to American pragmatism; but then we must keep in mind how different their arguments sound, and admit that in philosophy it is the sound which makes all the difference.

33. I am not, of course, denying that what you *say* depends upon what you intend to be saying. I am, rather, denying that intending is to be understood as a wanting or wishing. And I am suggesting that you could

not mean one thing rather than another (= you could not mean anything) by a given word on a given occasion without relying on a (general) meaning of that word which is independent of your intention on that occasion (unless what you are doing is *giving* the word a special meaning). For an analysis of meaning in terms of intention, see Grice, op. cit.

34. Or else it is a *special* report, like the one on p. 161 (last sentence); but it is still not a description of my wishes or intentions.

35. This may be summarised by saying that there is no such thing as *finding out* what a number, etc., is. This would then provide the occasion and the justification for logical construction.

36. Cf. D. F. Pears, 'Incompatibilities of Colours', in Flew (ed.), *Logic and Language*, Second Series, p. 19, n. 2.

37. One of the best ways to get past the idea that philosophy's concern with language is a concern with words (with 'verbal' matters) is to read Wisdom. Fortunately it is a pleasant way; because since the idea is one that you have to get past again and again, the way past it will have to be taken again and again.

38. As Austin explicitly says. See 'Excuses', p. 87 above.

39. This sometimes appears to be the only substantive disagreement between the philosophers who proceed from ordinary language and those who proceed by constructing artificial languages. But this may well be obscuring their deeper disagreements, which are, I believe, less about language than about whether the time has come to drag free of the philosophical traditions established in response to, and as part of, the 'scientific revolution' of the sixteenth and seventeenth centuries. I have found instruction about this in conversations with my friend and colleague Thomas S. Kuhn, to whom I am also indebted for having read (and forced the rewriting of) two shorter versions of this paper.

Chapter IX

1. The biographical information in this paragraph comes from the first of Moore's three papers called 'Wittgenstein's Lectures in 1930–33', *Mind*, LXIII (1954) and LXIV (1955); from R. R(hees)'s introduction to *The Blue and Brown Books*; and from a biographical sketch by G. H. von Wright, published together with Norman Malcolm's moving memoir, *Ludwig Wittgenstein* (Oxford, 1958).

2. Ludwig Wittgenstein, *The Blue and Brown Books* (Oxford, 1958). Cited here as *BB*.

3. London, 1958.

4. All references preceded by '§' are to paragraph numbers in Part I of *Philosophical Investigations*; references to Part II are preceded by 'II'.

5. What 'learning' and 'teaching' are here is, or ought to be, seriously problematic. We say a word and the child repeats it. What is 'repeating' here? All we know is that the child makes a sound which we accept. (How does the child recognise acceptance? Has he learned what that is?)

6. If we asked, 'In what kind of world would decision be unrelated to commitment and responsibility?' we might answer, 'In a world in which morality has become politicalised.' It is not secret that this has been happening to our world, and that we are perhaps incapable of what would make it stop happening. That is a personal misfortune of which we all partake. But the pain is made more exquisitely cruel when philosophers describe relations and conversations between persons as they would occur in a totally political world – a world, that is, in which relationships are no longer personal, nor even contractual – and call what goes on between such persons by the good (or bad) name of morality. That concedes our loss to have been not merely morality, but the very concept of morality as well.

7. It is significant that Wittgenstein thought of his methods as liberating. 'The real discovery is the one that makes me capable of stopping doing philosophy when I want to. – The one that gives philosophy peace, so that it is no longer tormented by questions which bring *itself* in question' (§133). The reason why methods which make us look at what we say, and bring the forms of language (hence our forms of life) to consciousness, can present themselves to one person as confining and to another as liberating is, I think, understandable in this way, recognising what we say, in the way that is relevant in philosophising, is like recognising our present commitments and their implications; to one person a sense of freedom will demand an escape from them, to another it will require their more total acceptance. Is it obvious that one of those positions must, in a given case, be right?

8. The importance and role of the sense of discovery in philosophical paradox (one of the constant themes in the philosophising of John Wisdom), in particular the pervasive significance of the fact that this sense is not accounted for by the familiar criticisms made by ordinary-language philosophers against the tradition, was brought in upon me in conversations with Thompson Clarke. He has also read this paper and done what he could to relieve its obscurities.

9. Austin, 'Other Minds', in A. G. N. Flew (ed.), *Logic and Language*, Second Series (London, 1953) p. 133.

10. The nature and extent of this fact, and of the different methods required in meeting it, is suggested by the differences of problems presented to psychoanalysts in the cases of neurotic and of psychotic communication (verbal and non-verbal). See, e.g., Frieda Fromm-Reichmann, *Principles of Intensive Psychotherapy* (Chicago, 1950) esp. ch. 8 and *passim*. Perhaps it is suggestive to say: the neurotic disguises the expression of particular communications (e.g. makes something fearful to him look and sound attractive), while the psychotic distorts his entire grammar. The neurotic has reason, and the strength, to keep what he means from himself; the psychotic has to keep what he knows he means from others. Wittgenstein is concerned with both of these kinds of incongruence.

11. Bernard Williams, in a review of Stuart Hampshire's *Thought and Action* in *Encounter*, xv (Nov 1960) pp. 38–42, suggests one important fact about what I have, parochially, called 'modern philosophy' (by which I meant the English and American academic traditions, beginning with

Descartes and Locke and never domesticating Hegel and his successors) which, I think, is related to its unconcern with the knowledge of persons and in particular with self-knowledge: viz., its neglect of history as a form of human knowledge.

Chapter X

1. This work was supported in part by the U.S. Army (Signal Corps), the U.S. Navy (Office of Naval Research), and the U.S. Air Force (Office of Scientific Research, Air Research and Development Command), and in part by the National Science Foundation (Grant G-13903).

2. Page references are to the reprint in this volume (Ed.).

3. Actually Cavell did not choose these examples himself but took them over from Mates against whom Cavell's arguments in M are directed.

4. The claim that the linguist must assume the truth of metalinguistic statements by native speakers in order to describe their language correctly is indefensible. Metalinguistic statements by native speakers appear in the linguist's corpus of the language, but this proves nothing about their truth because the corpus contains both true and false statements without discrimination. If the linguist had to separate the truths about the language from the falsehoods before he could begin to describe the language, he would have to know a great deal about the language before his descriptive work had even begun.

5. That is, what the speaker knows in each case are the general rules which structure the language. Precisely this point is made in M. Halle, 'Phonology in Generative Grammar', forthcoming in *Word*, where Halle demonstrates that the logical form of phonological rules is identical with the logical form of grammatical rules. Moreover, it is implicit in this article that the content of the latter rules must be stated in part in terms of phonological constructs. For an earlier but more detailed treatment of the phonological component of a grammar, cf. M. Halle, *Sound Patterns of Russian* (The Hague, 1959).

6. On p. 145 of M, Cavell uses this example, apparently without noticing that it contradicts S.

7. In fact, one need go no further than M to show the implausibility of Cavell's claim that we are rarely wrong about type 2 statements. In M Cavell notes that Ryle's type 2 statement about 'voluntary' is wrong, and we have seen (p. 145 of the present paper) that Cavell's espousal of S is likewise ill advised.

8. This is the way Cavell himself understands the occurrence of 'we' in type 1 and 2 statements. Cf. M, p. 160.

9. For a detailed discussion of this topic, cf. J. J. Katz and J. A. Fodor, 'The Structure of a Semantic Theory' (see Bibliography).

10. Cf. J. J. Katz and J. A. Fodor, 'What's Wrong with Philosophy of Language?' (see Bibliography; in part reprinted as Chapter XIV of the present volume).

11. This is the sort of point one is likely to overlook when one's philosophical attention is confined to single words to the exclusion of constructible expressions.

12. For a discussion of such failures of isomorphism between natural languages, and for further examples, see H. A. Gleason, *An Introduction to Descriptive Linguistics* (New York, 1955); B. L. Whorf, *Language, Thought and Reality* (Cambridge, 1956); R. Brown, *Words and Things* (Glencoe, Ill., 1958). Cf. also R. Brown and E. H. Lennenberg, 'A Study in Language and Cognition', *Journal of Abnormal and Social Psychology*, XLIX (1954) pp. 454–62.

13. To appreciate the importance and complexity of the problem of setting empirical constraints on the description of a natural language, the reader need only examine the extensive discussion this problem has received in the literature of descriptive linguistics.

14. We recognise that in M, Cavell is replying to Mates. But even so, the magnitude of his claims is such that they ought to have been defended against more tenable conceptions of empirical investigations in linguistics, for example the conception implicit in Chomsky's *Syntactic Structures* (The Hague, 1957).

Chapter XI

1. W refers throughout to 'The Availability of what we say', M to 'Must we mean what we say?' Page references are to the reprint in this volume (Ed.).

2. I am unable to assess the evidence (which, according to note 5 of W (see above), is contained in M. Halle's 'Phonology in a Generative Grammar', *Word*, XVIII (1962) pp. 54–72) for the entailment claimed in the above quotation from Fodor and Katz. Assuming that they are right in this claim, I suggest that a distinction between aspects of our knowledge of the sound system analogous to the distinction I shall draw below in regard to our semantical and syntactical knowledge will meet their argument.

3. It is not clear to me that 'native speaker' is exactly the characterisation which is needed here; having nothing better to offer, I follow Cavell. Surely *some* who are not (genetically speaking) native speakers would do as well; but of course generalisations about native speakers are not falsified if the same things can be said about some who are *not* native speakers.

4. In 'The Cult of Ordinary Usage', *British Journal for the Philosophy of Science*, III (1953) p. 305.

5. Note the considerable difference between 'remembering someone's *saying* "capable of murder" ', and 'remembering *that* one can say "capable of murder" '.

6. Thus the strenuous efforts of Wittgenstein, Malcolm, Austin, and other analysts to minimise this danger by constant reminders of the circumstances in which we do use certain philosophically troublesome locutions.

7. I am indebted to Robert C. Coburn for suggesting this consideration; whether my way of developing it is in harmony with his intentions is of course another question.

8. Cavell had remarked that philosophers make three types of statements about ordinary language:

> (1) There are statements which produce *instances* of what is said in a language ('We do say . . . but we don't say—'; 'We ask whether . . . but we do not ask whether—'). (2) Sometimes these instances are accompanied by *explications* – statements which make explicit what is implied when we say what statements of the first type instance us as saying ('When we say . . . we imply [suggest, say]—"; 'We don't say . . . unless we mean—"). Such statements are checked by reference to statements of the first type (M, p. 132 above).

I omit the third type because it seems to play no role in the subsequent arguments.

9. *Words and Things* (Glencoe, Ill., 1958).

10. A refers to 'The Availability of Wittgenstein's Later Philosophy' (Ed.).

11. One may say 'Pardon me' and in some sense mean 'You are very rude to stand for so long in my way'; and in other ways to numerous to deal with here, my statement requires expansion and qualification.

Chapter XII

1. Sections II–V and VII of this paper appeared in the *Journal of Philosophy*, LIV (1957) in a symposium with Professors Paul Henle and S. Körner entitled 'The Nature of Analysis'. The whole paper could not be printed there for reasons of space, and I am grateful to the editors of the *Journal* for permission to include in this revised version of the complete paper the extract already printed.

2. *An Empiricist's View of the Nature of Religious Belief* (Cambridge, 1955) p. 11.

3. *Eth. Nic.*, 1095 b2; *An. Post.*, 71 b33.

4. See my *The Language of Morals* (Oxford, 1952) pp. 124 ff.

5. See the remarks of Professor Ayer on Mr Wollheim's valuable paper 'La Philosophie Analytique et les Attitudes Politiques', in *La Philosophie Analytique*, ed Béra (Cahiers de Royaumont; Editions de Minuit, 1962), and compare also Aristotle, *An. Post.*, 100 a7, and *Eth. Nic.*, 1143 b4.

6. *Meno*, 80d.

7. Adapted from *Republic*, 331c.

Chapter XIII

1. Of course, there are other kinds of linguistic characterisations for which this description would not hold, e.g. 'the average American utters 2,432 words a day'. This is an empirical generalisation concerning the verbal behaviour of a group. I am not now concerned with such kinds of linguistic characterisation.

2. A similar point is made in a slightly different context by Noam Chomsky, *Aspects of the Theory of Syntax* (Cambridge, 1965) pp. 21–4.

3. i.e. Searle's *Speech Acts* (Cambridge, 1969) (Ed.).

Chapter XIV

1. J. J. Katz, *The Philosophy of Language*, p. 4, n.2.

2. Ibid., p. 8.

3. London, 1956.

4. i.e. *Linguistics in Philosophy* (Ithaca, N.Y., 1967) (Ed.).

5. P. Ziff, *Semantic Analysis* (Oxford, 1967).

6. J. A. Fodor and J. J. Katz, 'The Structure of Semantic Theory', in Fodor and Katz (eds), *The Structure of Language*.

7. Discussion and references in Chapter X above (Ed.).

8. N. Chomsky, *Syntactic Structures* (The Hague, 1957) Fodor and Katz (eds), *The Structure of Language*; Z. S. Harris 'Transformational Theory', *Language*, XLI (1965).

9. L. Wittgenstein, *Philosophical Investigations*, I, 90.

10. J. N. Findlay, 'Use, Usage and Meaning', *Proceedings of the Aristotelian Society*, supp. vol. XXXV (1961) pp. 231–42.

11. Tsu-lin Mei, 'Subject and Predicate, a Grammatical Preliminary', *Philosophical Review*, LXX (1961).

12. H. H. Dubs, 'Language and Philosophy', *Philosophical Review*, LXIV (1958).

13. See ch. vi of Vendler's *Linguistics in Philosophy* (Ed.).

14. *Philosophical Investigations*, I, 89.

15. Ibid., II, 223. The given translation, 'We cannot find our feet with them', is not literal enough.

16. In my own discussion, I am particularly indebted to M. Black, 'Necessary Statements and Rules', *Philosophical Review*, LXVI (1958) 313–41.

17. G. E. M. Anscombe, 'On Brute Facts', *Analysis*, XVIII (1957–58).

18. Aristotle, *Met.*, 1010a.

19. *Critique of Pure Reason*, A126 (N. Kemp Smith trans., p. 147).

20. See ch. 6 of Vendler's *Linguistics in Philosophy* (Ed.).

21. See Chomsky's symposium paper read at the Sixty-First Annual Meeting of the Eastern Division of the American Philosophical Association, Boston, 29 Dec 1964; also J. J. Katz, *The Philosophy of Language*, pp. 240–82.

328 *Notes*

helped by discussions with Professors S. Morgenbesser and J. J. Katz.

22. Concerning the points made in these two paragraphs I have been

23. These paragraphs anticipate conclusions reached in chs 5, 6 and 7 of Vendler's *Linguistics in Philosophy* (Ed.).

Chapter XV

1. Cf. J. L. Austin, 'Other Minds', *Proceedings of the Philosophical Society*, supp. vol. xx (1946), reprinted in A. G. N. Flew (ed), *Logic and Language*, Second Series (Oxford, 1953).

2. See Chapter VIII above, where Cavell makes just this claim, and see Chapter X for the reply by Fodor and Katz (Ed.).

3. H. Putnam, 'Minds and Machines', in S. Hook (ed.), *Dimensions of Mind* (New York, 1960) p. 166.

4. The ordinary-language analyst may complain that we have ignored the principle that similar cases are to be decided in a similar fashion. But this begs the question, since to specify what counts as relevant similarity is precisely to specify the generative principles that structure the sentences of the language.

5. For an important amendment to this view, see J. J. Katz, *The Philosophy of Language*, p. 4, n.2, and sections 3 and 4 of Chapter XIV above (Ed.).

6. This is not meant to imply that all the knowledge which enters into the production and comprehension of utterances comes under study in linguistics. Besides linguistic abilities and skills, factual information, memory, motives, etc., may determine what utterance is produced and how an utterance is understood. Linguistics is concerned to reconstruct only those of the speaker's abilities which are a function of his knowledge of the regularities of the language.

7. Chomsky writes: '. . . it is obvious that the set of grammatical sentences cannot be identified with any particular corpus of utterances obtained by the linguist in his field work. Any grammar of a language will *project* the finite and somewhat accidental corpus of observed utterances to a set (presumably infinite) of grammatical utterances. In this respect, a grammar mirrors the behaviour of the speaker who, on the basis of a finite and accidental experience with language, can produce or understand an indefinite number of new sentences' (in his *Syntactic Structures* (The Hague, 1957) p. 15).

8. Since there is no upper bound on the length of sentences in a natural language, a recursive assignment of meaning interpretations to sentences is the only possible way of giving each sentence a meaning.

Chapter XVI

1. London, 1949, pp. 149–53.
2. This distinction of achievement verbs from other classes has been carried out much more elaborately by F. N. Sibley, 'Seeking, Scrutinising and Seeing', *Mind*, LXIV (1955), and Z. Vendler, 'Verbs and Times', *Philosophical Review*, LXVI (1957). However, since Ryle's discussion is better known and since it contains within a small compass all sorts of moves I wish to consider, I have chosen to concentrate on it.
3. In *Syntactic Structures* (The Hague, 1957) pp. 15–16.
4. New York, 1958, pp. 207–8.
5. In A. G. N. Flew (ed.) *Logic and Language*, Second Series (Oxford, 1953) p. 81.
6. *Philosophical Review*, LXII (1953) p. 171; see also p. 45 above.
7. Of course there are serious questions into which I cannot go, as to the relation between such criteria and the elements and combinations so specified.
8. Hill, *Introduction to Linguistic Structures*, pp. 176 ff.
9. Reprinted in A. G. N. Flew (ed.), *Essays in Conceptual Analysis* (London, 1956).

Chapter XVII

1. There is a variety of ways of being naïve about the notion of having something in common (what aspirin and codeine have in common is not something you will discover just by inspection). But there are also various ways of being naïve about stating a rule. To say 'the situations must resemble one another' is not to state a rule. Not even if you add 'in a family way'.
2. Cf. J. A. Fodor and J. J. Katz, 'The Availability of What We Say' (Chapter X above). The arguments in the present paper presuppose the conclusions in that one, since one can sensibly raise the question 'In what circumstances is the informant right?' only if it is accepted that there are circumstances in which the informant is wrong.
3. Although this argument affords grounds for extreme caution in appealing to speakers' intuitions to distinguish symptoms from criteria, it cannot be considered conclusive since we might conceivably have *indirect* evidence in favour of the speaker's claims. For example, in certain simple cases we might be able so to deceive the speaker that he believes he has encountered a situation which is normal except that the relevant feature fails to obtain. We might then observe what a speaker so deceived is willing to say and what he is not. Somewhat more important is the consideration that we might have as a reason for accepting the speaker's claims about what he would say in situations we cannot observe cross-inductions based on the accuracy of the speaker's claims about what he would say in situations we can observe. Neither of these arguments would

appear to supply very strong reasons for trusting the speaker's intuitions, but they suffice to block the claim that there could exist no reasons whatever for doing so.

4. I assume throughout that the speaker's claims about what he would say should be understood as *predictions* as to what his verbal behaviour would be under the conditions enumerated. It is clear, however, that sometimes such claims are best understood as *decisions* as to what the best thing to say in such circumstances would be. This fact need not influence the present arguments, since the reasons for maintaining that the speaker's knowledge of his language does not supply adequate grounds for predicting what he would say in the critical cases are precisely the reasons for maintaining that the speaker's knowledge of his language does not supply adequate basis for a reasoned decision as to what he *ought* to say in those cases.

5. I use 'theory' very broadly to mean 'system of beliefs'. I would not use it at all except that it sounds odd to speak of 'devising and accepting a belief' and I wish to emphasise that, should our current beliefs break down in some important way, it would require serious inquiry to determine which new beliefs we ought to adopt. In particular, the results of such inquiry cannot be predicted on the basis of our current linguistic habits.

Bibliography

COLLECTIONS

J. Fodor and J. J. Katz, *The Structure of Language: Readings in The Philosophy of Language* (Englewood Cliffs, N.J., 1964).
R. Rorty, *The Linguistic Turn* (London, 1967).
The first of these leans towards the linguistics side of the linguistics/philosophy border, the latter inclines towards the philosophical side. The Rorty volume contains a remarkable bibliography.

BOOKS

N. Chomsky, *Syntactic Structures* (The Hague, 1957).
   Cartesian Linguistics (New York, 1964).
J. J. Katz, *The Philosophy of Language* (New York, 1964). A brief and relatively non-technical account of the way linguistic theory is developing.
W. V. O. Quine, *Word and Object* (Cambridge, Mass., 1960) esp. chs 1 and 2.
R. Quirk and J. Svartvik, *Investigating Linguistic Acceptability* (The Hague, 1966).
Z. Vendler, *Linguistics in Philosophy* (Ithaca, N.Y., 1967) (ch. 1 reprinted in this volume).
P. Ziff, *Semantic Analysis* (Ithaca, N.Y., 1960). A much more difficult philosophico-linguistic work.

ARTICLES

D. Bolinge, 'The Atomisation of Meaning', *Language*, XLI (1965).
J. J. Katz, 'The Relevance of Linguistics to Philosophy', *Journal of Philosophy*, LXII (1965).
   'Semantic Theory and the Meaning of "Good"', *Journal of Philosophy*, LXI (1964).
   and J. Fodor, 'The Structure of a Semantic Theory', in *Language*, XXXIX (1963) and in the Fodor and Katz collection.
N. Malcolm, 'Moore and Ordinary Language', in P. A. Schilpp (ed.), *The Philosophy of G. E. Moore*, 2nd ed. (New York, 1952) and reprinted in V. Chappell, *Ordinary Language* (Englewood Cliffs, N.J., 1964).

'Philosophy and Ordinary Language', *Philosophical Review*, LX (1951).

W. V. O. Quine, 'The Problem of Meaning in Linguistics', in *From a Logical Point of View* (Cambridge, Mass., 1961).

G. Ryle, 'Systematically Misleading Expressions', *Proceedings of the Aristotelian Society*, XXXII (1931–2), reprinted in Rorty, *The Linguistic Turn*, and Flew (ed.), *Logic and Language*, First Series.

J. Wisdom, 'Philosophical Perplexity', in *Proceedings of the Aristotelian Society*, XXXVII (1936–7), reprinted in Rorty, *The Linguistic Turn*.